CARL SANDBURG

ABRAHAM LINCOLN

THE PRAIRIE YEARS

AND

THE WAR YEARS

THE

ILLUSTRATED EDITION

FALL RIVER PRESS

New York

An Imprint of Sterling Publishing
387 Park Avenue South
New York, NY 10016

This 2011 edition published by Fall River Press.

ISBN 978-1-4351-3805-6

Distributed in Canada by Sterling Publishing
c/o Canadian Manda Group, 165 Dufferin Street
Toronto, Ontario, Canada M6K 3H6
Distributed in the United Kingdom by GMC Distribution Services
Castle Place, 166 High Street, Lewes, East Sussex, England BN7 1XU
Distributed in Australia by Capricorn Link (Australia) Pty. Ltd.
P.O. Box 704, Windsor, NSW 2756, Australia

For information about custom editions, special sales, and premium and corporate purchases, please contact Sterling Special Sales at 800-805-5489 or specialsales@sterlingpublishing.com.

Manufactured in China

2 4 6 8 10 9 7 5 3

www.sterlingpublishing.com

CARL SANDBURG

ABRAHAM LINCOLN

THE PRAIRIE YEARS

AND

THE WAR YEARS

THE

ILLUSTRATED EDITION

EDITED BY
EDWARD C. GOODMAN

FALL RIVER PRESS

New York

CONTENTS

Abraham Lincoln

PREFACE 6

INTRODUCTION 8

1. WILDERNESS BEGINNINGS 10
2. NEW SALEM DAYS 25
3. THE YOUNG LEGISLATOR 35
4. LAWYER IN SPRINGFIELD 41
5. "I AM GOING TO BE MARRIED" 49
6. RUNNING FOR CONGRESS 56
7. CONGRESSMAN LINCOLN 62
8. BACK HOME IN SPRINGFIELD 67
9. RESTLESS GROWING AMERICA 73
10. THE DEEPENING SLAVERY ISSUE 79
11. THE GREAT DEBATES 83
12. STRANGE FRIEND AND FRIENDLY STRANGER 93
13. "ONLY EVENTS CAN MAKE A PRESIDENT" 103
14. "MARY, WE'RE ELECTED" 111
15. THE HOUSE DIVIDING 121
16. "I BID YOU AN AFFECTIONATE FAREWELL" 126
17. AMERICA WITHER? — LINCOLN JOURNEYS TO WASHINGTON 131
18. LINCOLN TAKES THE OATH AS PRESIDENT 138
19. SUMTER AND WAR CHALLENGE — CALL FOR TROOPS 146
20. JEFFERSON DAVIS — HIS GOVERNMENT 154
21. TURMOIL — FEAR — HAZARDS 160
22. BULL RUN — MCCLELLAN — FRÉMONT — THE TRENT AFFAIR 167
23. THE POLITICS OF WAR — CORRUPTION 177
24. DONELSON — GRANT — SHILOH — MONITOR AND MERRIMAC — "SEVEN DAYS" — THE DRAFT 183
25. SECOND BULL RUN — BLOODY ANTIETAM — CHAOS 196
26. THE INVOLVED SLAVERY ISSUE — PRELIMINARY EMANCIPATION PROCLAMATION 203
27. MCCLELLAN'S "SLOWS" — ELECTION LOSSES — FREDERICKSBURG — '62 MESSAGE 209
28. THUNDER OVER THE CABINET — MURFREESBORO 214
29. FINAL EMANCIPATION PROCLAMATION, '63 219
30. HOOKER — CHANCELLORSVILLE — CALAMITY 225
31. WILL GRANT TAKE VICKSBURG? 230
32. DEEP SHADOWS — LINCOLN IN EARLY '63 234
33. THE MAN IN THE WHITE HOUSE 240
34. GETTYSBURG — VICKSBURG SIEGE — DEEP TIDES, '63 246

35. LINCOLN AT STORM CENTER 258
36. LINCOLN SPEAKS AT GETTYSBURG 263
37. EPIC '63 DRAWS TO A CLOSE 272
38. GRANT GIVEN HIGH COMMAND, '64 277
39. WILL HIS PARTY RENOMINATE LINCOLN? 283
40. CHASE THIRSTS TO RUN FOR PRESIDENT 287
41. SPRING OF '64 — BLOOD AND ANGEL 291
42. GRANT'S OFFENSIVE, '64 — FREE PRESS — LINCOLN VISITS THE ARMY 295
43. THE LINCOLN-JOHNSON TICKET OF THE NATIONAL UNION PARTY 299
44. WASHINGTON ON THE DEFENSIVE — PEACE BABBLINGS 303
45. "THE DARKEST MONTH OF THE WAR" — AUGUST '64 309
46. THE FIERCE FALL CAMPAIGN OF '64 314
47. THE MAN WHO HAD BECOME THE ISSUE 321
48. ELECTION DAY, NOVEMBER 8, 1864 326
49. LINCOLN NAMES A CHIEF JUSTICE 330
50. THE "LOST ARMY" — THE SOUTH IN FIRE AND BLOOD — WAR PRISONS 334
51. THE BITTER YEAR OF '64 COMES TO A CLOSE 342
52. "FOREVER FREE" — THE THIRTEENTH AMENDMENT 347
53. HEAVY SMOKE — DARK SMOKE 350
54. THE SECOND INAUGURAL 357
55. ENDLESS EXECUTIVE ROUTINE 367
56. LINCOLN VISITS GRANT'S ARMY — GRANT BREAKS LEE'S LINE 369
57. RICHMOND FALLS — APPOMATTOX 375
58. "NOT IN SORROW, BUT IN GLADNESS OF HEART" 385
59. NEGOTIATIONS — AN OMINOUS DREAM 388
60. THE CALENDAR SAYS GOOD FRIDAY 391
61. BLOOD ON THE MOON 395
62. SHOCK — THE ASSASSIN — A STRICKEN PEOPLE 410
63. A TREE IS BEST MEASURED WHEN IT'S DOWN 431
64. VAST PAGEANT — THEN GREAT QUIET 435

Lincoln Conspirators' Hanging by Edward C. Goodman 450

Lincoln Memorial by Edward C. Goodman 453

SOURCES AND ACKNOWLEDGMENTS 456

PHOTO CREDITS 457

INDEX 458

PREFACE

As a growing boy in an Illinois prairie town I saw marching men who had fought under Grant and Sherman; I listened to stories of old-timers who had known Abraham Lincoln. At twenty in 1898 I served in the 6th Illinois Volunteers, our expedition to Porto Rico being commanded by General Nelson A. Miles, a brigadier general in some of the bloodiest battles of the Army of the Potomac in 1864. Our uniforms were the same light blue trousers and dark blue jackets with brass buttons as worn by the troops of the Army of the Potomac. We took swims in the Potomac River and had our first salt water swim in Charleston Harbor in sight of Fort Sumter.

The Lincoln lore of that time and place was of the man in his Illinois backgrounds and settings. When for thirty years and more I planned to make a certain portrait of Abraham Lincoln, it was as the country lawyer and prairie politician. But when I finished my *Prairie Years* portrait, Lincoln the Man had grown on me so that I went on to write *The War Years*. Now twenty-eight years after publication of the two-volume *Prairie Years* and nearly fifteen years after publication of the four-volume *War Years*, I have tried to compress the essential story of Lincoln the Man and President into one volume.

I have in this work, of course, consulted and made use of such new materials and researches as throw added light on the life and personality of Lincoln. Since the writing of the *Prairie Years* in the early 1920's there have been some thirty years of fiercely intensive research on the life of Lincoln before he became president. In no thirty-year period since the death of Lincoln has so rigorous and thorough an examination been given the facts and myths of the life of Lincoln. Listed separately at the back of the book are my "Sources and Acknowledgments." One may with no harm quote from Paul M. Angle: "I am convinced that annotation irritates almost everyone except professional historians… Still, if he is to play fair with his readers, the historical writer can hardly omit all mention of the materials he has used." Or from James G. Randall the cryptic: "Perhaps in general footnotes should be held guilty unless proved innocent." In all but four instances the texts as written by Lincoln, or as published, are followed literally without the use of [*sic*]. In three of these instances Lincoln stuttered in writing, but it is certain he did not stutter in speaking.

Walt Whitman saw Lincoln as "the grandest figure on the crowded canvas of the drama of the nineteenth century." In the story of a great pivotal figure at the vortex of a vast dark human struggle, we meet gaps and discrepancies. The teller of the story reports, within rigorous space limits, what is to him plain, moving, revealing. Every biographer of Lincoln is under compulsion to omit all or parts of Lincoln letters and speeches that he would like to include; this in part explains why any Lincoln biography is different from any or all other Lincoln biographies; each must choose and decide what sentences or paragraphs shed the light needed for the Lincoln portrait and story. Supposing all could be told, it would take a far longer time to tell it than was taken to enact it in life.

Here and there exist Lincoln letters not yet published but there are no expectations that they will throw important fresh light. As recently as February 1954 came the first publication of letters of Lincoln to Judge David Davis, which I have used herein as throwing slightly deeper gleams on Lincoln as a master politician. A national event was the opening at midnight on July 26, 1947, the "unveiling" as some termed it, of the long secret Robert T. Lincoln Collection in the Library of Congress. The next five days I did my best at reporting in seven newspaper columns for a syndicate what was revealed in the 18,300 letters, telegrams, manuscripts, miscellaneous data. The fourteen Lincoln scholars and authors present agreed that while no new light of importance was shed on Lincoln, the documents deepened and sharpened the outlines of the massive and subtle Lincoln as previously known. When I mentioned to Paul Angle a cynical editorial writer referring to us as "hagiographers" (saint worshippers), Paul said, "We could use a few real saints in this country now. And it's nice to live in a country where you can pick the saints you prefer to worship so long as you don't interfere with other saint worshippers."

Having read the million-word record of Lincoln's speeches and writings several times, Roy P. Basler sets forth, "The more fully Lincoln's varied career is traced…the more his genius grows and passes beyond each interpretation." Yankee Gamaliel Bradford put it briefly: "He still smiles and remains impenetrable."

To Joseph Fifer, Civil War solider and later governor of Illinois, his favorite tribute to Lincoln was anonymous till after a six-year search he found that Homer Hoch of Kansas spoke it in the House of Representatives February 12, 1923:

"There is no new thing to be said about Lincoln. There is no new thing to be said of the mountains, or of the sea, or of the stars. The years go their way, but the same old mountains lift their granite shoulders above the drifting clouds; the same mysterious sea beats upon the shore; the same silent stars keep holy vigil above a tired world. But to the mountains and sea and stars men turn forever in unwearied homage. And thus with Lincoln. For he was a mountain in grandeur of soul, he was a sea in deep undervoice of mystic loneliness, he was a star in steadfast purity of purpose and service. And he abides."

On the 100th birthday anniversary of Lincoln, Brazilian Ambassador Joaquin Nabuco said: "With the increased velocity of modern changes, we do not know what the world will be a hundred years hence. For sure, the ideals of the generation of the year 2000 will not be the same of the generation of the year 1900. Nations will then be governed by currents of political thought which we can no more anticipate than the seventeenth century could anticipate the political currents of the eighteenth, which still in part sway us. But whether the spirit of authority, or that of freedom, increases, Lincoln's legend will ever appear more luminous in the amalgamation of centuries, because he supremely incarnated both those spirits."

CARL SANDBURG
Connemara Farm
Flat Rock, North Carolina
May 5, 1954

LINCOLN'S POET AND THE POET'S LINCOLN

The poets have always understood Lincoln," the historian Henry Steele Comager wrote in his review of Carl Sandburg's 1939 four-volume: *Abraham Lincoln: The War Years*, the monumental follow-up to his groundbreaking 1926 two-volume *Abraham Lincoln: The Prairie Years*. He cited Whitman and Emerson as well as Vachel Lindsay and Stephen Vincent Benét, all of whom had written about Lincoln, and then pronounced it "fitting that from the pen of a poet should come the greatest of all Lincoln biographies, one of the great biographies of our literature."

It was both a profound insight and a bold admission, coming as it did not from a poet but from a major American historian, and there was a good reason why it took a poet to understand Lincoln. "Poets are the unacknowledged legislators of the world," Shelley wrote in 1821, but it took a poet—the first in Comager's list—to understand that Abraham Lincoln, acknowledged *legislator*, was one of the great unacknowledged *poets* of the world. That was the connection Whitman formed with the president. He recognized in Lincoln an intense love of language, just as Sandburg later did. Young Lincoln, Sandburg wrote in *The Prairie Years*, "was hungry to understand the meaning of words" and would "lay awake hours at night thinking about the meaning of the meaning" of language. As an adult, Lincoln "enjoyed puns and folk sayings" and relished "the plain homespun language of a man of the people," Sandburg observed in *The War Years*.

That Sandburg, like Whitman, should rejoice in Lincoln's poetic love of language was only natural, for Sandburg rejoiced in Whitman's language and regarded himself as Whitman's disciple in the history of American literature. As a young poet in 1904, Sandburg journeyed to the Good Gray Poet's last home, in Camden, New Jersey—Whitman had died only a dozen years earlier—and asked directions to his house. The first man he encountered didn't know the name—"What is he, a machinist?" he asked—but Sandburg managed to find the place on Mickle Street and gave the woman who lived there twenty-five cents to show him through. At one point in the visit, she turned to Sandburg: "This Whitman," she said, "they say he was an infidel. Was he?" Sandburg replied: "He was nearer to God than any man that said that."

But Sandburg knew it was more than a love of language that had made Whitman a poet, just as Whitman had known it was more than his way with words that made Lincoln a legislator-poet. Sandburg took to his heart what Whitman had said in his Preface to *Leaves of Grass*, that "the United States themselves are

essentially the greatest poem," and, like Whitman, he believed Abraham Lincoln also imagined the nation this way. Like a great poem, Lincoln's America was the physical expression of an idea, mystical, spiritual, but very real—call it, as Whitman did, democracy, or as Lincoln called it in his *Second Annual Message to Congress*, "the last, best hope of earth."

So Lincoln was a poet in the grandest and deepest sense. Just before he started work on what became *The Prairie Years*," Sandburg penned a poem he never published:

> I make my acknowledgments to you,
> Jesus, Shakespeare, Lincoln.
> I say you dead are more real than people I
> see on streetcars, in offices and restaur-
> ants, in parks and cigar store hangouts.

Jesus, Shakespeare, Lincoln—all great poets, to be understood best by another great poet, and all more real, more present, more alive, than the living. As it had been with Whitman, who felt a bond with all humanity, living or dead (he therefore declared there really was no death), so it became for Sandburg in the instance of Abraham Lincoln. Lincoln was a presence. Through the four years consumed in writing *The Prairie Years* and the eleven in writing *The War Years*, Lincoln's life merged wholly with Sandburg's. "Your own character gets written into your work," Sandburg confessed to a friend about the Lincoln biography. When he finished the book, he spoke of having now to face the task of finding out just where Lincoln left off and Carl Sandburg began.

Carl August Sandburg was born just four years after Abraham Lincoln was murdered. He was born in Galesburg, Illinois, a town just 120 miles from Springfield, the state capital, where Lincoln had begun his career, practiced law, and served as a state legislator. He was born in a three-room frame house on Third Street, its boards so weathered and rough-hewn that a casual observer might have mistaken the place for a log cabin. Abraham Lincoln was very much a living presence in this part of Illinois, and young Carl grew up among people who had known him well and who spoke about him casually and often.

Carl Sandburg grew up in the world of Abraham Lincoln, but whereas Walt Whitman, living and working in Washington, D.C., had passed a formative portion of his adulthood in the presence of the adult Lincoln—Lincoln the war president—young

Sandburg's Lincoln was Lincoln the child, the youth, and the young man. It was almost as if they had come of age together, and so it was no accident that the very idea of writing a biography of Abraham Lincoln came to the poet Sandburg just after the success of *Rootabaga Stories*, a collection of children's stories he published in 1922. By this time, Sandburg was well established as poet who had brought a new muscular, homely realism to poetry—as in the already iconic "Chicago" of 1914: "Hog Butcher for the World, / Tool Maker, Stacker of wheat, / Player with Railroads and the Nation's Freight Handler: / Stormy, husky, brawling, / City of the Big Shoulders"—but, of late, he longed to escape the gritty grown-up realities of urban America for a sojourn, however temporary, in what he described in a letter to a friend as a "Far Country of make-believe." Besides, even an "established" poet makes little enough money writing verse. In *Rootabaga Stories*, Sandburg found his release, a journey back into childhood, and he also found a new and most welcome level of commercial success, which prompted him to write a pair of sequels, *Rootabaga Pigeons* and *Rootabaga Country*.

It also spurred him to begin organizing material he had been collecting for some years on Lincoln, and to begin thinking about it in a serious way as the basis of a children's biography of the childhood of the Great Emancipator. In this, Sandburg did what romantic poets had been doing at least since William Wordsworth at the end of the eighteenth century. He sought in childhood the innocence and freshness of imagination that lay at the root of poetic inspiration. And while the Lincoln book rapidly grew beyond the bounds of a standard juvenile biography—expanding into two volumes, beginning at birth and ending at the point of Lincoln's election to the presidency—it was still rooted in childhood. As Sandburg explained in his Preface to *The Prairie Years*, he had wanted to "sketch the country lawyer and prairie politician who was intimate with the settlers of the Knox County neighborhood where I grew up as a boy, and where I heard the talk of the men and women who had eaten with Lincoln, given him a bed overnight, heard his jokes and lingo, remembered his silences and his mobile face."

What began, then, as the continuation of an escape back into childhood soon became a labor of *love*, with the emphasis on labor. While he researched and wrote *Abraham Lincoln: The Prairie Years*, Sandburg held down a day job at the *Chicago Daily News* and had a bustling career as an itinerant lecturer and singer of folk ballads. He worked on the book at night, and, while traveling for his lectures, he collected original documents, old newspapers, and rare books. He especially craved the immediate reality of the papers that had passed through the hands of Lincoln or those near him. Sandburg met with New York businessman and Lincoln collector Frederick Hill Meserve, who owned some thirty thousand period photographs, including a wealth of Mathew Brady negatives and prints. During their time together, Meserve marveled at how Sandburg held up one negative and print after another, "exclaiming at their beauty" and "lingering over the faces of these men and women for he knew human stories behind those faces." As Whitman had said in "Song of Myself," there is no death—"If you want me again look for me under your boot-soles"—not when a living imagination makes contact with the products of the past and infuses them with life, as Carl Sandburg did in creating his Lincoln.

Over the years, some critics and historians have sniped and carped at the six volumes that, together, make up *Abraham Lincoln: The Prairie Years* and *Abraham Lincoln: The War Years*, complaining that Sandburg was no scholar, that he'd been taken in by certain forgeries, that he put words in Lincoln's mouth, that he imagined scenes for which there was no eyewitness documentation, that, in short, he put himself into the story of the life of another. To these charges, Sandburg consistently, even cheerfully, pleaded guilty, and he always acknowledged and thanked those who corrected his errors of fact, and he bowed to later scholars who had access to documents and other materials unavailable to him or of which he had simply been unaware. But for putting himself in Lincoln's story he never apologized, because that was the very reason he wrote the books: to put himself into a story he understood so well, a story he shared, the tale of a brother poet and, even more simply, of a brother.

"Can we accept as a Lincoln authority a poet, an author of fairy tales, a singer of folk songs, a man who thumbed his nose at the precepts of the historical professions, broke rules of literary composition with impunity and gloried in his unconventionality?" asked the historiographer Benjamin Thomas in his 1947 *Portrait for Posterity*, a survey of Lincoln and his many biographers. The answer, Thomas decided, was yes. "Like Lincoln," he wrote, Sandburg was "a common man with an uncommon mind. He has the same ideas about America that Lincoln had." No other Lincoln biography, no matter how thorough and authoritative in the best conventional scholarly style, gives readers what Sandburg's Lincoln gives them. It gives them Lincoln the man, grounded in hard fact but unabashedly imagined, and through the imagination, brought to life, today, now, and for as long as these volumes—now richly illustrated with the artifacts, documents, places, and people Lincoln knew so well—find willing eyes and minds and hearts.

ALAN AXELROD

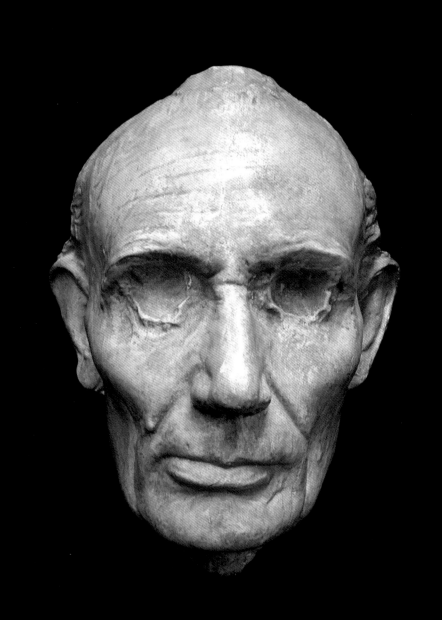

CHAPTER 1

WILDERNESS BEGINNINGS

Life mask of Abraham Lincoln cast in plaster in 1917 after the original cast in 1860 by Leonard Wells Volk.

WILDERNESS BEGINNINGS

IN THE year 1776, when the 13 American colonies gave to the world their famous Declaration of Independence, there was a captain of Virginia militia living in Rockingham County named Abraham Lincoln. He had a 210-acre farm deeded to him by his father, John Lincoln, one of the many English, Scotch, Irish, German, Dutch settlers who were taking the green hills and slopes of the Shenandoah Valley and putting their plows to unbroken ground long held by the Indians. These Lincolns in Virginia came from Berks County in Pennsylvania and traced back to Lincolns in New England and Old England.

Abraham Lincoln had taken for a wife Bathsheba Herring, who bore him three sons, Mordecai, Josiah and Thomas, and two daughters, Mary and Nancy. This family Abraham Lincoln moved to Kentucky in 1782. For years his friend Daniel Boone, coming back from trips to Kentucky, had been telling of valleys there rich with black land and blue grass, game and fish, tall timber and clear running waters. It called to him, that country Boone talked about, where land was 40 cents an acre. Abraham Lincoln sold his farm; they packed their belongings and joined a party heading down the Wilderness Road through Cumberland Gap and up north and west into Kentucky. Abraham Lincoln located on the Green River, where he filed claims for more than 2,000 acres.

One day about two years later, he was working in a field with his three sons, and they saw him in a spasm of pain fall to the ground, just after the boys had heard a rifle shot and the whine of a bullet. The boys yelled to each other, "Indians!" Mordecai ran to a cabin nearby, Josiah started across fields and woods to a fort to bring help. Six-year-old Tom stooped over his father's bleeding body and wondered what he could do. He looked up to see an Indian standing over him, a shining bangle hanging down over the Indian's shoulder close to the heart. Then Tom saw the Indian's hands clutch upward, saw him double with a groan and crumple to the ground. Mordecai with a rifle at a peephole in the cabin had aimed his shot at the shining bangle. Little Tom was so near he heard the bullet plug its hole into the red man.

Thomas Lincoln, while growing up, lived in different places in Kentucky with kith and kin, sometimes hiring out to farmers, mostly in Washington County. Betweenwhiles he learned the carpenter's trade and cabinetmaking. In his full growth he was about five feet nine, weighed about 185 pounds, his muscles and ribs close-knit. His dark hazel eyes looked out from a round face, from under coarse black hair. He could be short-spoken or reel off sayings, yarns, jokes. He made a reputation as a storyteller. He had little or no time for books, could read some, and could sign his name.

Thomas Lincoln at 19 had served in the Kentucky state militia. At 24 he was appointed a constable in Cumberland County. The next year he moved to Hardin County and served on a jury. He was trusted by a sheriff and paid by the county to guard a prisoner for six days. In the county jail he could see men bolted behind bars for not paying their debts and at the public whipping post both white and black men lashed on their naked backs. In 1803 Thomas Lincoln for "the sum of 118 pounds in hand paid" bought a 238-acre tract near Mill Creek, seven miles north of Elizabethtown, the county seat of Hardin County. In March 1805 he was one of four "patrollers" appointed in Hardin County to seize suspicious white characters or Negro slaves roving without permits. In March 1806 he was hired by Bleakley & Montgomery, storekeepers in Elizabethtown, to take a flatboat of their merchandise down the Ohio and Mississippi Rivers to New Orleans, earning 16 pounds in gold and a credit of 13 pounds in gold. Account books of the store had him occasionally buying "two twists of tobacco," one pound for 38 cents, and one pint of whisky for 21 cents.

Thomas Lincoln was in love and his wedding set for June 12, 1806, at Beechland in Washington County. Nancy Hanks, the bride-to-be, was a daughter of Lucy Hanks and was sometimes called Nancy Sparrow as though she was an adopted daughter of Thomas and Elizabeth Sparrow whose house was her home.

Lucy Hanks had welcomed her child Nancy into life in Virginia about 1784. The name of the child's father seems to have vanished from any documents or letters that may have

Lincoln family homestead in Rockingham County, Virginia, owned by Lincoln's grandfather also named Abraham. Photo by John Vachon.

existed. His name stayed unknown to baffle and mystify the seekers who for years searched for records and sought evidence that might bring to light the name of the father of the girl child Nancy Hanks.

Lucy traveled to Kentucky carrying what was to her a precious bundle. She was perhaps 19 when she made this trip. If Lucy was married when Nancy was born it seemed that her husband either died and she became a widow or he lived and stayed on in Virginia or elsewhere. In either case she and their child had to get along as best they could without him.

June 12, 1806, came and the home of Richard Berry at Beechland in Washington County saw men and women on horseback arriving for the wedding of 28-year-old Thomas Lincoln and 22-year-old Nancy Hanks. The groom was wearing his fancy beaver hat, a new black suit, his new silk suspenders. The bride's outfit had in it linen and silk, perhaps a dash somewhere of the

Stereoscopic view of the one-room cabin where Abraham Lincoln was traditionally born near Hodgenville, Kentucky, February 12, 1809.

The one-room cabin.

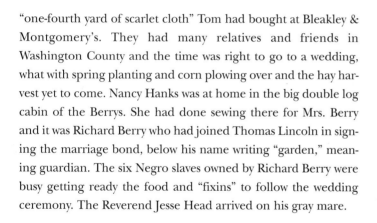

The symbolic log cabin at the Lincoln Birthplace National Historic Site.

"one-fourth yard of scarlet cloth" Tom had bought at Bleakley & Montgomery's. They had many relatives and friends in Washington County and the time was right to go to a wedding, what with spring planting and corn plowing over and the hay harvest yet to come. Nancy Hanks was at home in the big double log cabin of the Berrys. She had done sewing there for Mrs. Berry and it was Richard Berry who had joined Thomas Lincoln in signing the marriage bond, below his name writing "garden," meaning guardian. The six Negro slaves owned by Richard Berry were busy getting ready the food and "fixins" to follow the wedding ceremony. The Reverend Jesse Head arrived on his gray mare.

A hater of sin, he liked decency and good order and could pause in a sermon to step from the pulpit and throw out a disorderly mocker who had had a few drinks. The bride and groom stood up before him. He pronounced them man and wife and wrote for the county clerk that on June 12, 1806, Thomas Lincoln and Nancy Hanks had been joined together in the holy estate of matrimony "agreeable to the rites and ceremonies of the Methodist Episcopal Church."

The new husband put his bride on a horse and they rode away on the red clay road along the timber trails to Elizabethtown to make a home in a cabin close to the county courthouse. Tall, slender, dark-complexioned Nancy Hanks had happiness that year of 1806. One summer day she had news for her husband—a baby on the way! They rode out more often perhaps to the Little Mount Baptist Church where they were

members and spoke prayers more often of hope for the child to come. Perhaps an added dark zeal came in the brief grace Thomas spoke at meals.

On February 10, 1807, the child came wellborn and they named her Sarah. Nancy washed and nursed her baby, made her wishes and prayers for the little one. She read their Bible. One who knew her well said she was "a ready reader." She was a believer and knew so much of what she believed was yonder always yonder. She saw her husband in trouble in law courts. He took a contract to hew timbers and help put up a new sawmill for Denton Geoghegan, spent days of hard work on the job. When Geoghegan wouldn't pay him, Tom filed suit and won.

Detail of the symbolic log cabin at the Lincoln Birthplace National Historic Site. Photo by Lester Jones, August 22, 1940.

Geoghegan then started two suits against Lincoln, claiming the sawmill timbers were not hewn square and true. Tom Lincoln won both suits.

When he bought his second farm, 348 ½ acres on the South Fork of Nolin Creek, 18 miles southeast of Elizabethtown, he paid Isaac Bush $200 in cash and took on a small obligation due a former titleholder. This in 1808 made Tom Lincoln owner of 586 ½ acres of land, along with two lots in Elizabethtown and some livestock.

In May and the blossom-time of 1808, Tom and Nancy with the baby moved from Elizabethtown to the farm of George Brownfield, where Tom did carpenter and farm work.

The same year saw Tom Lincoln's family moved to his land on the South Fork of Nolin Creek, about two and a half miles from Hodgenville. He was trying to farm stubborn ground and make a home in a cabin of logs he cut from timber nearby. The floor was packed-down dirt. One door, swung on leather hinges, let them in and out. One small window gave a lookout on the weather, the rain or snow, sun and trees, and the play of the rolling prairie and low hills. A stick-clay chimney carried the fire smoke up and away.

One morning in February 1809, Tom Lincoln came out of his cabin to the road, stopped a neighbor and asked him to tell "the granny woman," Aunt Peggy Walters, that Nancy would

"Boyhood of Lincoln" by Henry Watson. Engraved by William M. Vander Weyde.

need help soon. On the morning of February 12, a Sunday, the granny woman was at the cabin. And she and Tom Lincoln and the moaning Nancy Hanks welcomed into a world of battle and blood, of whispering dreams and wistful dust, a new child, a boy.

A little later that morning Tom Lincoln threw extra wood on the fire, an extra bearskin over the mother, and walked two miles up the road to where the Sparrows, Tom and Betsy, lived. Dennis Hanks, the nine-year-old boy adopted by the Sparrows, met Tom at the door. In his slow way of talking Tom Lincoln told them, "Nancy's got a boy baby."

A half-sheepish look was in his eyes, as though maybe more babies were not wanted in Kentucky just then.

Dennis Hanks took to his feet down the road to the Lincoln cabin. There he saw Nancy Hanks on a bed of poles cleated to a corner of the cabin, under warm bearskins. She turned her dark head from looking at the baby to look at Dennis and threw him

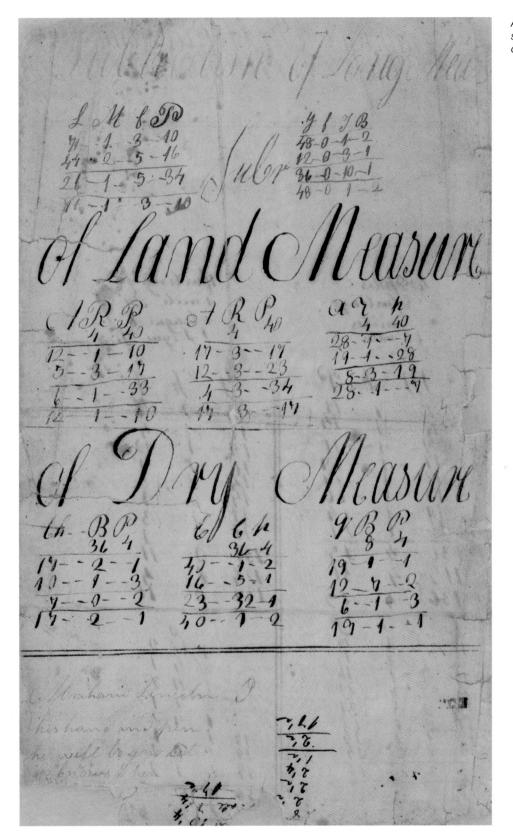

Abraham Lincoln's student sum book, ca. 1824-1826.

Lincoln studying by firelight. By Joseph Boggs Beale.

Young Lincoln studying in the fields.

WILDERNESS BEGINNINGS

a tired, white smile from her mouth and gray eyes. He stood watching the even, quiet breaths of this fresh, soft red baby. "What you goin' to name him, Nancy?" the boy asked.

"Abraham," was the answer, "after his grandfather."

Soon came Betsy Sparrow. She washed the baby, put a yellow petticoat and a linsey shirt on him, cooked dried berries with wild honey for Nancy, put the one-room cabin in better order, kissed Nancy and comforted her, and went home, saying she would come again in the morning.

Dennis rolled up in a bearskin and slept by the fireplace that night. He asked if he could hold the baby. Nancy, as she passed the little one into Dennis' arms, said, "Be keerful, Dennis, fur you air the fust boy he's ever seen." Dennis swung the baby back and forth, keeping up a chatter about how tickled he was to have a new cousin to play with. The baby screwed up its face and began crying with no letup. Dennis turned to Betsy Sparrow, handed her the baby and said, "Aunt, take him! He'll never come to much."

Whatever the exact particulars, the definite event on that 12th of February, 1809, was the birth of a boy they named Abraham after his grandfather who had been killed by Indians born in silence and pain from a wilderness mother on a bed of perhaps cornhusks and perhaps hen feathers with perhaps a laughing child prophecy later that he would "never come to much."

In the spring of 1811 Tom Lincoln moved his family ten miles northeast to a 230-acre farm he had bought on Knob Creek, where the soil was a little richer and there were more neighbors. The famous Cumberland Trail, the main pike from Louisville to Nashville, ran nearby the new log cabin Tom built, and they could see covered wagons with settlers heading south, west, north, peddlers with tinware and notions, gangs of slaves or "kaffles" moving on foot ahead of an overseer or slave trader on horseback, and sometimes in dandy carriages congressmen or legislative members going to sessions at Louisville.

Here little Abe grew out of one shirt into another, learned to walk and talk and as he grew bigger how to be a chore boy, to run errands, carry water, fill the woodbox, clean ashes from the fireplace. That Knob Creek farm in their valley set round by high hills and deep gorges was the first home Abe Lincoln remembered.

Again there were quiet and anxious days in 1812 when another baby was on the way; again came neighbor helpers and Nancy gave birth to her third child. They named him Thomas but he died a few days after and Sarah and Abe saw, in a coffin their father made, the little cold still face and made their first acquaintance with the look of death in a personal grief in their own one-room cabin.

Four miles a day Sarah and Abe walked when school kept and they were not needed at home. In a log schoolhouse with a dirt floor and one door, seated on puncheon benches with no backs, they learned the alphabet A to Z and numbers one to ten. It was called a "blab school"; the pupils before reciting read their lessons out loud to themselves to show they were busy studying.

Tom Lincoln worked hard and had a reputation for paying his debts. One year he was appointed a "road surveyor" to keep a certain stretch of road in repair, another time was named appraiser for an estate, and an 1814 tax book listed him as 15th among the 98 property owners named. In 1816 he paid taxes on four horses. In 1814, however, because of a flaw in title he sold his Mill Creek farm for 18 pounds less than he had paid for it; the tract survey in one place read "west" where it should have read "east." Another suit involved his title to the Nolin Creek farm, still another aimed to dispossess him of the Knob Creek farm. Meantime slavery was on the rise and in 1816 there were 1,238 slaves on the tax lists of Hardin County, one taxpayer owning 58 Negro slaves, men, women and children, on the books valued along with horses, cows and other livestock. So when Tom Lincoln in 1816 decided to move to Indiana it was, as Abe later wrote, "partly on account of slavery; but chiefly on account of the difficulty in land titles."

In December 1816, Tom Lincoln with Nancy, Sarah, Abe, four horses and their most needed household goods, made their breakaway from Kentucky, moving north and crossing the Ohio River into land then Perry County, later Spencer County, Indiana. They had toiled and hacked their way through wilderness when about 16 miles from the Ohio River they came to a rise of ground somewhat open near Little Pigeon Creek. Here the whole family pitched in and threw together a pole shed or "half-faced camp," at the open side a log fire kept burning night and day. In the next weeks of that winter Tom Lincoln, with help from neighbors and young Abe, now nearly eight, erected a cabin 18 by 20 feet, with a loft. Abe later wrote that he "though very young, was large of his age, and had an axe put into his hands at once; and was almost constantly handling that most

Older Mrs. Thomas Lincoln (Sarah Bush Lincoln), Abe's stepmother.

useful instrument." The chinking of wet clay and grass ("wattle and daub") between the logs in the new cabin had not been finished in early February when something happened that a boy remembers after he is a grown man. Years later Abe wrote, "At this place A.[braham] took an early start as a hunter, which was never much improved afterwards. A few days before the completion of his eigth year, in the absence of his father, a flock of wild turkeys approached the new log-cabin, and A.[braham] with a rifle gun, standing inside, shot through a crack and killed one of them." Then came another sentence, "He has never since pulled a trigger on any larger game," making it clear that when they had deer or bear meat or other food from "larger game," it was not from his shooting. He didn't like shooting to kill and didn't care for a reputation as a hunter.

When Tom Lincoln built this cabin he didn't own the land it stood on. He was a "squatter." Not until October 15, 1817, after a 90-mile overland trip to Vincennes did he enter his claim for a quarter section of land, paying a first installment of $16 then and in December $64. The Government was selling him the land at $2.00 an acre; the $80 he had paid was one-fourth of the purchase price and he would have a clear title when he paid the other three-fourths. It had been a hard year, "pretty pinching times," as Abe put it later. They had to chop down trees, clear away underbrush, on what few acres they planted after plowing the hard unbroken sod. Their food was mostly game shot in the woods nearby, deer, bear, wild turkeys, ducks, geese. Wild pigeons in flocks sometimes darkened the sky. Their cabin lighting at night was from fire logs, pine knots, or hog fat. Sarah and Abe went barefoot from late spring till autumn frosts, brought home nuts and wild fruits, watched sometimes in the excitement of their father smoking out a bee tree for the honey. One drawback was water supply. Abe or Sarah had to walk nearly a mile to fetch spring water. Tom dug several wells but they all went dry.

Some of those who came were hungry, even lustful, for land. Some were hunters, adventurers, outlaws, fugitives. Most were hoping for a home of their own. In December 1816, when the Lincolns came to Pigeon Creek, enough settlers had arrived in Indiana for it to be "admitted to the Union." It could be about then little Abe asked the solemn question, "The Union? What is the Union?"

A wagon one day late in 1817 brought into the Lincoln clearing their good Kentucky neighbors Tom and Betsy Sparrow and the odd quizzical 17-year-old Dennis Friend Hanks. For some years Dennis would be a chum of Abe's and on occasion would make free to say, "I am base born," explaining that his mother bore him before she married one Levi Hall. The Sparrows were to live in the Lincoln pole shed till they could locate land and settle. Hardly a year had passed, however, when Tom and Betsy Sparrow were taken down with the "milk sick," beginning with a whitish coat on the tongue, resulting, it was supposed, from cows eating white snakeroot or other growths that poisoned their milk. Tom and Betsy Sparrow died and were buried in September on a little hill in a clearing in the timbers nearby.

Soon after, there came to Nancy Hanks Lincoln that white coating of the tongue; her vitals burned; the tongue turned brownish; her feet and hands grew cold and colder, her pulse slow and slower. She knew she was dying, called for her children, and spoke to them her last dim choking words. Death came October 5, 1818, the banners of autumn flaming their crimsons over tall oaks and quiet maples. On a bed of poles cleated to the corner of the cabin, the body of Nancy Hanks Lincoln lay in peace and silence, the eyelids closed down in unbroken rest. To the children who tiptoed in, stood still, cried their tears of want and longing, whispered and heard only their own whispers answering, she looked as though new secrets had come to her in place of the old secrets given up with the breath of life.

Tom Lincoln took a log left over from the building of the cabin, and he and Dennis Hanks whipsawed it into planks, planed the planks smooth, and made them of a measure for a box to bury the dead wife and mother in. Little Abe, with a jack-knife, whittled pine-wood pegs. And while Dennis and Abe held the planks, Tom bored holes and stuck the whittled pegs through the holes. This was the coffin they carried next day to the little timber clearing nearby, where a few weeks before they had buried Tom and Betsy Sparrow.

So Nancy Hanks Lincoln died, 34 years old, a pioneer sacrifice, with memories of monotonous, endless everyday chores, of mystic Bible verses read over and over for their promises, of blue wistful hills and a summer when the crab-apple blossoms flamed white and she carried a boy child into the world.

A hard year followed with 12-year-old Sarah as housekeeper and cook, and Tom Lincoln with the help of Dennis and Abe trying to clear more land, plant it, and make the farm a go. It was the year Abe was driving a horse at the mill. While he was putting a whiplash to the nag and calling, "Git up, you old hussy; git up, you old hussy," the horse let fly a fast hind foot that knocked Abe down and out of his senses just as he yelled, "Git up." He lay bleeding, was taken home, washed, put to bed, and lay all night unconscious. He spoke of it afterward as a mystery of the human mind, and later wrote of himself, "In his tenth year he was kicked by a horse, and apparantly killed for a time." Instead of dying, as was half expected, he came to, saying, "You old hussy," thus finishing what he started to say before he was knocked down and out.

Lonesome days came for Abe and Sarah in November when their father went away, promising to come back. He headed for Elizabethtown, Kentucky, through woods and across the Ohio River, to the house of the widow Sarah Bush Johnston. They said he argued straight-out: "I have no wife and you no husband. I came a-purpose to marry you. I knowed you from a gal and you knowed me from a boy. I've no time to lose; and if you're willin' let it be done straight off." She answered, "I got a few little debts," gave him a list and he paid them; and they were married December 2, 1819.

Abe and Sarah had a nice surprise one morning when four horses and a wagon came into their clearing, and their father jumped off, then Sarah Bush Lincoln, the new wife and mother, then her three children by her first husband, Sarah Elizabeth (13), Matilda (10), and John D. Johnston (9 years old). Next off the wagon came a feather mattress and pillows, a black walnut bureau, a large clothes chest, a table, chairs, pots and skillets, knives, forks, spoons.

The one-room cabin now sheltered eight people to feed and clothe. At bedtime the men and boys undressed first, the women and girls following, and by the code of decent folk no one was abashed. Dennis and Abe climbed on pegs to the loft for their sleep and liked it when later the logs were chinked against the rain or snow coming in on them. Dennis said "Aunt Sairy," the new mother, "had faculty and didn't 'pear to be hurried or worried none," that she got Tom to put in a floor and make "some good beds and cheers. Abe, like Dennis, said "cheers"; if he said "chairs" he would be taken as "uppety" and "too fine-haired."

Eleven-year-old Abe went to school again. Years later he wrote of where he grew up, "There were some schools, so called; but no qualification was ever required of a teacher, beyond 'readin', writin', and cipherin' to the Rule of Three. If a straggler supposed to understand latin, happened to sojourn in the neighborhood, he was looked upon as a wizzard." School kept at Pigeon Creek when a schoolmaster happened to drift in, usually in winter, and school was out when he drifted away.

Boyhood National Memorial which preserves the Lincoln City, Indiana, farm site where Abraham Lincoln lived from 1816 to 1830.

Andrew Crawford taught Abe in 1820, James Swaney two years later, and after a year of no school Abe learned from Azel Dorsey. The schoolmasters were paid by the parents in venison, hams, corn, animal skins and other produce. Four miles from home to school and four miles to home again Abe walked for his learning, saying later that "all his schooling did not amount to one year."

Having learned to read Abe read all the books he could lay his hands on. Dennis, years later, tried to remember his cousin's reading habits. "I never seen Abe after he was twelve 'at he didn't have a book some'ers 'round. He'd put a book inside his shirt an' fill his pants pockets with corn dodgers, an' go off to plow or hoe.

They heard Abe saying, "The things I want to know are in books; my best friend is the man who'll git me a book I ain't read." One fall afternoon he walked to see John Pitcher, a lawyer at Rockport, nearly 20 miles away, and borrowed a book he heard Pitcher had. A few days later, with his father and Dennis and John Hanks he shucked corn from early daylight till sundown. Then after supper he read the book till midnight, and next day at noon hardly knew the taste of his corn bread because of the book in front of him. So they told it.

He read many hours in the family Bible, the only book in their cabin. He borrowed and read *Aesop's Fables, Pilgrim's Progress, Robinson Crusoe*, Grimshaw's *History of the United States*, and Weems' *The Life of George Washington, with Curious Anecdotes, Equally Honorable to Himself and Exemplary to His Young Countrymen*. Books lighted lamps in the dark rooms of his gloomy hours.

The years pass and Abe Lincoln grows up, at 17 standing six feet, nearly four inches, long-armed with rare strength in his muscles. At 18 he could take an ax at the end of the handle and hold it out from his shoulders in a straight horizontal line, easy and steady. Often Abe worked alone in the timbers, daylong with only the sound of his own ax, or his own voice speaking to himself, or the crackling and swaying of branches in the wind, or the cries and whirrs of animals, of brown and silver-gray squirrels, of partridges, hawks, crows, turkeys, grouse, sparrows and the occasional wildcat.

Education came to the youth Abe by many ways outside of schools and books. As he said later, he "picked up" education. He was the letter writer for the family and for neighbors. As he wrote he read the words out loud. He walked 30 miles to a courthouse to hear lawyers speak and to see how they argued and acted. He heard roaring and ranting political speakers—and mimicked them. He listened to wandering evangelists who flung their arms and tore the air with their voices—and mimicked them.

His stepmother was a rich silent force in his life. The family and the neighbors spoke of her sagacity and gumption, her sewing and mending, how spick-and-span she kept her house, her pots, pans and kettles. Her faith in God shone in works more than words, and hard as life was, she was thankful to be alive. She understood Abe's gloomy spells better than anyone else and he named her as a deep influence in him. "Abe never spoke a cross word to me," she said and she found him truthful.

When Abe's sister Sarah, a year after marrying Aaron Grigsby, died in childbirth in 1828, it was Sarah Bush Lincoln who spoke comfort to the nearly 19-year-old son of Nancy Hanks at the burial of his sister. Yet somehow the stepmother couldn't lessen the bitterness Abe held toward Aaron Grigsby, whether he blamed Grigsby for neglect of his sister or something else.

A mile across the fields from the Lincoln home was the Pigeon Creek Baptist Church, a log meetinghouse put up in 1822. On June 7, 1823, William Barker, who kept the minutes and records, wrote that the church "received Brother Thomas Lincoln by letter." He was elected the next year with two neighbors to serve as a committee of visitors to the Gilead church, and served three years as church trustee. Strict watch was kept on the conduct of members and Tom served on committees to look into reported misconduct between husbands and wives, brothers and sisters, of neighbor against neighbor.

Most of the church people could read only the shortest words in the Bible, or none at all. They sat in the log meetinghouse on the split-log benches their own axes had shaped, listening to the preacher reading from the Bible.

The Sabbath was not only a day for religious meetings. After the sermon, the members, who rode horses many miles to the meetinghouse, talked about crops, weather, births and deaths, the growing settlements, letters just come, politics, Indians and land titles.

Young Abraham Lincoln saw certain of these Christians with a clean burning fire, with inner reckonings that prompted them to silence or action or speech, and they could justify themselves with a simple and final explanation that all things should be done decently and in order.

CHAPTER 2

New Salem Days

NEW SALEM DAYS

I N FEBRUARY 1831, John Hanks had made an agreement with a man named Denton Offutt, a frontier hustler big with promises and a hard drinker, that he, Abe Lincoln and John D. Johnston would take a flatboat of cargo to New Orleans. Offutt was to have the flatboat and cargo ready and they were to meet him on the Sangamon River near the village of Springfield as soon as the snow should go off. With traveling by land made difficult by floods, they bought a large canoe. And so, with his mother's cousin and his stepbrother, in the spring of 1831, Abraham Lincoln, 22 years old, floated down the Sangamon River, going to a new home, laughter and youth in his bones, in his heart a few pennies of dreams, in his head a rag bag of thoughts he could never expect to sell.

Leaving their canoe at Judy's Ferry and not finding Denton Offutt there, they walked to Springfield and at Andrew Elliott's Buckhorn Tavern found Offutt lush with liquor and promises and no flatboat. He hired them at $12 a month and sent them to Government timberland, where they cut down trees, got logs to Kirkpatrick's mill for planks and gunwales. Near their shanty and camp on the Sangamon River where the flatboat was shaping, the Sangamon County assessor, Erastus Wright, saw Lincoln in April with his "boots off, hat, coat and vest off. Pants rolled up to his knees and shirt wet with sweat and combing his fuzzie hair with his fingers as he pounded away on the boat."

In about four weeks they launched the boat, 80 feet long and 18 feet wide, loaded the cargo of barreled pork, corn and live hogs, and moved downstream from Sangamo Town, steering away from snags and low water, Lincoln on deck in blue homespun jeans, jacket, vest, rawhide boots with pantaloons stuffed in, and a felt hat once black but now, as the owner said, "sunburned till it was a combine of colors." Lincoln, Hanks and John D. Johnston floated down the Mississippi River, meeting strings of flatboats and other river craft. Hanks, away from home longer than expected, left them at St. Louis.

Lincoln on a flat boat on trip to New Orleans. By Joseph Boggs Beale.

Stepping off the flatboat at New Orleans, Lincoln walked nearly a mile, on flatboats, to reach shore. In New Orleans, Lincoln could read advertisements of traders, one giving notice: "I will at all times pay the highest cash prices for Negroes of every description, and will also attend to the sale of Negroes on commission, having a jail and yard fitted up expressly for boarding them." There were sellers advertising, "For sale several likely girls from 10 to 18 years old, a woman 24, a very valuable woman 25, with three very likely children," while buyers indicated after the manner of one: "Wanted—I want to purchase twenty-five likely Negroes, between the ages of 18 and 25 years, male and female, for which I will pay the highest prices in cash." After a month or so, with Johnston, he took a steamboat north.

From New Orleans up the Mississippi on the steamboat and from St. Louis walking overland Lincoln must have wondered about New Salem village, the people there, his new job, the new life he was moving into. Offutt had rented the gristmill at the Sangamon River dam below the hilltop village and in St. Louis was buying a stock of goods for a new store. Lincoln was to be clerk in charge of store and mill at $15 a month and a back room to sleep in. Arriving in late July Lincoln walked the village street, looked over its dozen or more cabins, searched faces he expected to see many times for many months.

On August 1, 1831, he cast his first ballot. The polls were in the home of John Camron where Lincoln was boarding and getting acquainted with Camron's 11 daughters who teased him about his long legs and arms and heard him admit he "wasn't much to look at." Voting by word of mouth, each voter spoke to the election judges his candidates' names. A judge then called out the voter's name and his candidates, clerks recording the names "on poll sheets." Lincoln voted for a Henry Clay Whig for Congress—and against Joseph Duncan, then a Jackson man serving in Congress. He stayed around the polls most of the day talking cheerily, telling stories, making friends and getting acquainted with the names and faces of nearly all the men in the New Salem neighborhood.

Boarding in the John Camron house Lincoln could hear at the eating table or in candlelight before bedtime how young was the village, how it was built on hope and promise. It was only in January 1829 that Camron and his partner James Rutledge had permission from the state legislature to build the dam that Lincoln had come to know so well. They had a survey made the following October, named the place New Salem, and in December that year they had sold their first lot for $12.50; on Christmas Day 1829 they had their post office in the new store of Samuel Hill and John McNeil.

Far up in northern Illinois was a young village named Chicago, also built on hope and promise, like New Salem having about a dozen log cabins and a population of 100. The wide stretch of prairie between New Salem and Chicago was yet to have its tall grass and tough grass roots broken for crops from rich black soil. In southern Illinois the pioneers chose to farm where the sod was easier to break and near timber for firewood, fences, logs for cabins. These pioneers came mostly from Kentucky and Tennessee and had yet to see what crops could be raised on treeless prairies. A young and growing country and no one more sure and proud of New Salem's future than Denton Offutt, promoter, booster and boomer. He saw Lincoln as honest and able, picked him as a manager, told people, "He knows more than any man in the United States." Somehow at this particular time Offutt had an influence on Lincoln for good, perhaps made Lincoln feel more sure of himself. Lincoln never joined those who later blamed and belittled Offutt. There was something near tenderness in the way that, years later, Lincoln wrote, "Offutt, previously an entire stranger, conceived a liking for A.[braham] and believing he could turn him to account."

On a lot Offutt bought for $10, he and Lincoln built a cabin of logs for the new store. Offutt's goods arrived and Lincoln stacked shelves and corners. Soon stories got going about Lincoln's honesty, how he walked six miles to pay back a few cents a woman had overpaid for dry goods, and finding he had used a four-ounce weight instead of an eight, he walked miles to deliver to a woman the full order of tea she had paid for.

Offutt talked big about Lincoln as a wrestler and Bill Clary, who ran a saloon 30 steps north of the Offutt store, bet Offutt $10 that Lincoln couldn't throw Jack Armstrong, the Clary's Grove champion. Sports from miles around came to a level square next to Offutt's store to see the match; bets of money, knives, trinkets,

tobacco, drinks, were put up. Armstrong, short and powerful, aimed from the first to get in close to his man and use his thick muscular strength. Lincoln held him off with long arms, wore down his strength, got him out of breath, surprised and "rattled." They pawed and clutched in many holds and twists till Lincoln threw Armstrong and had both shoulders to the grass. Armstrong's gang started toward Lincoln with cries and threats. Lincoln stepped to the Offutt store wall, braced himself, and told the gang he would fight, race or wrestle any who wanted to try him. Then Jack Armstrong broke through the gang, shook Lincoln's hand, told them Lincoln was "fair," and, "the best feller that ever broke into this settlement."

One sure action everybody remembered was that Jack Armstrong gave Lincoln a warm handshake and they were close friends ever after. The Clary's Grove boys called on him sometimes to judge their horse races and cockfights, umpire their matches, and settle disputes.

In spare hours Lincoln had sessions with Mentor Graham, the local schoolmaster, who told him of a grammar at John C. Vance's, six miles off; he walked the six miles, brought back the book, burned pine shavings at night in the Onstot cooper shop to light Samuel Kirkham's *English Grammar*. As he went further, he had Bill Greene hold the book and ask him questions. In the New Salem Debating Society, Lincoln in his first speech opened in a tone of apology, as though he wasn't sure of himself. He surprised both himself and those hearing him. James Rutledge, president of the society, was saying there was "more than wit and fun" in Abe's head.

In his work at the store, and in hours after work, he was meeting people, characters, faces, voices and motives, close up in a range and variety as never before in his life. James Rutledge, 50 years old, of medium height, warmhearted, square in dealings, religious, born in South Carolina, had lived in Georgia, Tennessee, Kentucky, in White County, Illinois, on Concord Creek seven miles north of New Salem. The third of his nine children, Ann Mayes Rutledge, was 18, had auburn hair, blue eyes, a fair face, and Lincoln was to meet and know her. John M. Camron, Rutledge's partner and ten years younger, was a nephew of Mrs. Rutledge, had lived with or near them in White County

Lincoln at New Orleans Slave Market. By Joseph Boggs Beale.

and on Concord Creek. He was a massive, powerful man, had learned the millwright's trade, had become an ordained Cumberland Presbyterian minister, and sometimes preached in and around New Salem.

Young Mr. Lincoln in late 1831 and early 1832 studied a book of legal forms, signed as a witness to four deeds, wrote in his own hand several legal documents, a bill of sale and a bond, each beginning "Know all men by these presents." With the help of his good friend, Bowling Green, the justice of the peace, he was edging into law and how to write the simpler documents.

On March 9, 1832, came the boldest and most important paper he had ever written, telling the public he was stepping into politics as a candidate for the legislature of the State of Illinois. The *Sangamo Journal* at Springfield printed it and it was issued as a handbill. There was in it the tone of a young man a little bashful about what he was doing—and yet unafraid of his ideas and his platform, ready to debate them with any comer. A railroad for the service of New Salem would cost too high; her one hope was steamboat traffic; therefore he favored all possible improvement of the Sangamon River; "if elected, any measure in the legislature having this for its object, which may appear judicious, will meet my approbation, and shall receive my support." He came out strong for education, books, religion, morality. "That every man may receive at least, a moderate education, and thereby be enabled to read the histories of his own and other countries, by which he may duly appreciate the value of our free institutions, appears to be an object of vital importance, even on this account alone, to say nothing of the advantages and satisfaction to be derived from all being able to read the scriptures and other works, both of a religious and moral nature, for themselves." Thus, for the benefit of any who might have heard otherwise, the young politician showed himself as favoring books, schools, churches, the Scriptures, religion, morality.

One morning in April 1832 a rider got off his mud-spattered, sweating horse in New Salem and gave notice of Governor John Reynolds calling for 400 thirty-day volunteers from the Sangamon County state militia to report at Beardstown April 24. The Illinois frontier, like nearly every other state to the east, was to have an Indian war. The 67-year-old Black Hawk, war leader of the Sauk and Fox tribes, on April 6 had crossed the Mississippi River into Illinois, saying his people would plant corn along the Rock River.

Lincoln borrowed a horse and rode nine miles to Richland Creek to join a company of friends and neighbors, mostly Clary's Grove boys. Voting for a captain, each man of the company stepped out and stood by either Lincoln or one William Kirkpatrick. Three-fourths of the men at once went to Lincoln—and then one by one those standing by Kirkpatrick left him till he was almost alone. Lincoln was to write, years later, that he was "surprized" at this election and had "not since had any success in life which gave him so much satisfaction." He at once appointed Jack Armstrong first sergeant, and nine days later promoted from the ranks his rival William Kirkpatrick. They marched to Beardstown and went into camp, part of an army of 1,600 mobilizing there.

They marched to camp near the mouth of the Rock River where on May 9 Lincoln's company, with others, was sworn into the Federal service. The next day while the U.S. Regular Army troops moved on boats, the 1,500 militia marched 26 miles in swamp muck and wilderness brush along the left bank of the river, pushing and pulling when horses and wagons bogged. When night rains came the tents didn't shed water and Lincoln heard fagged men wail and curse, along with talk of deserting.

They marched up Rock River, then to Stillman's battlefield, then back along the Rock River, some men believing they were being kept busy to lessen grumbling. On May 21 came news of an Indian party near Ottawa that killed, mangled and scalped three families, 15 persons, and took away alive two girls of 17 and 15. They marched up Sycamore Creek, arrived at Pottawatomie Village where spies the day before had found a number of scalps. At this point mutiny came, troops demanding discharge. Governor Reynolds called a conference of captains, including Lincoln, and had them vote on whether to follow the enemy or go home. A tie vote was announced and General Whiteside's temper blazed in saying he would no longer lead such men except to be discharged. Four days later, after marching to Ottawa, Lincoln's company and others were mustered out of the service. Lincoln certified his muster roll, marking three men as "absent without leave."

The militia under General James D. Henry and other officers proved themselves equal and at times superior to the Regulars as they drove Black Hawk north, marching in storm and night rains, performing an epic of endurance and valor, outguessing the red men who had earlier tricked them. And the end? Black Hawk, the prisoner, was taken to Washington, in the Executive Mansion facing President Jackson, the red man saying to the white, "I am a man and you are another. . . I took up the hatchet to avenge injuries which could no longer be borne. . . I say no more of it; all is known to you."

Election Day was 18 days off, on August 6, and Lincoln traveled over Sangamon County, gave the arguments in his long address issued in the spring. At Pappsville, where a crowd had come to a sale, as he stepped on a box for his speech he saw fellow citizens on the edge of the crowd in a fist fight. He noticed his pilot friend Rowan Herndon getting the worst of it, stepped off the box, shouldered his way to the fight, picked a man by the scruff of the neck and the seat of the breeches, and threw him. Back on his box, he swept the crowd with his eyes in a cool way as though what had happened sort of happened every day, and then made a speech. Campaigning among farmers, he pitched hay and cradled wheat in the fields and showed the farmers he was one of them; at crossroads he threw the crowbar and let the local wrestlers try to get the "crotch hoist" on him. He closed his campaign with a speech in the county courthouse at Springfield. On Election Day Lincoln lost, running eighth in a field of 13 candidates. But in his own New Salem precinct, he polled 277 of the 300 votes cast.

He bought Rowan Herndon's interest in the partnership of Herndon and William F. Berry, merchants, giving Herndon his promissory note. Then Berry and Lincoln bought a stock of goods under peculiar conditions. Reuben Radford at his store had spoken threats to Clary's Grove boys and one day went away from his store telling his younger brother that if Clary's Grove boys came in they should have two drinks apiece and no more. The boys came, took their two drinks, stood the young clerk on his head, helped themselves at jugs and barrels, wrecked the store, broke the windows and rode away yelling on their ponies. Radford looked the wreck over and on the spot sold the stock to William G. Greene. The price was $400 which Greene made up by paying Radford $23 in cash and giving two notes for $188.50 each, secured by a mortgage on a New Salem lot. Lincoln drew

and witnessed the mortgage, and on the same day he and Berry bought the stock from Greene, paying $265 cash, assuming Greene's notes to Radford, and throwing in a horse to boot. Thus Greene made a profit of $242 and one horse. Across later months there was more financing, several lawsuits and court judgments. They did nothing, as Lincoln said later, "but get deeper and deeper in debt" and "the store winked out."

He had bought at an auction in Springfield a copy of Blackstone, the first of the law books to read. One morning he sat barefoot on a woodpile, with a book. "What are you reading?" asked Squire Godbey. "I ain't reading; I'm studying." "Studying what?" "Law." "Good God Almighty!"

Business dropped off. Berry took out a license in March 1833 for Berry and Lincoln to keep a tavern and sell retail liquors. The required bond had both names, Lincoln and Berry, but neither signature was in Lincoln's well-known handwriting. The license specified they could sell whisky at 12 ½ cents a pint, brandies, gins, wine and rum, at various prices. A few weeks after the firm got its license, Lincoln, in a deal of some kind, turned his interest in the store over to Berry.

On May 7, 1833, as Lincoln told it, he "was appointed Postmaster at New-Salem—the office being too insignificant, to make his politics an objection." The pay would run about $50 a year, in commissions on receipts. He had to be in the office at Hill's store only long enough to receive and receipt for the mail which came twice a week by postrider at first and later by stage. Letters arrived written on sheets of paper folded and waxed, envelopes not yet in use. The sender of a letter paid no postage; that fell on whoever the letter was addressed to. Postage on a one-sheet letter was six cents for the first 30 miles, ten cents for 30 to 80 miles, and so on to 25 cents for more than 400 miles. Two sheets cost twice as much, three sheets three times as much, and with every letter Lincoln had to figure how many sheets, how far it had come, then mark the postage in the upper right corner of the outside sheet. If anyone didn't like his figuring as to the number of sheets the receiver could open the letter before the postmaster and settle the question.

Lincoln was free to read newspapers before delivering them, and he read "the public prints" as never before. The habit deepened in him of watching newspapers for political trends and issues. And he could find excitement at times in reading the

*Hannah Armstrong,
who sewed and
cooked for Lincoln in
New Salem.*

speeches made in Congress at Washington as reported in full in the *Congressional Globe* subscribed for by John C. Vance. It was no pleasure for him to write later to the publishers, Blair & Rives, "Your subscriber at this place *John C. Vance,* is dead; and no person takes the paper from the office." It seemed he wasn't strict about regulations, and when George Spears sent a messenger with postage money for his newspapers and a note telling Lincoln he wanted a receipt, Lincoln replied he was "surprised" and, "the law requires News paper postage to be paid in advance and now that I have waited a full year you choose to wound my feelings by intimating that unless you get a receipt I will probably make you pay it again."

Lincoln signed as witness to petitions and deeds, signed honorable discharges for members of his Black Hawk War company,

accepted when after the war he was elected captain of militia in Clary's Grove, drew and attested mortgages, served as clerk with $1.00 of pay at September and November elections in New Salem, received $2.50 for taking poll books 18 miles to Springfield.

For earning a living, jobs at common labor were plenty; he worked as rail splitter, mill hand, farm hand, helped out at the Hill store. Meanwhile he read or dipped into Volney's *The Ruins of Empire,* Gibbon's *Decline and Fall of the Roman Empire,* Paine's *The Age of Reason.* And his debts haunted him. They added up to more when his former partner, William F. Berry, died on short notice in January 1835, his estate practically nothing, leaving Lincoln responsible for their joint obligations. Thus his debts ran to a total of $1,100—and they wouldn't laugh away. They were little rats, a rat for every dollar, and he could hear them in the night when he wanted to sleep.

Squire Bowling Green proved a friend and counselor, explained to Lincoln what he knew of the Illinois statutes, allowed Lincoln without fee to try small cases, examine witnesses and make arguments. The squire, not yet 50, weighed 250 pounds and was nicknamed "Pot" for his paunch. He held court wearing only a shirt and pants and once when two witnesses swore a hog didn't belong to Jack Kelso and Kelso swore it did, Squire Green decided, "The two witnesses we have heard have sworn to a damned lie. I know this shoat, and I know he belongs to Jack Kelso."

In the fall of 1833 came Lincoln's entry into the most highly technical and responsible work he had known. Writing of it later, he said, "The Surveyor of Sangamon [County], offered to depute to A[braham] that portion of his work which was within his part of the county. He accepted, procured a compass and chain, studied Flint, and Gibson a little, and went at it. This procured bread, and kept soul and body together." There were farm sections, roads and towns needing their boundary lines marked clear and beyond doubt on maps—more than the county surveyor, John Calhoun, could handle. On the suggestion of Pollard Simmons, a farmer and Democratic politician living near New Salem, Calhoun, a Jackson Democrat, appointed Lincoln, who went 18 miles to Springfield to make sure he wasn't tied up politically and could speak as he pleased.

In six weeks, however, he had mastered his books, and Calhoun put him to work on the north end of Sangamon County. The open air and sun helped as he worked in field and timberland with compass and measurements. His pay was $2.50 for "establishing" a quarter section of land, $2.00 for a half-quarter, 25 cents to 37 ½ cents for small town lots. He surveyed the towns of Petersburg, Bath, New Boston, Albany, Huron, and others. He surveyed roads, school sections, pieces of farm land from four-acre plots to 160-acre farms. His surveys became known for care and accuracy and he was called on to settle boundary disputes. In Petersburg, however, he laid out one street crooked. Running it straight and regular, it would have put the house of Jemima Elmore and her family into the street. Lincoln knew her to be working a small farm with her children and she was the widow of Private Travice Elmore, honorable in service in Lincoln's company in the Black Hawk War.

For his surveying trips he had bought a horse, saddle and bridle from William Watkins for $57.86, and for nonpayment Watkins on April 26, 1834, got judgment in court and levied on Lincoln's personal possessions. It looked as though he would lose his surveying instruments. Then Bill Greene showed up and turned in a horse on the Watkins judgment—and James Short came from Sand Ridge to the auction Lincoln was too sad to attend and bid in the saddle, bridle, compass and other surveying instruments. When Short brought them to Lincoln it hit him as another surprise in his young life. Short liked Lincoln as a serious student, a pleasant joker, and said that on a farm "he husks two loads of corn to my one."

In January 1834, after a survey for Russell Godbey, Lincoln bought two buckskins from Godbey and took them to Hannah Armstrong, the wife of Jack, who "foxed his pants," sewed leather between ankles and knees for protection against briars. The Armstrongs took him in two or three weeks at a time when he needed a place to stay, Hannah saying, "Abe would drink milk, eat mush, corn-bread and butter, rock the cradle while I got him something to eat. I foxed his pants, made his shirts. He would tell stories, joke people at parties. He would nurse babies—do anything to accommodate anybody."

Lincoln worked at occasional odd jobs when there was no surveying but he made it a point to find time to keep up his political connections. On March 1, 1834, he was secretary of a public meeting at New Salem which resolved on General James D. Henry, former sheriff of Sangamon County, as their choice for governor. General Henry had become a high name in the history of the Black Hawk War, a proven strategist and a soldier of courage who shared hardships with his men. He died of tuberculosis in New Orleans four days after the New Salem meeting that favored him and Lincoln couldn't stay away from a memorial service for Henry on April 20 in the courthouse at Springfield.

In those New Salem days were some saying Lincoln would be a great man, maybe governor or senator, anyhow a great lawyer, what with his studying of law. Others saw him as an awkward, gangly giant, a homely joker who could go gloomy and show it. It was noticed he had two shifting moods, one of the rollicking, droll story, one when he lapsed silent and solemn beyond any bystander to penetrate.

In late summer or early fall of 1834 many people in New Salem, Lincoln included, wondered what had become of John McNeil. It was two years since he had left New Salem. Before leaving he had sold his interest in the Hill-McNeil store to Hill, but at 32 he was the owner of farms steadily rising in value and was rated one of the shrewdest and richest traders in New Salem. In money and looks he was considered by girls "a good catch." On December 9, 1831, Lincoln with Charles Maltby witnessed two deeds given by John Camron to John McNamar and it was then, if not earlier, that Lincoln learned John McNeil's real name was John McNamar. This also explained to Lincoln why as election clerk he didn't see McNeil's name on the poll books; the man was keeping his real name off election records. He said that he had left his family in New York State rather bad off and, setting out to make a fortune, he didn't want his family to trace and interfere with him, but he would in good time go back and help them when he had made his money.

The one person most anxious about him when he went away from New Salem in 1832 was, in all probability, the 19-year-old Ann Rutledge. They were engaged to marry and it was understood he would straighten out affairs of his family in New York State and in not too long a time would come back to her for the marriage. He rode away on a horse that had seen service in the Black Hawk War and it was said that he wrote to Ann from Ohio of a serious three weeks' sickness there and again had written her from New York, and she had answered his letters—and that was all.

A few months after he left in September 1832, James Rutledge and John M. Camron, the two founders of New Salem, having failed in business affairs, moved with their families into the double-log house of a farm near Sand Ridge that McNamar owned through payment to Camron of $400. It could have been that McNamar was showing goodness of heart to the family of his betrothed, at the same time acquiring trusted and responsible caretakers of his property while he was away. Possibly, too, he believed Ann's feeling about him would have added assurance out of her living on his land, the same land she might live on after their marriage. McNamar was a careful and exact man, insisted on clear understandings in all bargains—and a betrothal to him was a bargain between a man and a woman and their joint properties. What they wrote to each other about motives and intentions was in letters not kept and saved.

And Lincoln, who called McNamar "Mack," who had surveyed the land McNamar owned, and who had lived under the same roof with Ann during the months "Mack" was a boarder at the Rutledge tavern, could hardly have been unaware of what she was going through. Her well-known betrothed had gone away saying he would be back soon; two years had gone by and except for a few weeks at the beginning no word had come from him. Did she talk over with Lincoln the questions, bitter and haunting, that harassed her? Had death taken her betrothed? Or was he alive and any day would see him riding into New Salem to claim her? And again, possibly, she kept a silence and so did Lincoln, and there was some kind of understanding beneath their joined silence.

Lincoln was to go away and stay away for months on important duties, writing her no letters that she kept and saved, she writing him no letters that he laid by as keepsakes. During the six weeks he mastered the surveying books, he could have seen her for only brief moments, if at all. And his surveying, as he said, "procured bread, and kept body and soul together." So definitely he was no man of property who like McNamar could offer her land and money, the creature comforts of life. He had arrived in New Salem "a piece of floating driftwood," as he later wrote, and was haunted by debts that had crept high on him. He was aware of large families, nine Rutledge children, 11 Camron daughters, Matthew Marsh writing "twelve is the least number," and a comment that central Illinois was "a hard country for women and cattle." His stepmother, Sarah Bush Lincoln, said he liked people in general, children and animals, but "he was not very fond of girls."

Did he tell Ann of any dream, daydream or reverie that came to him about love in general or a particular love for her? Or did he shrink from such talk because she might be clinging to some last desperate hope that her betrothed would return? Or did she lean to a belief that McNamar was gone for all time, then shifting to another awful possibility that he would surely come back to his land and properties, perhaps bringing a wife with him? Two years of silence could be heavy and wearing. She was 21 and Lincoln 25 and in the few visits he had time for in this year when surveying and politics pressed him hard, he may have gone no further than to be a comforter. He may have touched and stroked her auburn hair once or more as he looked deep into her blue eyes and said no slightest word as to what hopes lay deep in his heart.

CHAPTER 3

THE YOUNG LEGISLATOR

THE YOUNG LEGISLATOR

ON APRIL 19, 1834, Lincoln's name ran again in the *Sangamo Journal* as a candidate for the state legislature. Before that and after, he attended all sorts of political powwows, large and small, and those for whom he surveyed, and those he delivered letters to, did not fail to hear he was in the running. He had become a regular wheel horse of the Whig party backed by John T. Stuart, a Springfield lawyer and county Whig leader. This time Lincoln gave out no long address on issues as two years before. With no presidential ticket in the field, voters were freer in personal choice. Bowling Green, a local Democratic leader, out of his liking for and belief in Lincoln, offered him the support of fellow Democrats. Lincoln hesitated, talked it over with Stuart, then accepted.

So Lincoln played along with the Jackson Democrats who were after Stuart's scalp and with the Bowling Green Democrats who loved him for his own sake—speaking little on issues, and showing up, when there was time, any place he could meet voters face to face, shake hands, and let them know what he was like as a man, at Mechanicsburg taking a hand where fists were flying and ending the fight.

In the election for members of the Ninth General Assembly August 4, 1834, Lincoln ran second among 13 Sangamon County candidates, John Dawson having 1,390 votes, Lincoln, 1,376. Stuart ran fourth, with 1,164 votes, nosing out the one Democrat Stuart had "concentrated" against. Now at 25, Lincoln had won his first important political office, with better pay than ever before in his life, where he would train in the tangled and, to him, fascinating games of lawmaking and parliamentary management amid political labyrinths. After election he ran the post office, made surveys and appraisals, clerked in an October election, made court appearances in connection with his debts, and November 22 was elected a delegate to the State Education Convention to be held in Vandalia December 5.

He roomed with Stuart whose leadership made their room a Whig center. Here and in the legislature Lincoln was to meet men, most of them young, who would become governors,

Congressmen, U.S. Senators, men of influence and portent. Here he would meet a short and almost dwarfish man, a little giant, thick of body with a massive head, 21 years old and absolutely confident of himself—Stephen A. Douglas lobbying for his selection as state's attorney of the First Circuit. Many members had their wives and daughters along and there was a social life new to Lincoln—parties, cotillions, music and flowers, elegant food and liquor, a brilliance of silk gowns and talk that ranged from idle gabble to profound conversation about the state and nation. Around the public square in candlelighted taverns, coffee rooms and hangouts, could be heard the talk and laughter of men eating, smoking, drinking, greeting, getting acquainted, and no lack of office seekers on the hunt.

On December 1, in a two-story ramshackle brick building facing the public square, meeting on the lower floor, the House was called to order, the members sitting in movable chairs, three to a table—cork inkstands, quill pens and writing paper on each table—and on the floor a sandbox as spittoon. A fireplace and stove heated the room. Three tin dippers hung over a pail of drinking water. Evening sessions were lighted by candles in tall holders. Ceiling plaster crashed down occasionally during speeches and roll calls; members got used to it.

Among the 54 representatives Lincoln could feel that if he was a greenhorn, so were the other 35 first-term members; there were 17 second-termers, and only one veteran of three previous terms. Three-fourths of them were born in Southern states, only one member a native of Illinois. Seven members had, like Lincoln, been captains in the Black Hawk War; many had been privates. More than half were farmers, one-fourth lawyers, with a sprinkling of merchants and mechanics. A "whole-hog" Jackson man was elected speaker, Lincoln with other Whigs voting for a less than "whole-hog" Jackson Democrat. Not till the seventh ballot did the House elect a doorkeeper, several candidates being hungry to be doorkeeper. In the next few days the House heard routine reports and joined in inaugurating Governor Joseph Duncan of Jacksonville, an

1812 war veteran who at 17 enlisted in the U.S. Infantry and performed heroic service, a Democrat who had known President Jackson personally when serving in Congress and was slowly moving toward joining the Whigs. Of the 11 standing committees Lincoln was appointed to the Committee on Public Accounts and Expenditures and he was to serve on several special committees.

On December 5 Lincoln stood up, unfolded to his full height, and gave notice of a bill he would introduce. And according to the rules, three days later he laid before them a bill to limit the jurisdiction of justices of the peace. The members were interested because they had that week rejected a proposal to give the justices wider powers. Days passed into weeks and Lincoln's bill was rewritten in select committee, reported to the House where a proposed amendment was debated, and the bill referred to a special committee, Lincoln being named to the committee. When finally reported with an amendment it passed the House 39 to 7 and was sent to the Senate where it died of indefinite postponement.

He worked and voted for incorporation of a new state bank in Springfield, the start of an alliance that would go further. He voted for a canal to connect the Illinois River with Lake Michigan, looking toward waterway hauls from mid-Illinois to the Atlantic. His votes generally ran with those of Stuart and the Whig minority. Several times members put in bills that were in Lincoln's handwriting and it seemed his hand was in more affairs than he openly showed.

The House shook nearer storm on the National Bank issue than on any other. President Jackson had gone into open battle with the Bank, refusing to favor it with a recharter, charging it was a "money power" that bought newspapers, politicians and Congressmen. Henry Clay, Daniel Webster and other leading Whigs clashed with Jackson, who made it an issue in 1832 when farmer and labor ballots gave Jackson 219 votes in the electoral college as against 49 for Clay. When the U.S. Senate denounced Jackson's course as lawless and unconstitutional, Jackson replied with a fierce protest which the Senate refused to print in its journal. Lincoln heard many hours of hot partisan debate on pro-Jackson and anti-National Bank resolutions. He voted with the Whigs on all such resolutions except once when he indicated he believed the U.S. Senate ought to have allowed Jackson's answer to the Senate to be printed in its journal.

Before midnight of February 13 the last batch of hacked and amended bills was passed and Lincoln in two days of below-zero weather rode the stage to New Salem.

After the fixed programs and schedules of Vandalia, the smoke-filled rooms and hullabaloo, Lincoln now rode lonely country roads and walked in open winter air over fields he was surveying. He had seen lawmaking and politics at a vortex and vague resolves deepened in him. And as he wrote later, he "still mixed in the surveying to pay board and clothing bills"; his law books, "dropped" when a legislature met, "were taken up again at the end of the session." *The Sangamo Journal* had announced he was its New Salem agent and would take "Meal, Buckwheat, flour, pork on newspaper accounts."

After March he seemed to have little surveying work over the rest of 1835. During that year, of whatever letters he wrote only three were kept and saved and they were scant and perfunctory, shedding no light on his personal life or love or growth. It was certain that Ann Rutledge and Lincoln knew each other and he took an interest in her; probably they formed some mutual attachment not made clear to the community; possibly they loved each other and her hand went into his long fingers whose bones told her of refuge and security. They were the only two persons who could tell what secret they shared, if any. It seemed definite that she had had letters from McNamar and probable that after a time she had once written him that she expected release from her pledge. Summer of 1835 came and in September it would be three years since McNamar had gone, more than two years since any letter had come from him.

There seemed to have been an understanding between Ann and Lincoln, with no pledges, that they would take what luck might hand them in whatever was to happen, while they advanced their education. Lincoln had his debts, his law studies, his driving political ambitions, while she had her quandaries related to John McNamar. They would see what time might bring. August came and corn and grass stood stunted for lack of rain. Settlers came down with chills, fever, malaria, Lincoln for his aches taking spoonfuls of Peruvian bark, boneset tea, jalap and calomel.

Soon New Salem heard that Ann Rutledge lay fever-burned, her malady baffling the doctors. Many went out to the Rutledge place.

Days passed. Her cousin, McGrady Rutledge, a year younger than Ann, rode to New Salem and told Lincoln of her sickness growing worse. Lincoln rode out and they let him in for what might be his last hour with her. A few days later, on August 25, 1835, death came to Ann Rutledge and burial was in nearby Concord cemetery. Whether Lincoln went to her funeral, whether he wept in grief with others at the sight of her face in the burial box, no one later seemed to know. Her cousin, McGrady Rutledge, wrote far later, "Lincoln took her death verry hard." A letter of Matthew Marsh September 17 had a tone as though the postmaster Lincoln was in good health and cheer. But this tells us nothing of Lincoln's inner feelings.

It was to come to pass that 30 years later New Salem villagers soberly spoke and wrote that Lincoln went out of his mind, wandered in the woods mumbling and crazy, and had to be locked up, all of which was exaggeration and reckless expansion of his taking Ann's death "verry hard." Woven with the recollections of his "insanity" were also the testimonies of what a deep flaming of lyric love there had been between him and Ann.

In a snowfall over hills and rolling prairie Lincoln rode a stage, arriving to see Vandalia blanketed white. A special session of the legislature opened December 7, 1835. The senators on the upper floor were not feeling good about fresh large cracks down the walls, the north wall bulging out and snow sifting down on the floor which at its center had sunk half a foot. Over the next six weeks 139 bills came up in the House; 17 railroads chartered for Illinois towns that wanted to see the cars and hear the whistles. Half the bills introduced were passed, the most important the one for the Illinois and Michigan Canal, whereby wheat selling in Illinois at 50 cents the bushel, after the Great Lakes haul, would bring $1.25 in Buffalo.

At all times national politics boiled and seethed. Under orders from President Jackson a Democratic national convention had nominated Martin Van Buren for President, Illinois Whigs favoring a former Jackson man, Hugh White of Tennessee. The Whigs fought against resolutions praising Jackson and Van Buren, and most of all against approval of nominating conventions, a new way of naming candidates. Lincoln and Stuart were pleased that John Dawson, Sangamon County Democrat, was switching to the Whigs. He collected $262 as his pay for the

session and after adjournment January 18 rode the stage homeward in that occasional fair and warmer Illinois winter weather that whispers of spring on the way.

On March 24 the Sangamon Circuit Court recorded him as a person of good moral character, his first step toward admission to the bar and law practice. He advertised that 64 persons had uncalled-for letters which unless called for would be sent to the dead-letter office. On May 30 he handed out mail as postmaster for the last time and told his New Salem public that their post office was moved to Petersburg.

The convention system not yet operating, he put himself in the running in June as a candidate for the legislature, writing in the *Sangamo Journal,* "I go for all sharing the privileges of the government, who assist in bearing its burthens . . . admitting all whites to the right of suffrage, who pay taxes or bear arms, (by no means excluding females.)" And next November, "if alive," he would vote for Hugh L. White, the Whig candidate for President. He stumped the county, often speaking as one of a string of Whig candidates.

In the election August 1 the county gave Lincoln the highest vote of 17 candidates for the legislature. Sangamon County was taken by the Whigs, having now seven representatives and two senators.

Soon after this sweeping victory Lincoln in stride took his bar examination before two justices of the Supreme Court, passed, gave a dinner to his examiners, and on September 9, 1836, held in his hands a license to practice law in all the courts of Illinois.

In October and November he made three more known surveys and said good-by to surveying.

The tall Whigs from Sangamon County averaged six feet in height, Lincoln the longest, and were nicknamed the "Long Nine." Riding the stage to Vandalia two days, they talked about schemes and strategy that would carry through the legislature the one law more important to them than any other, an act to make Springfield the capital of Illinois. Arriving, they saw that Vandalia citizens, scared by the talk of moving the capital, had torn down the old building and were just finishing a new capitol in the center of the public square. Lincoln looked it over, stepping around workmen still on the job, tool sheds and piles of scaffolding lumber, piles of unused sand, brick and stone, perhaps laughing at the building hardly large enough to hold the new legislature, with no look toward future needs.

The legislature opened December 5, 1836, old members and 66 new ones smelling a pungent odor of fresh damp plaster. Governor Duncan's message advised state financial support for "all canals and railroads." On the 17 railroads and two canals chartered at the last session not a track had been laid nor a spade of dirt dug. The new dynamic member, Stephen A. Douglas, brought in a huge omnibus bill from the Committee on Internal Improvements. Nearly every town in the state wanted a railroad or canal and this bill would give it to them at a cost of $10,000,000, the state to sell bonds of that amount. On the same day the session began, this $10,000,000 program had been approved by an Internal Improvement State Convention, its delegates businessmen of wealth and power, including Thomas Mather, president of the State Bank in Springfield, of which bank Lincoln was continuously an active friend. As chairman of the Finance Committee Lincoln reported that the state had balanced its budget and had a surplus of $2,743.18, being strictly solvent.

In three ballots for U.S. Senator, Lincoln voted for Archibald Williams of Quincy, a lawyer from Kentucky who had switched from Democrat to Whig. Election went to Richard M. Young, a circuit judge and a "milk-and-cider" Jackson man who ran ahead of a "whole-hog" Jackson man, Williams running third. In celebration fine wines and liquors flowed at a supper where dishes and goblets went flying and Stephen A. Douglas and James Shields danced on a table to the length of it amid cigar smoke, ribald songs and the laughter and follies of drinking men. Judge Young was pleased next day to pay $600 for the supper, cigars, drinks and damages.

Of Archibald Williams, Lincoln was to see more. They were tall and angular, alike in homely looks and humor. Williams' clothes were so careless that once a hotel clerk, seeing him loaf in a chair, begged pardon and asked, "Are you a guest of this hotel?" and Williams in a cool snarl, "Hell, no! I am one of its victims, paying five dollars a day!"

In the House were 64 Democrats to 27 Whigs but in the Senate the roll was 22 Democrats to 18 Whigs. Through Lincoln's strategy the Senate first took up a bill to "permanently locate the seat of government of the State of Illinois." The bill passed and went to the House where maneuver and debate began to rage. Then suddenly a motion was made to table the bill "until next Fourth of July." And the motion passed by 39 to 38! Lincoln and the seven of the Long Nine in the House voted Nay. It looked like the end for their hope of making Springfield the new capital.

That night Lincoln called his Sangamon County colleagues into conference and gave each an assignment. They went out into the driving snow and knocked on doors. They found five members who had voted to table and brought them to change their vote in the morning. They located absentees of the afternoon who favored the bill and got their word to be surely on hand in the morning. Next morning, February 18, Enloe moved the bill "be re-considered." A roll call demanded by Douglas showed 42 Yea and 40 Nay. Over the next week came more amendments and harassing tactics, including a motion to postpone selection of a new capital till December 1839. On the third reading of the bill February 24, 1837, the House passed it by 46 to 37. The House and Senate then held a joint session on location and the fourth ballot gave Springfield 73, Vandalia 16, Jacksonville 11, Peoria 8, Alton 6, Illiopolis 3—Henry Mills of Edwards voting for Purgatory on the third ballot. The losers charged "bargain and corruption." But it was all over and Springfield put on a jubilee; citizens howled and danced around a big bonfire blazing at the old whipping post on the public square till that relic was ashes.

In the Southern States it was against the law to speak against slavery; agitators of slave revolts would be hanged and had been. The 3,000,000 Negro workers in the Southern States on the tax books were livestock valued at more than a billion dollars. In political parties and churches, in business partnerships and families, the slavery question was beginning to split the country in two. The secret "Underground Railway" ran from Slave States across Free States and over the line into Canada. An antislavery man would keep a runaway slave in his house, cellar or barn, and at night or in a load of hay in the daytime, pass him along to the next "station." Officers and slaveowners came north with warrants hunting their runaway property; Illinois was seeing them often. Also bogus slave hunters in southern Illinois kidnaped free Negroes, took them to slave soil and sold them. The governor had sent a brief note with memorials from six states notifying the House that the slavery question was becoming a burning issue.

Amid this welter, Lincoln could understand his fellow members in resolutions declaring: "We highly disapprove of the formation of abolition societies; . . . the right of property in slaves is sacred to the slave-holding States by the Federal Constitution, and . . . they cannot be deprived of that right without their consent . . ."

Lincoln voted against these resolutions, joined by only five other members, one of them Dan Stone, a Yankee graduate of Middlebury College, a lawyer and a member of the Ohio Legislature before coming to Springfield in 1833. Stone and Lincoln, three days before the legislature adjourned March 6, recorded this protest in language completely courteous but quietly unmistakable in meaning:

Resolutions upon the subject of domestic slavery having passed both branches of the General Assembly at its present session, the undersigned hereby protest against the passage of the same.

They believe that the institution of slavery is founded on both injustice and bad policy; but that the promulgation of abolition doctrines tends rather to increase than abate its evils.

They believe that the Congress of the United States has no power under the constitution, to interfere with the institution of slavery in the different States.

They believe that the Congress of the United States has the power under the constitution, to abolish slavery in the District of Columbia; but that that power ought not to be exercised unless at the request of the people of said District.

The difference between these opinions and those contained in the said resolutions, is their reason for entering this protest.

In December of this winter, Lincoln had written a drawling, hesitant, half-bashful letter to the daughter of a rich farmer in Green County, Kentucky, Miss Mary Owens, four months older than Lincoln, plump-faced, with a head of dark curly hair, large blue eyes, five feet five inches high. On her first visit to New Salem three years before, she had interested Lincoln; her sister, Mrs. Bennett Abell, at whose house Lincoln had stayed, played matchmaker and wanted the two to get married. When starting for a visit with her sister in Kentucky, Mrs. Abell, perhaps only joking, said she would bring her sister back if Lincoln would marry her. And Lincoln said, perhaps only joking, that he accepted the proposal to become Mrs. Abell's brother-in-law.

When Miss Owens came back to New Salem with her sister in November 1836, Lincoln saw three years had worked changes, Miss Owens having lost bloom, lost teeth, and become stout. He made love to her, it seemed, in a rather easy careless way. And she held him off as one trained in Kentucky schools for refined young ladies, dressed in what one of the Greens called "the finest trimmings I ever saw."

He puzzled her; in some things he was so softhearted. They had some vague understanding that they might marry.

In April he packed his saddlebags to leave New Salem where six years before he had arrived, as he said, "a piece of floating driftwood," being now a licensed lawyer, a member of the state legislature and floor leader of the Whig party. The hilltop village, now fading to become a ghost town, had been to him a nourishing mother, a neighborhood of many names and faces that would always be dear and cherished with him, a friendly place with a peculiar equality between man and man, where Bill Greene was nearly correct in saying, "In New Salem every man is a principal citizen." Bitter hours but more sweet than bitter he had had. Here he had groped in darkness and grown toward light. Here newspapers, books, mathematics, law, the ways of people and life, had taken on new and subtle meanings for him.

CHAPTER 4

LAWYER IN SPRINGFIELD

Early portrait of Abraham Lincoln.

LAWYER IN SPRINGFIELD

Joshua Fry Speed, Lincoln's partner in their general store.

SPRINGFIELD with 1,400 inhabitants in 1837 was selling to 18,000 people of the county a large part of their supplies, tools, groceries, and buying grain, pork and farm produce. There were 19 dry-goods besides other general stores, six churches, 11 lawyers and 18 doctors. Farm women coming to town wore shoes where they used to be barefoot; men had changed from moccasins to rawhide boots and shoes. Carriages held men in top boots and ruffled silk shirts, women in silks and laces. It was no wilderness that Abraham Lincoln, 28 years old, saw as he rode into Springfield April 15, 1837. Many of its people had come from Kentucky by horse, wagon and boat, across country not yet cleared of wolves, wildcats and horse thieves. A Yankee antislavery element in the Presbyterian Church had seceded to form a Second Presbyterian Church. And there were in Sangamon County 78 free Negroes, 20 registered indentured servants and six slaves.

Lincoln pulled in his horse at the general store of Joshua Speed. He asked the price of bedclothes for a single bedstead, which Speed figured at $17. "Cheap as it is, I have not the money to pay," he told Speed. "But if you will credit me until Christmas, and my experiment here as a lawyer is a success, I will pay you then. If I fail in that I will probably never pay you at all." Speed said afterward: "The tone of his voice was so melancholy that I felt for him . . . I thought I never saw so gloomy and melancholy a face in my life." Speed offered to share his own big double bed upstairs over the store. Lincoln took his saddlebags upstairs, came down with his face lit up and said, "Well, Speed, I'm moved." A friendship, to last long, began, as with William Butler, clerk of the Sangamon Circuit Court, who told Lincoln he could take his meals at the Butler home and there would be no mention of board bills.

The circuit courtroom was in a two-story building in Hoffman's Row, and upstairs over the courtroom was the law office of the new firm of Stuart & Lincoln: a little room with a few loose boards for bookshelves, an old wood stove, a table, a chair, a bench, a buffalo robe and a small bed. Stuart was running for Congress, so Lincoln most of the time handled all of their law practice in range of his ability. Between law cases he kept up his political fences, writing many letters.

Yet his own peace of mind was clouded 18 days later when again he wrote Mary Owens. She would have to be poor and show her poverty, if she married him. He was willing to marry, if she so wished. His advice would be not to marry.

That summer Mary Owens and Lincoln saw each other and came to no understanding.

Later when Mrs. Abell visited her sister in Kentucky, Miss Owens told neighbors that Abe Lincoln said to Mrs. Abell, in Springfield, "Tell your sister that I think she was a great fool because she did not stay here and marry me." If true, he was as baffling to them as to himself in heart affairs.

The 1837 business panic had come, banks failing, depositors out of luck, loans called and money tight, the *Sangamo Journal* saying the "groan of hard times is echoed from one end of the country to the other." The State Bank in Springfield had "suspended specie payments"; you could have folding paper money but no coin, no hard money.

After two weeks he was back in Springfield joining in the dirtiest mud-slinging campaign that Springfield politics had ever seen, "no holds barred," many old friendships to go on the rocks.

In law office routine Lincoln took depositions, drew deeds, filed declarations, bills of complaint, praecipes, perhaps taking an afternoon off when the famous Whig, Daniel Webster, made an hour and a half speech at a barbecue in a grove west of town. An official of the Post Office Department came one day to Springfield and asked about a certain amount of dollars and cents that had come into the hands of Lincoln as postmaster at New Salem. Lincoln brought out a sack and counted the money in it, the exact amount asked for by the inspector, who took the money, gave a receipt, and went away satisfied.

Into nearby Alton had moved a 35-year-old abolitionist Presbyterian minister, after editing a paper in St. Louis. His printing press arrived on a Sunday and that night was dumped into the Mississippi River by unknown persons. Friendly citizens bought him another printing press which a mob took and threw into the river, as they did a third printing press after he had helped organize an Illinois antislavery society. Word came that Ohio abolitionists were sending him another printing press. It arrived and was moved into a warehouse where a guard was kept. A night mob stormed the warehouse November 7, 1837, and failing to get in, tried to set the warehouse on fire. Elijah Parish Lovejoy rushed out to stop the attempt at arson and fell dead from a mob bullet. His brother, Owen Lovejoy, a Congregational minister, knelt at the grave and vowed "never to forsake the cause that had been sprinkled with my brother's blood." Lincoln over at Springfield could not know that in years to come, amid inscrutable political labyrinths, he and Owen Lovejoy would understand and cling to each other, Lincoln to write, "To the day of his death, it would scarcely wrong any other to say, he was my most generous friend."

In a carefully written address, "The Perpetuation of Our Political Institutions," before the Young Men's Lyceum of Springfield in January 1838, Lincoln's theme was the spirit of violence in men overriding law and legal procedure. He pointed to the men of the Revolution who, at cost of death and mutilation, had won the liberties of men now being violated, saying, "whenever the vicious portion of population shall be permitted to gather . . . and burn churches, ravage and rob provision stores, throw printing presses into rivers, shoot editors, and hang and burn obnoxious persons at pleasure, and with impunity; depend on it, this Government cannot last." It was Lincoln's masterpiece of thought and speech up to this, his 29th year. No quotes from it could indicate the main closely woven fabric of the address. He dealt with momentous sacred ideas, basic in love of the American Dream, of personal liberty and individual responsibility. They were seeds in his mind foreshadowing growth. He spoke a toleration of free discussion; even abolitionists, keeping within the law, could have their say, a viewpoint not agreeable to the dominant southern element of Sangamon County who, if not in the listening audience, could read the printed text in the *Sangamo Journal.*

Again running for the legislature in the summer of 1838, Lincoln spent most of the campaign speaking for Stuart who was running for Congress against Douglas. Once when Stuart took sick, Lincoln went to Bloomington and debated with Douglas. Once in Archer G. Herndon's store, over a sloppy wet floor, Stuart and Douglas tussled and mauled each other, "fought like wildcats." And three days before election a Douglas speech in front of the Market House riled the tall, supple Stuart, who got a neck hold on the short, thick Douglas and dragged him around the Market House. Stuart came out of it with a scar for life where Douglas put a deep bite in his thumb. In the August 6 election Lincoln led in a field of 17 candidates. In a total of 36,495 votes, Stuart won over Douglas by the slim majority of 36 votes. Douglas cried for a recount but couldn't get it.

In Vandalia in December the Whigs nominated Lincoln for speaker of the House, and failing of election he worked as Whig floor leader. Again his maneuvers and votes favored the Internal Improvements spending, partly because he with others had so earnestly promised the funds for improvements to members who voted for Springfield as the new capital.

After adjournment March 4 he rode out of Vandalia with perhaps a last backward look at the city he had helped rub off the map as the state capital.

He had seen the convention system working well for the Democrats and helped organize the first state Whig convention. It met in Springfield, named him one of five presidential electors for Illinois and a member of the State Central Committee.

Lincoln the lawyer.

Miss Mary Todd.

In December he made a speech of nearly two hours, an elaborate, intricate financial discussion of President Van Buren's scheme to replace the National Bank by a sub-treasury. In closing he registered an oath:

"Before High Heaven, and in the face of the world, I swear eternal fidelity to the just cause, as I deem it, of the land of my life, my liberty and my love." In a letter to Stuart he wrote, "Well, I made a big speech, which is in progress of printing in pamphlet form. I shall send you a copy."

In this December, the new capitol unfinished, the Senate met in the Methodist Church, the House in the Second Presbyterian Church. The Whigs had a majority of one in the House, each party 18 members in the Senate. He voted against repeal of the big Internal Improvements Bill. This jungle of finance had by now brought the state into debt $17,000,000 and in less than two years the state was to stop payment of interest. Little was saved out of the vast wreck except the Illinois and Michigan Canal which Lincoln helped to save, and in time by able refinancing it was made a paying project. Lincoln and others kept the main colossal but crumbling scheme alive and Lincoln wrote to Stuart, to no avail, asking him to try to get action on Lincoln's plan of a

previous session for the state to buy and sell public lands at a profit.

The national Whig convention in December 1839 nominated for President William Henry Harrison of Ohio, former Congressman and U.S. Senator, an 1812 war veteran and above all the commander and victor in the Battle of Tippecanoe defeating Chief Tecumseh. Nor did the Whigs fail to tell the country, howsoever true it might be, that Harrison lived in a plain log cabin and his drink was cider. Little mention was made that Harrison had lost his seat in Congress by voting against Missouri's admission to the Union unless as a Free and not a Slave State, which had its appeal to Lincoln as an early boomer of Harrison. Lincoln joined in the debating tournament in Springfield that ran eight straight evenings in December, Springfield learning, in a way, where Whig and Democrat stood. Lincoln as a four-time candidate for the legislature stumped his own district, and down into southern Illinois and over into Kentucky for the national ticket, often making two-hour speeches, at times debating with Douglas.

The wild campaign ended with Harrison as winner, with 234 electoral votes against Van Buren's 60, Harrison the first northern and western man to be sent to the White House. It was a famous campaign proving that sometimes the American democracy goes on a rampage and shows it has swift and terrific power, even though it is not sure what to do with that power.

Among Illinois Whigs were regrets. They carried their national ticket, but lost the state to the Democrats. This put a new color on a case they were interested in. Months earlier they had charged the Democrats with fraud in voting; thousands of Irish workmen in the canal zone had started a test action before a circuit judge who ruled that foreign-born inhabitants must be naturalized before they could vote. The Democrats took the case to the Supreme Court, knowing that if they lost the case they would lose thousands of votes.

Then came the newly elected legislature into session, with a Democratic majority. Douglas wrote a bill which became law. It set up five new supreme court judgeships; these with the four old judges would be the supreme court of the state besides doing the work of the circuit court judges, who were thrown out. The bill passed the Senate by a vote of 22 to 17, and the House by a vote of 45 to 43. By this move the Democrats saved the canal zone vote for their party, appointed Democrats as clerks in half the counties of the state as provided in the bill. Stephen A. Douglas, no longer register of the land office under a Whig national administration, was appointed a Supreme Court judge. The reply of the Whig party was a calm address issued by a committee of which Lincoln was a member, declaring "that the independence of the Judiciary has been destroyed – that hereafter our courts will be independent of the people, and entirely dependent upon the Legislature – that our rights of property and liberty of conscience can no longer be regarded as safe from the encroachments of unconstitutional legislation."

Several days in January 1841 Lincoln was in his seat only part of the day's session, on January 12 answering only two of the four roll calls; then for five straight days he was absent from the legislature.

Ninian W. Edwards of the Long Nine, a polished aristocrat and son of a former governor of Illinois, was the same age as Lincoln, and they had campaigned together and joined in Whig conferences. The Edwards' house, built of brick, stood two stories high and could have held a dozen prairie-farmer cabins. To this house in 1839 came a young woman from Lexington, Kentucky. She had been there two

Robert S. Todd, father of Mary Todd Lincoln in a daguerreotype of a painting, ca. 1836.

years before on a short visit. Now she had come to stay, Miss Mary Todd, a younger sister of Elizabeth, the wife of Ninian W. Edwards. Granddaughters of Todds who had fought through the American Revolution, their father, Robert Smith Todd, had been a captain in the War of 1812, had been clerk of the House and a state Senator, and was president of the Bank of Kentucky in Lexington.

Miss Mary Todd was 21, plump, swift, beaming. With her somewhat short figure sheathed in a gown of white with black stripes, low at the neck and giving free play to her swift neck muscles, the skirt fluffed out in a balloonish hoop, shod in modish ballroom slippers, she was a center of likes and dislikes among those who came to the house of her sister. For Lincoln, as he came to know her, she was lighted with magnets, the first aggressively brilliant feminine creature who had crossed his path so that he lost his head. One woman remarked that he didn't go as much as other young men for "ladies company." He saw in Mary Todd, with her pink-rose smooth soft skin, light brown hair hinting of bronze, ample bosom, flying glimpses of slippers, a triumph of some kind; she had finished schools where "the accomplishments" were taught; she spoke and read French. She had left her home in Kentucky because of a dispute with her stepmother. She was impetuous, picked the ridiculous angle, the weak point of anyone she disliked and spoke it with thrust of phrase. Her temper colored her; she could shine with radiance at a gift, a word, an arrival, a surprise, an achievement of a little cherished design, at winning a withheld consent. A shaft of wanted happiness could strike deep in her. Mary Todd was read, informed and versed in apparel and appearance. She hummed gay little ditties putting on a flowered bonnet and tying a double bowknot under her chin. A satisfying rose or ostrich plume in her hair was a psalm.

Her laughter could dimple in wreaths running to the core of her; she was born to impulses that rode her before she could ride them. After excesses of temper had worn her to exhaustion, she could rise and stand up to battle again for a purpose definitely formed. In the Edwards' circle they believed there were clues to her character in a remark she passed at a fireside party one evening. A young woman married to a rich man along in years was asked, "Why did you marry such a withered-up old buck?" and answered, "He had lots of houses and gold." And the quick-tongued Mary Todd in surprise: "Is that true? I would rather marry a good man, a man of mind, with a hope and bright prospects ahead for position, fame, and power than to marry all the houses, gold, and bones in the world."

In 1840 Lincoln and Mary Todd were engaged to be married. Ninian W. Edwards and his wife had argued she was throwing herself away; it wasn't a match; she and Lincoln came from different classes in society. Her stubborn Covenanter blood rose; she knew her own mind and spoke it; Lincoln had a future; he was her man more than any other she had met.

The months passed. Lincoln, the solitary, the melancholy, was busy, lost, abstracted; he couldn't go to all the parties, dances, concerts Mary Todd was going to. She flared with jealousy and went with other men; she accused him; tears; misunderstandings. They made up, fell out, made up again. The wedding was set for New Year's Day, 1841.

And then something happened. The bride or the groom, or both, broke the engagement. It was a phantom wedding, mentioned in hushes. There was gossip and dispute about whether the wedding had been set for that date at all. Lincoln was a haunted man. Was he sure he didn't love her? He was seeing Dr. Henry often, and wrote Stuart, "Whether I shall ever be better I can not tell; I awfully forbode I shall not. To remain as I am is impossible; I must die or be better, it appears to me. The matter you speak of on my account, you may attend to as you say, unless you shall hear of my condition forbidding it. I say this, because I fear I shall be unable to attend to any business here, and a change of scene might help me. If I could be myself, I would rather remain at home with Judge Logan. I can write no more." He begged Stuart to go the limit in Washington toward the appointment of Dr. Henry as postmaster in Springfield.

The legislature adjourned. Josh Speed was selling his store and going back to his folks in Kentucky. Lincoln in a struggle to come back traveled to Louisville in August and staying with Speed some three weeks shared talk and counsel with that rare friend. Speed recalled Lincoln saying he had done nothing to make any human being remember that he had lived; he wished to live to connect his name with events of his day and generation and to the interest of his fellow men. Slowly, he came back. A sweet and serene old woman, Joshua Speed's mother, talked with him, gave him a mother's care, and made him a present of an Oxford Bible.

CHAPTER 5

"I Am Going To Be Married"

"I Am Going To Be Married"

JOSHUA SPEED, deep-chested, broad between the ears, had spots soft as May violets. And he and Abraham Lincoln told each other their secrets about women. "I do not feel my own sorrows much more keenly than I do yours," Lincoln wrote Speed in one letter. And again: "You know my desire to befriend you is everlasting."

The wedding day of Speed and Fanny Henning had been set; and Speed was afraid he didn't love her; it was wearing him down; the date of the wedding loomed as the hour for a sickly affair. He wrote Lincoln he was sick. And Lincoln wrote what was wrong with Speed's physical and mental system, a letter tender as loving hands swathing a feverish forehead, yet direct in its facing of immediate facts. It was a letter showing that Lincoln in unlucky endings of love affairs must have known deep-rooted, tangled, and baffling misery.

Speed's wedding day came; the knot was tied. And soon he read lines from Lincoln at Springfield: "When this shall reach you, you will have been Fanny's husband several days . . . But you will always hereafter, be on ground that I have never occupied, and consequently, if advice were needed, I might advise wrong. I do fondly hope, however, that you will never again need any comfort from abroad. But should I be mistaken in this—should excessive pleasure still be accompanied with a painful counterpart at times, still let me urge you, as I have ever done, to remember in the depth and even the agony of despondency, that very shortly you are to feel well again. I am now fully convinced, that you love her as ardently as you are capable of loving. Your ever being happy in her presence, and your intense anxiety about her health . . . would place this beyond all dispute in my mind.

A month passed and Lincoln had news from Speed that the marriage was a complete success and bells rang merrily, Speed far happier than he ever expected to be. To which Lincoln replied: "I know you too well to suppose your expectations were not, at least sometimes, extravagant; and if the reality exceeds them all, I say, enough, dear Lord. I am not going beyond the truth, when I tell you, that the short space it took me to read your last letter, gave me more pleasure, than the total sum of all I have enjoyed since that fatal first of Jany. '41."

Mrs. Simeon Francis, wife of the editor of the *Sangamo Journal*, invited Lincoln to a party in her parlor, brought Lincoln and Miss Todd together and said, "Be friends again." Whatever of fate or woman-wit was at work, and whatever hesitations and broodings went on in Lincoln's heart, they were friends again. But they didn't tell the world so.

At the meetings of Lincoln and Mary Todd in the Francis home, Miss Todd made it clear to him that if another date should be fixed for a wedding, it should not be set so far in the future as it was the time before. Lincoln agreed and early in October wrote to Speed: "You have now been the husband of a lovely woman nearly eight months. That you are happier now than you were the day you married her I well know . . .and the returning elasticity of spirits which is manifested in your letters. But I want to ask a closer question—'Are you now, in *feeling* as well as *judgement*, glad you are married as you are?' From any body but me, this would be an impudent question not to be tolerated; but I know you will pardon it in me. Please answer it quickly as I am impatient to know." Speed answered yes and yes, his marriage had brought happiness. A few weeks later, Lincoln came to the room of James Matheny, before Matheny was out of bed, telling his friend, "I am going to be married today."

On the street Lincoln met Ninian W. Edwards and told Edwards that he and Mary were to be married that evening. Edwards gave notice, "Mary is my ward, and she must be married at my house." When Edwards asked Mary Todd if what he had heard was true, she told him it was true and they made the big Edwards house ready.

Lincoln took all care of a plain gold ring, the inside engraved: "Love is eternal." At the Edwards house on the evening of November 4, 1842, the Reverend Charles Dresser in canonical

House where Abraham Lincoln married Mary Todd, November 4, 1842.

"I Am Going To Be Married"

Law office of Lincoln & Herndon.

Law office in Springfield, Illinois, where Lincoln practiced with William Herndon.

"I Am Going To Be Married"

William Herndon, 16 years the law partner of Lincoln in Springfield.

L. C. Handy Studios

HERNDON ABOUT 1870

This is the earliest known picture of Herndon, who was camera-shy. On May 23, 1870, he wrote Ward Hill Lamon: "I never had a photog taken — dont know how it would look." A drawing based on the above likeness appeared in Lamon's *Life of Abraham Lincoln* in 1872.

robes performed the ring ceremony of the Episcopal church for the groom, 33, and the bride, soon to be 24.

Afterward in talk about the wedding, Jim Matheny said Lincoln had "looked as if he was going to slaughter." Gossip at the Butler house where Lincoln roomed had it that, as he was dressing, Bill Butler's boy came in and asked, "Where are you going?" Lincoln answering, "To hell, I suppose." However dubious such gossip, Lincoln, seven days after his wedding, wrote to Sam Marshall at Shawneetown, discussed two law cases, and ended the letter: "Nothing new here, except my marrying, which to me, is matter of profound wonder."

The Lincoln couple boarded and roomed at $4.00 per week in the plain Globe Tavern, where their first baby came August 1, 1843, and was named Robert Todd. Soon after, they moved into their own home, bought for $1,500, a story-and-a-half frame house a few blocks from the city center. The framework and floors were oak, the laths hand-split hickory, the doors, door frames and weatherboarding black walnut. The house was painted, wrote one visitor, "a Quaker tint of light brown." In the back lot were a cistern, well and pump, a barn 30 by 13 feet, a carriage house 18 by 20. Three blocks east the cornfields began and farms mile after mile.

In the nine, and later, 15 counties of the Eighth Judicial District or "Eighth Circuit," Lincoln traveled and tried cases in most of the counties, though his largest practice was in Logan, Menard, Tazewell and Woodford, which were part of the Seventh Congressional District. Over the Eighth Circuit area, 120 miles long and 160 miles wide at its limit, ranging from Springfield to the Indiana line, Lincoln met pioneer frontier humanity at its best and worst, from the good and wise to the silly and aimless.

Since joining Logan, Lincoln had more cases in the higher courts in Springfield. In December 1841 he argued 14 cases in the Supreme Court, losing only four. Of 24 cases in that court during 1842 and 1843 he lost only seven. But Logan was taking a son into partnership, and he saw, too, that Lincoln was about ready to head his own law firm. And Logan, a Whig, elected a member of the legislature in 1842, had an eye on going to Congress, as did Lincoln. The firm had, on Lincoln's advice, taken in as a law student a young man, William H. Herndon, nine years younger than Lincoln, who had clerked in the Speed store and slept upstairs. Shortly after Herndon's admittance to law practice in December 1844, Lincoln and he formed a partnership and

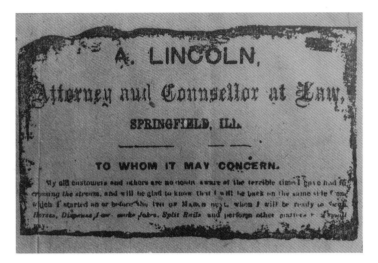

Business card of Abraham Lincoln.

opened their office. The younger man had spoken amazement at Lincoln's offer to take him on, Lincoln saying only, "Billy, I can trust you and you can trust me." From then on for years he was "Billy" and called the other man "Mr. Lincoln."

Herndon was intense, sensitive, had hair-trigger emotions. His grandfather in Virginia had given slaves their freedom; his father, a former store and tavern keeper, in politics had fought to make Illinois a Slave State. The son knew tavern life, and was near vanity about how he could read men by their eyes. He was of medium height, rawboned, with high cheekbones, dark eyes set far back, his shock of hair blue-black. He knew rough country boy talk and stories, tavern lingo, names of drinks, the slang of men about cards, horse races, chicken fights, women. Yet he was full of book learning, of torches and bonfires, had a flamboyance about freedom, justice, humanity. He was close to an element in Sangamon County that Lincoln termed "the shrewd wild boys." He liked his liquor, the bars and the topers and tipplers of the town. He was a Whig, was plain himself and was loved by many plain people. Lincoln, in a political letter, had referred to his own arrival in Sangamon "twelve years ago" as "a strange [r], friendless, uneducated, penniless boy, working on a flat boat—at ten dollars per month" and was now astonished "to learn that I have been put down here as the candidate of pride, wealth, and arristocratic family distinction." There was a factor of politics as well as law in his choosing for a partner the money-honest, highfalutin, whimsical, corn-on-the-cob, temperamental, convivial Bill Herndon.

CHAPTER 6

RUNNING FOR CONGRESS

*Rev. Peter Cartwright who ran
unsuccessfully against Lincoln for
the U.S. House of Representatives.*

RUNNING FOR CONGRESS

"**N**OW IF you should hear any one say that Lincoln don't want to go to Congress, I wish you as a personal friend of mine, would tell him you have reason to believe he is mistaken." Thus Lincoln was writing in mid-February 1843 to an active Whig, Richard S. Thomas. As a state party leader, with other Whigs, he wrote in March a campaign circular, an "Address to the People of Illinois," analyzing national issues, favoring a tariff for revenue rather than direct taxation, the National Bank opposed by the Democrats, a state income by sale of public lands; he warned hesitant Whigs they must use the convention system for nominations or go on losing to "the common enemy"; he pleaded for party unity, writing that "he whose wisdom surpasses that of all philosophers, has declared 'a house divided against itself cannot stand.'"

Edward D. Baker, U.S. Senator. Lincoln named his 2nd son Edward in his honor.

At the district convention in Pekin, a third rival, John J. Hardin, had a majority at hand for the nomination. Lincoln, for the sake of party unity, moved the nomination be made unanimous. Tall, well-tailored, having an air of command, a Transylvania University graduate, Hardin had been Lincoln's rival for Whig floor leadership in the legislature. In speech he stammered but had an ease and grace about it so no one minded.

The Kentucky son of a distinguished U.S. Senator, a Black Hawk War veteran, a brigadier general of state militia, he had a paying law practice in Jacksonville and an ever-keen eye for a seat in Congress.

Lincoln engineered passage of a resolution by 18 votes to 14, whereby the convention, as individuals, recommended E. D. Baker as the Whig party nominee for Congress in 1844, subject to the decision of the convention then. It seemed that Lincoln, with Baker and Hardin, had made an arrangement that Baker would follow Hardin in 1844 as the nominee and Lincoln would follow Baker in 1846. Lincoln was later to remind Hardin of "the proposition made by me to you and Baker, that we should take a turn a piece." Hardin would claim the purpose of the resolution was "to soothe Baker's mortified feelings," Lincoln being certain that was not "the sole" object. Some delegates came away understanding that three Whig leaders had agreed on a rotation, "a turn a piece" in Congress.

He tried to get the Sangamon County delegates to a district convention to endorse him for Congress, but the convention had pledged them to Edward D. Baker. Born in London, England, a Black Hawk War private, a lawyer certified in Carrollton, Illinois, once a state senator, Baker was one of the inner circle of Springfield Whigs, a brilliant and dramatic speaker who could shift modulations from hard ringing steel to rose and rainbow, a stubborn fighter moving with dash and gallantry. When "Ned" Baker loved a man or a cause, he could pour it out in lavish speech. And Lincoln's heart went out in admiration and affection for Ned Baker as perhaps to no other man in Springfield. Named a delegate to the district convention, pledged to support Baker, Lincoln wrote to Speed, "I shall be 'fixed' a good deal like a fellow who is made groomsman to the man what has cut him out, and is marrying his own dear 'gal'."

Lincoln pledged himself to party harmony and when Hardin won his seat in Congress at the August election, Sangamon County gave him three times the majority of his own Morgan County. Nevertheless, when Lincoln voted August 7 he spoke out the names of only two candidates, constable and justice of the peace. Why he didn't vote for Hardin for Congress, nor for, nor against, any Whig candidates for the county offices, had no explanation from him. It was the more odd because in Whig circulars he had strictly urged all Whigs to go to the polls and vote for all Whigs. Possibly the election clerks were slovenly incomplete in recording what they heard. If he failed to vote for Hardin, it went unnoticed by opponents or rivals who could have used it against him. Hardin went to Congress, followed the Whig party line, and in 1844 stepped aside and let Baker have nomination and election.

Early in the 1844 presidential campaign, after bloody riots in Philadelphia, and Democratic forces blaming Whigs as wishing hate and violence toward "foreigners and Catholics," Lincoln at a public meeting in Springfield moved passage of resolutions he had written, "That the guarantee of the rights of conscience, as found in our Constitution, is most sacred and inviolable, and one that belongs no less to the Catholic, than to the Protestant; and that all attempts to abridge or interfere with these rights, either of Catholic or Protestant, directly or indirectly . . . shall ever have our most effective opposition." In late October he spoke in Indiana for the national ticket and Henry Clay, the third-time Whig candidate for President. Election Day found him in Gentryville, Indiana. In this November, James K. Polk of Tennessee won by 170 electoral votes over 105 for Clay, his Illinois majority 12,000.

When Baker came back from Washington, he hesitated about telling Lincoln he wouldn't run again, because of the chance Hardin might run and they both might lose out. Soon after, however, he told Lincoln that he would decline nomination, and when the next year another baby boy arrived at the Lincoln home, he was named Edward Baker Lincoln.

As Lincoln had feared and foreseen, Hardin wanted to run again. When Hardin later saw county delegations moving toward Lincoln, he proposed that instead of nominating by convention the Whigs should poll the counties of the district, with no candidate allowed to electioneer outside his own county. Lincoln

wrote to Hardin, "I am entirely satisfied with the old system under which you and Baker were successively nominated and elected to congress; and because the whigs of the District are well acquainted with that system."

Hardin began to feel outguessed and outplayed and wrote to Lincoln complaining. Lincoln, on February 7, 1846, answered with the longest political letter he had ever written, a masterpiece of merciless logic. Point by point he cornered Hardin, writing at its close, "In my letter to you, I reminded you that you had first at Washington, and afterwards at Pekin, said to me that if Baker succeeded he would most likely hang on as long as possible, while with you it would be different." Nine days later Hardin drew out of the contest, and the district convention at Petersburg, May 1, by acclamation nominated Lincoln for Congress in the one district in Illinois more certain than any other of Whig victory.

Against Lincoln the Democrats put up Peter Cartwright, a famous and rugged old-fashioned circuit rider, a storming evangelist, exhorter and Jackson Democrat. He was 61 and Lincoln 37, both of them very human. He had lived near New Salem, held camp meetings near there, and Lincoln had seen him and heard of his ways. Cartwright's men kept reports going: Lincoln's wife was a high-toned Episcopalian; Lincoln held drunkards as good as Christians and church members; Lincoln was a "deist" who believed in God but did not accept Christ nor the doctrines of atonement and punishment; Lincoln said, "Christ was a bastard." Lincoln put out a handbill giving the most complete and specific statement he had ever made publicly regarding his religion. It read:

A charge having got into circulation in some of the neighborhoods of this District, in substance that I am an open scoffer at Christianity, I have by the advice of some friends concluded to notice the subject in this form. That I am not a member of any Christian Church, is true; but I have never denied the truth of the Scriptures; and I have never spoken with intentional disrespect of religion in general, or of any denomination of Christians in particular. It is true that in early life I was inclined to believe in what I understand is called the "Doctrine of Necessity," that is, that the human mind is impelled to action, or held in rest by some power, over which the mind itself has no control; and I have sometimes (with one, two or three, but never publicly) tried to maintain this opinion in argument. The habit of arguing thus however, I have, entirely left off for more than five years. And I add here, I have always understood this same opinion to be held by several of the Christian denominations. The foregoing, is the whole truth, briefly stated, in relation to myself, upon this subject.

Whig friends raised $200 for his personal campaign expenses. After the election he handed them back $199.25, saying he had spent only 75 cents in the campaign. The count of ballots gave Lincoln 6,340 votes, Cartwright 4,829, Walcott (Abolitionist) 249.

He wrote to Speed, "Being elected to Congress, though I am very grateful to our friends, for having done it, has not pleased me as much as I expected."

Eleven days after Lincoln's nomination in May, Congress had declared a state of war between the United States and Mexico, authorizing an army of 50,000 volunteers and a war fund of $10,000,000 to be raised. In speeches Lincoln seemed briefly to advise all citizens to stand by the flag of the nation, supply all needs of the brave men at the fighting fronts, till an honorable peace could be secured. Trained rifle companies of young men offered service; of 8,370 volunteers in Illinois only 3,720 could be taken; they went down the Mississippi, across the Gulf to Texas, and on into baking hot deserts of Mexico. The war now declared was, in part, for the boundary claimed by Texas, the Rio Grande.

The dream was of "an ocean-bound republic," an America "from sea to sea." A Democratic editor saw this surge as Manifest Destiny; nothing could stop it. President Polk ordered American troops in "protective occupation" on a strip of land in dispute at the Rio Grande. The inevitable clashes came-and the all-out war was on. Though the Americans were outnumbered four to one in nearly all actions, they had better cannon, riflemen and strategy. The battles ended September 14, 1847, when Mexico City was taken. The two outstanding generals, Winfield S. Scott and Zachary Taylor, were both Whigs. Texas, New Mexico and California came into the U.S. domain. The long and bitter dispute with Great Britain over the Oregon boundary, bringing war threats on both sides, was settled by Polk backing down from the cry of "54° 40' or fight" to 49°. So there was Manifest Destiny, "America from sea to sea."

Chicago was a four-day stage trip and Lincoln arrived in that city of 16,000 in July 1847, one of hundreds of delegates to the River and Harbor Convention, run by Whigs, and aimed to promote internal improvements and to rebuke laxity of the Polk administration. Here Lincoln met Tom Corwin of Ohio, Edward Bates and Thomas Hart Benton of Missouri, and Thurlow Weed, a Whig party boss in New York State. The notable New York lawyer David Dudley Field, spoke against certain internal improvements as unconstitutional; Horace Greeley wrote to his New York Tribune that "Hon. Abraham Lincoln, a tall specimen of an Illinoisan . . . was called out, and spoke briefly and happily."

Lincoln had his first look at mighty Lake Michigan, blue water moving on to meet the sky, a path for ship transport of wheat to New York and Europe. Farmers and wheat-buyers were hauling wheat to Chicago from 250 miles away; lines of 10 to 20 wagons headed for Chicago were common. Lincoln had no regrets over his long efforts for the canal to connect the Illinois River and Lake Michigan.

Lincoln's term in Congress was to start in December 1847; he went on riding the Eighth Circuit, driving a rattletrap buggy or on horseback, sometimes perhaps as he tied his horse to a hitching post, hearing a voice across the street, "That's the new Congressman Lincoln." His yearly income ranged from $1,200 to $1,500, comparing nicely with the governor's yearly $1,200 and a circuit judge's $750.

Lincoln had begun wearing broadcloth, white shirts with white collar and black silk cravat, sideburns down three-fourths the length of his ears. Yet he was still known as carelessly groomed, his trousers mentioned as creeping to the ankles and higher, his hair rumpled, vest wrinkled, and at the end of a story putting his arms around his knees, raising his knees to his chin and rocking to and fro. Standing he loomed six feet four inches;

seated he looked no taller than average, except for his knees rising above the chair's seat level.

In the small clique of Springfield Whigs who had come to wield party controls, the opposition dubbed Lincoln the "Goliath of the Junto."

Leasing his Springfield house for a yearly rental of $90, "the North-upstairs room" reserved for furniture storage, Lincoln on October 25, 1847, with wife, four-year-old Robert and 19-month-old Eddie, took stage for St. Louis, and after a week of steamboat and rail travel, arrived in Lexington, Kentucky. There relatives and friends could see Mary Todd Lincoln and her Congressman husband she took pride in showing. They stayed three weeks. Lincoln saw the cotton mills of Oldham, Todd & Company, worked by slave labor, driving out with his brother-in-law, Levi Todd, assistant manager.

He got the feel of a steadily growing antislavery movement in Kentucky.

Lincoln saw in the Todd and other homes the Negro house servants, their need to be clean, their handling of food and linen, the chasm between them and Negro field hands who lived in "quarters." He read books in the big library of Robert Todd, went to many parties and in the capital city of Kentucky met leading figures of the state and nation. He heard Henry Clay on November 13 before an immense audience: "Autumn has come, and the season of flowers has passed away . . . I too am in the autumn of life, and feel the frost of age," terming the Mexican War one of "unnecessary and offensive aggression," holding, "It is Mexico that is defending her firesides, her castles and her altars, not we." For the United States to take over Mexico and govern it, as some were urging, Clay saw as impossible, and there would be danger in acquiring a new area into which slavery could move.

CHAPTER 7
CONGRESSMAN LINCOLN

Portrait of Congressman Lincoln. Photo
by Nicholas H. Shepherd, ca. 1848.

Congressman Lincoln

BY STAGE and rail the Lincoln family traveled seven days to arrive in Washington December 2, staying at Brown's Hotel, then moving to Mrs. Sprigg's boardinghouse on ground where later the Library of Congress was built. They saw a planned city with wide intersecting streets, squares, parks, a few noble buildings on spacious lawns, yet nearly everywhere a look of the unfinished, particularly the Capitol with its dark wooden dome, its two wings yet to be built. Cobblestoned Pennsylvania Avenue ran wide from the Capitol to the White House yet a heavy rain on Polk's inauguration day brought mudholes where parading soldiers slipped and sprawled.

Here lived 40,000 people, among them 8,000 free Negroes and 2,000 slaves. Here were mansions and slums; cowsheds, hog pens and privies in back yards; hogs, geese and chickens roving streets and alleys. Sidewalks were mostly of gravel or ashes. Thirty-seven churches of varied faiths competed with outnumbering saloons, card and dice joints, houses where women and girls aimed to please male customers. Ragged slaves drove produce wagons; gangs of slaves sold or to be sold at times moved in chains along streets. Lincoln saw a jail near the Capitol which he was to term "a sort of negro livery-stable," where Negroes were kept to be taken south "precisely like a drove of horses." Yet here too were libraries, museums, fountains, gardens, halls and offices where historic and momentous decisions were made, ceremonials, receptions, balls, occasions of state and grandeur, and all the dialects of America from Louisiana to Maine, the Southern drawl, the Yankee nasal twang, the differing western slang.

Lincoln liked Mrs. Sprigg's place, the lodgings and meals, the Whig anti-slavery members of Congress who ate there, especially the abolitionist war horse from Ohio, Joshua R. Giddings. When Lincoln couldn't referee a table dispute, he could usually break it up with an odd story that had point. But Mrs. Lincoln couldn't find company, attractions, women, social events of interest to her, and with her husband one of the busiest men in Congress, missing only seven roll calls in the long session that was opening,

after three months of it she traveled with the two boys to her father's home in Lexington.

In the Hall of Representatives, after the oath of office, Lincoln drew a seat in the back row of the Whig side. Many faces and names in the House and over in the Senate became part of him, part of his life then and in years after. George Ashmun, John G. Palfrey and Robert Winthrop of Massachusetts, John Minor Botts of Virginia, Howell Cobb and Alexander Stephens of Georgia, Andrew Johnson of Tennessee, Robert C. Schenck of Ohio, Caleb B. Smith of Indiana, Jacob Thompson of Mississippi, David Wilmot of Pennsylvania-Lincoln could have no dim forevision of the events and tumults where those men would be joined or tangled with him.

He could see at one desk a little man with delicate sideburns, a mouth both sweet and severe. Eighty years old, this man had been professor of rhetoric at Harvard, U.S. Senator from Massachusetts, President of the United States from 1825 to 1829, after which he was in Congress for 17 years. In the foreign service in Paris he had seen Napoleon return from Elba. This was John Quincy Adams, one of the foremost and fiery Whigs to cry that the war with Mexico was instigated by slaveholders for the extension of slave territory. Over in the Senate Lincoln could see the Illinois wonder boy who had had two terms in the House, had been elected to a third, but resigned before taking his seat to start his first term in the upper chamber. Stephen A. Douglas quoted Frederick the Great, "Take possession first and negotiate afterward," and declared, "That is precisely what President Polk has done."

In an emotion-drenched speech February 2, Alexander Stephens voiced the depths of Whig scorn of the President, in somewhat the vein of parts of Lincoln's speech some three weeks earlier. "The principle of waging war against a neighboring people to compel them to sell their country, is not only dishonorable, but disgraceful and infamous. What! shall it be said that American honor aims at nothing higher than land? Lincoln wrote to Herndon: "I just take up my pen to say, that Mr. Stephens of Georgia, a little slim, pale-faced, consumptive man, with a voice like Logan's, has just concluded the very best speech, of an hour's length, I ever heard. My old, withered, dry eyes, are full of tears yet. If he writes it out any thing like he delivered it, our people shall see a good many copies of it."

A new Senator from Mississippi, who at Buena Vista had stayed in his saddle with a bleeding foot till the battle was won, a cotton planter, Jefferson Davis, was saying Mexico was held by "title of conquest," that Yucatan should be annexed or England would take it, and if the American advance to the Isthmus was resisted, he favored war with Britain. His bill for ten regiments to garrison Mexico passed the Senate by 29 to 19 but was pigeon-holed in the House, where Whigs controlled. The need of the South for new areas into which slavery could spread, and by which the South would have political representation to match that of the growing North, had brought splits and factions in both parties north and south.

Senator John C. Calhoun of South Carolina believed, "People do not understand liberty or majorities. The will of the majority is the will of a rabble. Progressive democracy is incompatible with liberty." His mantle of leadership seemed to be falling on Jefferson Davis who in this year of 1848 told the Senate that if folly, fanaticism, hate and corruption were to destroy the peace and prosperity of the Union, then "let the sections part . . . and let peace and good will subsist." With this readiness to break up the Union, the Southern Whigs, Toombs, Stephens, and above all Henry Clay, could not agree. In the North the Democrats were losing unity in several states on the issue of whether slavery should be extended into the new vast territories acquired and being settled.

Over the country those having ears had heard of the Wilmot Proviso cutting across party lines, setting Southern Whigs against Northern, Southern Democrats angry with the Northern. Thirty-four-year-old David Wilmot of Pennsylvania, a Jacksonian Democrat who had fought for the rights of labor and against imprisonment for debt, had in 1846 offered a rider to the appropriations bill, a proviso that slavery would be shut out from all lands acquired by the Mexican War. Since then, over and over, this proviso had been moved as an amendment to this and that bill before Congress. Lincoln voted for the proviso, so he wrote, "at

least" 40 times, he was sure. This hammering away at no further spread of slavery brought movements, outcries of injustice and interference, and threats of secession from Southern leaders.

One February morning John Quincy Adams stood up to speak, suddenly clutched his desk with groping fingers, then slumped to his chair, was carried out to linger and die, saying, "This is the last of earth, but I am content." In a final hour Henry Clay in tears had held the old man's hand. Lincoln served with a committee on arrangements; there was a funeral of state, many saying Mr. Adams could have no fear of the Recording Angel.

In a dignified speech June 20 Lincoln questioned intentions to amend the Constitution indicated in the Democratic platform. He advised, "No slight occasion should tempt us to touch it. Better not take the first step, which may lead to a habit of altering it ... New provisions, would introduce new difficulties, and thus create, and increase appetite for still further change. No sir, let it stand as it is."

Distinct, irrevocable events of 1848 were throwing shadows pointing to events lurking in farther shadows dark beyond reading. In February the Mexican War ended with a treaty; New Mexico and Upper California were ceded to the United States; the lower Rio Grande from its mouth to El Paso became the boundary of Texas; for territory acquired the United States was to pay Mexico $15,000,000. Calhoun, Davis, Rhett and others of the South were openly trying to organize secession of the Southern States from the Union. In the North was explosive force in the Free-Soil party which nominated the former Democratic President Martin Van Buren for President and Charles Francis Adams, son of John Quincy Adams, for Vice-President. Names that counted were in the new party, Salmon P. Chase of Ohio, Charles Sumner of Massachusetts, William Cullen Bryant, Longfellow, Lowell, Whittier, David Wilmot and others. Antislavery Whigs and Democrats were pouring into the new party in some states saying here was a cause to fight for, whereas the Whig and Democratic party platforms straddled, weasled and stood for nothing on any issue of the hour.

The great Whig hero, Daniel Webster, had a certain majesty but "lacked popular appeal." The other idolized veteran Whig hero, Henry Clay, had run three times and lost. And Lincoln, with Stephens and others, in a clique calling themselves "The Young Indians," served in the forefront of those who saw Zachary

Taylor as the one candidate to win in the coming campaign. True enough, Taylor was owner on his Louisiana plantation of more than a hundred slaves, was naive and somewhat ignorant of politics; he had never voted for President but said that had he voted for President in 1844 it would have been for Clay; he saw the Wilmot Proviso as "a mere bugbare" of agitators and it would disappear; he cautioned, "I am not an ultra Whig." But the name of "Old Zach" at 64 carried magic; he was honest, rugged, plain; against terrific odds his armies, by his keen strategy and dogged courage, had won for him the beloved nickname of "Old Rough and Ready." He had spoken of the war as uncalled-for and had moved his troops into action only under direct orders which he obeyed as a trained and loyal soldier.

Because of the Whig party's "turn about is fair play" policy, Lincoln was not running for re-election to Congress. When news came to him of the August 7 election in Illinois, Stephen T. Logan, running for Lincoln's seat, had lost by 106 votes to a Mexican War veteran. Lincoln at headquarters of the national Whig committee was busy franking documents, helping edit a Whig paper *The Battery*, getting out campaign literature, writing political letters. He was assigned to speak in New England where the Free-Soilers had a threatening strength. By "steam cars" to New York and probably boat to Norwich he made the three-day trip that had him September 12 in Worcester, Massachusetts, where he declared that Taylor was "just the man to whom the interests, principles and prosperity of the country might be safely intrusted." At Tremont Temple in Boston he spoke after Governor William H. Seward of New York who was soon to be elected U.S. Senator. At their hotel Lincoln told Seward he had been thinking about Seward's speech, and, "I reckon you are right. We have got to deal with this slavery question, and got to give much more attention to it hereafter."

Election returns (exclusive of South Carolina, where the legislature chose electors) gave a popular vote for Taylor 1,360,752; Cass 1,219,962; Van Buren 291,342. Ohio elected six Free-Soilers to Congress, other states six more, which forebode the slavery issue would blaze on. Cass had carried Illinois but there was comfort that Ned Baker, who had moved to Galena, was elected to Congress. Lincoln had written of him, "He is a good hand to raise a breeze." It counted a little, too, that his congressional district had given a whopping majority of more than 1,500 for Taylor. And the new legislature elected a new U.S. Senator, James Shields, a Democrat, with whom Lincoln had more than a slight acquaintance.

In late November 1848 Lincoln left Springfield for St. Louis and by steamboat up the Ohio River and then by rail reached Washington and took his seat in the House December 7, three days after the Thirtieth Congress had convened. While traveling, he wrote that he took "very extra care" of a letter containing money. "To make it more secure than it would be in my hat, where I carry most all my packages, I put it in my trunk."

He proposed that no new slaves could be brought into the District to live there, except temporarily the slaves, "necessary servants," of Government officers from slaveholding states. After January 1, 1850, all children born of slave mothers should be free, should be "reasonably supported and educated" by the owners of their mothers though owing "reasonable service" to such owners until arriving at an age to be determined. By these two provisions— no new slaves to be brought in and all children born of slaves to be free—and all living slaves in the District certain to die sometime, there would be a definite, calculable day when slavery would have vanished from the District. The President, Secretary of State and Secretary of the Treasury should be a board to determine the value of such slaves as owners "may desire to emancipate." Yet Congress must not impose its will on the District; therefore let it provide an election where all "free white male" voters could say whether they wanted such emancipation.

One proviso was to make trouble for Lincoln then and for years after. Washington authorities would be "empowered and required" to arrest and deliver to owners "all fugitive slaves escaping into said District." He had begun waiting for unforeseen events sure to come.

He saw "Old Zach" inaugurated March 4, did his best at reaching the new Whig President and having him appoint Ned Baker to the Cabinet, but it didn't come off.

Admitted March 7 to practice before the U.S. Supreme Court he argued a case appealed from an Illinois court, and lost it.

Back in Springfield, for months he carried on a furious and snarled campaign of letter writing, conferences, wirepulling, aimed at getting for himself or for some other Illinois Whig, the appointment of Commissioner of the General Land Office at Washington, salary $3,000 a year. In June in Washington wearing a linen duster, he offered reasons why he, an original Taylor man, should be named over the Clay man who landed it. Justin Butterfield won through northern Illinois and Chicago influence, besides that of Daniel Webster and Henry Clay.

CHAPTER 8

BACK HOME IN SPRINGFIELD

BACK HOME IN SPRINGFIELD

BACK in Springfield picking up law practice again he still had his sense of humor and the advice he had long ago given Speed that when feeling sad work is a cure. He liked the law. He was a born lawyer. He went to it, later writing, "From 1849 to 1854, both inclusive, I practiced law more assiduously than ever before." He traveled the Eighth Circuit, staying two days to two weeks in each county seat, in some years from September till Thanksgiving and from March till June away from his Springfield home.

In February 1850 the four-year-old boy Edward Baker Lincoln died. He could call to Eddie and the boy had no living ears to hear. The mother took it hard and it was his place to comfort and restore, if he could, a broken woman.

From the funeral sermon by the Reverend James Smith of the First Presbyterian Church, a friendship grew between the Lincoln family and Mr. Smith. He had been a wild boy in Scotland, a scoffer at religion, then a preacher in Kentucky; he could tell a story—he and Lincoln were good company. The Lincolns rented a pew; Mrs. Lincoln took the sacrament, and joined in membership. Mr. Smith presented Lincoln with his book, *The Christian's Defense*, a reply to infidels and atheists. Lincoln read the book, attended revival meetings, was interested, but when asked to join the church he said he "couldn't quite see it."

Over the year 1850 Lincoln could read in newspapers and the *Congressional Globe* of the tumults and hazards of political drama in Washington. Only by slender circumstance and hair-trigger chances was the Union saved. In Senate and House men of both sides of the Great Compromise shook their fists and cried threats. In January Henry Clay, whom Lincoln was to term "my beau ideal of a statesman," had introduced the omnibus bills and argued that only by compromise, by give and take, by each side north and south making concessions, could the Union be saved. As his bills came out of a special committee they would let California into the Union as a Free State; New Mexico and Utah would become territories, without reference to slavery; Texas would be paid for giving up boundary claims in New Mexico and having her other boundaries fixed; the slave trade in the District of Columbia would be abolished but slavery would continue so long as it was insisted on by Maryland, which had ceded the District land to the Federal Government. Last and most fiercely disputed was the proposed new Fugitive Slave Law, "with teeth in it"; the Negro claimed as a slave could not have a jury trial and could not testify; a Federal official would be empowered to decide ownership and if he decided for the Negro his fee was $5.00 but if his decision was for the owner his fee was $10; also anyone helping a runaway Negro was made liable to fine and imprisonment.

Daniel Webster on March 7 made a three-hour speech to crowded galleries. The eyes of the audience left him a few moments when the foremost interpreter of the doctrine of states' rights and secession, the aged John C. Calhoun, who was to die 24 days later, had his gaunt and bent form in a black cloak helped to the seat he had held so many years. Webster spoke for the Great Compromise, bill by bill, as the only agreement by which the Union could be held together. Mr. Lincoln out in Illinois must have dwelt with keen eyes on Mr. Webster's passionate exclamations toward his close: "Secession! Peaceable secession! Sir, your eyes and mine are never destined to see that miracle. The dismemberment of this vast country without convulsion! The breaking up of the great deep without ruffling the surface! Who is so foolish . . . as to expect to see any such thing? . . . There can be no such thing as a peaceable secession." Webster had tried, in private conferences, to provide jury trial for the fugitive slave, but that was one of many matters to which in that hour he could not refer. Webster, wrote one of his intimate friends, was "a compound of strength and weakness, dust and divinity."

Lincoln and son Tad. Photo by Alexander Gardner, 1865.

President Taylor was 65 and scandals, quarrels and insoluble problems had worn him. He sat three hours in the hot sun near the Washington Monument ceremonial on the Fourth of July, listening to orations calling for conciliation and national harmony. He drank ice water, went home to the White House and ate from a basket of cherries, disobeyed his doctor and drank goblets of iced milk and ate more cherries. He died July 9, saying, "I have endeavored to do my duty." With his death hope ran higher of passing the Great Compromise.

Serving as floor captain for the worn men, Clay and Webster, was Senator Douglas; he traded and rounded up votes; he framed provisions of the three most important bills; he maneuvered against the outspoken threats of immediate secession, made speeches for an ocean-to-ocean republic. He replied in anger and scorn to the Massachusetts Free-Soiler, Senator Charles Sumner, who called Douglas "a Northern man with Southern principles." Douglas heard and would never forget and would come back to it again and again that the Whig Senator from New York, William H. Seward, declared, ". . . there is a higher law than the Constitution, which regulates our authority . . . " He kept a wary eye on new Free-Soil Senators who held the Fugitive Slave Law to be infamous and said so. Douglas kept close to the new Whig President, Millard Fillmore, chubby-faced, moderate, suave, doing his best for the Great Compromise. By majorities of about one-third or more, the omnibus bills, some of them slightly modified, passed and became law. From January on through part of August the great debate had raged in Washington and spread over the country. Now cannons boomed over Washington, bonfires blazed, processions roared through the streets, stopping for speeches at the homes of Webster, Douglas and others. Lincoln, two years later, in eulogizing Clay, would say of this new peace, "The nation has passed its perils, and is free, prosperous, and powerful."

When word came of his father on the Coles County farm dying in January 1851 Lincoln wrote to his stepbrother John D. Johnston:

I feel sure you have not failed to use my name, if necessary, to procure a doctor, or any thing else for Father in his present sickness. My business is such that I could hardly leave home now, if it were not, as it is, that my own wife is sick-abed. (It is a case of baby-sickness, and I suppose is not dangerous.)

I sincerely hope Father may yet recover his health; but at all events, tell him to remember to call upon, and confide in, our great, and good, and merciful Maker; who will not turn away from him in any extremity.

When death came close, with a murmur from deep rivers and a cavern of dark stars, Lincoln could use Bible speech. The father died January 17, 1851, and the only son, with a crowded court calendar, including three Supreme Court cases, did not go to the funeral. Lincoln's final somber words to his father could be construed several ways. To be at the deathbed of one for whom you have even a small crumb of affection is definitely "more painful than pleasant." Thomas Lincoln to the last was a churchgoing, religious man, his invariable grace at meals, as reported by a local paper: "Fit and prepare us for humble service, we beg for Christ's sake. Amen."

When a third boy baby come to the Lincoln family in 1850 he was named William Wallace: the fourth one in 1853 was named Thomas after his grandfather, so Mrs. Lincoln wrote in a letter to Sarah Bush.

To this was added a postscript which might be termed the only known letter Lincoln wrote to his beloved stepmother, who was to say, "Abe was the best boy I ever saw. His mind and mine, what little I had, seemed to run together, more in the same channel." The postscript read:

A word for Mother:

Chapman tells me he wants you to go and live with him. If I were you I would try it awhile. If you get tired of it (as I think you will not) you can return to your own home. Chapman feels very kindly to you; and I have no doubt he will make your situation very pleasant. Sincerely your Son A. Lincoln.

After 11 years of marriage Lincoln and Mary Todd had stood together at the cradles of four babies, at the grave of one. For these little ones Lincoln was thankful. To handle them, play with them and watch them grow, pleased his sense of the solemn and the ridiculous.

Mary had sewed her own clothes, had sewed clothes for the children; he let her manage the house In Springfield she was quoted as once saying, "Money! He never gives me any money; he leaves his pocketbook where I can take what I want."

In many matters Lincoln trusted her judgment. Herndon wrote much against her yet he noted: "She was an excellent judge of human nature, a better reader of men's motives than her husband and quick to detect those who had designs upon and sought to use him. She was, in a good sense, a stimulant. She kept him from lagging, was constantly prodding him to keep up the struggle. She wanted to be a leader in society. Realizing that Lincoln's rise in the world would elevate and strengthen her, she strove in every way to promote his fortunes, to keep him moving, and thereby win the world's applause."

Talk about her over Springfield ran that she economized in the kitchen to have fine clothes; she had a terrible temper and tongue. That her husband had married her a thousand dollars in debt, that he charged low fees and had careless habits, that he trusted her and let her have her own way in the household economy, didn't fit well into the gossip. That she was at times a victim of mental disorder, that she was often sorry and full of regrets after a wild burst of temper, didn't make for exciting gossip.

In July 1850 and in Chicago on a law case, Whigs pressed Lincoln to memorialize Zachary Taylor. He spoke as a Whig to Whigs, by inference defending the Whig policy toward the Mexican War.

When Henry Clay died in June 1852, Springfield stores closed, and after services in the Episcopal Church, a procession moved to the Hall of Representatives where Lincoln sketched Clay's long life, how Clay on occasions by his moderation and wisdom had held the Union together when it seemed ready to break. He quoted Clay on the American Colonization Society: "There is a moral fitness in the idea of returning to Africa her children, whose ancestors have been torn from her by the ruthless hand of fraud and violence. Transplanted in a foreign land, they will carry back to their native soil the rich fruits of religion, civilization, law and liberty." How desperate this hope, Lincoln was to learn at cost. Over the South were 3,204,000 slaves valued on tax books at more than one and one-half billion dollars. How to pay for them as property, if that were conceivable, and then "transplant" them to Africa, was the problem.

Lincoln in 1852 had for 20 years been a loyal Whig party leader who had shaken hands with nearly all active local Whig leaders over Illinois. He seemed to be merely a party wheel horse in his seven speeches in the 1852 campaign, discussing candidates and personalities rather than any great issues.

He belittled statements of Douglas with a relentless logic that became comic and had an audience splitting its sides. He had never read Seward's "supposed proclamation of a 'higher law'" but if it was intended to "foment a disobedience to the constitution, or to the constitutional laws of the country, it has my unqualified condemnation." He praised General Winfield Scott, a hero of two wars, the third military candidate of the Whigs for President. He had seen Southern Whigs favoring the Whig President Fillmore for the nomination but Seward and the extreme antislavery Whigs had swung the nomination to Scott. When Scott in the November election carried only four states, the question was asked by good Whigs, "Is the party falling to pieces?"

Herndon wrote that Lincoln was "the most secretive man" he ever knew. About the year 1850, wrote Herndon, he and Lincoln were driving in Lincoln's one-horse buggy to the Menard County Court. The case they were to try would touch on hereditary traits. "During the ride he spoke, for the first time in my hearing, of his mother, dwelling on . . . qualities he inherited from her. He said, among other things, that she was the illegitimate daughter of Lucy Hanks and a well-bred Virginia farmer or planter; and he argued that from this last source came his power of analysis, his logic, his mental activity, his ambition. . . The revelation—painful as it was—called up the recollection of his mother, and, as the buggy jolted over the road, he added "ruefully, 'God bless my mother; all that I am or ever hope to be I owe to her,' and immediately lapsed into silence . . . We rode on for some time without exchanging a word."

Herndon in 1840 had married Mary Maxcy, the daughter of Virginia-born James Maxcy, the first town constable of Springfield. Her quiet beauty was likened to a summer daisy in a meadow corner. She bore him six children, read books for him, gave him ease after his restless hours. Their home held rare happiness, and in a sense, they had a lifelong romance.

Older Harriet Beecher Stowe who wrote "Uncle Tom's Cabin" against slavery published in serial from 1851-1852.

Little Harriet Beecher Stowe in 1852 had published a novel, *Uncle Tom's Cabin*, and by the device of dramatizing a black Christ lashed by a Yankee-born Satan, had led millions of people to believe that in the Slave States south of the Ohio River was a monstrous wrong. She ended her book with a prophecy: "This is an age of the world when nations are trembling and convulsed. A mighty influence is abroad, surging and heaving the world, as with an earthquake. And is America safe? Every nation that carries in its bosom great and unredressed injustice has in it the elements of this last convulsion."

Emerson, the Concord preacher, saw war, revolution, violence, breeding in the antagonisms of bold, powerful men. "Vast property, gigantic interests, family connection, webs of party, cover the land with a network that immensely multiplies the dangers of war."

Lincoln caught the feel of change in the national air. He had seen the frontier move far west. He had seen St. Louis,

with its 5,000 people, grow to 74,000 in 20 years, and Springfield from 700 to 6,000. Senator Douglas was telling of "a power in this nation greater than either the North or the South, a growing, increasing, swelling power, that will be able to speak the law to this nation, and to execute the law as spoken. That power is the country known as the great West—the Valley of the Mississippi."

Between 1850 and 1860, the country's 23,000,000 people become 31,000,000, this being 2,000,000 more than Great Britain. In ten years 2,600,000 people arrive from overseas, in a single year 400,000. The East grows 21 per cent, the South 28 per cent, the Northwest 77 per cent, in population. Little towns peep up on the prairies where before were only gophers and jack rabbits.

The transcontinental railroad, the iron-built, ocean-going steamship, the power-driven factory-the owners and managers of these are to be a new breed of rulers of the earth. Between seaboard and the Mississippi comes the "iron horse" hauling pork and grain of the West to factory towns of the East, to vessels sailing to Europe; the cars return with sewing machines, churns, scissors, saws, steel tools. New reaping and threshing machinery comes.

A territory of Kansas is organized, and from slave-soil Missouri, men with rifles ride over into Kansas and battle with abolitionists from New England for political control of Kansas. Emerson peers into years ahead and cries, "The hour is coming when the strongest will not be strong enough." On a late afternoon of any autumn day in those years, Abraham Lincoln in his rattletrap buggy over the prairie might have been lost deep in the swirl of his thoughts and his hope to read events to come.

He wrote of the legitimate object of government being "to do for the people what needs to be done, but which they can not, by individual effort, do at all, or do so well, for themselves," such as "Making and maintaining roads, bridges, and the like; providing for the helpless young and afflicted; common schools; and disposing of deceased men's property." Military and civil departments were necessary. "If some men will kill, or beat, or constrain others, or despoil them of property, by force, fraud, or noncompliance with contracts, it is a common object with peaceful and just men to prevent it."

CHAPTER 9

RESTLESS GROWING AMERICA

RESTLESS GROWING AMERICA

THE CALIFORNIA "gold rush" of 1849 and what followed had the eyes of the world. San Francisco had become a world port. Sacramento, four lone houses in April 1849, became in six months a roaring crazy city of 10,000. Ten men in one week had shaken from the gravel in their hand-screens a million dollars in gold nuggets. More than once a single spade had sold for $1,000. Courts and law broke down in San Francisco and a Committee of Vigilantes took over the government.

Over the Great Plains moved wagon trains, a traveler counting 459 wagons in ten miles along the Platte River. A Peoria newspaper in 1854 counted 1,473 wagons in one month, movers going to Iowa. In a single week 12,000 immigrants arrived on railroad trains in Chicago. Cyrus McCormick's Chicago factory in 1854 sold 1,558 farming machines, mostly for both reaping and sowing, and was planning for 3,000 machines in 1855. The Department of State reported that Irish immigrants alone had in three years sent back to the old country nearly $15,000,000 for their kinfolk. A restless young growing America was moving toward a future beyond reading.

The peace of the Great Compromise had held up fairly well, broken by the endless crying of antislavery men against the new Fugitive Slave Law.

Amid these changing scenes and issues, Douglas had become the foremost dramatic leader of the Democratic party, speaking, as he said, for "Young America" as against "Old Fogies," meaning Cass, Buchanan and other figures of hesitation. A younger element of the party boomed him for President in 1852 and he was only 39 when in the Democratic national convention on the 30th and 31st ballots he had more votes than any other candidate. He made his home in Chicago, where he bought land for a few dollars and sold one tract for $80,000, To the young University of Chicago he donated ten acres. He was close to all interests that wanted a railway to the Pacific. His tenacity had brought a rail route from the Great Lakes to the Gulf; the Illinois Central was thankful to him and let him have private cars for travel.

Stephen A. Douglas, a political opponent of Lincoln. Portrait by Lussier, ca. 1870.

After the death of his wife in early 1853, when he went back to Congress he was noticed as bitter, bad-tempered, a sloven in dress, chewing tobacco and careless where he spat. He went abroad several months, seeing Russia and the Near East, and came back the oldtime Douglas who could put his hands on the shoulders of an old colleague or a young precinct worker and say, as though they were chums, "I count on your help." He was three years later to marry Adéle Cutts, a great-niece of Dolly Madison, a beautiful, warmhearted woman who proved to be a perfect helpmeet for a combative and furiously active husband.

In early 1854 came a bold, challenging action of Douglas that set the slavery issue boiling in a wild turmoil, Douglas having predicted, "It will raise a hell of a storm." Now 41, a battler, magnetic, with flashing blue eyes, chin drawn in, pivoting, elusive, he made a daring, spectacular play for reasons better known to himself than any he gave to the public. His lionlike head, his black pompadour swept back in waves, his deep bass voice, were seen and heard. Toiling, sweating, crying, he had coaxed, guided and jammed through Congress the Nebraska Bill, as it came to be known. It created two territories, Kansas on the south, Nebraska on the north; in each the voters would decide whether it should be free or slave soil. Nebraska then stretched far and wide, its area including all or part of the later states of Nebraska, North and South Dakota, Wyoming and Montana. There, in the future, under "popular sovereignty," said Douglas, "they could vote slavery up or down." Southern members had insisted on, and got, a provision expressly repealing the hitherto sacred Missouri Compromise; the line it drew between slave and free soil was wiped out.

As the news went across the country, not in the memory of living men had there been such recoils and explosions of opinion and passion over a political act and idea. Lincoln was roused as "by the sound of a fire-bell at night." In New England, 3,050 clergymen signed a widely published memorial to the U.S. Senate: "IN THE NAME OF ALMIGHTY GOD, AND IN HIS PRESENCE," we "solemnly protest against the passage of . . . the Nebraska bill." In Chicago 25 clergymen signed a like protest, followed by 500 ministers in the Northwest. Several longtime Democratic party leaders in Illinois gave it out that they were anti-Nebraska men. Traveling to Illinois, Douglas could see from his car window the burning of dummies bearing his name; in Ohio some women managed to present him with 30 pieces of silver. In Chicago in front of North Market Hall, on the hot night of September 1, he defied and insulted those against him; a crowd of 8,000 interrupted with questions, hisses, groans, boos, catcalls. They howled and hooted him till he looked at his watch, jammed his silk hat on his head, and left.

Among those who led in hooting Douglas were the Know-Nothings, members of the secret "Order of the Star Spangled Banner." When asked what the order stood for, members answered, "I know nothing." Each member on joining swore he would never vote for a foreigner or a Catholic for any office. Their slogans were, "Americans must rule America" and "No papacy in the Republic."

Before the year closed the Know-Nothings would surprise the country by electing mayors of Philadelphia and Washington. In alliance with Free-Soilers and former Whigs, they were to sweep Massachusetts with 63 per cent of all ballots, electing a Know-Nothing governor and legislature. They would have swept New York State but for the longtime proven friendships of Seward and Weed with groups of foreigners and Catholics.

On a State Fair day in Springfield thousands who hated or loved Douglas stood in the cool night air of October 2 to see him on the Chenery House porch, torches lighting his face. His eyes flashed and lips trembled. "I tell you the time has not yet come when a handful of traitors in our camp can turn the great State of Illinois, with all her glorious history and traditions, into a negro-worshiping, negro-equality community." The next afternoon Douglas spoke three hours in the Statehouse. Had not the Missouri Compromise been practically wiped out by the Omnibus Bill of 1850? Was not the real question whether the people should rule, whether the voters in a territory should control their own affairs?

The next afternoon Lincoln spoke to the same crowd. "Wherever slavery is, it has been first introduced without law." He gave reasons for hating it as a "monstrous injustice," and added: "When southern people tell us they are no more responsible for the origin of slavery, than we; I acknowledge the fact. When it is said that the institution exists; and that it is very difficult to get rid of it, in any satisfactory way, I can understand and appreciate the saying. I surely will not blame them for not doing what I should not know how to do myself . . . What next? Free them, and make them politically and socially, our equals? My own feelings will not admit of this, and if mine would, we well know that those of the great mass of white people will not. Whether this feeling accords with justice and sound judgment, is not the sole question, if indeed, it is any part of it. A universal feeling, whether well or ill-founded, can not be safely disregarded."

And yet, while he could not say what should be done about slavery where it was already established and operating, he was sure it would be wrong to let it spread north. And what should be done first of all? "The Missouri Compromise ought to be restored. For the sake of the Union, it ought to be restored." In Peoria 12 days later, he gave much the same speech to a crowd of thousands, wrote it out for publication, and it became widely known as the "Peoria Speech."

In the October elections of 1854, anti-Nebraska voters of all shades-former Whigs and Democrats, Know-Nothings, Fusionists—won by startling majorities.

At meetings in Ripon, Wisconsin, and Jackson, Michigan, citizens opposed to slavery extension, and coming from all parties, resolved in favor of a new party with a new name gathering anti-Nebraska Whigs and Democrats, also Free-Soilers, under one banner, and, "we will cooperate and be known as 'Republicans.'" In Wisconsin and Vermont conventions the name Republican was adopted. The New York *Tribune*'s Whig Almanac designated the 21 Congressmen from Ohio as Republicans, and in October 1854 Greeley was writing, "We consider the Whig party a thing of the past." In several county and congressional districts over Illinois the name Republican had been adopted, an Ottawa Democratic paper saying the Republican convention there was made up of "Whigs, abolitionists, know nothings, sore heads, and fag ends."

A group of radical abolitionists met in Springfield October 5 to organize an Illinois Republican party. Later when Lincoln was named a member of the new state central committee of the new Republican party, he declined the honor, as without his authority, and refused to attend their meetings.

In the November 7 election the Democrats elected only four of the nine Illinois Congressmen, and to the legislature only 41 regular Democrats against 59 anti-Nebraska members of differing shades. Lincoln wrote the names of all members in alphabetical order and studied his chances for election to the seat of U.S. Senator James Shields. Late in 1854 he sent out many letters in the tone of one: "I have really got it into my head to try to be United States Senator; and if I could have your support my chances would be reasonably good." In February 1855 he watched in the Statehouse the election for U.S. Senator. He got 45 votes. Six more would have elected him. The balloting went on, his vote slumped to 15.

Lincoln wrote to a friend: "I regret my defeat moderately, but I am not nervous about it." By not being stubborn he had won friends. He gave a dinner for all anti-Nebraska members of the legislature. Mrs. Lincoln had watched the balloting from the gallery and was bitter about it. Julia Jayne, the wife of Trumbull, had been bridesmaid at her wedding; they had joined in writing

Portrait of young Lincoln by Thomas Hicks, ca. 1848 .

verse and letters to the *Sangamo Journal*, but forever after the night of Trumbull's election Mrs. Lincoln refused to speak to Julia or to receive a call from her.

In August 1855 Lincoln wrote to Owen Lovejoy, "Not even *you* are more anxious to prevent the extension of slavery than I; and yet the political atmosphere is such, just now, that I fear to do any thing, lest I do wrong." Know-Nothing elements would be needed to combat the pro-Nebraska Democrats. "About us here, they [the Know-Nothings] are mostly my old political and personal friends; and I have hoped their organization would die out without the painful necessity of my taking an open stand against them. Of their principles I think little better than I do of those of the slavery extensionists. Indeed I do not perceive how any one professing to be sensitive to the wrongs of the negroes, can join in a league to degrade a class of white men."

In 1856, on the Missouri and Kansas border, 200 men, women and children were shot, stabbed or burned to death in the fighting between free- and slave-state settlers and guerrillas. The money loss, in crops burned, cattle and horses stolen or killed, ran about $2,000,000. Each side aimed to settle Kansas with voters for its cause. In May, as the first state convention to organize the Republican party of Illinois was meeting in Bloomington, the town of Lawrence, Kansas, had been entered by riding and shooting men who burned the Free State Hotel, wrecked two printing offices and looted homes.

Senator Charles Sumner of Massachusetts, speaking on "The Crime Against Kansas," had lashed verbally South Carolina Senator Andrew P. Butler, saying Butler "has chosen a mistress . . . who, though ugly to others, is always lovely to him—I mean the harlot, Slavery." And Congressman Preston Brooks, a nephew of Butler, had walked into the Senate chamber, and over the head and backbone of the seated Sumner had rained blows that broke to pieces a gutta-percha cane, beating his victim near to death. Over the North raged a fury almost tongue-tied. In the South was open or secret exultation; the man they hated and loathed more than any other in Congress had met punishment and would leave the Senate and suffer years before his wounds healed.

These events were in the air when political elements of Illinois and other states were holding conventions to organize state parties and to get up a national Republican party. The convention met in Major's Hall, upstairs over Humphrey's Cheap Store, near the courthouse square. The platform denounced Democratic policies and declared Congress had power to stop the extension of slavery and should use that power. After several delegates spoke, there were calls for Lincoln. He stood up. There were cries, "Take the platform," which he did. He observed, according to a Whitney version written many years later, "We are in a trying time"; then suddenly came the thrust, "Unless popular opinion makes itself very strongly felt, and a change is made in our present course, *blood will flow on account of Nebraska, and brother's hand will be raised against brother!* . . . We must not promise what we ought not, lest we be called on to perform what we cannot . . . We must not be led by excitement and passion to do that which our sober judgments would not approve in our cooler moments." He noted that the delegates had been collected from many different elements. Yet they were agreed, *"Slavery must be kept out of Kansas."* The Nebraska Act was usurpation; it would result in making slavery national. "We are in a fair way to see this land of boasted freedom converted into a land of slavery in fact."

He summarized history to show that freedom and equality, sacred to the men of the American Revolution, had become words it was fashionable to sneer at. He rehearsed current violent events. Should force be met with force? He could not say. "The time has not yet come, and if we are true to ourselves, may never come. Do not mistake that the ballot is stronger than the bullet." Applause came regularly. He was saying what the convention wanted said. He was telling why the Republican party was being organized. As applause roared and lingered, the orator walked slowly toward the back of the platform, looked at notes in his hand, took a fresh start and worked toward the front. To Bill Herndon and others he seemed taller than ever before. "He's been baptized," said Herndon, hearing Lincoln declare that no matter what was to happen, "We will say to the Southern disunionists, *We* won't go out of the Union, and you *shan't.*" The delegates rose from their seats, applauded, stamped, cheered, waved handkerchiefs, threw hats in the air, ran riot. He was their tongue and voice. He had deepened the passions and unified the faith of adherents of a partisan cause.

He made safe, moderate investments. Speculations beckoned to others, but not to him. At hotels he took what was offered him with no complaint. He told his fellow lawyer Joe Gillespie he never felt easy when a waiter or a flunky was around. Before posing for an ambrotype he ran his fingers through his hair to rumple it; on the stump or in jury speeches his hands wandered over his head and put the hair in disorder. Always, it was noticed, the linen he wore was clean; his barbers didn't let the sign of a beard start; he blacked his own boots. As to haircuts, grammar and technicalities, he wasn't so particular. In jury arguments and before a big crowd in Springfield, he wiped sweat from his face with a red silk handkerchief.

Friendships with Swett, Whitney and others on the circuit grew and deepened for Lincoln, and particularly that with fair-haired and pink-faced Judge David Davis, six years younger, five inches shorter, a hundred pounds heavier. A graduate of Kenyon College, Davis had come west and grown up with Bloomington. He had a keen eye for land deals and owned thousand-acre tracts. On his large farm near Bloomington he had a frame mansion where Lincoln stayed occasionally. In many ways the destinies of Davis and Lincoln were to interweave.

CHAPTER 10

THE DEEPENING SLAVERY ISSUE

THE DEEPENING SLAVERY ISSUE

THE DEMOCRATIC national convention opened June 2, 1856, in Cincinnati, gave unanimous endorsement to the Nebraska Act, voted 138 to 120 against a Pacific railway, and after the 15th ballot went into a deadlock with 168 ½ votes for James Buchanan for President, 118 ½ for Douglas, a two-thirds vote being required to nominate. Douglas sent a letter saying the "embittered state of feeling" was a danger to the party and as Buchanan had a majority he was entitled to the nomination. On the 17th ballot Buchanan was nominated by unanimous vote. Buchanan had been away as minister to England, had taken no hand in the Kansas-Nebraska mess, and was rated a "safe" candidate. He and the platform faced to the past. The most human touch in the platform struck at the Know-Nothings; "a political crusade . . . against Catholics and foreign-born" had no place in the American system.

A fresher air and new causes moved the first national Republican convention in Philadelphia in mid-June. The newly born party's platform faced to the future; no extension of slavery, admission of Kansas as a Free State, "a railroad to the Pacific Ocean, by the most central and practicable route." No delegates came from the Deep South, only a few from the Border States; the party was sectional.

The nomination for President went to John C. Fremont; he had served as U.S. Senator from the Free State of California; as an explorer and "pathfinder" in western wilds he had made a name for daring and enduring hardship. He was overly dignified, an egotist, a greenhorn in politics, yet somehow he had never said or done anything radical that could harm him or the party. He was nominated by 359 votes, 196 going to U.S. Supreme Court Justice John McLean. Lincoln had favored the veteran Whig McLean as the man to draw the votes of the conservative Old Line Whigs. For Vice-President William L. Dayton of New Jersey, an able lawyer and former U.S. Senator, was nominated, the first ballot giving him 259 votes and Abraham Lincoln 110. The news reaching Lincoln, he laughed that it must be "some other Lincoln."

A February convention of Know-Nothings in Philadelphia had declared that only "*native-born* citizens" should hold office, and the foreign-born should vote only after "continued residence of twenty-one years." This political convention of the American party took a proslavery stand in endorsing the Kansas-Nebraska Bill, an antislavery faction walking out. Millard Fillmore, while in Europe, was nominated for President, and coming home, accepted. Fillmore had been a Whig Vice-President, had become a Whig President on the death of President Taylor, had a strong Whig following that would vote for him. And Lincoln in letters and in more than 50 speeches hammered it home that a Whig vote for Fillmore was a vote against the Republicans and a vote for Buchanan, the Democrat. He mentioned Fremont often but never with any slight flowering of praise. Also he handled Fillmore respectfully and tenderly, with no belittlement, saying nothing of the Know-Nothings who created and sponsored Fillmore as a candidate. He kept quiet about a convention of Old Line Whigs, presided over by Judge Edward Bates of Missouri, which in September endorsed Fillmore, "without adopting the peculiar doctrines" of the American party.

At Galena July 23, 1856, Lincoln went radical. He spoke there in what was probably the tone of his "Lost Speech." In no other published speech did he refer to the naked might and force that could in the future be called into play. Fillmore in an Albany speech had charged that if the Republicans elected a President the event would dissolve the Union. "Who are the dis-unionists, you or we?" Lincoln asked. "We, the majority, would not strive to dissolve the Union; and if any attempt is made it must be by you, who so loudly stigmatize us as disunionists. But the Union, in any event, won't be dissolved. We don't want to dissolve it, and if you attempt it, *we won't let you.* With the purse and sword, the army and navy and treasury in our hands, and at our command, you *couldn't do it* . This Government would be very weak, indeed, if a majority, with a disciplined army and navy, and a well-filled treasury, could not preserve itself, when attacked by an unarmed, undisciplined, unorganized minority. All this talk about the dissolution of the Union is humbug—nothing but folly. *We won't dissolve the Union, and you shan't.*" Thus it was published in Galena and Springfield newspapers.

His law practice got little of his time as he rode on trains, in buggies and wagons, to speak at many points including Bloomington, Urbana, Sterling, Paris, Grand View, Charleston, Oregon, Vandalia, Decatur, Lacon, the State Fair at Alton, Ottawa, Joliet, Peoria, Clinton, Pittsfield, Jacksonville, four speeches in Springfield, occasionally two speeches in one day. A crowd of 10,000 heard him in Kalamazoo, Michigan, where an abolitionist wrote he was "far too conservative and Union-loving."

In his own home Lincoln's arguments failed. Mrs. Lincoln wrote to a sister: "My weak woman's heart was too Southern in feeling to sympathize with any but Fillmore . . . he made so good a President & is so just a man & feels the *necessity* of keeping foreigners within bounds."

When the October and November election returns were all in, Buchanan had 174 electoral votes, Fremont 114, Fillmore 8. The popular vote was 1,838,169 for Buchanan, 1,341,264 for Fremont, 874,534 for Fillmore. Buchanan carried all the Slave States except Maryland, which Fillmore carried. Lincoln's fears of the Fillmore vote were seen in Illinois where the vote was 105,000 for Buchanan, 96,000 for Fremont, and 37,000 for Fillmore. Yet there was comfort. The Republicans had elected a Mexican War veteran, Colonel William H. Bissell, governor, and the state ticket had swept in.

At a Chicago banquet Lincoln spoke the toast: "*The Union*—the North will maintain it—the South will not depart therefrom." All who didn't vote for Buchanan made a majority of 400,000. "We were divided between Fremont and Fillmore. Can we not come together, for the future . . . Let bygones be bygones. Let past differences, as nothing be." The central idea should be not "all citizens as citizens are equal" but the broader and better "all *men* are created equal." He was sure, "The human heart *is* with us—God is with us."

On March 6, 1857, in the U.S. Supreme Court room on the ground floor of the north wing of the Capitol, a hushed crowd listened to get every word read for three hours from a document by a man out of the past, an 81-year-old man, thin of body and furrowed of face, frail and fading, his voice at times a whisper. He had been Attorney General and Secretary of the Treasury under President Jackson who appointed him Chief Justice. He was Roger Brooke Taney, Maryland-born, a devout Catholic, free from scandal, highly respected in his profession, one lawyer terming him "apostolic" in conduct.

He read for three hours the Supreme Court decision in the case of Dred Scott, a slave suing for freedom because he had been taken into territory where slavery was illegal under the Missouri Compromise; the Supreme Court of Missouri had sent him back into slavery because he had voluntarily returned to a Slave State. Four of the nine judges of the U.S. Supreme Court dissented, five being from Slave States. The decision declared that Congress did not have power to prohibit slavery in the Territories; the Missouri Compromise was unconstitutional; a slave was property and if a slaveowner took his property into a territory where the U.S. Constitution was the high law, his property could not be taken from him; a Negro slave or a free Negro whose ancestors were slaves, could not become a U.S. citizen. Negroes "were not intended to be included under the word 'citizens'" in the Constitution. Quoting from the Declaration of Independence "that all men are created equal," Taney read: "The general words above quoted would seem to embrace the whole human family . . . But it is too clear for dispute that the enslaved African race were not intended to be included."

Taney had hoped good would come from this decision but it set the slavery question seething. The New York *Tribune* said 6,000,000 people in the South had more weight in the Supreme Court than 16,000,000 people in the Free States. Lincoln, from now on for years, was to stress more than ever what he believed the Declaration of Independence meant by the clause "that all men are created equal." The question would recur, "If those who wrote and adopted the Constitution believed slavery to be a good thing, why did they insert a provision prohibiting the slave trade after the year 1808?" Into Lincoln's speech was to come more often that phrase "the Family of Man" as though mankind has unity and dignity.

Never ending for months had been the unrest and the high crying over "Bleeding Kansas." Between November 5, 1855, and

December 1, 1856, about 200 persons had been killed and far more wounded from guns and knives. The Emigrant Aid Society, with large eastern funds, had sent out thousands of antislavery settlers and the legislature was strongly antislavery. But by registration trickery in test oaths, by thousands of ballots from counties having only a few score of settlers, by threats of violence, and by refusal of thousands of antislavery voters to vote in a special election where they said their votes wouldn't be counted, the proslavery party "elected" a constitutional convention which met in Lecompton under Federal troop guard. The Lecompton constitution which they wrote, proslavery in its mumbo-jumbo clauses, was sent to Washington for approval by Congress.

Guerrillas, bushwackers, roving outlaw gangs were more common after the "Pottawatomie Creek Massacre," Tall, bearded John Brown, 56 years old, haunted by five free-state men killed, made a decision. He would kill five slave-state men, saying to one of his men, Townley, who didn't like the idea, "I have no choice. It has been decreed by Almighty God, ordained from eternity, that I should make an example of these men." On the night of May 24, 1857, he took two men and his four obedient sons, Owen, Frederick, Salmon and Oliver, each with a rifle, pistol and cutlass, and they went to three different cabins. In the Doyle cabin, the wife and mother begged to be let alone, but out into the night they dragged her husband and two sons, found next morning on the grass 200 yards from the cabin, the father shot in the head and stabbed in the breast, one son with arms and fingers cut off and a hole in his throat, the other son with holes in side, head and jaw. At Wilkinson's cabin past midnight they forced him to open the door, heard his sick wife plead, but he was found next day dead, with gashes in head and side. At the third cabin they took William Sherman who was found next morning with his skull split open and left hand cut off. The butchery was done mainly with two-edged cutlasses Brown had brought from Ohio.

Over the country in press and pulpit, on the platform, on sidewalks and in cigar stores and saloons, each side made its claims on the basis of distorted and incomplete reports. The sad fact that didn't come out till complete evidence was in made it clear that the victims slaughtered so coldly were merely plain illiterate farmers making a scant living and definitely not pro-slavery agitators. One son of Brown who didn't go along asked his father, "Did you have anything to do with that bloody affair on the Pottawatomie?" And John Brown: "I approved of it." The son: "Whoever did it, the act was uncalled for and wicked." And John Brown: "God is my judge. The people of Kansas will yet justify my course."

Three months later when Buchanan was throwing out of office men put in by Douglas, postmasters, marshals, land and mail agents, Herndon wrote to Trumbull, "Lincoln and I are glad to death that Douglas has been crushed." But Douglas was far from crushed. With his Democratic following in Congress, joined with Republicans, he defeated Buchanan's proslavery measures for Kansas. Over the nation and in a large segment of his party Douglas had never before had such a peculiarly high and honorable standing. Many, however, in Republican and other circles, held that he was no particular hero in having done what he had to do; when Buchanan wanted to make a mockery of "popular sovereignty," his only course was to oppose Buchanan, even if it should smash party unity. He kept on saying he didn't care "whether slavery was voted up or down," and in that posture he was the same old Douglas.

CHAPTER 11
THE GREAT DEBATES

The Great Debates

THE POLITICAL letters of Lincoln early in 1858 showed more and more a rare skill in the management of men. He wrote Lovejoy that he had been in Lovejoy's district and the danger had been that the Democrats "would wheedle some Republican to run against you."

Many Republicans were saying when their state convention met in Springfield June 16, 1858, "We know Douglas, we have fought him for years, and now we're going to give him the run of his life." On a unanimous vote the resolution passed, saying, "Abraham Lincoln is the first and only choice of the Republicans of Illinois for the U.S. Senate as the successor of Stephen A. Douglas." In the evening in the hall of the House of Representatives, Lincoln came, bowed to applause and cheers, murmured, "Mr. President and Gentlemen of the convention." Then he read a speech from manuscript. He had worked harder on it, revised it with more care, than any other speech in his life; he had read it the evening before to a group of party leaders who advised him not to deliver it. Now he read:

"If we could first know *where* we are, and *whither* we are tending, we could better judge *what* to do, and *how* to do it. We are now far into the *fifth* year, since a policy was initiated, with the *avowed* object, and *confident* promise, of putting an end to slavery agitation. Under the operation of that policy, that agitation has not only, *not ceased*, but has *constantly augmented*. In my opinion, it will not cease, until a crisis shall have been reached, and passed. 'A house divided against itself cannot stand.' I believe this government cannot endure, permanently half *slave* and half *free*. I do not expect the Union to be *dissolved*. I do not expect the house to *fall*, but *I do* expect it will cease to be divided. It will become *all* one thing, or *all* the other."

The speaker read on: "Either the *opponents* of slavery, will arrest the further spread of it, and place it where the public mind shall rest in the belief that it is in the course of ultimate extinction; or its *advocates* will push it forward, till it shall become alike lawful in *all* the States, *old* as well as *new*, *North* as well as *South*."

He put together this and that circumstance and argued that while on the face of them the people could not be sure there was a conspiracy on foot to nationalize slavery, yet explanations were required. "Put *that* and *that* together, and we have another nice little niche, which we may, ere long, see filled with another Supreme Court decision, declaring that the Constitution of the United States does not permit a *state* to exclude slavery from its limits . . . Such a decision is all that slavery now lacks of being alike lawful in all the States." What interested the country most, as many newspapers published the speech in full, was its opening paragraph. It became known as the "House Divided" speech. It went far.

Douglas started west in June, his daily movements watched by the country. The Chicago *Times* reprinted from the Philadelphia *Press*: "Senator Douglas, accompanied by his beautiful and accomplished wife, arrived at the Girard House, en route for Chicago." Sixty miles out from Chicago, a special Illinois Central train with a brass band, flags and pennants met the Douglas party July 9 and escorted the statesman to Chicago. As he stepped out on the Lake Street balcony of the Tremont House that night, rockets and red fire lit the street. Lincoln heard Douglas refer to him as "a kind, amiable, and intelligent gentleman, a good citizen and an honorable opponent." He heard Douglas say to the swarming thousands on the street: "Mr. Lincoln advocates boldly and clearly a war of sections, a war of the North against the South, of the free States against the slave States, a war of extermination to be continued relentlessly until the one or the other shall be subdued, and all the States shall either become free or become slave."

The next night Lincoln spoke from the same Tremont House balcony to a crowd somewhat smaller; rockets blazed; the brass band of the German Republican Club from the Seventh Ward rendered music. And amid much on issues of the day Lincoln said: "I do not pretend that I would not like to go to the United States Senate, I make no such hypocritical pretense, but I do say to you that in this mighty issue, it is nothing

Abraham Lincoln two weeks before the final Lincoln-Douglas debate. Photo by Calvin Jackson, October, 1858.

Abraham Lincoln, head-and-shoulders portrait, facing front, by T. Painter Pearson, 1858.

THE GREAT DEBATES

Lincoln immediately prior to Senate nomination. Photo by Alexander Hesler, Chicago, 1857.

to you: nothing to the mass of the people of the nation whether or not Judge Douglas or myself shall ever be heard of after this night."

It was in this same month that A. P. Chapman wrote Lincoln of "Grand Mother Lincoln" (Sarah Bush) doing well, and, "I often take my Republican papers and read Extracts from them that Eulogise you you can hardly form an idea how proud it makes her. She often says Abram was always her best child & that he always treated her like a son. I told her I was a going to write you to day & and she says tell you she sent a heap of love to you & wants to see you once more very much . . . "

Lincoln wrote a challenge to debate and Douglas accepted. The two men would meet on platforms and clash on issues in cities in seven different parts of the state, all Illinois watching, the whole country listening. By the shorthand writing newly invented, reporters would give the country "full phonographic verbatim reports," newspapers told their readers.

In the Ottawa public square 12,000 listeners sat or stood in a broiling summer sun August 21 for the first debate. For three

hours they listened. A train of 17 cars had come from Chicago. By train, boat, wagon, buggy and afoot people had arrived, waved flags, paraded and escorted their heroes.

Acres of people listened and, the speaking ended, they surged around their heroes and formed escorts. A dozen grinning Republicans lifted Lincoln to their shoulders, and a Republican crowd headed by a brass band saw him carried to Mayor Glover's home. "With his long arms about his carriers' shoulders, his long legs dangling nearly to the ground, his long face was an incessant contortion to wear a winning smile that succeeded in being only ghastly," said a Democratic newspaper. Next came Freeport, far in the northwestern corner of Illinois. A torchlight procession met Douglas; the Chicago *Times* counted 1,000 torches, the Chicago *Press* and *Tribune*.

Lincoln rode to the speaking stand in a covered wagon drawn by six big white horses. Fifteen thousand people sat and stood listening through three hours of cloudy, chilly weather; mist and a fine drizzle drifted across the air. Some had come on the new

Poster for a reenactment of the Lincoln-Douglas debate to be held at the DuPage County Centennial, 1939.

Lincoln and Douglas met at the Bryant Cottage, now a State Historical Site, to work out the details of their debates in 1858. Photo by Virginia Dahms.

sleeping cars from Chicago the night before. One train on the Galena road had 16 cars and 1,000 passengers.

Then debaters and shorthand reporters dropped south 300 miles, to a point south of Richmond, Virginia. The Jonesboro crowd numbered about 1,400, most of them rather cool about the great debate. The place was on land wedged between the Slave States of Kentucky and Missouri; several carloads of passengers had come from those states to listen.

On October 7, in the itinerary, came Galesburg, in Knox County. Twenty thousand people and more sat and stood hearing Lincoln and Douglas speak while a raw northwest wind tore flags and banners to rags. The damp air chilled the bones of those who forgot their overcoats. For three hours the two debaters spoke to people who buttoned their coats tighter and listened.

Six days later, in Quincy, on the Mississippi River, 12,000 people came from Illinois, Iowa, Missouri, and sat and stood three hours hearing the debaters. And two days later, farther down river,

looking from free-soil Illinois across to slave-soil Missouri, the debaters had their final match, in Alton, before 6,000 listeners.

Two men had spoken in Illinois to audiences surpassing any in past American history in size and in eagerness to hear. Yet they also spoke to the nation. The main points of the debates reached millions of readers. Newspapers in the larger cities printed the reports in full. A book of passion, an almanac of American visions, victories, defeats, a catechism of national thought and hope, were in the paragraphs of the debates. A powerful fragment of America breathed in Douglas' saying at Quincy: "Let each State mind its own business and let its neighbors alone! . . . If we will stand by that principle, then Mr. Lincoln will find that this republic can exist forever divided into free and slave States . . . Stand by that great principle and we can go on as we have done, increasing in wealth, in population, in power, and in all the elements of greatness, until we shall be the admiration and terror of the world, . . . until we make this continent one ocean-bound republic."

Those who wished quiet about the slavery question, and those

Lincoln-Douglas debates about allowing slavery in free territory in 1858.

U.S. postage stamp issued on the centennial of the Lincoln-Douglas debates, 1958.

who didn't, understood Lincoln's inquiry: "You say it [slavery] is wrong; but don't you constantly . . . argue that this is not the right place to oppose it? You say it must not be opposed in the free States, because slavery is not here; it must not be opposed in the slave States, because it is there; it must not be opposed in politics, because that will make a fuss; it must not be opposed in the pulpit, because it is not religion. Then where is the place to oppose it? There is no suitable place to oppose it."

Lincoln cited a Supreme Court decision as "one of the thousand things constantly done to prepare the public mind to make property, and nothing but property, of the negro in all the states of this Union." Why was slavery referred to in "covert language" and not mentioned plainly and openly in the U.S. Constitution? Why were the words "negro" and "slavery" left out? Was it not always the single issue of quarrels? "Does it not enter into the churches and rend them asunder? What divided the great Methodist Church into two parts, North and South? What has raised this constant disturbance in every Presbyterian General Assembly that meets?" It was not politicians; this fact and issue of slavery operated on the minds of men and divided them in every avenue of society, in politics, religion, literature, morals. "That is the issue that will continue in this country when these poor

tongues of Judge Douglas and myself shall be silent. It is the eternal struggle between these two principles . . . The one is the common right of humanity and the other the divine right of kings. It is the same . . . spirit that says, 'You work and toil and earn bread, and I'll eat it.' No matter in what shape it comes, whether from the mouth of a king who seeks to bestride the people of his own nation and live by the fruit of their labor, or from one race of men as an apology for enslaving another race, it is the same tyrannical principle."

On October 30, several thousand farmers out around Springfield hitched up their teams and drove into town to a Republican rally; Lincoln was to make his last speech of the campaign. Nine cars had come from Jacksonville and way stations. The Chicago & Alton brought 32 cars from McLean and Logan Counties, seats and aisles full, tops of the cars and two engine pilots crowded with passengers. Ten thousand swarmed around the Statehouse square, waves of people facing toward the speakers' stand.

He knew Galesburg to the north would vote about two to one for him and Jonesboro to the south three to one against him. He faced toward Jonesboro and all the South rather than Galesburg and the North. "The legal right of the Southern people to

Stephen A. Douglas, ca. 1855-1865.

reclaim their fugitives I have constantly admitted. The legal right of Congress to interfere with their institution in the states, I have constantly denied ... To the best of my judgment I have labored for, and not against the Union."

And in the same tone, he ended. "Ambition has been ascribed to me. God knows how sincerely I prayed from the first that this field of ambition might not be opened. I claim no insensibility to political honors; but today could the Missouri restriction be restored, and the whole slavery question replaced on the old ground of 'toleration' by necessity where it exists, with unyielding hostility to the spread of it, on principle, I

would, in consideration, gladly agree, that Judge Douglas should never be out, and I never in, an office, so long as we both or either, live."

November 2, Election Day, arrived, wet and raw in northern Illinois. And though Lincoln had a majority of 4,085 votes over Douglas, Douglas because of a gerrymander held a majority of the legislature. Lincoln wrote to loyal friends, "Another explosion will soon come." Douglas managed to be supported as the best instrument both to *break down* and to *uphold* the slave power. "No ingenuity can keep this deception . . . up a great while." He was glad he made the race. "Though I now sink out of view, and shall be forgotten, I believe I have made some marks which will tell for the cause of civil liberty long after I am gone." And he joked; he was like the boy who stubbed his toe, "It hurt too bad to laugh, and he was too big to cry."

On January 5 the legislature elected Douglas. After the news Lincoln sat alone in his law office with his thoughts a while, blew out the light, locked the door, stepped down to the street, and started home. The path, worn pig-backed, was slippery. One foot slipped and knocked the other foot from under him. He was falling. He made a quick twist, caught himself, and said with a ripple, "It's a slip and not a fall!" The streak of superstition in him was touched. He said it again, "A slip and not a fall!"

And far off in Washington, Stephen A. Douglas was reading a telegram, from the *State Register*, "Glory to God and the Sucker Democracy, Douglas 54, Lincoln 46."

In November 1858 the *Illinois Gazette* at Lacon, the Chicago *Democrat*, the Olney, Illinois, *Times*, nominated Lincoln for President. The Cincinnati *Gazette* printed a letter nominating him, and a mass meeting at Sandusky, Ohio, called for him to head the Republican ticket in 1860.

In Bloomington, in December, Jesse Fell saw Lincoln coming out of the courthouse door. Fell was a land trader in thousand-acre tracts, a railroad Promoter, a contractor for large lots of railroad ties off his timberland holdings. He was of Quaker blood, antislavery, Republican, a little below medium height, smooth-faced, honest-spoken, trusted and liked in Bloomington. He stepped across the street and asked Lincoln to go with him to the law office of his brother, Kersey H. Fell. A calm twilight was deepening, as Fell said: "Lincoln, I have been East, . . . travelling in all the New England States, save Maine; in New York, New Jersey, Pennsylvania, Ohio, Michigan, and Indiana; and everywhere I hear you talked about.. . . I have a decided impression, that if your popular history and efforts on the slavery question can be sufficiently brought before the people, you can be made a formidable, if not a successful, candidate for the Presidency."

Lincoln heard and, as Fell told it, replied: "Oh, Fell, what's

the use of talking of me for the Presidency, whilst we have such men as Seward, Chase, and others, who are . . . so intimately associated with the principles of the Republican party. Everybody knows them. Nobody, scarcely, outside of Illinois, knows me."

And Fell went on, "Now, Mr. Lincoln, I come to the business part of this interview. I want to get up a well-considered, well-written newspaper article, telling the people who you are, and what you have done, that it may be circulated not only in that state, but elsewhere, and thus help in manufacturing sentiment in your favor. I know your public life and can furnish items that your modesty would forbid, but I don't know much about your private history: when you were born, and where, the names and origin of your parents, what you did in early life, what were your opportunities for education, etc., and I want you to give me these. Won't you do it?"

Lincoln had been listening and said: "Fell, I admit the force of much that you say, and admit that I am ambitious, and would like to be President; I am not insensible to the compliment you pay me, and the interest you manifest in the matter, but there is no such good luck in store for me, as the Presidency of these United States; besides, there is nothing in my early history that would interest you or anybody else; and as Judge Davis says, 'It won't pay.'"

Rising, Lincoln wrapped a thick gray and brown wool shawl around his bony shoulders, spoke good night, and started down the stairway, with Fell calling out that Lincoln must listen and do as he asked. Newspapers in small towns in Midwest states had begun asking, "Why not Abraham Lincoln for President of the United States?" Calls for Lincoln to speak, as the foremost Republican figure of the West, were coming from Kansas, Buffalo, Des Moines, Pittsburgh. Thurlow Weed, the New York boss, wired to Illinois, "Send Abram Lincoln to Albany immediately." Long John Wentworth, editor of the Chicago *Democrat*, a Republican paper, saw Lincoln looming, and told him he "needed somebody to run him"; in New York Seward had Weed to run him. Lincoln laughed, "Only events can make a President."

CHAPTER 12
STRANGE FRIEND AND
FRIENDLY STRANGER

STRANGE FRIEND AND FRIENDLY STRANGER

LINCOLN was 51 years old. With each year since he had become a grown man, his name and ways, and stories about him, had been spreading among plain people and their children. So tall and so bony, with so peculiar a slouch and so easy a saunter, so sad and so haunted-looking, so quizzical and comic, as if hiding a lantern that lighted and went out and that he lighted again—he was the Strange Friend and the Friendly Stranger. Like something out of a picture book for children—he was. His form of slumping arches and his face of gaunt sockets were a shape a Great Artist had scrawled from careless clay.

In Springfield and other places, something out of the ordinary seemed to connect with Abraham Lincoln's past, his birth, a mystery of where he came from. The wedding certificate of his father and mother was not known to be on record. Whispers floated of his origin as "low-flung," of circumstances so misty and strange that political friends wished they could be cleared up and made respectable. The wedding license of Thomas Lincoln and Nancy Hanks had been moved to a new county courthouse—where no one had thought to search.

When Tad was late bringing home the milk he hunted the boy and came home with Tad on his shoulders and carrying the milk pail himself. Once he chased Tad and brought the little one home, holding him at arm's length; the father chuckled at his son's struggle to kick him in the face. Once as he lugged the howling Willie and Tad, a neighbor asked, "Why, Mr. Lincoln, what's the matter?" The answer: "Just what's the matter with the whole world. I've got three walnuts and each wants two."

Though the years had passed, he still believed, "Improvement in condition—is the order of things in a society of equals." And he still struggled under the load of that conundrum of history he had written ten years back: "As Labor is the common *burthen* of our race, so the effort of *some* to shift their share of the burthen on to the shoulders of *others*, is the great, durable, curse of the race."

The name of the man had come to stand for what he was, plus beliefs, conjectures and guesses. He was spoken of as a "politician" in the sense that politics is a trade of cunning, ambitious, devious men. He chose a few issues on which to explain his mind fully. Some of his reticences were not evasions but retirements to cloisters of silence. Questions of life and destiny shook him close to prayers and tears in his own hidden corners and byways; the depths of the issues were too dark, too pitiless, inexorable, for a man to open his mouth and try to tell what he knew.

There was a word: democracy. Tongues of politics played with it. Lincoln had his slant at it. "As I would not be a *slave*, so I would not be a *master*. This expresses my idea of democracy. Whatever differs from this, to the extent of the difference, is no democracy."

What he said to a crowd at Lewistown one August afternoon of 1858 had been widely printed and many a reader found it deeply worth reading again and again. His theme was the Declaration of Independence and its phrase, "that all men are created equal," and have unalienable rights to "life, liberty and the pursuit of happiness." That document was a "majestic" interpretation:

This was their lofty, and wise, and noble understanding of the justice of the Creator to His creatures. [Applause.] Yes, gentlemen, to *all* His creatures, to the whole great family of man . . . They grasped not only the whole race of man then living, but they reached forward and seized upon the farthest posterity . . . Wise statesmen as they were, they knew the tendency of prosperity to breed tyrants, and so they established these great self-evident truths, that when in the distant future some man, some faction, some interest, should set up the doctrine that none but rich men, or none but white men, were entitled to life, liberty and the pursuit of happiness, their posterity might look up again to the Declaration of Independence and take courage to renew the battle which their fathers began . . . I charge you to drop every paltry and insignificant thought for any man's success. It is nothing; I am nothing; Judge Douglas is nothing. *But do not destroy that immortal emblem of Humanity—the Declaration of American Independence.*

Somewhere in this period Milton Hay of Springfield heard Lincoln speak offhand a rule or maxim in politics. Hay later

Front parlor of Lincoln home in Springfield, Illinois, from Leslie's Illustrated *newspaper, v.11, n.276, p.245.*

Exterior of the Lincoln home in Springfield, Illinois.

The Lincoln writing-desk in his Springfield home.

This stereoscope was one of the boys' toys in the sitting room. They would open the top to allow light into the box, insert a card into the stereoscope which had two nearly identical photographs side-by-side, and then would peer through the two holes in front.

passed it on to Joseph Fifer of Bloomington who found it so simple and so nicely singsong that he couldn't forget it: "You can fool some of the people all of the time, and all of the people some of the time, but you can't fool all of the people all of the time."

Herndon believed Lincoln cloaked his ways with women by a rare and fine code, writing, "Mr. Lincoln had a strong, if not terrible passion for women. He could hardly keep his hands off a woman, and yet, much to his credit, he lived a pure and virtuous life. His idea was that a woman had as much right to violate the marriage vow as the man—no more and no less. His sense of right—his sense of justice—his honor forbade his violating his marriage vow. Judge Davis said to me, 'Mr. Lincoln's honor saved many a woman.' This I know. I have seen Lincoln tempted and I have seen him reject the approach of woman!"

A curious friend and chum of Lincoln was Ward Hill Lamon,

his Danville law partner, a young Virginian, dauntless, bull-necked, melodious, tall, commanding, often racy and smutty in talk, aristocratic and, drinking men said, magnificent in the amount of whisky he could carry. The first time he and Lincoln met, Lamon wore a swallow-tailed coat, white neckcloth, and ruffled silk shirt, and Lincoln: "Going to try your hand at law, are you? I don't think you would succeed at splitting rails." As the years passed a strange bond of loyalty between the two men grew. "Sing me a little song," was Lincoln's word to Lamon, who brought out a banjo and struck up the lively "Cousin Sally Downard," or "O Susanna," or the sad "Twenty Years Ago."

Herndon told of his partner coming to the office sometimes at seven in the morning when his usual hour to arrive was nine. Or of Lincoln at noon, having brought to the office a package of crackers and cheese, sitting alone eating. Mrs. Lincoln and Herndon hated each other. While Herndon was careless as to

Lincoln's shaving mirror. Abraham Lincoln was clean shaven until 1860, when he received a letter from a young girl who told him that he would gain more votes with a beard. He took her advice and became the first American president in office with a beard.

where he spat, she was not merely scrupulously neat and immaculate as to linen and baths, she was among the most ambitious women in Springfield in the matter of style and fashion. She knew of such affairs as Herndon getting drunk with two other men and breaking a windowpane that her husband had to hustle the money for so that the sheriff wouldn't lock up his law partner. She didn't like it that her husband had a drinking partner reckless with money, occasionally touching Lincoln for loans. She carried suspicions and nursed misgivings as to this swaggering upstart, radical in politics, transcendentalist in philosophy, antichurch.

At parties, balls, social gatherings, she moved, vital, sparkling, often needlessly insinuating or directly and swiftly insolent. If the music was bad, what was the need of her making unkind remarks about the orchestra? Chills, headaches, creepers of fear came; misunderstandings rose in waves so often around her; she was alone, so all alone, so like a child thrust into the Wrong Room.

There were times when she made herself pretty for him. One picture of her after 15 years of marriage shows dark ringlets of hair down her temples and about her ears, a little necklace circling her bare neck, three roses at her bosom, and a lily in her shapely hands.

She was often anxious about her boys, had mistaken fears about their safety or health, exaggerated evils that might befall them. She gave parties for them and wrote with her own pen, in a smooth and even script, gracious invitations.

Mary Todd had married a genius who made demands; when he wanted to work, it was no time for interruptions or errands. For this brooding and often somber man she was

Despite the presence of hired help, Mary usually prepared the evening meals and served them in the dining room.

Formal parlor where the Lincolns entertained important guests. It was here, on May 19, 1860, where Lincoln was officially asked to run for the Presidency.

wife, housekeeper, and counselor in personal and political affairs in so far as he permitted. She watched his "browsing" in the pantry and tried to bring him to regular meals. She had kept house years ago, too poor for a hired girl; they burned wood then; now they had a coal cookstove with four lids and a reservoir to warm rain water. She had chosen the beautiful, strong black-walnut cradle, into which she had put, one after the other, four boy babies.

With their rising income and his taking place as the outstanding leader of his party, Mary Lincoln in the late 1850's enjoyed

For a time, Mary shared her room with her two youngest children, Willie and Tad. When Mary and Abraham shared a bedroom, they would have also shared it with Bobbie and Eddie as well. This was a common sleeping arrangement during this time. When the children were considered old enough, they received their own room. In Willie's and Tad's case, this meant moving across the hallway.

giving parties occasionally for two or three hundred people. Isaac N. Arnold noted of these evenings "everything orderly and refined," and "every guest perfectly at ease," with a table "famed for the excellence of many rare Kentucky dishes, and in season, loaded with venison, wild turkeys, prairie chickens, quail and other game." She had moved with him from lean years to the comforts of the well-to-do middle class. With ownership of his house and lot, with farm lands, and collectible bills he had out, Lincoln in 1859 had property worth perhaps $15,000 or more.

The Lincolns' sitting room is similar to a modern family room. Here the parents held parties for Willie and Tad including one for which they invited fifty children.

CHAPTER 13

"ONLY EVENTS CAN MAKE
A PRESIDENT"

"Only Events Can Make a President"

LINCOLN'S name had spread far as a speaker and thinker. In 1859 he made speaking trips in Illinois, Indiana, Ohio, Wisconsin, Iowa, Kansas, and had to refuse many invitations to speak. On these trips he met leading men of the Republican party. They could judge whether he was presidential timber. He had said, "Only events can make a president," and there were friends saying events might dictate that each other candidate was either too old, too radical or too conservative and that Lincoln was on points the one most available. Also on these speaking trips Lincoln kept in touch with undercurrents of politics and public feeling; he met men who were to be delegates to the national Republican party convention the next year.

He tried to guide party policy, writing in June 1859 to Governor Chase about the Ohio Republican party platform demand for the "repeal of the atrocious Fugitive Slave Law." The proposition was "already damaging us here" in Illinois. If brought up in the next Republican national convention it would "explode" the convention and the party.

In May 1859 banker Jacob Bunn handling the deal, Lincoln bought for $400 the weekly German-language newspaper of Springfield, the *Illinois Staats-Anzeiger*. By the contract, Lincoln owned the type, press and other equipment, and Theodore Canisius, the editor, was to continue publishing a Republican paper in German with occasional articles in English. Those handling the deal kept it a secret; Lincoln said nothing of it to Herndon; no news of it was published. Editor Canisius had written Lincoln asking where he stood on the Massachusetts Act of 1859 providing that no foreign-born naturalized citizen could hold office or vote until two years after his naturalization. Lincoln wrote, "I am against it's adoption in Illinois, or in any other place, where I have a right to oppose it." The census of the next year would show 1,300,000 foreigners in the country, 700,000 of them Germans, chiefly in the Northern States. They held a balance of political power in many states. Their editors and political leaders were many of them German university graduates who had taken a hand in the revolutions of 1830 or 1848 in

Germany; some had served prison terms or escaped; they had been hunted men, coming to America as refugees and fugitives; they had their bitterness over the Fugitive Slave Law. One of the hunted was Lincoln's friend at Belleville, Gustave Koerner, who to escape arrest, fled Germany to France, then to St. Louis, later to become a Supreme Court justice in Illinois and lieutenant governor. Lincoln was now openly allying himself with these men. He had helped Germans write a resolution passed by the Republican state convention in 1856 declaring that "our naturalization laws . . . being just in principle, we are opposed to any change being made in them intended to enlarge the time now required to secure the rights of citizenship." This resolution a German editor had taken to the Philadelphia national convention of the Republican party where it was, in substance, adopted.

Herndon brought from Boston a book that Lincoln read, *The Impending Crisis of the South,* by Hinton Rowan Helper, who came from a slaveholding family that had lived a hundred years in the Carolinas. Helper gave formidable statistics showing that under the free labor system the North was growing richer and the people of the South sinking deeper in debt and poverty.

Abolitionists had stood up and interrupted church services to cry out it was a crime that the U.S. Constitution sanctioned slavery. Garrison had publicly burned a copy of the Constitution of the United States, calling it "a covenant with hell"; Henry Ward Beecher had held mock auctions of Negro women in his Brooklyn church; Uncle Tom's Cabin had sold in many editions and as a stage play held audiences breathless. The next census was to show that the 3,204,000 slaves of 1850 had increased to 3,953,500.

John Brown, who fought to free the slaves at Harpers Ferry, Virginia. Engraved by Small, Maynard & Co.

John Brown

"ONLY EVENTS CAN MAKE A PRESIDENT"

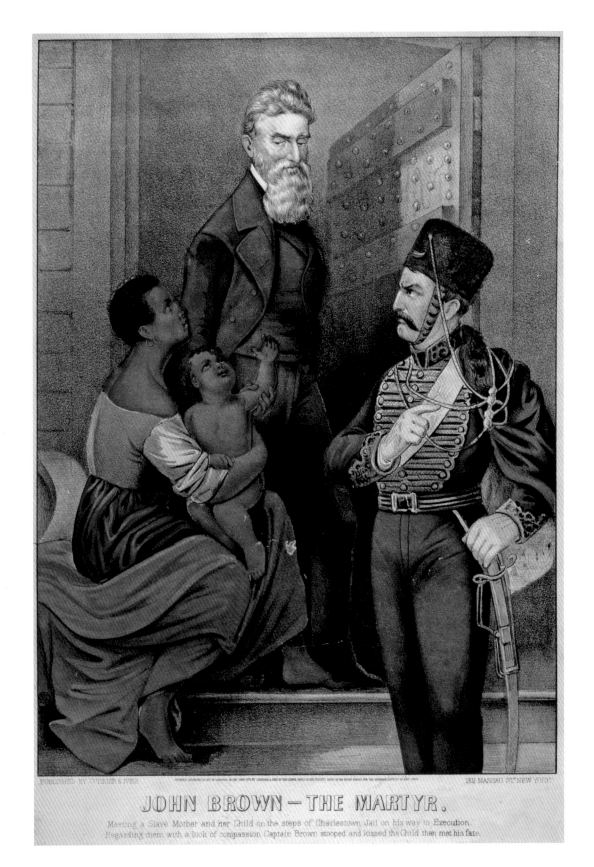

PUBLISHED BY CURRIER & IVES.   152 NASSAU ST. NEW YORK.

JOHN BROWN — THE MARTYR.

Meeting a Slave Mother and her Child on the steps of Charlestown Jail on his way to Execution.
Regarding them with a look of compassion Captain Brown stooped and kissed the Child then met his fate.

Out of Kansas came a man who ran slaves to freedom, burned barns, stole horses, and murdered men and boys without trial or hearing. He had come to Kansas from Ohio and New York, a descendant of Mayflower Pilgrim Fathers; two of his grandfathers fought in the Revolutionary War; at his house his 19 children partook in prayer and Scripture reading morning and night. He told eastern abolitionists action was the need, bold deeds. He had a saying: "One man and God can overturn the universe." Funds for rifles, pikes, wagons and stores were raised by wealthy and respectable citizens who in secret code termed the affair a "speculation in wool."

On Monday, October 17, 1859, the telegraph carried strange news. At the junction of the Shenandoah and Potomac Rivers, where Virginia and Maryland touch borders, in the rocky little town of Harpers Ferry, a U.S. Government arsenal and arms factory had been captured, the gates broken and watchmen made prisoners, slaveholders taken prisoner and their slaves told to spread the word of freedom to slaves everywhere—all of this between Sunday night and Monday daybreak.

Would the next news tell of slaves in revolt repeating the Nat Turner insurrection, with men, women and children butchered, homes looted and burned? The country breathed easier on Tuesday's news that Colonel Robert E. Lee, commanding 80 marines, had rushed a little engine-house fort where 18 men inside had fought till all were dead or wounded except two.

In a corner of the engine house, an old man with a flowing long beard said his name was John Brown. "Who sent you here?" they asked. "No man sent me here. It was my own prompting and that of my Maker." "What was your object?" "I came to free the slaves. I think it right to interfere with you to free those you hold in bondage." "And you say you believe in the Bible?" "Certainly I do." "Don't you know you are a seditionist, a traitor?" "I was trying to free the slaves." "You are mad and fanatical." "And I think you people of the South are mad and fanatical. Is it sane to think such a system can last? Is it sane to talk of war rather than give it up?"

Imaginary engraving of John Brown meeting the Slave Mother and her child on his way to execution, after painting by Louis Ransom. Engraved by Currier & Ives.

The State of Virginia gave him a fair trial on charges of murder, treason and inciting slaves to rebellion; Northern friends sent him able lawyers; he was found guilty and sentenced to be hanged. He spoke calmly to the court. "Had I taken up arms in behalf of the rich, the powerful, the intelligent . . . or any of their class, every man in this court would have deemed it an act worthy of reward rather than of punishment . . . I see a book kissed here which is the Bible, and which teaches me that all things that I would have men do unto me, so must I do unto them. I endeavored to act up to that instruction. I fought for the poor; and I say it was right, for they are as good as any of you . . . God is no respecter of persons . . . Now, if it be deemed necessary that I should forfeit my life for the furtherance of the ends of justic . . . I say, let it be done."

Friends planned to steal him away from the death watch. He sent them word he would be more useful to freedom when dead. He wished to be a memory among young men. He was 59, but the average age of those who fought and died for his cause was a little over 25. He wrote in the Charles Town jail a last message before going to the gallows: "I, John Brown, am now quite certain that the crimes of this guilty land will never be purged away but with blood. I had, as I now think, vainly flattered myself that without much bloodshed it might be done." Beyond the 3,000 guardsmen with rifles and bayonets, he could see blue haze and a shining sun over the Blue Ridge Mountains. "This is a beautiful country; I never had the pleasure of really seeing it before."

John Brown's ghost did walk. The governor of Virginia, the jailer, spoke of how he died, without a quaver, cool, serene. Emerson, Thoreau, Victor Hugo compared him to Christ, to Socrates, to the great martyrs. Wendell Phillips said, "The lesson of the hour is insurrection." Abolitionists acclaimed him and spoke for disunion. The antislavery men had regrets; they knew the South was lashed and would retaliate. Senator Douglas called for a law to punish conspiracies, quoting Lincoln's House Divided and Seward's Irrepressible Conflict speeches to indicate that Republican politicians and their "revolutionary doctrines" had incited John Brown.

Lincoln warned the Southern element, according to the Leavenworth *Register*, "If constitutionally we elect a President, and therefore you undertake to destroy the Union, it will be our duty to deal with you as old John Brown has been dealt with."

On December 20 Lincoln sent Jesse Fell the requested auto-biography. His father and mother came from "second families." Indiana, where he grew up, "was a wild region." And his schooling? "There was absolutely nothing to excite ambition for education. Of course when I came of age I did not know much. Still somehow, I could read, write, and cipher to the Rule of Three; but that was all. I have not been to school since. The little advance I now have upon this store of education, I have picked up from time to time under the pressure of necessity."

Letters kept coming about the House Divided speech. Just what did it mean? He would quote its opening paragraph, and write: "It puzzles me to make my meaning plainer. Look over it carefully, and conclude I meant all I said and did not mean anything I did not say, and you will have my meaning." And to close, "If you . . . will state to me some meaning which you suppose I had, I can, and will instantly tell you whether that was my meaning."

In December came a letter from high Republican leaders in Ohio asking "for publication in permanent form" of the great debates of 1858. Lincoln wrote December 19 he was grateful for "the very flattering terms" of their request and, "I wish the reprint to be precisely as the copies I send, without any comment whatever." In January the Chicago *Press & Tribune* carried news that Ohio Republicans were publishing the Lincoln-Douglas debates as a campaign document, the Springfield *Journal* clipping it and adding it was "a most delicate and expressive compliment . . . The name of 'Old Abe,' the leader of the great Republican army of the Northwest, has become a word of power and might." Other newspapers chimed in. That the book would come off the press and go to an immense audience of readers gave Lincoln a quiet pride in the first book for which he had furnished a manuscript.

The title page read: "Political Debates between Hon. Abraham Lincoln and Hon. Stephen A. Douglas, in the Celebrated Campaign of 1858, in Illinois," the publishers Follett, Foster & Company, Columbus, Ohio. The book held the awesome heave and surge of the slavery issue and its companion, the dark threat of the Union dissolved. It gave the passionate devotion of Douglas to an ocean-bound republic of free white men, with what he termed "the inferior races," the Negro, the Indian, the Chinese coolie, barred from citizenship—and Lincoln's thousand-faceted defense of the clause, "that all men are created equal," and his

high cries against the spread of slavery. In a sense, the book was a master mural of the American people in a given year.

Lincoln one October morning in 1859 "came rushing into the office," wrote Herndon, in his hands a letter inviting him to lecture in Brooklyn, in Plymouth Church, on the platform of Henry Ward Beecher. He thought it over, consulted with Herndon and others, and wrote the committee chairman, "I believe, after all, I shall make a political speech of it." Then over the winter weeks of late 1859 and early 1860 he toiled on the speech, at the State Library sinking himself in the *Congressional Globe*, the *Annals of Congress*, fingering through old mellowed newspaper files, in his office worming his way through his own six-volume Elliot's *Debates on the Federal Constitution*. This was to be no stump speech to prairie farmers. He would face a sophisticated metropolitan audience. The Chicago *Press & Tribune* on February 16, 1860, had sweepingly endorsed Lincoln for president, his character "the peer of any man yet named . . . more certain to carry Illinois and Indiana than any one else . . . great breadth and acuteness of intellect" and Lincoln would "never be President by virtue of intrigue and bargain." On February 23, as Lincoln left Springfield for New York, the *Illinois State Register* took its fling as to the coming speech: "Subject, not known, Consideration, $200 and expenses. Object, presidential capital. Effect, disappointment."

Arriving in New York he learned that the Young Men's Republican Union of New York City had arranged for his speech to be given in Cooper Union. At the Astor House he saw visitors, refused invitations to speak in New Jersey, went on working at his speech, noticed the *Tribune* called him "a man of the people, a champion of free labor." A Springfield Democrat, M. Brayman, wrote a letter February 27 telling of being at dinner with Lincoln, and admirers came to their table. "He turned half round and talked 'hoss' to them—introduced me as a Democrat, but one so good tempered that he and I could 'eat out of the *same rack, without a pole between us.*'"

A snowstorm interfered with traffic, and on the night of February 27 the Cooper Union audience didn't fill all the seats. About 1,500 people came, most of them paying the 25 cents admission; the door receipts were $367. The *Tribune* said that "since the days of Clay and Webster" there hadn't been a larger assemblage of the "intellect and moral culture" of the city of New York.

Crowds about Lincoln's carriage.

"ONLY EVENTS CAN MAKE A PRESIDENT"

The eminent attorney, David Dudley Field, escorted the speaker to the platform, where among distinguished guests sat the innocent-faced Horace Greeley. William Cullen Bryant, editor of the *Evening Post*, author of "Thanatopsis" and "To a Waterfowl," told the audience of Lincoln's majority for the senatorship in Illinois and the legislative apportionment that elected Douglas. Bryant closed, "I have only, my friends, to pronounce the name of Abraham Lincoln of Illinois [loud cheering], to secure your pro-foundest attention."

A tall, gaunt frame came forward, on it a long, new suit of broadcloth, hanging creased and rumpled as it came out of his satchel. Applause began; the orator smiled, put his left hand to the lapel of his coat, and so stood as the greeting slowed down. "Mr. *Chee*man," he said with Kentucky tang in his opening. He was slow getting started. There were Republicans not sure whether to laugh or feel sorry. As he got into his speech there came a change. They saw he had thought his way deeply among the issues and angers of the hour. He quoted Douglas: "Our fathers, when they framed the Government under which we live, understood this question [of slavery] just as well, and even better, than we do now." And who might these "fathers" be? Included must be the 39 framers of the original Constitution and the 76 members of the Congress who framed the amendments. And he went into a crisscross of roll calls, quotations, documents in established history, to prove "the fathers" held the Republican party view of restricting slavery. Did any one of "the fathers" ever say that the Federal Government should *not* have the power to control slavery in the Federal Territories? "I defy any man to show that any one of them ever, in his whole life, declared that." He said "neither the word 'slave' nor 'slavery' is to be found in the Constitution, nor the word 'property' even." They called the slave a "person." His master's legal right to him was phrased as "service or labor which may be due." Their purpose was "to exclude from the Constitution the idea that there could be property in man."

The wide wedges of faces between were listening. "And now, if they would listen—as 1 suppose they will not—I would address a few words to the Southern people."

He reasoned: "All they ask, we could readily grant, if we thought slavery right; all we ask, they could as readily grant, if they thought it wrong. Their thinking it right, and our thinking it wrong, is the precise fact upon which depends the whole controversy. Thinking it right, as they do, they are not to blame for desiring its full recognition, as being right; but, thinking it wrong, as we do, can we yield to them? Can we cast our votes with their view, and against our own?" To search for middle ground between the right and the wrong would be "vain as the search for a man who should be neither a living man nor a dead man." He finished: "Let us have faith that right makes might, and in that faith, let us, to the end, dare to do our duty as we understand it."

Applause came, outcries and cheers; hats went in the air and handkerchiefs waved; they crowded to shake the speaker's hand; a reporter blurted, "He's the greatest man since St. Paul" and scurried away to write: "No man ever before made such an impression on his first appeal to a New York audience."

In the morning Lincoln saw that four papers printed his speech in full, and learned there would be a pamphlet reprint of it. Brady photographed him; as the picture came out he looked a little satisfied with himself; it wasn't his usual sad face. But people liked it.

Lincoln spoke for his party in New England and visited his boy, Robert, in school at Exeter, New Hampshire.

He made speeches in Providence, Concord, Manchester, Dover, New Haven, Meriden, Norwich, and finally in Bridgeport on March 10, usually to "capacity audiences," several times escorted by brass bands and torchlight processions of cheering Republicans. He thanked James A. Briggs for a $200 check for the Cooper Union speech, begged off any more speaking dates, but on March 11 did go with Briggs to hear Beecher preach in Brooklyn and to attend the Universalist Church of Edwin H. Chapin in New York. The next day he took the Erie Railroad for Chicago and two days later was home in Springfield, arriving, said the *Journal*, "in excellent health and in his usual spirits."

CHAPTER 14

"Mary, We're Elected"

"Mary, We're Elected"

WILLIAM H. SEWARD, eight years older than Lincoln, leading all other candidates for the Republican presidential nomination, was a New Yorker of Welsh-Irish stock, a slim, middle-sized man, stooped, white-haired, with a pointed nose, a slouching walk, a plain conversational tone in public speaking, "eyes secret but penetrating, a subtle, quick man, rejoicing in power." His friend and manager, Thurlow Weed, publisher of the Albany *Evening Journal,* ran a Seward publicity bureau, was in touch with large special interests and made free use of money in promoting Seward.

When governor of New York, Seward had brought into effect laws requiring jury trial for fugitive slaves, with defense counsel fees paid by the state. In the U.S. Senate, replying to Webster, Seward had said, ". . . there is *a higher law* than the Constitution, which regulates our authority over the domain." In October 1858 he spoke of the slavery issue as not "the work of fanatical agitators," but rather, "It is an *irrepressible conflict* between opposing and enduring forces, and it means that the United States must and will, sooner or later, become either entirely a slaveholding nation, or entirely a free-labor nation."

Handsome, portly, overdignified Salmon P. Chase of Ohio, antislavery, radical, had twice been governor and served a term as U.S. Senator; he would get delegates from Ohio and elsewhere but didn't seem formidable. Judge Edward Bates of Missouri would have that state's delegates and a scattered following from elsewhere. He was 67, had married a South Carolinian's daughter who bore him 17 children. He had been a Whig Congressman and his backers said that as a Free-Soil Whig from a Border Slave State he would avert secession. He was smallish, bearded, a moderate Old Line Whig who kept a diary that whispered to him he would be President. In 1856 he had been a leader in an Old Line Whig convention at Baltimore which endorsed the American [Know-Nothing] party and he didn't know the full force of German editors and political leaders who had axes out for him and would throw a fierce strength against him.

John McLean, an Ohio Democrat, appointed associate justice of the U.S. Supreme Court by President Jackson, was in the running, his dissenting opinion in the Dred Scott case being in his favor. He was 75, and Lincoln wrote to Trumbull, "I do not believe he would accept it [the nomination]; . . . If he were ten years younger he would be our best candidate." McLean's health was failing and he was to die within a year, but he was mentioned in reckonings that did not include Lincoln.

Before mid-May the Lincoln-Douglas debates book, at 50 cents in paper or $ 1.00 clothbound, was to go into four editions; the pamphlet reprints of the Cooper Union speech were selling at one cent the copy, and there was a growing legend spreading wider of the tall homely man who was log-cabin born and had been flatboatman and rail splitter, struggling on to where his speech and thought were read nationwide. All this had created an aura about Lincoln that in the few weeks now left before the national Republican convention in May was to be the more effective because it was no forced growth. It had a way of dawning on men, "Why, yes, come to think of it, why not Lincoln? The more you look at him the more he is the man."

Into the state Republican convention at Decatur on May 9 came John Hanks carrying two fence rails tied with flags and streamers, with the inscription, "Abraham Lincoln, the Rail Candidate far President in 1860: Two rails from a lot of 3,000 made in 1830 by Thos. Hanks and Abe Lincoln—whose father was the first pioneer of Macon County." Shouts followed: "Lincoln! Lincoln! Speech!" He thanked them with a sober face. Cheers: "Three times three for Honest Abe, our next President." Shouts from the convention: "Identify your work!" "It may be that I split these rails," and scrutinizing further, "Well, boys, I can only say that I have split a great many better-looking ones."

Thus the Rail Candidate was brought forth, and the nickname of Rail Splitter. The idea came from Richard Oglesby, a Decatur

Judge David Davis who assisted in Lincoln's presidential campaign of 1860 and was later appointed to the U.S. Supreme Court.

Hannibal Hamlin, Lincoln's first term Vice-President from 1861-1865.

lawyer, Kentucky-raised, a plain and witty man, who shared Lincoln's belief in the people. He had hunted out John Hanks and planned the dramatization of Lincoln as "the Rail Splitter." Far more important was it that the convention instructed its delegates to the Chicago convention to vote as a unit for Lincoln; 7 of the 22 delegates personally preferred Seward, and Orville H. Browning's choice was Bates.

Two weeks earlier, at the national Democratic convention in Charleston, South Carolina, where the Douglas delegates held a majority control, but lacking the necessary two-thirds to nominate their hero, slavery men had split the party, and two separate wings of it were to hold conventions in June. The answers of Douglas to Lincoln in the Freeport debate and his break with the Buchanan administration had lost nearly all former trust of the South in him.

On May 9 in Baltimore was organized the new Constitutional Union party with a short platform calling for the maintenance of the Constitution, the Union and law enforcement. For President they nominated John Bell of Tennessee, a former Whig Congressman and U.S. Senator, for Vice-President, Edward Everett, a former Secretary of State and president of Harvard University. Not much was expected from them; their platform was not merely simple but too simple.

Illinois delegates were outfitting with silk hats and broadcloth suits for the Chicago Republican convention May 16. Lincoln was saying, "I am a little too much a candidate to stay home and not quite enough a candidate to go." Judd and others had made a special point of getting the convention for Chicago. They told the national committee that holding the convention in an eastern city would "run a big chance of losing the West." Chicago had become

HON. ABRAHAM LINCOLN, OF ILLINOIS.   HON. HANNIBAL HAMLIN, OF MAINE,

FOR PRESIDENT,   FOR VICE PRESIDENT.

THE REPUBLICAN BANNER FOR 1860.

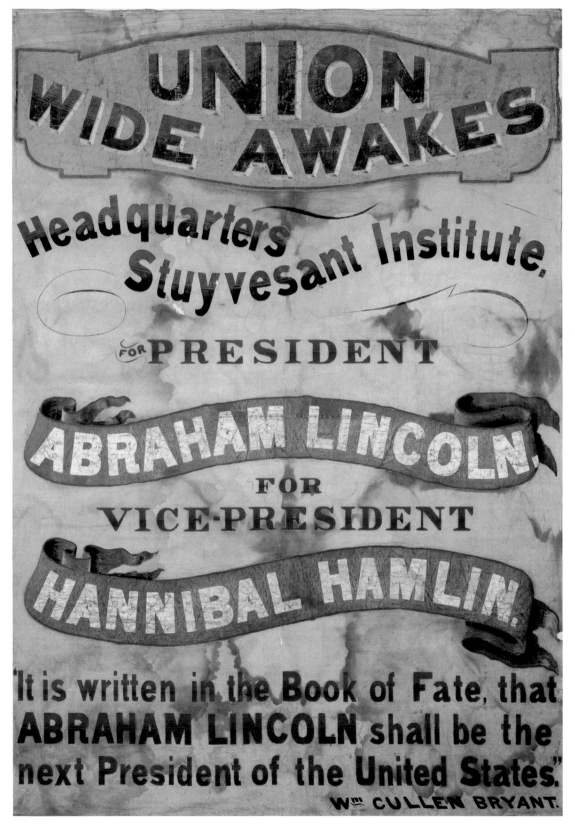

The Wide Awakes political clubs of young men rallied for Lincoln in the 1860 campaign.

Lincoln-Hamlin campaign banner, 1860.

Lincoln-Hamlin campaign flag, 1860.

a symbol for audacity, enterprise and onward stride. Its population of 29,000 in 1850 had become 80,000 in 1855, and 109,000 in 1860; it betokened the "great Northwest" that had wrought transformations in American national politics. Its trade in hogs, cattle, wheat, corn, farm machinery, and the associated finance and transportation, made it the depot and crossroads for thousand-mile prairies. Out of it ran 15 railway lines with 150 railroad trains a day; on May 16, 1860, they had brought an estimated 40,000 strangers and 500 delegates to the convention. At the corner of Lake and Market Streets the Sauganash Hotel had been torn down, and a huge rambling lumber structure, to hold 10,000 people, had been put up and named the Wigwam. Chicago girls and women, with the help of young men, had made the big barnlike interior gay and brilliant with flags, bunting and streamers of red, white and blue.

The day before the convention opened, May 15, Davis and Dubois wired Lincoln: "We are quiet but moving heaven & Earth. Nothing will beat us but old fogy politicians." The next day Judd's message was: "Don't be frightened. Keep cool. Things is working." On the afternoon of May 17 the platform was adopted in a sweep of yells and cheers. The Seward men then wanted to ballot on candidates; a motion to that effect was made but the chair said "the tally-sheets had not been prepared" and on a quick motion to adjourn and by a light unrecorded vote, Chairman George Ashmun announced the motion prevailed and the convention was adjourned. The moment was fateful; Seward men believed they could have nominated their man that afternoon. That May 17 the main Lincoln backers worked all night and clinched important deals. Davis telegraphed Lincoln: "Am very hopeful. Don't be Excited. Nearly dead with fatigue. Telegraph or write here very little."

When the platform was adopted the day before, leaving out mention of the Declaration of Independence, old Joshua R. Giddings arose, and said it was time to walk out of the Republican party. Then young George William Curtis of *Harper's Weekly* stood up and shamed the convention; the principle of the equality of men was written in and Giddings stayed on.

Seward victory was in the air; champagne fizzed at the Richmond House. Straw votes on all incoming railroad trains had given Seward overwhelming majorities. Michigan, Wisconsin, Minnesota, were a unit for Seward, as were the New York,

Lincoln and Hamlin campaign button.

Massachusetts (except four who were for Lincoln) and California delegations. Horace Greeley wired his New York *Tribune* that Seward seemed sure to win. Lincoln workers were saying with clenched fists and blazing eyes that the Republicans were beaten at the start if Seward headed the ticket. They scared a definite element who wanted to win; and again there were antislavery men such as Bryant of the New York *Evening Post* who believed Seward to be the same type as Daniel Webster, much intellect, little faith, none of the "mystic simplicity" of Lincoln.

On the first two days of the convention's routine business the Seward men were allowed by the Chicago managers to have free run of the floor. But on May 18, when sunrise saw thousands milling about the Wigwam doors, the Lincoln shouters were shoved through the doors till they filled all seats and standing room; hundreds of New York hurrah boys couldn't squeeze in. Lamon and Fell got a thousand men recruited for their lung power; they had been given tickets and were on hand. They watched their leaders, two men located on opposite sides of the Wigwam.

Seward had 173 ½ votes, Lincoln 102, and favorite sons and others the remainder of the votes on the first ballot. On the

Abraham Lincoln. Photo by Alexander Hesler, 1860.

second ballot, Lincoln jumped to 181 as against Seward's 184 ½. On the third ballot, of the 465 votes Lincoln swept 231 ½ while Seward dropped to 180. Medill of the *Tribune* whispered to Cartter of Ohio, "If you can throw the Ohio delegation for Lincoln, Chase can have anything he wants." "H-how d'-d'ye know?" stuttered Cartter, Medill answering, "I know, and you know I wouldn't promise if I didn't know."

Cartter called for a change of four votes from his state to Lincoln. Other delegates announced changes of votes to Lincoln. As the tellers footed up the totals, and the chairman waited for the figures, the charter of 10,000 people stopped, the fluttering of ladies' fans ended, the scratching of pencils and the clicking of the telegraph dot-dash dash-dot-dash could be heard. The 900 reporters from everywhere in America clutched their pencils.

The chairman spoke. Of 465 votes, 364 were cast for the candidate highest, and "Abraham Lincoln, of Illinois, is selected as your candidate for President of the United States."

Hannibal Hamlin, the Maine senator, a former Democrat, was nominated for Vice-President, and thanks voted to the convention chairman, George Ashmun of Massachusetts. Seward's manager, Thurlow Weed, pressed the temples of his forehead to hold back tears but the tears came. Greeley wrote it was a fearful week he hoped never to see repeated. "If you had seen the Pennsylvania delegation, and known how much money Weed had in hand, you would not have believed we could do so well as we did . . . We had to rain red-hot bolts on them, however, to keep the majority from going for Seward."

Knapp telegraphed Lincoln: "We did it. Glory to God," and Fell: "City wild with excitement. From my inmost heart I congratulate you." Swett warned, "Don't let any one persuade you to come here," Dubois and Butler saying: "Do not come without we telegraph you," Judd more brief: "Do not come to Chicago," and Koerner briefest of all: "Don't come here."

On May 18 Lincoln walked from home to his office and was talking with two law students when the office door burst open and the *Journal* editor, Baker, told him of the first ballot in Chicago. They walked to the telegraph office, found no later news, and at the *Journal* office met a crowd shouting good news would be coming. Lincoln slouched in a chair but straightened up at the next news of his big gains on the second ballot. And when the wires sang that his nomination had been made unanimous, he knew that a great somber moment had come to him and the firing of 100 jubilant guns made a shadowed music. He read a flurry of gay telegrams, shook hands all round, then went home to tell the news and see his wife's face beam and glow. In the afternoon he shook hands with many callers.

Bonfires of boxes, barrels and brushwood lighted up the Sangamon River country that Friday night. A brass band and a cheering crowd at the Lincoln house surged to the front porch and called for a speech. He saw the honor of the nomination not for him personally but as the representative of a cause; he wished his house big enough so he could ask them all inside. Shouts and yells of hurrah parties broke on the night till the gray dawn of the morning after.

Judge Davis answered a question on what the wild week cost: "The entire expense of Lincoln's nomination, including headquarters, telegraphing, music, fare of delegations, and other incidentals, was less than $700."

The notification committee at his house formally told Lincoln he was nominated for President. He formally replied, and later, after reading the platform, sent a letter of acceptance. He would co-operate, "imploring the assistance of Divine Providence."

In June the adjourned Democratic national convention met in Baltimore, and after bitter and furious debates, nominated Douglas of Illinois for President and Herschel Johnson, a Georgia unionist, for Vice-President. Delegates from 11 slave states walked out, bolted their old party, and nominated John C. Breckinridge of Kentucky for President and Joseph Lane of Oregon for Vice-President. They rejected with scorn and hate Douglas' "popular sovereignty" and his leadership; they believed with John Randolph who 40 years earlier had advised secession, saying, "Asking a state to surrender part of her sovereignty is like asking a lady to surrender part of her chastity." When Stephens of Georgia was asked what he was thinking, "Why, that men will be cutting one another's throats in a little while. In less than twelve months we shall be in a war, and that the bloodiest in history."

Wide-Awake clubs of young men in uniforms marched in torchlight processions. Seward spoke across the Northern States; Lincoln went to the railway station to pay him a cordial greeting when he passed through Springfield. Batteries and flotillas of orators spoke. They argued, threatened, promised, appealed to statistics, passions, history. But the high chosen spokesman of the party had little or nothing to say.

Five hack biographies sprouted in June. Later came more pretentious and competent biographies, bound in boards, one by William Dean Howells, the best by D. W. Bartlett, a 354-page volume with a steel engraving of Lincoln. Six editions were printed of the New York *Tribune's* impressive *Political Text Book for 1860*, 248 pages of the most notable speeches and documents of all parties. In campaign literature the Republicans far surpassed the Democrats. Medals and coins were struck, one medal praising soap on one side and the candidate on the other. Requests for autographs flooded in. Wendell Phillips was asking, "Who is this huckster in politics?" Seward was saying, "No truer defender of the Republican faith could have been found."

John Locke Scripps, a Chicago *Tribune* editor, had a long interview with Lincoln, and on his request Lincoln wrote for his use a 2,500-word autobiography. From this Scripps wrote a 32-page close-print pamphlet titled "Life of Abraham Lincoln." Scripps wrote to a brother, "I have been getting out a campaign Life of Lincoln for the million which is published simultaneously by us [the Chicago *Tribune*] and by the *New York Tribune*." Though Scripps was rushed, and wrote against time, he produced a little book packed with a charming readable story having documents and dignity. A million copies at five cents apiece meant millions of readers now had a few answers to, "Who and what is Abraham Lincoln, his folks, his ways, his looks, his home, his beliefs and policies?"

In this summer of 1860 Lincoln saw a powerful young political party shaping his figure into heroic stature, coloring his personality beyond reality. From hundreds of stump orators and newspapers came praise and outcry for "Abe," "Old Abe," "the Rail Candidate," "the Backwoodsman," "Honest Abe," "the Man of the People," the sagacious, eloquent Man of the Hour, one who starting from a dirt-floor cabin was to move on into the Executive Mansion in Washington.

Douglas stumped the country in what seemed for him a losing fight; he went on tireless, men amazed at the way he wore out, went to bed, and came back fighting. At Norfolk, Virginia, in late August he told an audience of 7,000 that he wanted no votes except from men who desired the Union to be preserved. On a slip of paper handed him was the question whether, if the South seceded, he would advise resistance by force. To this he flashed, "I answer emphatically that it is the duty of the President of the United States and all others in authority under him to enforce the laws of the United States as passed by Congress and as the courts expound them . . . In other words, I think the President of the United States, whoever he may be, should treat all attempts to break up resistance to its laws as Old Hickory treated the Nullifiers in 1832." At Raleigh, North Carolina, he said he would "hang every man higher than Haman" who resisted Constitutional law. No Illinoisan would ever consent to pay duty on corn shipped down the Mississippi. "We furnish the water that makes the great river, and we will follow it throughout its whole course to the ocean, no matter who or what may stand before us."

The campaign came to its last week. As the summer and fall drew on he was to those who met him the same friendly neighbor as always—but with more to think about. He shook hands with Whitney in a big crowd, and a half-hour later, seeing Whitney again, he shook hands and called him by name. "He didn't know me the first time," said Whitney.

Millions of people had by this time read his words of two years ago in the House Divided speech. They struck the soft, weird keynote of the hour. "If we could first know *where* we are, and *whither* we are tending, we could then better judge *what* to do, and *how* to do it"

Early reports on election evening, November 6, gave Douglas 3,598 votes and Lincoln 3,556 in Sangamon County while in Springfield Lincoln had 1,395 against 1,326 for Douglas. From nine o'clock on he sat in the Springfield telegraph office. Lincoln with friends stepped across the street to where the Republican Ladies' Club had fixed a supper. The ladies rushed him. "How do you do, Mr. President?" Hardly were the men seated when a messenger rushed in waving a telegram. New York had gone Republican. Lincoln's election was clinched.

In the streets, and around the Statehouse, crowds surged, shouting themselves hoarse. The jubilee was still going as Lincoln walked home to say to a happy woman, "Mary, we're elected." The local *Journal* was saying, "Our city is as quiet as a young lady who has just found out that she is in love."

The national count gave Lincoln 1,866,452 votes; Douglas, 1,376,957; Breckinridge, 849,781; Bell, 588,879. Lincoln had majorities in 17 Free States, Breckinridge carried 11 Slave States, Bell 3 Slave States. In the electoral college Douglas had only the 3 votes of New Jersey and the 9 of Missouri. The total electoral college votes looked a little silly, giving dim light on the popular balloting, with Lincoln, 180; Breckinridge, 72; Bell, 39; Douglas, 12. In a total of some 4,700,000 votes the other combined candidates had nearly a million more votes than Lincoln. Fifteen states gave him no electoral votes; in ten states of the South he didn't get a count of one popular vote. He was the most sectionally elected President the nation had ever had and the fact would be dinned into his ears.

CHAPTER 15
THE HOUSE DIVIDING

THE HOUSE DIVIDING

President-Elect Lincoln in Chicago.
Photo by Alexander Hesler, 1860.

LINCOLN'S election was a signal. The Atlanta newspaper, *Confederacy*, spoke for those who had visions of violence: "Let the consequences be what they may—whether the Potomac is crimsoned in human gore, and Pennsylvania Avenue is paved ten fathoms deep with mangled bodies, or whether the last vestige of liberty is swept from the face of the American continent, the South will never submit to such humiliation and degradation as the inauguration of Abraham Lincoln." This was in part bravado and blowoff and in part hope and determination.

South Carolina legislators voted to raise and equip 10,000 volunteer soldiers; Georgia voted $1,000,000 and Louisiana $500,000 for guns and men. Robert Toombs was saying: "It is admitted that you seek to outlaw $4,000,000,000 of property of our people . . . Is not that a cause of war?" But was secession the safest immediate way of managing this property? Jefferson Davis had hopes and doubts. And Alexander Stephens had written, "I consider slavery much more secure in the Union than out of it if our people were but wise."

On the way to Chicago November 21 Lincoln made a two-minute speech at Bloomington, referred to the expressed will of the people, and, "I think very much of the people, as an old friend said he thought of woman. He said when he lost his first wife, who had been a great help to him in his business, he thought he was ruined—that he could never find another to fill her place. At length, however, he married another . . . and that his opinion now was that *any woman would do well who was well done by.*"

In Chicago, as he had arranged by letters, he met Vice-President-elect Hamlin and Joshua Speed. He wasn't sure he had ever before met Hamlin but he had heard him speak in the Senate. Hamlin couldn't remember having met Lincoln but he had heard him in the House in a speech that had "auditors convulsed with laughter." People so crowded in on the two important men in the Tremont House that they went for their conference to a private home. Lincoln wished in appointments to hold a balance between Whigs who had turned Republican and Democrats who had turned Republican. He would trust Hamlin to name the New England member of his Cabinet for Secretary of the Navy, giving Hamlin three names he inclined to favor, Hamlin deciding on a former Jackson Democrat, Gideon Welles, a Hartford editor. They both favored Seward for Secretary of State.

Thurlow Weed came from Albany, on Swett writing him that Lincoln wanted to see him about Cabinet matters. Lincoln had long trained himself to put men at their ease while pumping them with quiet questions, learning by asking, and asking with keen, soft persistence. He knew that Weed was in touch with such men of power as A. T. Stewart, leading New York merchant, and August Belmont, New York representative of the Rothschilds, international bankers, and one of the northern capitalists to whom the South was in debt $200,000,000. Salmon P. Chase, newly elected U.S. Senator from Ohio, came by invitation. Lincoln said he "wasn't exactly prepared" to appoint Chase Secretary of the Treasury, but if he did, would Chase accept? Chase wouldn't promise. He'd think it over. And he went away to line up friends to put pressure on Lincoln to appoint him.

President-Elect Hon. Abraham Lincoln. Engraved by Currier & Ives, 1860.

Simon Cameron came and after long talks left with a letter signed by Lincoln:

I think fit to notify you now, that by your permission, I shall, at the proper time, nominate you to the U.S. Senate, for confirmation as Secretary of the Treasury, or as Secretary of War—which of the two, I have not definitely decided. Please answer at your own earliest convenience.

Cameron's enemies brought evidence to Lincoln intended to show that Cameron was "the very incarnation of corruption" and his fortune "acquired by means forbidden to the man of honor."

Winfield Scott, hero of the Mexican War, in charge of security at Lincoln's 1st inauguration, 1861.

churchman, as manager of the Charleston Bible Society, as vice-president of the Young Men's Temperance Society, as secretary of the Charleston Port Society for promoting the Christian gospel among seamen, as the father of 12 children, the driving motive of Rhett's life was to win secession and Southern independence, build a confederacy on the cornerstone of African slavery, and restore the African slave trade outlawed by the U.S. Constitution as of 1808. Rhett organized "minutemen" and vigilance committees, to make sure of delegates pledged to secession. He wrote the ordinance of disunion, and in secret session the convention's 169 delegates in St. Andrew's Hall at Charleston, December 16, 1860, passed it without debate in 45 minutes. A newly adopted flag brought a great shout, rocked the hall, and from lowlands to upcountry were bells, bonfires, torchlights, parades, shotgun salutes and cries of jubilee. One by one the six other Cotton States of the lower South joined South Carolina in leaving the Union.

Senators and Representatives from the South spoke sad and bitter farewells to Congress; U.S. postmasters, judges, district attorneys, customs collectors, by the hundreds sent their resignations to Washington. Of the 1,108 officers of the U.S. Regular Army, 387 were preparing resignations, many having already joined the Confederate armed forces. The U.S. mint at New Orleans and two smaller mints were taken over by the Confederate States, as were post offices and customhouses. Governors of seceded states marched in troops and took over U.S. forts that had cost $6,000,000.

Lincoln wrote Cameron another letter; things had developed which made it impossible to take him into the Cabinet. Would he write a letter publicly declining any Cabinet place? And Cameron's answer was a bundle of recommendations outnumbering the opposition three to one; Lincoln later wrote Cameron that he wouldn't make a Cabinet appointment for Pennsylvania without consulting him.

"Resistance to Lincoln is Obedience to God" flared a banner at an Alabama mass meeting; an orator swore that if need be their troops would march to the doors of the national Capitol over "fathoms of mangled bodies."

Against Southern advice that South Carolina wait till President Buchanan's term ended, Robert Barnwell Rhett and his forces had manipulated the precise dramatic event of secession. As a Congressman of six terms and a U.S. Senator of one term, as editor of the Charleston *Mercury*, as lawyer and

Reports flew that Southern forces would seize Washington, Lincoln to be sworn in at some other place. Twenty-two carloads of troops were starting from Fort Leavenworth across Missouri for Baltimore. Cameron of Pennsylvania was saying, "Lincoln, if living, will take the oath of office on the Capitol steps." Dr. William Jayne of Springfield wrote to Trumbull, "Lincoln advised he would rather be hanged by the neck till he was dead on the steps of the Capitol than buy or beg a peaceful inauguration." Newly organized artillery companies were drilling in Chicago. A thousand Negro slaves were throwing up fortifications in Charleston, South Carolina. Governor Yates notified the legislature, "Illinois counts among her citizens 400,000 who can bear arms." Five million dollars and a hundred thousand troops would be offered by their state, Pennsylvania legislators were saying.

"The Revolution" was the top headline under which a New York daily paper assembled the news of the country. Nine columns were required on one day to report declarations of Southern conventions, and resignations from the Army, Navy and training academies. Stephens of Georgia had dug into history. "Revolutions are much easier started than controlled, and the men who begin them, even for the best purposes and object, seldom end them."

The New York *Herald*, circulating 77,000 copies daily, earning profits of 1300,000 a year, advised in an editorial, "A grand opportunity now exists for Lincoln to avert impending ruin, and invest his name with an immortality far more enduring than would attach to it by his elevation to the Presidency. His withdrawal at this time from the scene of conflict, and the surrender of his claims to some national man who would be acceptable to both sections, would render him the peer of Washington in patriotism." And the *Herald* added: "If he persists in his present position . . . he will totter into a dishonoured grave, driven there perhaps by the hands of an assassin, leaving behind him a memory more excrable than that of Arnold—more despised than that of the traitor Catiline."

Senator Jefferson Davis, pale and just risen from a sickbed, in January spoke his words of parting: "I offer you my apology for any thing I may have done in the Senate, and I go remembering no injury I have received." His regrets coupled to a warning: "There will be no peace if you so will it."

In the very air of the City of Washington was coming a sense of change, of an impending program to be wrought out on historic anvils in smoke and mist, of old bonds and moorings broken, of a formerly confident and dominant class giving way to an element a little raw and new to government and diplomacy, young and strange in its champing and chafing.

In the White House Buchanan suggested gently, "The election of any one of our citizens to the office of President does not of itself afford just cause for dissolving the Union."

He argued that seceded states had no right to secede, yet the Federal Government had no right to use force to stop them from seceding. He urged, however, the right of the Federal Government to use force against individuals, in spite of secession, to enforce Federal laws and hold Federal property. Yet his words lacked action to give them force.

One comfort to him was his niece, Harriet Lane, robust, with golden-brown hair, violet-blue eyes, a graduate of the Visitation Convent near Washington. A warship had been named for her, also a race horse, a flower, a fashionable gown and many a new-born girl child. "No American woman ever had more offers of marriage than Harriet Lane."

While a hurricane was preparing, these two careful persons lived with their mild secrets in the White House. "Be quiet and discreet and say nothing"—the written advice of the old man to his niece was his own guiding motto.

With inauguration day a few weeks off, letters warned Lincoln he would be killed before he reached Washington. He sent Thomas S. Mather, adjutant general of Illinois, to Washington to sound Winfield Scott on his loyalty. Mather came back to report he had found the Mexican War hero propped up with pillows, in bed, an old worn man with flesh in rolls over face and neck. His breathing heavy, he half choked and wheezed out the words: "Say to him that, when once here, I shall consider myself responsible for his safety. If necessary I'll plant cannons at both ends of Pennsylvania Avenue, and if any show their hands or even venture to raise a finger, I'll blow them to hell."

Delegates at Montgomery, Alabama, on February 4 organized a provisional government named the Confederate States of America, electing Jefferson Davis of Mississippi as President and Alexander Stephens of Georgia as Vice-President. Second to Robert Barnwell Rhett as a torch of revolution was William Lowndes Yancey of Alabama. And yet, in the seats of high power sat neither Yancey nor Rhett. Yancey and other extremists would have liked Rhett to be President. But a moderate element took the power, men who would rather have waited, who would have held a convention and presented demands to the North. In their newly adopted constitution they struck directly at Rhett, Yancey and the slave traders, and bid for international good will by expressly forbidding the African slave trade for all time.

It was sunset and dawn, moonrise and noon, dying time and birthing hour, dry leaves of the last of autumn and springtime blossom roots.

CHAPTER 16

"I Bid You an Affectionate Farewell"

John Hay, one of Lincoln's two private secretaries. Photo by C.M. Gilbert.

"I Bid You an Affectionate Farewell"

WHEN a Brooklyn hatter one January day presented Lincoln with a black silk hat, he turned to say, "Well, wife, if nothing else comes out of this scrape, we are going to have some new clothes." Such attentions pleased Mrs. Lincoln. She had a sprightly manner of saying, "We are pleased with our advancement." In the hustle of deciding what to take along to the White House, when asked about many things to be done or not done, she would sometimes burst out, "God, no!" One winter morning she was burning papers in the alley when Jared P. Irwin, a neighbor, asked if he could have some of them. She said he was welcome and Irwin scraped from the fire several of the most interesting letters written by Mr. and Mrs. Lincoln to each other.

She spoke of fears about her health, would mention "my racked frame" to other women, and say she hoped the chills she suffered from in earlier years would not return in Washington. She might find Washington a city of tears and shadows. She would go there with new clothes, fresh ribbons, and see. She made a trip in January to New York City, there meeting Robert, who came down from Harvard. She had as good a time as possible for her, choosing and buying gowns, hats, footwear and adornments becoming to one to be called "the First Lady of the Land."

Lincoln rode to Mattoon, missed connections with a passenger train, and took the caboose of a freight train to Charleston. With a shawl over his shoulders, and his boots in slush, mud and ice, he picked his way in the late evening dusk alongside the tracks the length of the freight train to the station, where a buggy was ready. Friends took him to the house where he stayed overnight. Next day he drove eight miles out to an old farm. Sally Bush Lincoln and he put their arms around each other and listened to each other's heartbeats. They held hands and talked, they talked without holding hands. Each looked into eyes thrust back in deep sockets. She was all of a mother to him. He was her boy more than any born to her. He gave her a photograph of her boy, a hungry picture of him standing and wanting, wanting. He

stroked her face a last time, kissed good-by and went away. She knew his heart would go roaming back often, that even when he rode in an open carriage in New York or Washington with soldiers, flags and cheering thousands along the streets, he might just as like be thinking of her in the old log farmhouse out in Coles County, Illinois.

His regular secretary was a trusted, reliable, accurate, scrupulous young man, sober as a work horse, earnest as the multiplication table; he had freckles and reddish hair; a young Bavarian from the *Pike County Sucker*. This was John G. Nicolay, secretive, dependable, often carrying messages not to be written but whispered.

The other or second secretary, not strictly engaged as such, was going to Washington. Lincoln had said, "We can't take all Illinois with us down to Washington, but let Hay come." A keen and whimsical lad, John Hay. He had been class poet at Brown University, graduated, gone home to Warsaw, Illinois, then to Pike County, and later to Springfield to study law with his Uncle Milton, who had an office on the same floor as Lincoln & Herndon. He wrote notes in French to a sweetheart, and had a handsome, careless elegance all the girls in Springfield liked.

"Lincoln is letting his whiskers grow," men were saying in January, when his upper lip and cheeks were shaved but a stubble left on the chin. Then in February hair had grown over jaws, chin and throat, the upper lip shaven. This facial design was wrought by William Florville, a Haitian-born colored man, known as "Billy the Barber" whose shop in Springfield dated back to 1831. Why Lincoln took to whiskers at this time nobody seemed to know. A girl in New York State had written begging him to raise a beard. An October letter from New York signed only "True Republicans" pleasantly but seriously asked him to "cultivate whiskers and wear standing collars." But something more than these random wishes guided him. Herndon, Whitney, Lamon, Nicolay, heard no explanation from him as to why after 52 years with a smooth face he should now change.

John G. Nicolay, Lincoln's private secretary, photographed by Mathew Brady, 1861.

In a dusty third-story locked room over the store of his brother-in-law, C. M. Smith, Lincoln, with a few books and documents he consulted, had hidden away from all callers while he worked on his inaugural address for March 4, in Washington, amid the cannon to be planted by General Scott. Two printers, sworn to secrecy, had in January set up and run off 20 copies of the address. Weeks had gone by. Nobody had told or been careless. The inaugural text was still a well-kept secret.

Lamon was called from Bloomington and told: "Hill, it looks as if we might have war. I want you with me, I must have you." And Lamon was going along, banjo, bulldog courage and all.

A queer dream or illusion had haunted Lincoln at times through the winter. On election evening he had thrown himself on a haircloth sofa at home, soon after the telegrams reported him President-elect. Looking into a bureau mirror across the room he saw himself full length, but with two faces. It bothered him; he got up; the illusion vanished; but when he lay down again there in the glass were two faces again, one more pale than the other. He got up again, mixed in the election excitement, forgot about it; but it haunted him. He told his wife and she said it was a sign he would be elected to a second term, and the death pallor of one face meant he wouldn't live through his second term.

A cold drizzle of rain was falling February 11 when Lincoln and his party of 15 were to leave Springfield on the eight o'clock at the Great Western Railway station. Chilly gray mist hung the circle of the prairie horizon. A short locomotive with a flat-topped smokestack stood puffing with a baggage car and special passenger car coupled on; a railroad president and superintendent were on board.

Then he spoke slowly, amid the soft gray drizzle from the sky. Later, on the train he wrote with a pencil about half of his speech, dictating to Nicolay the remainder of his good-by words to Springfield: "My friends—No one, not in my situation, can appreciate my feeling of sadness at this parting. To this place, and the kindness of these people, I owe every thing. Here I have lived a quarter of a century, and have passed from a young to an old man. Here my children have been born, and one is buried. I now leave, not knowing when, or whether ever, I may return, with a task before me greater than that which rested upon Washington. Without the assistance of that Divine Being, who ever attended him, I cannot succeed. With that assistance I cannot fail. Trusting in Him, who can go with me, and remain with you and be every where for good, let us confidently hope that all will yet be well. To His care commending you, as I hope in your prayers you will commend me, I bid you an affectionate farewell."

CHAPTER 17

AMERICA WHITHER?—LINCOLN JOURNEYS TO WASHINGTON

AMERICA WHITHER? — LINCOLN JOURNEYS TO WASHINGTON

MERICA whither?" was the question, with headache and heartache in several million homes, as Lincoln began his winding journey to Washington. There Congress had not yet, after canvass of electoral results, declared and certified him President-elect. There coming events were yet to unlock a box of secrets. In the hair-trigger suspense General Scott was saying to an aide, "A dog fight now might cause the gutters to run with blood." And he was putting guards at doorways and vantage points to make sure of order when the electoral vote for President would be canvassed February 13.

The journey from Springfield to Washington brought Lincoln face to face with the governors and legislators of five states. He set foot in key cities; spoke with important men controlling politics, money, transportation, supplies; delivered more than 20 speeches; shook the hands of thousands of people; took his own look at immense crowds who wanted their look at the pivotal figure of the American scene.

Persons on board the Wabash Railroad train carrying the President-elect over the Indiana cornlands included press correspondents, old Eighth Circuit lawyers Ward Hill Lamon, Orville H. Browning, Jesse K. Dubois, Judge David Davis, Norman B. Judd of Chicago, four uniformed Regular Army officers, and 24-year-old Colonel Elmer Ephraim Ellsworth, whose Zouaves had swept the country, won championship colors, performed at West Point for Regular Army officers, and on the White House lawn.

Not yet had Congress declared Lincoln President. Excitement ran high in Washington February 13. Crowds climbed up Capitol Hill for gallery seats, at every doorway finding armed guards. "No one could pass except Senators and Representatives, and those who had the written ticket of admission signed by the Speaker of the House or the presiding officer of the Senate," wrote

Lincoln raising a flag on Independence Hall,
Philadelphia on Feb. 22, 1861. By Joseph Boggs Beale.

L. E. Chittenden. "Even members of Congress could not pass in their friends." A Washington militia colonel in civilian clothes said his men and their rifles were with in easy call. Pennsylvania Avenue, "choked with a howling angry mob," saw much street fighting and many arrests.

Tellers read the certificates state by state. John C. Breckinridge, the Vice-President, a Kentuckian whose heart lay deep with the secession cause, pronounced:

Abraham Lincoln, of Illinois, having received a majority of the whole number of electoral votes, is elected President of the United States for four years, commencing the 4th of March, 1861 . . .

Lincoln that day rode on his special train on the Little Miami Railroad to the capital of Ohio. To the state legislature at Columbus that night Lincoln made a speech peculiar from several angles: "I cannot but know what you all know, that, without a name, perhaps without a reason why I should have a name, there has fallen upon me a task such as did not rest even upon the Father of his Country . . . I turn, then, and look to the American people and to that God who has never forsaken them . . . "

The Lincoln special reached Pittsburgh February 14. He thanked Mayor Wilson and the citizens for a "flattering reception," again said he would speak on the country's "present distracted condition" when the time arrived, hoped that when he did finally speak he would say nothing to disappoint the people generally throughout the country, and once more threw out soothing words of a bright outlook, further baffling the better-informed philosophers.

Lincoln remembered a little girl who had written suggesting his face should have whiskers. He had answered it might look like a piece of "silly affec[ta]tion." Her town was Westfield, New York, and there he told the crowd, "I have a correspondent in this place, and if she is present I would like to see her." No one came forward. "Who is it? Give us her name," came from the crowd. "Her name is Grace Bedell." And Grace was led and carried to the platform, Lincoln saying, "She wrote me that she thought I would be better looking if I wore whiskers." He looked down at the little girl, "You see, I let these whiskers grow for you, Grace." Then he kissed her. Far and wide went the press item. The New York *Tribune* headlined "Old Abe Kissed by Pretty Girl."

While Lincoln crossed the Empire State from west to east February 18, news came over the wires that down in Montgomery, Alabama, amid thundering cannon and cheers from an immense crowd, Jefferson Davis took his oath as President of the Confederate States of America, six today and more tomorrow. For the first time since leaving home, Lincoln publicly admitted weariness, ending a short speech from the steps of the capitol at Albany, "I have neither the voice nor the strength to address you at any greater length."

The personal humility he had spoken in five states reached its lowest shrinking-point in the Hall of Assembly of the New York capitol: ". . . It is true that while I hold myself without mock modesty, the humblest of all individuals that have ever been elevated to the Presidency, I have a more difficult task to perform than any one of them. When the time comes I shall speak as well as I am able for the good of the present and future of this country—for the good both of the North and the South . . ."

Down the Hudson River, with greetings at Troy, Hudson, Peekskill. Then New York, the Front Door to America, where tall ships came in from the seven seas to one of the great world ports; where the 35,000 votes for Lincoln for President were a third of the total ballots; where had grown up the financial center of the country, with vast controls over trade, manufacture, transportation; where Mayor Fernando Wood had declared that New York should establish itself as a free city, separate from the Union, sovereign in itself like the seceded states of the South, thereby holding its trade and continuing "uninterrupted intercourse with every section" of the country; where they owned the New York *Daily News* and openly advocated the rights of the Confederate States.

Lincoln rode in a procession of 30 carriages led by a platoon of mounted police. His open carriage, a barouche, had accommodated the Prince of Wales a few months before. At the Astor House 500 policemen held the crowds in line. For the first time on his journey Lincoln faced a crowd of peculiar curiosity, its silence having a touch of the sinister. The cheers and shouts were not like Buffalo, Columbus, Indianapolis.

In the City Hall next morning, surrounded by aldermen and writers for the press, Lincoln faced Mayor Wood, spoke thanks for the reception "given me . . . by a people who do not by a majority agree with me. He was talking past Wood and to the country in saying: "This Union should never be abandoned unless it fails and the probability of its preservation shall cease to exist without throwing the passengers and cargo overboard."

White kid gloves were then in style for wear at opera but Lincoln, in a box at the new and sumptuous Academy of Music on Fourteenth Street and Irving Place, wore *black* kids on his large hands contrasting with the red-velvet box front. The word spread, and the press commented on the one pair of black gloves in the packed house.

Mrs. Lincoln the same evening was holding a fairly successful reception in the parlors of the Astor House. Newspapers mentioned Mrs. August Belmont as among those present, which caused Mrs. Belmont to send a note to the newspapers saying she wished it known that she was not present. Tad and Willie went with a nursemaid and saw a play at Laura Keene's Theatre. With mother and father they saw Barnum's museum and its mammoth monstrosities and concatenated curiosities.

He arrived in Philadelphia at four o'clock. In the hotel parlor Lincoln stood handshaking that night for an hour or two. Later in Norman B. Judd's room Lincoln met Allan Pinkerton, a railroad detective in the service of the Philadelphia, Wilmington & Baltimore Railroad, to guard trains and bridges and circumvent threatened explosions and fires. Pinkerton opened: "We have come to know, Mr. Lincoln, and beyond the shadow of a doubt, that there exists a plot to assassinate you. The attempt will be made on your way through Baltimore, day after tomorrow. I am here to help in outwitting the assassins." Lincoln sat with legs crossed, a good-natured curiosity on his face fading to a sober look. "I am listening, Mr. Pinkerton."

A barber named Fernandina was foremost among the conspirators, according to Pinkerton's spies, who, he said, had been at work for weeks and had become "bosom friends and inseparable companions" of the plotters.

Pinkerton went personally to Baltimore, purporting to be a Georgia secessionist, and "Fernandina cordially grasped my

Ward H. Lamon, self-appointed bodyguard of Lincoln.
Photo by Mathew Brady.

Charles Sumner, abolitionist Senator from Massachusetts.

hand, and we all retired to a private saloon." Fernandina was asked if there was no other way to save the South than by killing Lincoln. He replied, in the Pinkerton report: "No, as well might you attempt to move the Washington Monument yonder with your breath, as to change our purpose. He must die—and die he shall." With another drink by this time, he was asked about the police. He had fixed that, too: "They are

all with us. I have seen the Chief Marshal of Police, and he is all right. In a week from today, Lincoln will be a corpse." Also it seemed that Pinkerton detected another conspirator named Hill, who also drank heavy and often, and also was ready, in his talk, to kill Lincoln. He said, in the Pinkerton report, "I shall immortalize myself by plunging a knife into Lincoln's heart."

Lincoln interrupted with many questions. Supporting Pinkerton's viewpoint were the practical Judd and the equally practical Samuel M. Felton, a railroad president who considered the evidence positive of a plot to burn railroad bridges, blow up trains, "and murder Mr. Lincoln on his way to Washington." Pinkerton gave details of a wild-eyed plot. The police chief at Baltimore was arranging to send only a small force to the railroad depot, where a gang of toughs would start a fight to draw off the policemen. Then the Fernandina assassins would close round the President-elect and deliver the fatal shot or knife thrust. "We propose," said Pinkerton, "to take you on to Washington this very night, Mr. President, and steal a march on your enemies."

Lincoln deliberated, then: "Gentlemen, I appreciate the suggestions, and while I can stand anything essential in the way of misrepresentation, I do not feel I can go to Washington tonight. Tomorrow morning I have promised to raise the flag over Independence Hall, and after that to visit the legislature at Harrisburg. Whatever the cost, these two promises I must fulfill. Thereafter I shall be ready to consider any plan you may adopt."

At six o'clock that morning of February 22, Washington's Birthday, Lincoln amid cannon salutes and crowd applause pulled a rope and raised a flag over Independence Hall. Inside Independence Hall he spoke to an audience crowding all corners and overflowing. He had often pondered over the "dangers" incurred by the men who had assembled there and framed the Declaration. Not merely separation from a motherland, but liberty as a hope to all the world, for all future time, was the sentiment guiding them. "It was that which gave promise that in due time the weights should be lifted from the shoulders of all men, and that *all* should have an equal chance . . ." He asked if the country could be saved on that basis. If so he would consider himself one of the happiest men in the world. "But, if this country cannot be saved without giving up that principle—I was about to say I would rather be assassinated on this spot than surrender it." He could see no need of bloodshed and war. "And I may say in advance, there will be no blood shed unless it be forced upon the Government. . . "

Judd had been up nearly the whole night in a conference with Pinkerton and other men. They arranged for Lincoln to journey from Harrisburg on a two-car train that night under conditions they believed would deliver him safely in Washington the next morning. In Harrisburg, amid guns and platoons, Lincoln replied to Governor Curtin's welcome that under the weight of his great responsibility he brought an honest heart, but "I dare not tell you that I bring a head sufficient for it." He would lean on the people. "If my own strength should fail, I shall at least fall back upon these masses, who, I think, under any circumstances will not fail."

Close to six o'clock Lincoln was called from the dinner table, went upstairs to his room, changed his dinner dress for a traveling suit, and came down with a soft felt hat sticking in his pocket, and a folded shawl on his arm. A carriage was ready. Then, as Judd told it: "Mr. Lamon went first into the carriage; Col. Sumner of the regular army, was following close after Mr. Lincoln; I put my hand gently on his shoulder; he turned to see what was wanted, and before I could explain the carriage was off. The situation was a little awkward." Judd had tricked Colonel Sumner into a moment of delay, and to the Colonel's furious words Judd replied, "When we get to Washington, Mr. Lincoln shall determine what apology is due you."

In Philadelphia shortly after ten a carriage with Detective Pinkerton and Superintendent Kenney of the P. W. & B. Railroad met Lincoln and Lamon at the Pennsylvania Railroad station and took them to the P. W. & B. station, where they were put on the last car of the New York-Washington train. A woman detective working for Pinkerton had reserved rear berths of a sleeping-car, one for her "invalid brother" to be occupied by Lincoln, who was quickly in his berth with the curtains carefully drawn.

Lincoln was not heard from during the night, according to Lamon. At six in the morning the President-elect stepped off the train in Washington.

On February 4, 1861, the Peace Convention in Washington had begun its sessions behind closed doors. Though an air of secret and important deliberation was desired by many of the delegates, the main proceedings reached newspapers from day to day. Twenty-one Border and Northern States sent delegates; Michigan, Wisconsin and Minnesota let it be known they expected only useless or mischievous talk.

Lincoln had breakfast with Seward the morning he arrived and at 11 called with Seward at the White House, chatted with

President Buchanan, and shook hands with the Cabinet. In the afternoon he met the Illinois Congressmen and Senators, headed by Stephen A. Douglas. At seven he dined at Seward's home on F Street and at ten o'clock he received "reciprocal" calls from the Buchanan Cabinet members, also plenty of private citizens. Betweenwhiles he had held interviews with General Scott, Francis P. Blair, Sr., Montgomery Blair, many officials and would-be officials. Tomorrow was Sunday.

Mrs. Lincoln and the three Lincoln boys took their first Washington breakfast with husband and father next morning. And Lincoln went with Seward to St. John's Church (Episcopal) that Sunday morning.

Sumner and Lincoln were getting acquainted. Up to Lincoln, Sumner would stride to tell him this or that *must* be done. The Senator from Massachusetts, the scholar in politics, the most elegantly tailored man in House or Senate, wearing maroon vests, fawn gaiters, blue-violet neckties, high silk hat, cape over shoulders, gold-headed cane, gold watch chain, was born in Boston to money and leisure. He had a handsomely modeled head, wavy locks of hair, sideburns; he was a beau, scholar, zealot, bachelor, 50 years old.

In his Senate seat, after a session had closed and nearly all the members had left the chamber, Sumner had been struck on the head with a cane. The blows rained till the cane broke in pieces. Bruised and lacerated without warning or a chance to fight back, he struggled to rise and get at his unseen assailant, nearly wrenching loose his desk from the iron screws that held it to the floor, he was so powerful physically. The assailant, Congressman Preston Brooks of South Carolina said he had only wanted to half-kill Sumner and watch him live and suffer. He had resigned his seat, had been re-elected by his constituents and presented with more canes and wishes that he would use them as he knew how.

On Sunday, March 3rd, the House clock indicated nearly ten that night when Stanton called up his Force Bill for consideration. After two attempts to move adjournment, by Illinois Republican Washburne and Pennsylvania Republican Hickman, the floor was obtained by New York Republican John Cochrane, who before taking his seat renewed the motion to adjourn. By a vote of 77 to 60 the House adjourned and, wrote Boteler, "the Thirty-Sixth Congress expired on the following Monday of March 4, without having given to Mr. Lincoln the power to call out the militia and to accept the services of volunteers."

In those closing hours of Congress a bill was passed to forbid the Federal Government forever from interfering with slavery in any manner whatsoever in any Slave State—requiring three-fourths of the states of the Union to approve the measure as an amendment to the Constitution. This was as far as Congress could go within its powers to guarantee the South that whatever it intended to do as to slavery extension in the Territories, its policy was to let slavery alone in the Slave States. The act was in line with the Republican party platform and Lincoln's public and private declarations.

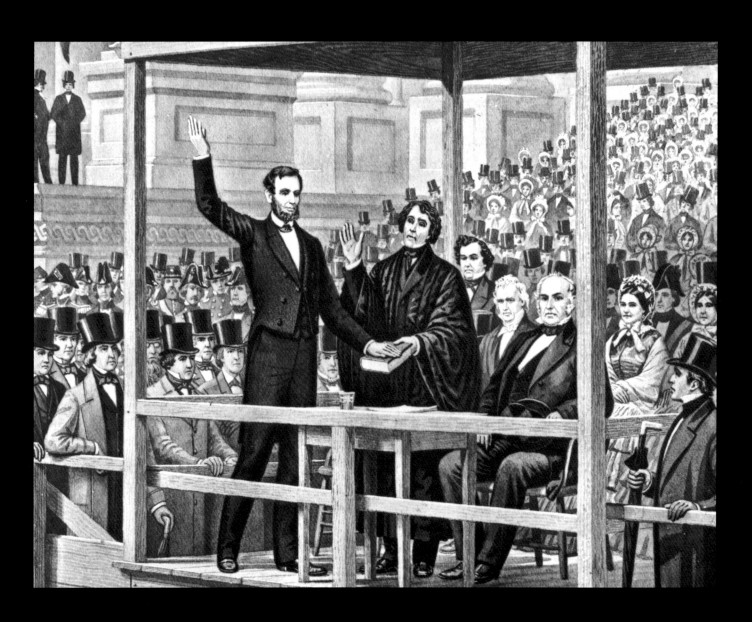

CHAPTER 18

LINCOLN TAKES THE OATH
AS PRESIDENT

Lincoln's First Inauguration, March 4, 1861.
By Joseph Boggs Beale.

LINCOLN TAKES THE OATH AS PRESIDENT

MARCH 4 dawned with pleasant weather that later turned bleak and chilly for the 25,000 strangers roving Washington. With hotels and rooming houses overcrowded, hundreds had slept on the porches of public buildings and on street sidewalks. Thousands filled the street around Willard's as the forenoon wore away. General Scott and Colonel Stone had arranged for riflemen in squads to be placed in hiding on the roofs of certain commanding houses along Pennsylvania Avenue. From windows of the Capitol wings riflemen were to watch the inauguration platform.

President Buchanan drove with Senator Baker of Oregon and Senator Pearce of Maryland from the White House to Willard's in an open carriage. Buchanan stepped out and soon returned arm in arm with Lincoln as police kept a path for them. Then the procession moved down Pennsylvania Avenue with representations from all branches of the Government. A new procession was formed to escort the President-elect to the east portico and the platform outdoors, where a crowd of at least 10,000 that had waited long gave its applause and scattering cheers.

Ned Baker's silver-bell voice rang out: "Fellow-citizens, I introduce to you Abraham Lincoln, the President-elect of the United States." The applause was a slight ripple. Then came the inaugural address; Lincoln drew the papers from an inside coat pocket, slowly pulled spectacles from another pocket, put them on, and read deliberately the fateful document.

Then stepped forward Chief Justice Taney, worn, shrunken, odd, with "the face of a galvanized corpse," said Mrs. Clay of Alabama. His hands shook with age, emotion, both, as he held out an open Bible toward the ninth President to be sworn in by him. Lincoln laid his left hand on the Bible, raised his right hand, and repeated after the Chief Justice the oath prescribed by the Constitution: "I do solemnly swear that I will faithfully execute the office of President of the United States, and will, to the best of my ability, preserve, protect, and defend the Constitution of the United States."

The artillery over on the slope boomed with all its guns a salute of thunder to the 16th President of the United States. That was all. The inauguration was over.

The inaugural address itself, as a state paper from the first administration of a new party, as a definition of policy and viewpoint, as a breaking of Lincoln's long silence, was the high point of the day. Beyond the immediate hearers was the vast unseen audience that would read the address in cold print. Never before in New York had such crowds waited at newspaper offices and jammed and scrambled for the first sheets wet from the press. In its week of delivery it was the most widely read and closely scrutinized utterance that had ever come from an American President. No previous manuscript from Lincoln's hand had been so carefully written by him, rearranged, modified. The draft made in Springfield underwent important changes, mainly deletions, under the suggestions of Seward and Browning, with Lincoln's added light as he traveled and events shifted.

The finished address Lincoln gave the world went to readers who searched and dug into every line and phrase. Reason and emotion wove through it—and hopes, fears, resolves. Parts of it read:

. . . Apprehension seems to exist among the people of the Southern States, that by the accession of a Republican Administration, their properly, and their peace, and personal security, are to be endangered. There has never been any reasonable cause for such apprehension. Indeed, the most ample evidence to the contrary has all the while existed, and been open to their inspection. It is found in nearly all the published speeches of him who now addresses you. I do but quote from one of those speeches when I declare that "I have no purpose, directly or indirectly, to interfere with the institution of slavery in the States where it exists. I believe I have no lawful right to do so, and I have no inclination to do so." Those who nominated and elected me did so with full knowledge that I had made this, and many similar declarations, and had never recanted them . . .

Lincoln's inauguration ceremony, March 4, 1861.

LINCOLN TAKES THE OATH AS PRESIDENT

Abraham Lincoln's Inauguration. Photo by Benjamin B. French, March 4, 1861.

There is much controversy about the delivering up of fugitives from service or labor. The clause I now read is as plainly written in the Constitution as any other of its provisions:

"No person held to service or labor in one State, under the laws thereof, escaping into another, shall, in consequence of any law or regulation therein, be discharged from such service or labor, but shall be delivered up on claim of the party to whom such service or labor may be due." . . .

There is some difference of opinion whether this clause should be enforced by national or by state authority; but surely that difference is not a very material one . . .

A disruption of the Federal Union heretofore only menaced, is now formidably attempted.

I hold, that in contemplation of universal law, and of the Constitution, the Union of these States is perpetual. Perpetuity is implied, if not expressed, in the fundamental law of all national governments. It is safe to assert that no government proper, ever had a provision in its organic law for its own termination . . .

The Union is much older than the Constitution. It was formed in fact, by the Articles of Association in 1774. It was matured and continued by the Declaration of Independence in 1776. It was further matured and the faith of all the then thirteen States expressly plighted and engaged that it should be perpetual, by the Articles of Confederation in 1778. And finally, in 1787, one of the declared objects for ordaining and establishing the Constitution, was "*to form a more perfect Union.*" . . .

It follows from these views that no State, upon its own mere motion, can lawfully get out of the Union—that *resolves* and *ordinances* to that effect are legally void; and that acts of violence, within any State or States, against the authority of the United States, are insurrectionary or revolutionary, according to circumstances.

I therefore consider that, in view of the Constitution and the laws, the Union is unbroken; and, to the extent of my ability, I shall take care, as the Constitution itself expressly enjoins upon me, that the laws of the Union be faithfully executed in all the States. Doing this I deem to be only a simple duty on my part; and I shall perform it, so far as practicable, unless my rightful masters, the American people, shall withhold the requisite means, or, in some authoritative manner, direct the contrary. I trust this will not be regarded as a menace, but only as the declared purpose of the Union that it *will* constitutionally defend, and maintain itself.

In doing this there needs to be no bloodshed or violence; and there shall be none, unless it be forced upon the national authority. The power confided to me, will be used to hold, occupy, and possess the property, and places belonging to the government, and to collect the duties and imposts; but beyond what may be necessary for these objects, there will be no invasion—no using of force against, or among the people anywhere . . .

If a minority, in such case, will secede rather than acquiesce, they make a precedent which, in turn, will divide and ruin them; for a minority of their own will secede from them, whenever a majority refuses to be controlled by such minority. For instance, why may not any portion of a new confederacy, a year or two hence, arbitrarily secede again, precisely as portions of the present Union now claim to secede from it. All who cherish disunion sentiments are now being educated to the exact temper of doing this . . .

Plainly, the central idea of secession, is the essence of anarchy . . .

One section of our country believes slavery is *right*, and ought to be extended, while the other believes it is *wrong*, and ought not to be extended. This is the only substantial dispute . . .

Physically speaking, we cannot separate. We cannot remove our respective sections from each other, nor build an impassable wall between them. A husband and wife may be divorced, and go out of the presence, and beyond the reach of each other; but the different parts of our country cannot do this . . . Suppose you go to war, you cannot fight always; and when, after much loss on both sides, and no gain on either, you cease fighting, the identical old questions as to terms of intercourse, are again upon you.

This country, with its institutions, belongs to the people who inhabit it. Whenever they shall grow weary of the existing government, they can exercise their *constitutional* right of amending it, or their *revolutionary* right to dismember, or overthrow it. I cannot be ignorant of the fact that many worthy, and patriotic citizens are desirous of having the national constitution amended. While I make no recommendation of amendments, I fully recognize the rightful authority of the people over the whole subject, to be exercised in either of the modes prescribed in the instrument itself . . . I understand a proposed amendment to the Constitution—which amendment, however, I have not seen, has passed Congress, to the effect that the federal government, shall never interfere with the domestic institutions of the States, including that of persons held to service. To avoid misconstruction of what I have said, I depart from my purpose not to speak of particular amendments, so far as to say that, holding such a provision to now be implied constitutional law, I have no objection to its being made express, and irrevocable . . .

Why should there not be a patient confidence in the ultimate justice of the people? Is there any better, or equal hope, in the world? In our present differences, is either party without faith of being in the right? If the Almighty Ruler of nations, with his eternal truth and justice, be on your side of the North, or on yours of the South, that truth, and that justice, will surely prevail, by the judgment of this great tribunal, the American people . . .

While the people retain their virtue, and vigilence, no administration, by any extreme of wickedness or folly, can very seriously injure the government, in the short space of four years.

My countrymen, one and all, think calmly and *well*, upon this whole subject. Nothing valuable can be lost by taking time . . . Intelligence, patriotism, Christianity, and a firm reliance on Him, who has never yet forsaken this favored land, are still competent to adjust, in the best way, all our present difficulty.

In *your* hands, my dissatisfied fellow countrymen, and not in *mine*, is the momentous issue of civil war. The government will not assail *you*. You can have no conflict, without being yourselves the aggressors. *You* have no oath registered in Heaven to destroy ihe government, while *I* shall have the most solemn one to "preserve, protect and defend" it.

Thus flowed the reasonings, explanations, watchwords that ended Lincoln's long silence. He finished: "I am loth to close. We are not enemies, but friends. We must not be enemies. Though passion may have strained, it must not break our bonds of affection. The mystic chords of memory, stretching from every battle-field, and patriot grave, to every living heart and hearthstone, all over this broad land, will yet swell the chorus of the Union, when again touched, as surely they will be, by the better angels of our nature."

The Montgomery *Advertiser* in Alabama was sure the inaugural meant war, nothing less would satisfy "the abolition chief," and the artfully worded address was written by a pen more skillful than the Rail Splitter wielded.

"To twenty millions of people," said the New York *Tribune* of the address, "it will carry tidings, good or not, as the case may be, that the federal government of the United States is still in existence, with a Man at the head of it." Not one "fawning expression" could be found in it, observed the Boston *Transcript*. "The language is level to the popular mind, the plain, homespun language of a man accustomed to talk with the 'folks' and the 'neighbors,' whose words fit his facts and thoughts."

The New York *Herald* commented, "It would have been almost as instructive if President Lincoln had contented himself with telling his audience yesterday a funny story and letting them go"; however, the inaugural was "not a crude performance," for "it abounds with traits of craft and cunning." The Baltimore *Sun* read in the inaugural that "it assumes despotic authority, and intimates the design to exercise that authority to any extent of war and bloodshed. If it means what it says, it is the knell and requiem of the Union, and the death of hope." The Baltimore *Exchange* believed "the measures of Mr. Lincoln mean war"; while Douglas said publicly, "It is a peace offering rather than a war message."

The Richmond *Enquirer* saw in it "the cool, unimpassioned, deliberate language of the fanatic . . . Sectional war awaits only the signal gun . . . The question, 'Where shall Virginia go?' is answered by Mr. Lincoln. She must go to *war*." The Charleston *Mercury* announced, "It is our wisest policy to accept it as a declaration of war."

Inauguration night saw an attempt at gaiety, the Union Ball, in a new building on Judiciary Square, the hall light-flooded by five large gas chandeliers. Lincoln shook hands from 8:15 till 10:30. The estimate was 25 hands a minute. His gloves were now *white* kids. He looked absent-minded, as young Henry Adams saw him, as though "no man living needed so much education as the new President but all the education he could get would not be enough."

The Marine Band played "Hail to the Chief" at 11. Lincoln entered leading the grand march, arm in arm with Mayor Berret, followed by Mrs. Lincoln arm in arm with Senator Stephen A. Douglas. Lincoln avoided waltz and square dance, but Mrs. Lincoln and Douglas were partners in a quadrille. Hundreds of women in crinoline trod the waltz, schottische, polka, mazurka. Mrs. Lincoln wore a new blue gown, a large blue feather in her hair. Many said it must be her happiest night of life, the realization of dreams long awaited. The ball over, Mr. and Mrs. Lincoln went for the first night in their new house of presences, shadows, ghosts.

As Lincoln slept that night, relays of ponies and men were rushing west from St. Joe, Missouri, with his inaugural address.

They would be seven days and 17 hours reaching Sacramento, California, with his plea for the east and west coasts, the Great Lakes and the Gulf, the Rio Grande and the Penobscot, to belong to one common country.

Thus far Lincoln's Cabinet slate, with two minor exceptions, stood as he had framed it late on election night in the Springfield telegraph office. When told, "They will eat you up," he replied, "They will be just as likely to eat each other up."

At noon on March 5 the Senate received and approved the new President's nominations: Secretary of State, William H. Seward; Secretary of the Treasury, Salmon P. Chase; Secretary of War, Simon Cameron; Secretary of the Navy, Gideon Welles; Secretary of the Interior, Caleb B. Smith; Attorney General, Edward Bates; Postmaster General, Montgomery Blair, The new Cabinet had four old-line Democrats (Chase, Cameron, Welles, Blair) and three old-line Whigs (Seward, Bates, Smith), a wrong balance, Lincoln heard many times, and made clear: "I'm something of an old-line Whig myself and I'll be there to make the parties even." These Cabinet men he would see and hear often; they would be stubborn with him and he with them.

At Willard's the main-floor corridors surged with office seekers, overflowing up the staircases into halls, reading room, barbershop, writing room, out on the porch and steps. From all over the North "the triumphant Republicans had winged their way to the prey." Many wore the new paper collars, some had linen. They crowded the Willard bar morning and night.

In mid-March Senator John Sherman of Ohio introduced to Lincoln his brother William Tecumseh Sherman who, having just resigned as head of the Louisiana Military Academy, seeing war ahead, "may give you some information you want." Lincoln asked, "How are they getting along down there?" On Sherman fiercely replying, "They are preparing for war," the President said, "Oh, well, I guess we'll manage to keep house." Had Lincoln known of the steeled loyalty of this Ohio man, he would have met Sherman with a different greeting. However, the President was in a mood when he chose to show no anxiety, and this worried Sherman.

In the Cabinet, Chase, Cameron and Blair had their friends and allies to take care of in about the same proportion as Seward, a hundred asking an office that could go to only one. Among many wanting office was a belief that either money or influence could bring it, while Lincoln guessed he had "ten pegs where there was one hole to put them in."

The Union was weaker than a month before because the administration had exhibited "a blindness and a stolidity without a parallel in the history of intelligent statesmanship," said the New York *Times*. This lent support to the *Herald*'s repeated jabs: "the Lincoln Administration is cowardly, mean, and vicious," the blame resting on "the incompetent, ignorant, and desperate 'Honest Abe.'" William Cullen Bryant in a New York *Evening Post* editorial took the *Tribune* and *Times* outbursts as nervous and pevish. To frame in 30 days a clear policy for so complex a national situation was a hard matter, as Bryant saw it, and furthermore, how could the facile critics know that Lincoln had not fixed upon his policy, with a decision to make it known to the world by action instead of a windy proclamation?

CHAPTER 19

SUMTER AND WAR CHALLENGE— CALL FOR TROOPS

Fort Sumter bombing, April 12, 1861, by Conrad Wise Chapman, ca. 1865.

Sumter and War Challenge — Call for Troops

THE MORNING after inauguration Lincoln had studied dispatches from Major Robert Anderson, commander of Fort Sumter in Charleston Harbor, reporting that his food supplies would last four weeks or by careful saving perhaps 40 days. The Confederates stood ready to batter Fort Sumter and run down its flag whenever the word came from their Government at Montgomery.

When the Senate on March 25 requested from the President the Anderson dispatches to the War Department, the President replied, "I have, with the highest respect for the Senate, come to the conclusion that at the present moment the publication of it would be inexpedient." The Senators from Virginia, North Carolina, Tennessee, Arkansas, Texas, were in their seats answering roll call from day to day, their states not having officially and formally seceded.

Lincoln had called his Cabinet for its first meeting March 9 and put a written question, "Assuming it to be possible to now provision Fort Sumter, under all the circumstances, is it wise to attempt it?" The Cabinet members went away, returning March 16 with written answers. Seward advised No: it was not a time for the use of force. Chase advised Yes and No; Yes if it meant peace, No if the attempt was to bring on civil war, armies, million-dollar budgets. Cameron advised No, seeing that "no practical benefit will result to the country." Welles advised No: "I entertain doubts." Smith advised No: giving up Fort Sumter would cause "surprise and complaint" but it could be "explained and understood." Bates advised No: "I am willing to evacuate Fort Sumter." Blair was the only one with an unmodified Yes: Buchanan had hesitated and failed; Jackson had acted and won; provisioning the fort would "vindicate the hardy courage of the North, and the determination of the people and their President to maintain the authority of the Government." Thus the seven new counselors stood five against sending food to Anderson, one for it, and one neither for nor against it.

Lamon had arrived from a trip to Charleston. From the Governor of South Carolina he brought the message to Lincoln: "Nothing can prevent war except the acquiescence of the President of the United States in secession . . . Let your President attempt to reinforce Sumter, and the tocsin of war will be sounded from every hilltop and valley in the South."

The President on March 28 met his Cabinet in secret session. He read to them a memorandum from General Scott discouraging attempts to reinforce Sumter and advising, "The giving up of Forts Sumter and Pickens may be justified."

At noon next day the Cabinet met to discuss going to war. Bates wrote he would reinforce Fort Pickens, and "As to Fort Sumter, I think the time is come to either evacuate or relieve it." The President asked the others to write their views. Seward wrote: "I would at once, and at every cost, prepare for a war at Pensacola and Texas" and "I would instruct Major Anderson to retire from Fort Sumter forthwith." Chase would maintain Fort Pickens and provision Fort Sumter. Welles would make Fort Pickens impregnable, and as to Sumter, the Government was justified in "a peaceable attempt to send provisions to one of our own forts." Smith seemed to believe he would defend Fort Pickens and evacuate Fort Sumter, recognizing it as risky politically. Blair would hold Fort Pickens and fight "the head and front of this rebellion" at Fort Sumter. Cameron was absent. So the Cabinet stood three for and three against the evacuation of Sumter.

On April 1, 1861, Nicolay brought to Willard's a package of papers which he handed to Secretary Welles, who lived there. Welles read the papers; then, as Welles told it: "Without a moment's delay I went to the President with the package in my hand. He was alone in his office and, raising his head from the table at which he was writing, inquired, '*What have I done wrong?*'"

Then came the unraveling of a tangled affair. In Welles' hands were two papers signed by Lincoln, who after reading

Gideon Welles, Secretary of the Navy, 1861-1869.

them said he was surprised he had sent such a document to the Secretary of the Navy. He had signed the papers without reading them, he told Welles; Seward with two or three young men had been at the White House through the day on a subject Seward had in hand. "It was Seward's specialty, to which he, the President, had yielded, but as it involved considerable details, he had left Mr. Seward to prepare the necessary papers."

Lincoln did not know when signing this appointment, nor Seward when advising Lincoln to sign it, that the man thereby appointed, Captain Samuel Barron, supposedly of the U.S. Navy, had five days before accepted a commission as a commodore in the Confederate States Navy! Nor could Lincoln or Seward under the circumstances have guessed that two weeks later Captain Barron would go to Richmond, take the oath of

Confederate loyalty, and enter actively into building coast fortifications to defend Virginia and North Carolina against ships whose officers would have been detailed by him had he managed to get into the place to which Lincoln appointed him and from which Lincoln removed him the day Welles entered Lincoln's office in such anger that Lincoln's greeting was, "What have I done wrong?"

A naval lieutenant, Gwathmey, arrived in Secretary Welles' office and took from a belt strapped around his body under his shirt a letter from Captain Adams, senior naval officer in command of Fort Pickens. Welles learned that Adams was operating in obedience to an armistice negotiated by the Buchanan administration by which the U.S. Government was not to reinforce Fort Pickens provided the Confederate forces did not attack it.

John Worden, a naval lieutenant whose loyalty to the Union was vouched for, received from the Secretary of the Navy a dispatch and was advised to memorize it, burn it, and on arriving in Florida make a certified copy as he remembered it. Worden did this, and Fort Pickens was reinforced the night of April 12.

Fort Sumter, three miles out from Charleston, rising almost sheer with the rock walls of its island, was being ringed round with batteries, guns and 5,000 recruits under General P. G. T. Beauregard, constantly in touch with Governor F. W. Pickens of South Carolina and Secretary L. P. Walker of the Confederate War Department at Montgomery. Visitors to the U.S. Army officers or soldiers at Fort Sumter were challenged by Confederate pickets, had to show passes from Governor Pickens.

The doubts of long months were at an end. Thus Lincoln framed an issue for his country and the world to look at and consider. Sumter was a symbol. Jefferson Davis called his advisers into session at Montgomery to consider Lincoln's message to Governor Pickens, which had been telegraphed on. Robert Toombs, Secretary of State, read Lincoln's letter, and said, "The firing on that fort will inaugurate a civil war greater than any the world has yet seen; and I do not feel competent to advise you . . . You will wantonly strike a hornet's nest which extends from mountains to ocean; legions, now quiet, will swarm out and sting us to death . . ." President Davis, however, decided in favor of attacking the fort, leaving to Beauregard the choice of time and method.

Beauregard on April 11 sent a little boat out to Sumter. A note to Anderson from Beauregard, his old-time affectionate pupil in artillery lessons at West Point, read: "I am ordered by the Government of the Confederate States to demand the evacuation of Fort Sumter . . . All proper facilities will be afforded for the removal of yourself and command . . ." Major Anderson wrote in answer: " . . . It is a demand with which I regret that my sense of honor, and of my obligations to my Government, prevent my compliance . . ." As Major Anderson handed this note to Beauregard's aides, he made the remark, "Gentlemen, if you do not batter us to pieces, we shall be starved out in a few days."

Now four men from Beauregard went in a boat out to Sumter. Past midnight they handed Major Anderson a note saying there would be no "useless effusion of blood" if he would fix a stated time for his surrender. Anderson called his officers; from one till three they consulted. And at 3:15 that morning Anderson gave his answer: "Cordially uniting with you in the desire to avoid the useless effusion of blood, I will, if provided with the proper and necessary means of transportation, evacuate Fort Sumter by noon on the 15th instant, and I will not in the meantime open my fire on your forces unless compelled to do so by some hostile act against this fort or the flag of my Government . . . should I not receive prior to that time controlling instructions from my Government or additional supplies."

Within five minutes they gave Anderson a written answer:

Fort Sumter, S. C., April 12, 1861—3:20 A.M.

Sir:

By authority of Brigadier-General, commanding the Provisional Forces of the Confederate States, we have the honor to notify you that he will open the fire of his batteries on Fort Sumter in one hour from this time.

We have the honor to be, very respectfully, your obedient servant,

James Chestnut, Jr.,
 Aide-de-Camp.
STEPHEN D. LEE,
 Captain, C. S. Army, Aide-de-Camp.

The four men got into their boat, with Chestnut musing over Major Anderson's parting words, "If we do not meet again on earth, I hope we may meet in Heaven."

Encircling batteries let loose all they had. The mortars and howitzers laughed. Wood fires on hulks at the inner harbor entrance and daybreak lighted one lonesome relief ship from Lincoln; it and two others arriving later could be of no help. Through daylight of the 12th and through the rain and darkness of the night of the 13th, the guns pounded Sumter with more than 3,000 shot and shell. Smoke, heat, vapor, stifled the garrison; the men hugged the ground with wet handkerchiefs over mouths and eyes till they could breathe again. The last biscuit was gone; they were down to pork only for food. The storm and dark of the early morning on the 13th ended with clear weather and a red sunrise.

Again offered the same terms of surrender as before, Anderson, after 33 hours of bombardment, gave up the fort. On Sunday, the 14th, he marched his garrison out with colors flying, drums beating, saluting his flag with 50 guns. They boarded one of the relief ships and headed north for New York Harbor. They had lost one man, killed in the accidental explosion of one of their own cannon. In their last glimpse of Fort Sumter they saw the new Confederate flag, Stars and Bars, flying. In his trunk Major Anderson had the flag he had defended; he wished to keep this burnt and shot flag and have it wrapped round him when laid in the grave.

On that Sunday of April 14, the White House had many visitors in and out all day. Senators and Congressmen came to say their people would stand by the Government, the President. The Cabinet met. A proclamation was framed. It named the States of South Carolina, Georgia, Alabama, Florida, Mississippi, Louisiana and Texas as having "combinations too powerful to be suppressed" by ordinary procedure of government.

"Now therefore, I, Abraham Lincoln, President of the United States, in virtue of the power in me vested by the Constitution and the laws, have thought fit to call forth, and hereby do call forth, the militia of the several States of the Union, to the aggregate number of seventy-five thousand, in order to suppress said combinations, and to cause the laws to be duly executed."

He called on "all loyal citizens" to defend the National Union and popular government, "to redress wrongs already long enough endured." The new army of volunteer soldiers was to retake forts and property "seized from the Union." Also, "in every event, the utmost care will be observed, consistently with the objects aforesaid, to avoid any devastation, any destruction of, or interference with, property, or any disturbance of peaceful citizens."

Also the proclamation called both Houses of Congress to meet at noon on the Fourth of July. The war of words was over and the naked test by steel weapons, so long foretold, was at last to begin.

The dilemma of a divided country Lincoln and Douglas discussed at the White House that Sunday of April 14, just after the flag came down at Sumter. Now Lincoln could be thankful that across the years of political strife between him and Douglas, the two had so spoken to and of each other that their personal relations had never reached a breaking point. The two foremost American political captains were closeted for a two-hour confidential talk, with only Congressman Ashmun in the room. Douglas read the proclamation to be published next morning, gave it his approval, though advising that he would call for 200,000 rather than 75,000 troops.

Douglas, at Willard's, wrote out a dispatch which next day went to the country through the Associated Press. He had called on the President and had "an interesting conversation on the present condition of the country," the substance of which was, on the part of Mr. Douglas, "that while he was unalterably opposed to the administration in all political issues, he was prepared to fully sustain the President in the exercise of all his constitutional functions, to preserve the Union, maintain the Government, and defend the capital. A firm policy and prompt action was necessary. The capital was in danger, and must be defended at all hazards, and at any expense of men and money." He added that he and the President "spoke of the present and future without any reference to the past." Douglas was a hoarse and worn man of dwindling vitality, but he struck with decisive words that sank deep in every one of his old loyal followers. He knew he had trumpets left, and he blew them to mass his cohorts behind Lincoln's maintenance of the Union.

Now came the day of April 15, 1861, for years afterward spoken of as "the day Lincoln made his first call for troops." What happened on that day was referred to as the Uprising of the People; they swarmed onto the streets, into public squares, into meeting halls and churches. The shooting of the Stars and Stripes off the Sumter flagstaff—and the Lincoln proclamation—acted as a vast magnet on a national multitude.

In a thousand cities, towns and villages the fever of hate, exaltation, speech, action, followed a similar course. Telegrams came notifying officers and militiamen to mobilize. Newspapers cried in high or low key the war song. Then came mass meetings, speeches by prominent citizens, lawyers, ministers, priests, military officers, veterans of the War of 1812 and the Mexican War, singing of "The Star-spangled Banner" and "America," fife-and-drum corps playing "Yankee Doodle." Funds were subscribed to raise and equip troops, resolutions passed, committees appointed to collect funds, to care for soldiers' families, to educate or trouble the unpatriotic. Women's societies were formed to knit and sew, prepare lint and bandages.

In the large cities military units of the foreign-born were formed. Irishmen of New York made up four regiments: the 69th, Irish Zouaves, Irish Volunteers, St. Patrick Brigade. The Italian Legion made ready, also the Garibaldi Guards. Germans supplied the Steuben Volunteers, the German Rifles, the Turner Rifles, the De Kalb Regiment. The English and Irish Home Guards were proposed for men of former service in the British Army and Irish constabulary, while the British Volunteers were to recruit from British subjects in New York.

Astor, Vanderbilt, Aspinwall, A. T. Stewart, Belmont of the House of Rothschild, the millionaires who had been at the breakfast to Lincoln when he came through New York, they and their cohorts and lawyers were now for war.

On April 20, 50,000 people made their way to a Union mass meeting at Union Square in New York City.

On April 17 when Virginia seceded, her troops were set in motion for a surprise march on the U.S. fort and arsenal at Harpers Ferry, the most dramatic point northward for raising her new flag. They arrived April 18 and took the fort and arsenal without fighting. The barrels and locks of 20,000 pistols and rifles were sent to Richmond to be remade. Two days later the U.S. navy yard at Norfolk, Virginia, was threatened, or the commander was afraid it was, and guns, munitions, ships and war property valued at $30,000,000 went up in smoke.

Robert E. Lee, Virginian, resigned from the U.S. Army, gave up his stately home on Arlington Heights overlooking Washington, to take command of the Army of Virginia. Long ago he had opposed slavery. He favored the Union but couldn't fight against his native state. Before resigning he was interviewed by Francis P. Blair, Sr., who said later: "I told him what President Lincoln wanted him to do; he wanted him to take command of the army . . . He said he could not, under any circumstances, consent to supersede his old commander [General Scott]. He asked me if I supposed the President would consider that proper. I said yes . . . The matter was talked over by President Lincoln and myself for some hours on two or three different occasions . . . The President and Secretary Cameron expressed themselves as anxious to give the command of our army to Robert E. Lee." Now Lee had gone to Richmond.

A volunteer White House Guard gathered under Cassius M. Clay, who would delay sailing as the new Minister to Russia, and Senator James H. Lane, the new Senator from the new State of Kansas. Both men had commanded troops in the Mexican War, had faced mobs in their antislavery careers. Both expected the war to begin in Washington and were ready for a last-ditch fight at the White House doors.

From the governors of Border States came warlike answers to Lincoln's dispatch asking for quotas of troops: "Kentucky will furnish no troops for the wicked purpose of subduing her sister Southern States," replied Governor Beriah Magoffin. "Your requisition, in my judgment," replied Claiborne Jackson of Missouri, "is illegal, unconstitutional and revolutionary in its objects, inhuman and diabolical, and cannot be complied with."

President Davis at Montgomery announced that his Government would issue "letters of marque" giving authority to ships joining the Confederacy to seize U.S. vessels of commerce. Lincoln replied by proclaiming a blockade of ports of the seceded states.

Each day in bureaus and departments at Washington came new resignations, Southerners leaving to go south to fight.

On April 18 arrived 532 Pennsylvania boys from Pottsville, Lewistown, Reading, Allentown, whom Hay noted as "unlicked patriotism that has poured ragged and unarmed out of Pennsylvania." Now came word that the telegraph wires leading to the North were cut. The Baltimore telegraph office was in the hands of secessionists. The War Office said, "This stops all." With mails stopped, railroads crippled, bridges down, telegraph wires dead, it was not easy in Washington to laugh away the prediction of the New Orleans *Picayune* that Virginia's secession would result in "the removal of Lincoln and his Cabinet, and whatever he can carry away, to the safer neighborhood of Harrisburg or Cincinnati."

At what moment would some free-going body of Southern troops ride into the capital, seize the city, and kidnap the Government? These questions were asked in Washington. Then and later this was regarded as an easy possibility. There were Southerners eager for the undertaking.

Impatience was heard in the President's Cabinet. Chase wrote a belief that the President in lieu of any policy had "merely the general notion of drifting, the Micawber policy of waiting for something to turn up." Lincoln, however, was taking to himself one by one the powers of a dictator. He authorized a raid whereby at three o'clock the afternoon of April 20 U.S. marshals entered every major telegraph office in the Northern States and seized the originals of all telegrams sent and copies of all telegrams received during 12 months. Also the President dug into the Treasury of the United States for millions of dollars—without due and required authority of Congress. At a meeting held Sunday, April 21, in the Navy Department, away from any spies and all observers in the White House, the Cabinet members joined with Lincoln in the placing of immense funds.

"It became necessary for me to choose," said Lincoln later, "whether I should let the government fall at once into ruin, or whether . . . availing myself of the broader powers conferred by the Constitution in cases of insurrection, I would make an effort to save it." Government money orders for million-dollar amounts

Lincoln sent by private messengers, who went by way of Wheeling and Pittsburgh to New York.

In the Treasury building now were howitzers. At the Mint were howitzers. In the marble corridors of the Capitol were howitzers, muskets, provisions, munitions of war. In the Senate chamber slept the 6th Massachusetts boys. In the House of Representatives slept the Pennsylvania boys. At each Capitol doorway was a ten-foot barricade of sandbags, cement barrels, iron plate. The Georgetown flour mills' supply, 25,000 barrels, was seized as a war necessity.

On April 23 a little mail arrived—and newspapers. Anderson and his garrison had arrived in New York and the town had gone wild over them! A Union Square mass meeting with 50,000 people shouting for the Union! Processions, speeches, enlistments of more men than the President called for! Million-dollar appropriations for the war! The famous crack regiment, the dandy 7th of New York, had marched down Broadway between vast walls of cheering crowds, heading south for Washington! The Governor of Rhode Island sailing with troops and guns for Washington!

A locomotive whistle shrieking hallelujah the next day, April 25, was followed by the marching—left, right, left, right—up Pennsylvania Avenue of the 7th New York. Then came 1,200 Rhode Islanders and a brigade of 1,200 from Massachusetts. A crippled locomotive at Annapolis had been repaired by Massachusetts mechanics; volunteer tracklayers put the road from Annapolis in running order again. A troop route to the North had been found. In a few days Washington had 10,000 defense troops. Now, for a time, Lincoln knew that the capital would still be at Washington.

CHAPTER 20

JEFFERSON DAVIS—
HIS GOVERNMENT

Jefferson Davis, President of the Confederate States of America
as painted by Christian F. Schwerdt, ca. 1875.

Jefferson Davis—His Government

THE CONFEDERATE Government, strengthened by the finally seceded States of Arkansas, Tennessee, North Carolina and Texas, moved the last week in May from Montgomery, Alabama, to Richmond, Virginia, to be nearer the Border States and the expected heavy fighting. Into Richmond streamed regiments from all parts of the South. The cry in the South, "On to Washington!" snarled straight into the cry from the North, "On to Richmond!"

From the Potomac River to the Gulf Coast and the Rio Grande ran the recruiting ground of this Confederate Army. Its line zigzagged 1,500 miles from Chesapeake Bay through Kentucky and out to the corners of Kansas. Its brain and will centered in the capitol, the executive mansion, the departments, at Richmond. Its chief weapon of defense was an army of 100,000 troops. The controls of this Government were out of the hands of those who had first given it breath and fire. Rhett of the True Perpetual Separationists was now only a member of the Confederate Congress with no executive authority; the efforts to appoint him Secretary of War had failed.

Yancey was shelved as a commissioner to European nations, with no power to act and no special instructions.

A new and a young Government it was at Richmond. "Where will I find the State Department?" an Englishman asked Robert Toombs, Secretary of State. "In my hat, sir," replied Toombs, "and the archives in my coat pocket." The impulsive Toombs was soon to resign and take to the camp and battlefield. He should have been Secretary of War, said many, but that place went to Leroy Pope Walker of Alabama, a lawyer and politician, harassed by technical matters of how a people with ports restricted or closed, and with no gun or arms factories or powder mills, should create those requisites. He was soon to step from office to field service, and this Confederate War Department at Richmond took on as Acting Assistant Secretary of War one Albert Taylor Bledsoe, a West Point graduate who had become a Protestant Episcopal clergyman, later a professor of mathematics, though part of his ten years as a practicing lawyer was spent in Springfield, Illinois, with an office adjoining that of Lincoln & Herndon.

The Secretary of the Treasury, Christopher Gustavus Memminger, an orphan-asylum boy, a German Lutheran born in Württemberg, a lawyer, businessman, and politician of exceptional integrity, founder of the public school system in Charleston, was the one South Carolina name in the Cabinet. He arranged with Gazaway B. Lamar, the Southern secessionist president of the Bank of the Republic in New York, for a contract with the American Bank Note Company to engrave and print in New York the bonds and treasury notes of the Confederacy. "The work was handsomely executed on the best of bank note and bond paper," wrote Memminger, "but with all the precaution taken by Mr. Lamar, the entire issue fell into the hands of the Federal Government and was seized as contraband of war." Engravers rushed from Europe were therefore to direct the printing of Confederate money on paper brought from Baltimore by agents who ran the Federal picket lines.

The Navy head was Stephen R. Mallory of Florida, once chairman of the Committee on Naval Affairs of the U.S. Senate, and having, as President Davis wrote, "for a landsman much knowledge of nautical affairs." Mallory was the one Roman Catholic of the Cabinet. The one Jew was Judah P. Benjamin of New Orleans, whose wife was a French Roman Catholic. Twice elected U.S. Senator from Louisiana, in his advocacy of the legal grounds for slavery, he once came close to a duel with Jefferson Davis. Once when defending slavery Benjamin was classified by Senator Wade of Ohio as "a Hebrew with Egyptian principles." He had a rare legal mind, and as Attorney General and later as Secretary of State was one of the few trusted helpers of President Davis; he toiled in his Richmond office from eight in the morning till past midnight, and was sometimes referred to as "the brains of the Confederacy." The one Texan in the Cabinet was the Postmaster General, J. H. Reagan, former Congressman, Indian fighter, and Southwestern pioneer.

Mrs. Jefferson Davis (Varina Howell Davis).

Heading this Cabinet was a figure chosen as a military authority; he stood in the public eye as a moderate rather than a radical secessionist, having integrity and distinctively Southern qualities. This was the Mississippi cotton planter, West Point graduate, Black Hawk War lieutenant, Mexican War veteran wounded in service, U.S. Senator, Secretary of War under the Pierce administration, orator, horseman, man of fate—Jefferson Davis. He and Lincoln were both born in Kentucky, Davis a year earlier than Lincoln, one as a child carried north to free soil, the other as a suckling babe taken to the lower South.

When 17, Davis had replied to a sister's letter telling him of his father's death: "The intelligence contained in yours was more than sufficient to mar the satisfaction of hearing from anyone . . ." This formal manner, this icy perfection, was to stay with him. One of the rare times he dropped it was in his love letters to Sarah Knox Taylor, the 16-year-old daughter of Colonel Zachary Taylor at Fort Crawford, Wisconsin. She was too young to marry, the father frowned. But Miss Taylor visited a Kentucky aunt, the young Lieutenant resigned from the Army, the couple were married in

Kentucky and went to Mississippi near Vicksburg, to Brierfield, an 800-acre plantation given them by his brother, Joseph Davis, with 14 Negro slaves on credit. Malarial fever brought both of them down. In six weeks the bride of three months died in a delirium, singing an old hymn, "Fairy Bells," that she had from her mother.

An older brother brought to the plantation Miss Varina Howell, a 17-year-old girl from a well-to-do planter family at Natchez; she had soft liquid eyes, large curved eyebrows, with grace of speech and swift decisions. She was saved from mere prettiness by angular cheekbones and a full-lipped mournful mouth. She was 19 and he 37 when they married, and testimonies ran that she was the perfect helpmeet of a difficult man. She was health to him physically and mentally, in loyalty a tigress.

His national reputation in politics began with his service in the U.S. Senate in 1847, his clashes with Douglas, his denials of secession purposes clouded by arguments that states had a Constitutional right to secede. While Lincoln and Douglas were debating he said he wished they would tear each other to pieces

Robert Barnwell Rhett, II, Confederate Congressman.

Alexander H. Stephens, Vice-President of the Confederate States of America.

like the Kilkenny cats. When on November 6 Lincoln, though lacking a majority vote, had carried the electors of every Northern State except New Jersey, Davis on November 10 had sent a letter to Rhett: "If South Carolina has determined to secede, I advise her to do so before the Government passes into hostile hands." On a sickbed racked by neuralgia, his left eye lost, Senator Davis talked with Seward, and the news came that Lincoln had declared he would concede almost every point at issue with the South except that no more Slave States could be made from Territories. Mississippi seceded January 9, and 11 days later Davis told the Senate he was officially notified of the secession of his state and must resign.

Tears were in many eyes at his saying they parted "not in hostility to others, not to injure any section of the country, not even for our own pecuniary benefit, but from the high and solemn motive of defending and protecting the rights we inherited, and which it is our duty to transmit unshorn to our children . . . It only remains for me to bid you a final adieu."

On February 10, with a warm spring sun pouring down on leaf and petal, he and Varina were in a rose garden trimming and cutting, as though blood red roses carry ministrations. A messenger threaded his way through the bushes and handed Jefferson Davis a telegram. His wife tried to read his face while he read the telegram. His face took on grief and she was afraid evil news had arrived. "After a few minutes' painful silence he told me, as a man might speak of a sentence of death." The Montgomery delegates to the convention of the Confederate States of America had elected him provisional President, when so definitely he preferred campaign and battlefield to an administrative desk.

She wept a good-by and he rode to Montgomery, sleeping in his clothes, routed from the train by crowds roaring for their new President, calling for speeches, "bonfires at night, firing by day."

William Lowndes Yancey, Confederate Senator.

Christopher G. Memminger, Confederate Secretary of the Treasury.

After inauguration he wrote to her: "I thought it would have gratified you to have witnessed it, and have been a memory to our children."

Davis was a chosen spear of authority heading 11 states committed to him as against 23 states formally still in the Union with Lincoln, one side reckoned as having 9,000,000 people (including 3,900,000 slaves) as against 22,000,000 Northern people.

In the event of his death President Davis' place would be taken by a man who could himself have been President of the Confederate States by saying Yes to one condition. On the evening of February 8 delegates from six states came to Alexander Hamilton Stephens' room, their spokesman Robert Toombs, ever a warm personal friend of Stephens no matter how they disputed over politics.

"Aleck," said Toombs, "you are the choice of every man in Congress, and all of us are ready to pledge to help you form your Cabinet. There is only one point—those fellows from Virginia and the Border States want you to promise to strike the first blow.

Then slowly and distinctly, "No, I will never strike the first blow." Toombs roared, "Aleck!" and with a long look into the unflinching eyes of Stephens turned on his heel and with the other men strode from the room.

Stephens wanted retirement, peace, poetry, philosophy, time for friendly talks, time at his home in Liberty Hall to bathe the sore eyes of his old blind dog Rio. Yet Toombs and the others made him Vice-President of the Confederacy. He understood the North and its Lincoln, once writing of old friendships in Congress, "I was as intimate with Mr. Lincoln as with any other man except perhaps Mr. Toombs."

CHAPTER 21

TURMOIL—FEAR—HAZARDS

Stephen A. Douglas, 1813-1861, life-mask.
Photo by Leonard Volk.

TURMOIL—FEAR—HAZARDS

THE LINCOLN administration hammered away at shaping a new and huge war establishment. On May 3 the President issued a proclamation calling into service 42,034 three-year volunteers, 22,714 enlisted men to add ten regiments to the regular U.S. Army, 18,000 seamen for blockade service—bringing the total of the Army to 156,861 and the Navy to 25,000. Day and night the President and other anxious officers worked on grand strategy and petty details.

After May '61, the U.S. mail service no longer ran into the seceded states. In this month too the Confederate Congress authorized all persons owing debts in the United States (except in Delaware, Maryland, Kentucky, Missouri and the District of Columbia) to pay the amount of those debts into the Confederate Treasury. According to R. G. Dun & Company, the South owed Northern merchants about $211,000,000, of which $169,000,000 was due in New York City.

By May 9 some 20,000 troops were in Washington. They included Colonel Elmer E. Ellsworth and the regiment of Fire Zouaves he had recruited in ten days from New York City fire-department men. New Yorkers had raised a fund of $60,000 for uniforms and arms. Ten different patterns of rifles were carried by Ellsworth's red-trousered ranks.

In bright moonlight on May 24 at two o'clock in the morning, squads of cavalry crossed the bridges leading from Washington across the Potomac into Virginia, and were followed by infantry and by engineers, who began crowning every hill for miles with defense trenches for the protection of the ten-mile-square District of Columbia surrounded by Slave States.

In the Chicago Wigwam, Stephen A. Douglas had told an immense audience, "Before God it is the duty of every American citizen to rally around the flag of his country," and then gone home, to die.

The afternoon of June 3 his wife, holding his hand, asked if he had any last word for his boys and he answered, "Tell them to obey the laws and support the Constitution of the United States." These were telegraphed and generally recorded as his last words, though Chicago and New York newspaper accounts agreed in substance with that of the New York *Herald*: "When a few moments before his death, his wife leaned lovingly over him and sobbingly asked, 'Husband, do you know me? Will you kiss me?' he raised his eyes and smiled, and though too weak to speak, the movements of the muscles of his mouth evinced that he was making an almost dying struggle to comply with her request. His death was calm and peaceful; a few faint breaths after 9 o'clock; a slight rattling of his throat; a short, quick convulsive shudder, and Stephen A. Douglas passed into eternity."

Roll call of the Todd family of Lexington, Kentucky, found Mary Todd Lincoln's eldest brother Levi, and her half-sister Margaret Kellogg for the Union, while her youngest brother George and her three half-brothers Samuel, David and Alexander had joined the Confederate Army, and her half-sisters Emilie Helm, Martha White and Elodie Dawson were the wives of Confederate officers.

The fierce old Kentucky preacher and Union man, Robert Jefferson Breckinridge, could not get personal with his opposition. It included two of his own sons who were going into Confederate gray, one of them organizing a company for service under the Stars and Bars, and such kinsmen as his nephew John C. Breckinridge, and such illustrious Kentuckians as James B. Clay, the son of Henry Clay. Of his three sons only one was choosing the Stars and Stripes to fight under.

The Kentucky Legislature, after almost continuous session since January '61, adjourned sine die, proclaiming neutrality but still in the Union, and slowly drifting away from her sister Slave States to the south, who occasionally taunted Kentucky with "hesitation and cowardice." In the June balloting for members of the Congress Lincoln had called to meet July 4, Kentucky elected antisecessionists in nine out of the ten districts, the Union majority in the state being 54,700.

At Baltimore election of April 24, 1861, only one ticket had been in the field, "States' Rights." Of 30,000 voters in the city, only 9,244 went to the polls and they all voted for secessionist members of the Maryland Legislature, which was to assemble two days later.

What with Union regiments increasing daily at Annapolis, Governor Hicks could have pleased the secessionist element by calling the legislature to Baltimore. Instead he convened it at the town of Frederick, a Unionist community but without Union troops. Such decisions favoring the Unionists came regularly from Governor Hicks. Slowly it became clear that the strength of secession in Maryland lay chiefly in a furiously active minority in Baltimore.

A military department under Brigadier General Benjamin F. Butler was set up at Annapolis. In rain, darkness and thunder Butler moved 1,000 troops to Baltimore May 13, stacked arms on Federal Hill overlooking Baltimore, issued a proclamation that they were there to enforce respect and obedience to the laws of the United States. The North cheered Butler.

Butler when removed from Maryland and put in charge of Fortress Monroe in Virginia protested personally to Lincoln; the treatment of him implied reproaches. The President, according to Butler's report, said very kindly and courteously, "The administration has done everything to remove every thought of reproach upon you."

They shook hands and Butler left to spread word that they were "the warmest personal friends." Not yet had Butler discredited himself. His performances in Maryland had heartened the North, and he was on form worth the high commission Lincoln handed him. The Butler gift for expedients rang across the country again when in May fugitive slaves flocked by hundreds into his camp. The legal question Butler disposed of by his decision, "The negro must now be regarded as *contraband*" (like smuggled goods or anything forbidden to be supplied by neutrals to belligerents). The country picked up this word "contraband" as often untying knots of the Fugitive Slave Law. Many a runaway slave, after starving in timber and swamp, arrived in the Union lines to say with jubilation, "I'se contraband."

The next flare-up in Maryland ended with the Chief Justice of the U.S. Supreme Court tangled in dispute with the President. General George Cadwalader, in command of Fort McHenry near Baltimore, sent a squad of soldiers who at two o'clock the morning of May 25 roused one John Merryman from bed in his home at Hayfields and took him to Fort McHenry and locked him up "in close custody." Lawyers for Merryman appeared the same day before Roger B. Taney, who made his home in Baltimore. They denied that Merryman was guilty of reported charges of treason, prayed for a writ of habeas corpus. Chief Justice Taney issued the writ and commanded that General Cadwalader appear before him "and that you have with you the body of John Merryman."

Lincoln's reply to Chief Justice Taney was given to the country in a message to Congress on July 4:

Soon after the first call for militia, it was considered a duty to authorize the Commanding General, in proper cases, according to his discretion, to suspend the privilege of the writ of habeas corpus; or, in other words, to arrest, and detain, without resort to the ordinary processes and forms of law, such individuals as he might deem dangerous to the public safety . . . Of course some consideration was given to the questions of power, and propriety, before this matter was acted upon . . . Are all the laws, *but one*, to go unexecuted, and the government itself go to pieces, lest that one be violated? Even in such a case, would not the official oath be broken, if the government should be overthrown . . . It was not believed that any law was violated . . . It was decided that we have a case of rebellion . . . Now it is insisted that Congress, and not the Executive, is vested with this power. But the Constitution itself, is silent as to which, or who, is to exercise the power . . .

Queen Victoria's proclamation of May 13, 1861, took notice of hostilities "between the government of the United States of America and certain States styling themselves the Confederate States of America" and declared the "royal determination to maintain a strict and impartial neutrality in the contest between said contending parties."

The President and the Cabinet through the new and often bungling personnels of their old departments were wrestling with crazy patterns of military organization, red tape, confusions of counsels, inpouring brigades, telegrams exchanged daily or hourly with governors recruiting troops, the direction of four grades of troops: (1) regulars; (2) three-month volunteers; (3) state militia; (4) three-year volunteers; besides independent troop units in Border States still neutral.

John C. Breckenridge, U.S. Vice-President under Buchanan and Secretary of War for the Confederate States of America.

In commissioning major generals of volunteers the President seemed to rest chiefly on the judgment of Scott, who favored John E. Wool, John A. Dix, Henry W. Halleck, Don Carlos Buell. The appointment of John C. Fremont as a major general was mainly political, as were the appointments of Benjamin F. Butler and Nathaniel P. Banks. David Hunter, Edwin V. Sumner and John Pope, who had accompanied Lincoln from Springfield to Harrisburg, were commissioned as brigadiers. Among the May and June appointees as brigadiers nearly all had West Point training and Mexican War service records.

William Tecumseh Sherman came again to the White House and left with a colonel's commission. Sherman had amazed the President and given him a healthy laugh by refusing a brigadier's commission and saying he would rather work up from colonel.

Of a total of 1,108 U.S. Army officers, 387 had resigned to go South. These resigned Southerners, 288 of them West Point-trained, included promising officers, of actual field and battle service. Among West Pointers in Northern service were 162 born in Slave States. Among West Pointers gone South for service were

U.S. Maj. General Benjamin F. Butler, who occupied New Orleans.

19 Northern-born men. Lincoln was writing in a message to Congress: "It is worthy of note, that while in this, the government's hour of trial, large numbers of those in the Army and Navy, who have been favored with the offices, have resigned, and proved false to the hand which had pampered them, not one common soldier, or common sailor is known to have deserted his flag. Great honor is due to those officers who remain true…"

In his message to Congress Lincoln was writing no line or word dealing with any phase of the Negro and slavery. The President kept an official loyalty to the Fugitive Slave Act. On July 6, 1861, Secretary of War Cameron notified Lincoln that 64 volunteer regiments of 900 men each, besides 1,200 Regulars, were in readiness around Washington, and the troops enrolled elsewhere over the North made a total of 225,000. Of this army, one of the largest the earth had ever seen, Lincoln was Commander in Chief.

Pierre Gustave Toutant Beauregard, superintendent of the West Point Military Academy before he resigned the previous winter, a Mexican War veteran, was now commanding an army of 20,000 Confederate troops near Washington at Manassas

Junction. As the hero who had shot away the flag at Fort Sumter, he was called to Virginia to check Northern invasion. He began June 1 with a proclamation: "A reckless and unprincipled tyrant has invaded your soil. Abraham Lincoln, regardless of all moral, legal, and constitutional restraints, has thrown his Abolition hosts among you . . . All rules of civilized warfare are abandoned . . . Your honor and that of your wives and daughters, your fortunes, and your lives are involved in this momentous contest."

On July 4 when Congress assembled it was in the air that soon a battle would be fought near Washington. Greeley's *Tribune* clamored in headlines: "Forward to Richmond! Forward to Richmond! The Rebel Congress must not be allowed to meet there on the 20th of July! By that date the place must be held by the National Army!"

In his message to Congress the President gave a miniature history of the Fort Sumter affair, of how the fort was bombarded to its fall "without even awaiting the arrival of the provisioning expedition." It forced the questions: "Is there, in all republics, this inherent, and fatal weakness? . . . Must a government, of necessity, be too *strong* for the liberties of its own people, or too *weak* to maintain its own existence?" No choice was left but "to call out the war power of the Government." Applause swept the House at the recommendation "that you give the legal means for making this contest a short and decisive one" and for the work at least 400,000 men and $400,000,000.

The President then queried whether the Southern movement should be called "secession" or "rebellion," saying that the instigators of the movement understood the difference. The message was a brief for a client, a letter to the American people. The Northern press gave it greater approval than any utterance hitherto from Lincoln. The Senate confirmed the President's appointments. A new army bill gave the President more than he asked, authorizing 500,000 three-year volunteers. A joint resolution to make legal and valid the extralegal, dictatorial and proscriptive acts of the President in the emergencies since his proclamation of war in April met little direct opposition, but was held up and laid away amid unfinished business from day to day. He had gone out of his way to do so many things without the required authority from Congress. Now Congress politely refused to sanction all he had done.

CHAPTER 22
BULL RUN — MCCLELLAN — FRÉMONT — THE TRENT AFFAIR

Bull Run — McClellan — Frémont — The Trent Affair

THE PRESIDENT on June 29 had called a Cabinet meeting before which General Irvin McDowell laid his plans. His army of 30,000 was to fight the 21,900 Confederates at Manassas under General Beauregard. Another Confederate army over in the Shenandoah Valley was to be held by a Union army under General Robert Patterson, also in the valley, and stopped from joining Beauregard. General Scott approved McDowell's battle plan but favored waiting till a larger army, better trained and prepared, could win victories that would be destructive.

The Battle of Bull Run, Sunday, July 21, 1861, was to a large and eager public a sort of sporting event, the day and place of combat announced beforehand, a crowd of spectators riding to the scene with lunch baskets as though for a picnic. On horseback, in buggies and gigs, Senators Trumbull, Wade, Chandler, Grimes, Wilson, McDougall, besides Congressmen with emergency navy revolvers and pretty ladies in crinoline gowns, rode out to gaze on a modern battle. The word was that the Northern Shovelry would make Southern Chivalry bite the dust.

Lincoln went as usual that Sunday morning to the New York Avenue Presbyterian Church. During the afternoon he read telegrams from the battlefield, one every 10 or 15 minutes. A messenger from Scott arrived. All seemed favorable. The President went for a drive in his carriage, as usual of evenings. At six o'clock came Seward, pale, worn, hoarse, asking Nicolay and Hay, "Where is the President?" He had gone to drive, they told Seward, showing telegrams indicating victory. "Tell no one," came the words from Seward. "That is not true. The battle is lost," He had news that McDowell's army was retreating and calls were coming for General Scott to save Washington.

The President returned a half-hour later. Nicolay and Hay told him the news. "He listened in silence, without the slightest change of feature or expression, and walked away to army headquarters." There a dispatch from a captain of engineers read: "The day is lost. Save Washington and the remnants of this army.

The routed troops will not re-form." General Scott refused to believe it. The Cabinet was called. Now came a telegram from McDowell. His army had gone to pieces, and was "a confused mob."

McDowell's staff man, James B. Fry, recorded 16 officers and 444 men killed, 78 officers and 1,046 men wounded, 50 officers and 1,262 men missing, not including Congressman Alfred Ely of New York captured and sent to Libby Prison in Richmond. General Johnston officially reported Confederate losses at 378 killed, 1,489 wounded, and 30 missing.

But more than any other General Robert Patterson was blamed; if he had smashed at Johnston's army in the Shenandoah Valley, then Johnston's fresh regiments wouldn't have marched in and started the panic. "As for blame and causes," wrote George William Curtis in a private letter, "they are in our condition and character. We have undertaken to make war without in the least knowing how."

In a letter to Lincoln from Greeley in New York, the foremost American editor was ready for an armistice, a national convention, peace, disbandment of forces.

Probing, analyzing, approving of Lincoln but more often scolding, were Horace Greeley and his newspaper. Among the 50,000 subscribers of the New York *Tribune* were nearly all the editors and news writers of America. Greeley had arrived in New York 20 years old, with $10 in his pocket, a greenhorn from Vermont farms who had picked up the trade of printer. He edited the *New Yorker*, the *Jeffersonian*, the *Log Cabin*, and in 1841 started his penny morning paper, the New York *Tribune*, which for 21 years was at the forefront reporting, if not advocating, every reform, radical idea and "ism" that came to view. "Go West, young man" was his repeated advice, and in the westward flow of settlers a famous slogan.

Horace Greeley,
Editor of the New York Tribune.

BULL RUN—McCLELLAN—FRÉMONT—THE TRENT AFFAIR

U.S. General George B. McClellan, Commander of the Army of the Potomac. Photo by Mathew Brady.

At 25 he married Mary Y. Cheney, a Connecticut school-teacher whom he met at a vegetarian boardinghouse in New York. She was slight, girlish-looking, a brunette with long curls falling below her shoulders. Their first child was fair, with notable complexion and hair that fell as "a shower of ruddy gold" to his shoulders; he died at five in an Asiatic cholera plague that infected New York in 1848. Another boy died at six from croup. One girl died at six months of age. Two infants died at childbirth. Of the seven Greeley children two daughters were alive.

Lincoln gave his personal attention to the camps around Washington, kept close to men and officers, mixed with them. He rode in an open hack with Seward one day across the Potomac.

Colonel William Tecumseh Sherman at a roadside asked if they were going to his camp. "Yes," said Lincoln. "We heard that you had got over the big scare, and we thought we would come over and see the boys." He asked Sherman into the hack. At the camp, noted Sherman, "Mr. Lincoln stood up and made one of the neatest, best, and most feeling addresses I ever listened to, referring to our disaster, the high duties that still devolved on us, and the brighter days to come."

The Senate resolution to approve the President's unconstitutional acts done without approval of Congress during the emergency weeks, when Congress was not in session and could not then approve, was introduced the third day of the session. It would declare legal and valid the President's first call for state militia troops, his proclamation of blockade and action therein, his call for three-year volunteers and his increase of the Regular Army and the Navy, and not least of all his suspension of the ancient Anglo-Saxon writ of habeas corpus. By a vote of 37 to 5 it passed the Senate, and by 74 to 19 the House, the Nays being Border State votes, with help from Ohio and Indiana.

When Congress adjourned August 6, it had given the President nearly all the practical measures he needed to proceed with the war. He was more of an executive than most of them had expected.

The Army of the Potomac grew into 168,000 in November from 50,000 on July 22, when Washington had received its new commander, General George Brinton McClellan. McClellan was appointed by Lincoln by reason of an overwhelming weight of public and private opinion. He looked the part, with a well-modeled head, mustache and goatee, sat his saddle as a trained Man on Horseback, issued commands with authority, published proclamations modeled on Napoleon. Washington adopted him, the Army took to him, correspondents nicknamed him "Little Mac" and "the Young Napoleon."

Only the year before, he had married Ellen Mary Marcy, the daughter of a Regular Army officer, to whom he was now writing, "Who would have thought, when we were married, that I should so soon be called upon to save my country?" He had left her and a $10,000-a-year job as president of the Ohio & Mississippi Railroad at Cincinnati. He had been chief engineer and then vice-president of the Illinois Central Railroad, entertained Douglas in his Chicago home, and the only ballot he had ever cast was for Douglas. His *Manual on the Art of War*, his translation of a French book on bayonet exercises, were reputable. Commanding an army of 18,000 in West Virginia, he had overcome about two-thirds that number, giving the North the only actions thus far having semblance of military victories.

An illusion that the enemy outnumbered him kept growing. Day by day in personal interviews, in notes and letters, he called on the President, on Scott and others, for more and more men. "I am here in a terrible place; the enemy have from three to four times my force," he wrote his wife August 16, adding a few days later, "I do not *live* at all; merely exist, worked and worried half to death."

In November General Winfield Scott was retired on pay, with honors, and with tributes from the President and others. McClellan was now commissioned General in Chief, and at the White House Lincoln said to him, "I should be perfectly satisfied if I thought this vast increase of responsibility would not embarrass you." "It is a great relief, Sir!" said McClellan. "I feel as if several tons were taken from my shoulders today. I am now in contact with you, and the Secretary. I am not embarrassed by intervention." "Well," said Lincoln, as John Hay heard him, "draw on me for all the sense I have, and all the information. In addition to your present command, the supreme command of the army will entail a vast labor upon you." "I can do it all," McClellan said quietly.

McClellan's army now numbered more than 160,000; he had at least three times as many troops as the enemy at Manassas. Twice in that autumn of 1861 the spick-and-span platoons of the Army of the Potomac had passed in grand review before President Lincoln, the Cabinet, governors of states and ladies in silken crinoline. There had been autumn weather on which many commented—mild, pleasant days and cool nights, perfect weather for an army movement to redeem Bull Run, to end the war. Thus ran hope and talk.

Driving snow came with the last week in November. Winter weather was on. Wool coats, heavy blankets, firewood, tents, huts, were the need. The war was costing more than $1,000,000 a day. A hazard was in the air. Would the Young Napoleon slog through in a winter campaign and take Richmond? If he should, said men of the South at Richmond, he would find it as Napoleon did Moscow, a city in ashes.

The Kentucky Senator, John C. Breckinridge, once a Vice-President of the United States, had called at the White House to bid good-by to his kinswoman, Elizabeth Todd Grimsley. He was resigning as U.S. Senator and joining the Confederate Army as a brigadier general.

Nathaniel Lyon, short, bearded, with dark-red hair and fiery temperament, drove himself hard, some of his raw volunteer troops saying he talked to them as if they were mules. Lyon threw his army of 6,000 at more than twice that number of Confederates August 10, 1861, at Wilson's Creek, Missouri. Bullets struck him near the ankle, on the thigh; one cut his scalp to the bone; his horse was shot. Mounting another horse, his face white from loss of blood, he ordered a bayonet charge and led it, tumbling off his horse into the arms of his orderly with a bullet hole close to the heart. His army retired, the enemy not following. The losses were about 1,200 killed and wounded on each side. Missouri boys of both armies lay dead in the cornfields alongside Kentucky, Iowa and Illinois boys. The Confederates gave over the body of Lyon. Crowds came to view the coffin as it journeyed to Connecticut, where the general assembly mourned its "beloved son."

An outcry arose when Congressman Frank Blair and others put the blame for Lyon's death, Wilson's Creek and other losses on General John Charles Frémont, commander of the Department of the West, with headquarters, troops and munitions at St. Louis.

Frémont, in 1856 the first Republican party candidate for President, was born in Savannah, Georgia. Expelled from college in Charleston, South Carolina, for "continual disregard of discipline," he was an instructor of mathematics on a U.S. war sloop, a railroad surveyor in the Tennessee mountains, and became a lieutenant in the U.S. Topographical Corps. He led expeditions west, exploring the Rocky Mountains, South Pass, winning the first recorded climb up the highest point in the Wind River Mountains. Frémont Peak was named for him.

He clashed with the Spanish rulers of California, took a hand in overthrowing them and setting up the State of California, of which he was the first U.S. Senator. Then came land, gold mines, money pouring in at the rate of $75,000 a month, and Frémont's Mariposa estate of 46,000 acres, which had cost him $3,000, was estimated at $10,000,000. Though he was head of the Western Department on July 3, Frémont lingered in Washington, delayed in New York, arrived in St. Louis on July 25; he directed entrenchments thrown around St. Louis, wore out relays of telegraphers with messages to governors and troop commanders. Many days he worked from five in the morning till midnight.

From the southwest corner of Missouri had come a messenger from Lyon begging Frémont to send him men. Frémont answered, "If he fights it will be on his own responsibility." Frémont had urged Lyon to retreat to Rolla, which would be falling back about halfway to St. Louis. And he started two regiments toward Lyon. But Lyon never saw them. For him war was fighting; he sought out the enemy. Lyon died in the drawn battle at Wilson's Creek. The memory rankled with men like Frank Blair.

Frémont through the night of August 29 and far into the morning of August 30 worked on a proclamation. In pompous terms and with threats he didn't have power to enforce, he declared "martial law throughout the State of Missouri." Drawing the line of the Union Army across half the state, he promised that all persons north of this line caught "with arms in their hands" would be court-martialed and "if found guilty will be shot." Also "the property, real and personal, of all persons in the State of Missouri who shall take up arms against the United States, or who shall be directly proven to have taken an active part with their enemies in the field, is declared to be confiscated to the public use, and their slaves, if any they have, are hereby declared freemen."

"Lincoln's reply to Frémont September 11 pointed to the clause relating to confiscation of property and liberation of slaves, which "appeared to me to be objectionable, in it's nonconformity to the Act of Congress passed the 6th. of last August." He had therefore written his wish to Frémont that the clause be modified and now, "Your answer, just received, expresses the preference on your part, that I should make an open order for the modification, which I very cheerfully do."

Judges David Davis and Joseph Holt were appointed to direct an audit of accounts. War Secretary Cameron, with an adjutant general, went personally to St. Louis.

They all found extravagance, mismanagement, blunders, but no specific outstanding corruption. The total of contracts for food, guns, steamboats, uniforms, supplies, fortifications, ran to about $12,000,000. Nothing could be fastened on Frémont. He came through the search with a record for personal honesty. The Chicago Irish Brigade under Colonel James A. Mulligan defended Lexington eight days against 20,000 of the enemy and surrendered 1,600 men September 20. Blamed for this fresh loss of good troops,

Frémont had notified General Scott at Washington: "I am taking the field myself . . . Please notify the President immediately." General Scott replied, "The President is glad you are hastening to the scene of action; his words are, 'he expects you to repair the disaster at Lexington without loss of time.'" Yet Frémont went on losing time.

Thus on November 2 Frémont was removed from command. Lincoln's removal order, dated October 24, had gone to General S. R. Curtis at St. Louis with instructions that the order was not to

U.S. Major General Charles C. Frémont, commander of the Army of the West. Photo by Mathew Brady.

be handed Frémont if when reached by messenger "he shall then have, in personal command, fought and won a battle, or shall then be actually in a battle, or shall then be in the immediate presence of the enemy, in expectation of a battle."

Frémont had lasted in Missouri just 100 days. In that time he made himself a hero in the eyes of nearly all the antislavery elements of the Northern States and of Europe. Sober citizens pulled the portraits of Lincoln from their walls and trampled under foot the face of the President, according to the Cincinnati *Gazette*. Wendell Phillips estimated Lincoln as "not a man like Frémont, to stamp the lava mass of the nation with an idea." Honoring Frémont in person, Henry Ward Beecher in his Brooklyn church said, "Your name will live and be remembered by a nation of freemen." James Russell Lowell, Greeley and Bryant spoke deep offense at Lincoln's treatment of Frémont. The Chicago *Tribune* denounced the President's action and predicted grave humiliation unless the administration took a more vigorous policy.

Not for long could any man be the hero of the New York *Herald*. The foremost innovator in the journalism of his time, James Gordon Bennett, was studied by Lincoln as one of the powers to be kept on the Union side as far as possible. Self-announced as "daily daguerreotype of American manners and thought" the *Herald*'s 66-year-old owner and editor, born of Roman Catholic parents in Keith, Scotland, had trained for priesthood at Aberdeen, had starved as a bookseller in Boston, had lived shabbily as a hack writer in New York. He issued his first four-page penny New York *Herald* in 1835, doing all the work except the printing himself, writing and shaping the whole paper on an editorial desk of one board slung over two dry-goods boxes, "one poor man in a cellar against the world," as he phrased it.

After Bull Run the *Herald* counseled fresh determination and further preparations, almost in the tone of Lincoln's memoranda for immediate action; no panic, no bewilderment, as in the case of Greeley. Then on Lincoln's revoking Frémont's personal proclamation of Negro emancipation had come the *Herald*'s encomiums for Lincoln, praise in heaping measure, compliments that like fresh roses must soon wither and fade, petal by petal. With no cessation Bennett would

continue putting the blame for the war on "nigger worshippers," sprinkling his editorial page with that phrase, and steadily maintaining that antislavery agitators were hypocrites rather than heroes.

In November '61 came a dramatic clash of English-speaking nations. The *Trent*, a British Royal Mail packet, one day out from Havana, was steaming serenely along the Bahama Channel. At noon November 8 she came to where the channel narrows to a width of 15 miles. There the *San Jacinto*, a screw sloop of the American Navy, was waiting.

The *Trent* hoisted the British colors. The *San Jacinto* ran up the Union flag. Also the *San Jacinto* fired a shot across the bow of the *Trent*. And as the British steamer showed no signs of slowing down, the American sloop sent a shell that burst in front of the bow of the *Trent*. This brought her to. Captain Moir of the *Trent* lifted a trumpet to his lips, and sang out, "What do you mean by heaving my vessel to in this way?" No answer came.

Three boats were leaving the *San Jacinto* with officers, sailors, marines. They rowed to the *Trent* in a few minutes, and Lieutenant D. MacNeill Fairfax, speaking for the commander of the *San Jacinto*, asked for the passenger list of the *Trent*. He had information that James M. Mason and John Slidell, newly appointed Confederate commissioners to Great Britain and France respectively, were on board.

Mr. Slidell standing near stepped up to Lieutenant Fairfax. "I am Mr. Slidell; do you want to see me?" Mr. Mason, also being near, stepped up, and as he and Lieutenant Fairfax had been introduced years before there was no need for him to say who he was. Next the Lieutenant asked for the secretaries to Messrs. Mason and Slidell and they were lined up. At this point the American Lieutenant informed the British Captain that he had been sent by his commander to arrest Messrs. Mason and Slidell and take them as prisoners on board the U.S. vessel nearby. The two ships moved away toward different horizons and soon each was alone in the silence of the sea.

First Bull Run Battlefield, July 1861.

BULL RUN—MCCLELLAN—FRÉMONT—THE TRENT AFFAIR

When the *Trent* passengers reached London November 27, they found themselves accepted heroes and heroines who had undergone severe tests. The London *Morning Chronicle* tore its hair and gave the war party its cues: "Abraham Lincoln, whose accession to power was generally welcomed on this side of the Atlantic, has proved himself a feeble, confused and little-minded mediocrity. Mr. Seward, the firebrand at his elbow, is exerting himself to provoke a quarrel with all Europe."

On the intervention of Queen Victoria and Prince Albert, the severe instructions to Lord Lyons from Lord Palmerston, the Prime Minister, and Lord John Russell, Secretary for Foreign Affairs, were softened, and instead they framed a note for Seward and Lincoln to read. Mainly it asked whether Captain Wilkes had done what he did by his own wish and whim or at the command of his Government. If it was a Government order and in line with U.S. policy—then war! The ships of the best and biggest navy in the world were made ready. Eight thousand picked troops were put on transports and set sail for Canada.

That the U.S. Government had in its clutches John Slidell was exciting to antislavery men, for Slidell had led in repealing the Missouri Compromise, was an author of the Fugitive Slave Law, had lengthily examined John Brown in jail, seeking information that might convict New England financial backers of Brown. Mason's record ran close to that of Slidell. The two of them personified the doctrines justifying slavery. America trembled with war fever. Famous lawyers such as Caleb Cushing and Edward Everett justified Wilkes as having the law with him, though other good lawyers like Charles Sumner and Charles Francis Adams were sure he was in the wrong.

During the weeks of this fury Lincoln gave no inkling of what he would do. In his December message to Congress he made no reference to the matter. Gait, the Canadian financial Minister, in a White House visit asked the meaning of fortifications and depots of arms on the Great Lakes, Lincoln replying, "We must say something to satisfy the people." And what about the Mason and Slidell case? Gait inquired. "Oh, that'll be got along with," was the brief and equivocal response. Minister Lyons treasured the anecdote, and it was rehearsed in many legations that to a portentous diplomatic inquiry the American President had answered, "Oh, that'll be got along with."

From week to week Adams was helpless till one day the mail brought Seward's note calling for arbitration and saying the captured Southern commissioners "will be cheerfully liberated." Discussion of this note had run two days in Lincoln's Cabinet, and Bates wrote: "There was great reluctance on the part of some of the members of the cabinet—and even the President himself"—to give up the Southern commissioners. However, it was so ordered. The British reply later took exception to minor points and acknowledged satisfaction as to "the reparation which Her Majesty and the British nation had a right to expect." Mason and Slidell were let out of their comfortable jail in Boston and placed on board a British war vessel to cross the Atlantic.

CHAPTER 23
THE POLITICS OF WAR—
CORRUPTION

THE POLITICS OF WAR—CORRUPTION

THE WAR cost was mounting toward $1,500,000 a day as the winter of '61 set in. Money was pouring in and out in larger aggregates, bigger numbers, than Federal bookkeeping ever before recorded. A long-drawn battle, with money as ammunition, had been fought between the North and the South in Great Britain and on the continent of Europe. The fighting—with gold, moneybags, credit—was over war supplies. The North outbid and outbought the South.

On the revolutionary advances in communication a magazine writer had noted, "Today newspapers multiplied by millions whiten the whole country every morning like the hoar frost." Lincoln's message to Congress in December '61 swept the national horizons. Westward from Omaha gangs of linemen had strung wires to the coast. "The President's message," said a dispatch, "read in Congress at 12 o'clock on Tuesday, was received by telegraph at San Francisco, and published early on Wednesday morning."

The message maintained in austere tone throughout that the Union was intact and its Government would ride the crisis and enforce its will. Lincoln opened with "great gratitude to God for unusual good health, and most abundant harvests." Kentucky "is now decidedly, and, I think, unchangeably," ranged on the side of the Union. Missouri had passed beyond seizure by the insurrectionists. The three states of Maryland, Kentucky and Missouri, "neither of which would promise a single soldier at first, have now an aggregate of not less than forty thousand in the field, for the Union."

In this message Lincoln changed from referring to himself as "he" or "the executive." After nine months as President he was "I." Where before he had written, "The executive deems it of importance," he now wrote, "I deem it of importance."

Declaring friendship for two Negro national governments the President could see no good reason for "withholding our recognition of the independence and sovereignty of Hayti and Liberia."

The Confiscation Act, by which Negroes belonging, as property, to disloyal slaveholders became freemen, was scrupulously recited in terms of law. "The legal claims of certain persons to the labor and service of certain other persons have become forfeited." In such numbers had these liberated Negroes come into the Union army lines and become Federal dependents, and so sure was it that more of them would arrive for disposal, that it now became necessary to have a permanent policy for their disposal.

The message drew more approval and perhaps less hostile comment in general than either the first inaugural or the July 4 message to Congress. Its most original feature concerned Negro freedom. Delicately, tentatively, and in the strictest of legal terms pertaining to the management of property, Lincoln projected his policy of gradual compensated emancipation. In substance his proposal was that the Border Slave States might enact laws for selling their slaves to the U.S. Government, which in turn should free the slaves and then take steps to colonize them.

When in December Congress appointed a Committee on the Conduct of the War, Lincoln saw it as one extreme intended to check another. Among its members were D. W. Gooch of Massachusetts, George W. Julian of Indiana, John Covode of Pennsylvania and Moses F. Odell of New York. Chiefly radical antislavery Republicans, they were headstrong men of brains, courage, ability, of long training in politics and the antislavery struggle; of the group the gadfly was Julian. The chairman of the committee, Benjamin Franklin Wade, strode into the White House one day and stormily told Lincoln he must throw McClellan overboard. Lincoln asked who should then be put in McClellan's place. Snorted Wade, "Anybody!" Lincoln, coolly: "*Wade, anybody* will do for you but I must have *somebody*."

Short, deep-chested, defiant-looking Ben Wade was 61, of Puritan stock, his father a Revolutionary War soldier. Day laborer on the Erie Canal, farm hand, cattle-driver, schoolteacher, prosecuting attorney of Ashtabula County, he entered the Ohio

Legislature and put through a bill forbidding that body to grant divorces. He fought against passage of the Fugitive Slave Law and then fought against its enforcement. He entered the U.S. Senate in 1851 as one of the small group of antislavery men who first dared, on broad policy grounds, to challenge the Southerners.

Though Stevens limped with a clubfoot, he was a horseman and a swimmer. His tongue was often sharp and, men said, malicious and arrogant. In the Pennsylvania Legislature he had put through bills that won him the name of father of the free-school system of the state. In law practice, investments, iron and furnace projects, Thaddeus Stevens had made one fortune of $200,000, lost it, made another, and had a reputation for paying his debts to the last dollar. His recreation was gambling. An old-timer said he lost and won and didn't seem to care.

In January '62 it was six months since McClellan had been put at the head of the Army of the Potomac. Money, men, bread, beef, gunpowder, arms, artillery, horses, had been given McClellan on a colossal scale. The army under him in the public prints and in common talk was rated the largest and finest known in modern history. And with this well-trained force of fresh troops he settled into winter quarters, the enemy army only two days' easy march away.

His army was made up mainly of boys in the early 20's, thousands of them 19 and under. They wrote home about their winter huts, pork and beans, coffee and soup from tin cups, epidemics of measles and mumps, digging trenches, putting up telegraph wires, clearing range for artillery with pick and shovel, throwing up earthworks, driving beef to camp, hauling military stores, dysentery, sore feet, roaches in hardtack, target practice, washing shirts and underwear in creeks and rivers.

Late in December McClellan fell sick with typhoid fever and took to his bed for three weeks. During those weeks he ran his armies, from the Atlantic to the Mississippi and beyond, from his bed. Lincoln wrote Chase a card January 2, 1862: "I have just been with General McClellan; and he is very much better." Days followed, however, when others came to McClellan's bedside and did business—but the President was kept outside, and failed to get polite entry.

Lincoln, while refusing to remove McClellan from command,

as urged by radicals, was getting ready to let McClellan know who held authority. He issued on January 27 his General War Order No. 1, fixing February 22, 1862, as "the day for a general movement of the Land and Naval forces of the United States against the insurgent forces." He named the army "at & about, Fortress Monroe," the Army of the Potomac, the Army of Western Virginia, the army near Munfordville, Kentucky, the army and flotilla of gunboats at Cairo, Illinois, and a naval force in the Gulf of Mexico as ordered to be ready to move on that day. Department heads, commanders and subordinates "will severally be held to their strict and full responsibilities, for the prompt execution of this order." Four days later he followed this with "President's Special War Order No. 1" commanding that the Army of the Potomac, after providing for the defense of Washington, move on February 22 to seize and occupy Manassas Junction, "all details to be in the discretion of the general-in-chief." To this last he added a note to McClellan on February 3 urging his plan for a land attack on the Confederate army near Washington rather than an expedition by water for a peninsular attack on Richmond:

If you will give me satisfactory answers to the following questions, I shall gladly yield my plan to yours. Does not your plan involve a greatly larger expenditure of time, and money than mine? Wherein is a victory more certain by your plan than mine? Wherein is a victory more valuable by your plan than mine? In fact, would it not be less valuable, in this, that it would break no great line of the enemie's communications, while mine would? In case of disaster, would not a retreat be more difficult by your plan than mine?

McClellan replied on the same day with a long letter showing his belief that by rapid enveloping movements on the peninsula near Richmond he could take the Confederate capital. A direct land attack on the Confederate army near Washington he could not approve. But he did have a mental picture of what he was going to do, for, wrote Secretary Chase, he came February 13 and said, "In ten days I shall be in Richmond . . . The ten days passed away; no movement, and no preparation for a movement, had been made."

McClellan gave consent to Lincoln's plucking Fremont from his retirement. There was created the Mountain Department in West Virginia, where Fremont took command of 25,000 men, later reinforced by 10,000. He was to follow a pet plan of Lincoln's, which he approved. The idea was to march over the

Simon Cameron, U.S. Secretary of War, 1861-1862.

mountains into East Tennessee, lend strength to the Unionist sentiment which dominated there, and seize the railroad at Knoxville. McClellan had no objections. And for the time being Lincoln had found a niche for the political and military figure about whom there clung such an aura of romance that thousands of boy babies in antislavery families were named Fremont.

To a resolution directing that the Secretary of War furnish the Senate with information as to contracts, amounts, names of contractors, dates, payments of money, Cameron made no reply. Months passed and Cameron sent neither information nor excuses nor regrets nor acknowledgments to the Senate.

Part of the clamor that arose was political and aimed at smearing the administration. Part of it traced to the jealousy of contractors and special interests not in favor with Cameron. Of this Lincoln was keenly aware. A delegation of New York and Boston bankers called on him and urged the removal of Cameron.

Slowly the President had arrived at. his appraisal, given to Nicolay, that Cameron was utterly ignorant and, regardless of the course of things, obnoxious to the country, selfish, incapable of organizing details, and—least of all—"openly discourteous to the President."

The first open break between Lincoln and Cameron came in December '61 when the Secretary issued his annual report. Without having consulted the Executive, Cameron was thrusting himself forward as a spokesman of administration policy. The slave property of rebels should be confiscated, declared the paragraph that surprised and offended the President: "It is as clearly a right of the Government to arm slaves, when it may become necessary, as it is to use gunpowder taken from the enemy. Whether it is expedient to do so is purely a military question . . . If it shall be found that the men who have been held by the rebels are capable of bearing arms and performing efficient military service, it is the right, and may become the duty of the Government to arm and equip them, and employ their services against the rebels."

As Lincoln first glanced at the copy from the public printer placed in his hands, and his eye rested on the passage about arming the slaves, he was instantly aroused. And as the incident later

Edwin Stanton, U.S. Secretary of War, 1862-1868.

came to the painter Carpenter, Lincoln spoke decisively: "This will never do! General Cameron must take no such responsibility. That is a question which belongs exclusively to me!" Telegrams went to the postmasters of the leading cities. The Cameron report was mailed back to Washington. A new edition was printed with the closing paragraph of the first edition omitted and a new paragraph substituted.

Both Lincoln and Cameron knew they had come to the parting of the ways. Cameron began to hint that his War Department duties wearied him and he would prefer a foreign mission. Lincoln said nothing for several weeks. Then a note of January 11, 1862, written by Lincoln to Cameron was made public: "As you have, more than once, expressed a desire for a change of position, I can now gratify you, consistently with my view of the public interest. I therefore propose nominating you to the Senate, next Monday, as minister to Russia." Four days the Senate wrestled behind closed doors on the President's naming Cameron Minister to Russia. Cameron was confirmed January 17 by a vote of 28 to 14.

No other member of Lincoln's Cabinet seemed to have the complete approval accorded Edwin McMasters Stanton to replace Cameron. A Jackson Democrat replacing an ousted secessionist in President Buchanan's Cabinet as the Cotton States were seceding, he confidentially advised Seward and other Unionists of what went on in Cabinet meetings.

Stanton, the son of a widowed mother, at 13 years of age took care of her and a family of five. Working his way through Kenyon College, clerking in a bookstore in Columbus, Ohio, he met Mary Lamson, daughter of an Episcopal clergyman, carefully educated and, like himself, poor. They took their honeymoon in a 125-mile sleigh ride from Columbus to Cadiz, Ohio, where he began law practice, made money from the start, was known as stiff and proud rather than sociable, on occasion designated as "cheeky."

When his child Lucy died, after her body had been buried a year he had it exhumed, cremated, and placed the ashes in a metal box which he kept in his own room.

The wife of his youth died in childbirth in 1844 and Stanton insisted she must wear her wedding clothes for burial. For years he went twice a week to decorate her grave, on Sundays always going alone, "to meet her," he said. Twelve years passed before he married the daughter of a wealthy merchant in Pittsburgh.

At the War Department, at ten o'clock in the morning a room 15 by 20 feet began to fill up with claim agents, contractors, relatives of soldiers, Senators and Congressmen, all unable to get a private interview with the department head. At 11 there was a buzz and a stir and Stanton walked in, speaking to no one till he reached a high desk opposite the entrance. Then he picked out one by one those he would do business with.

Every day Stanton had his errands at the White House. At any hour he might be seen walking from the War Office taking telegrams, letters, official business, to the President. And Lincoln stepped over to the War Office nearly every day, sometimes during large troop movements or battles spending hours with his War Secretary over the latest wire news. The President gave wide and free play to Stanton's capacity for hard work and Stanton's enjoyment of personal power. In office less than two weeks, Stanton ordered the arrest of General Charles P. Stone in the Ball's Bluff disaster.

On Stanton's announcing to him the news of the arrest, the President said, "I suppose you have good reasons for it; and having good reasons, I am glad I knew nothing of it until it was done." Willie Lincoln lay sick with fever, and later in connection with the Stone affair the President wrote, "Owing to sickness in my family, the Secretary of War made the arrest without notifying me that he had it in contemplation." And Stone was held in Fort Lafayette prison 189 days, released without trial and without charges having been preferred against him, then again restored to his brigadier shoulder straps.

Yet the unremitting quest of individual profits and personal fortunes, behind war fronts where men were dying for proclaimed sacred causes, made a contrast heavy for the human mind to hold and endure.

CHAPTER 24

DONELSON—GRANT—SHILOH—
MONITOR AND *MERRIMAC*—
"SEVEN DAYS"—THE DRAFT

Donelson—Grant—Shiloh—*Monitor* and *Merrimac*—"Seven Days"—The Draft

LINCOLN called to Washington James B. Eads, a St. Louis man who had spent many days on the bottom sand and mud of the Mississippi River, salvaging ships with a diving bell he invented. Eads, back in St. Louis and under Government contract, got 4,000 men over the country working on his plans. In 100 days he had ready eight iron-plated, steam-propelled gunboats. These and more made up a flotilla commanded by Andrew H. Foote, a Connecticut Yankee Puritan sea dog, who in 1856 had lost 40 of his own men and killed 400 Chinese in the Canton River of China, who never swore nor drank nor allowed intoxicating liquor on shipboard; his prayer meetings and sermons among seamen were a topic in naval and other circles.

On February 6, 1862, Commodore Foote's gunboats escorted steamboats up the Tennessee River carrying 18 regiments under Brigadier General Ulysses S. Grant. They crowded the decks watching the scenery, 18,000 troops—cornhuskers, teamsters, rail splitters, shopmen, factory hands, college students, from Iowa, Nebraska, Illinois, Indiana, Ohio, Missouri, many of them not yet old enough to vote.

The gunboats stopped at Fort Henry, shelled it, and troops marched in and took its flag. The Confederate garrison had left for Fort Donelson on the Cumberland River. Grant marched his army 12 miles across country to Fort Donelson in fair weather, warm and balmy.

Foote took his gunboats down to the Ohio River, up the Cumberland, and exchanging shots with the Fort Donelson guns was disabled so that he had to steam downriver. This left Grant with 27,000 troops, counting new arrivals, to contest with 18,000 troops inside a fort. Before the fighting began a cold wind came, snow fell, the roads froze. In ten-above-zero weather men fired and loaded their muskets, and in the night huddled and shivered, seeking fences, brush, trees, logs, to keep off the wind. Neither side dared light a bivouac fire. Men and boys were found next morning frozen stiff.

On Sunday, February 16, telegrams began trickling into the War Department in Washington. General Simon B. Buckner, commanding Fort Donelson, had sent a messenger to Grant asking for "terms of capitulation" and Grant replied: "No terms except an unconditional and immediate surrender can be accepted. I propose to move immediately upon your works." And the Confederate commander was surrendering the fort and 13,828 prisoners. The battle losses were: Union, 500 killed, 2,108 wounded, 224 missing; Confederate, 231 killed, 1,534 wounded. The victory clinched Kentucky to the Union, gave a foothold in Tennessee, sent Union armies 200 miles forward into enemy territory. It lighted up the gloom of the North and the hopes of Lincoln.

Ulysses S. Grant, an Ohio boy, graduated at West Point as number 21 in a class of 39. At West Point he rode a horse over a hurdle six feet six, a new record. At Monterey in the Mexican War he went for ammunition relief, riding under fire in Comanche style, clinging to the saddle with one leg while holding his head and body close to the side of the horse away from the enemy. He was five feet eight in height, wore a full beard, was nearly always a little disheveled, even sat for his picture with coat or hair in disorder. He had quiet manners, gravity, gray eyes, and a face with economy of expression.

Grant had cleared land on 80 acres near St. Louis left to him by his wife's father. He became accustomed to two slaves given to his wife by her father, a slaveholder. He hauled wood ten miles into St. Louis at $10 a cord. He built himself a two-story house of logs, a masterpiece of simple design and craftsmanship, and named the place Hardscrabble. They traded Hardscrabble for a house and lot in St. Louis. As a real-estate salesman Grant failed. Friends said ague and rheumatism still held him; chills shook him on spring afternoons, weakened him so that he was dizzy and had to be helped to the omnibus he rode home in. He looked glum and felt useless. The family moved to Galena, Illinois, where he was selling hides to shoemakers and harness- and saddle-makers, his income $800 a year,

Portrait of Maj. General Ulysses S. Grant. Photo by Mathew Brady.

Confederate General Joseph E. Johnston.

General Ulysses S. Grant leading a charge at the Battle of Pittsburgh, Tenn. Engraved by Currier & Ives.

Battle of Shiloh, April 6-7, 1862, Tenn., Gen. Grant faced Generals Albert Johnston and P.G.T. Beauregard. Engraved by Thure de Thulstrup.

when the war commenced. He went to Springfield, Illinois, was made colonel, and took a regiment to Missouri.

The country had now nicknamed him "Unconditional Surrender" Grant. Against intrigue, connivance and slander, Lincoln gave to Grant the stars of a major general. The President was more than interested in this plain fighter who had given the Union cause its first victories worth mentioning. Lincoln saw among the driving motives in the Fort Donelson victory the passion of the Northwest, his own region, for nationalism, for an unbreakable Union of States.

The laughter at McClellan now was wry, bitter. The Western forces had battled and won big points sooner than commanded in Lincoln's order setting February 22 as the day for a general movement of land and sea forces. Washington's Birthday came while McClellan's colossal Army of the Potomac kept to its tents and winter huts around Washington. Johnston nearby at Manassas had in his Confederate army less than one man for McClellan's three.

Lincoln now stepped publicly into the handling of the Army of the Potomac, to the extent of publishing on March 7 and 8 his General War Orders No. 2 and No. 3. One directed McClellan to organize his army for active field operations into four corps, Lincoln naming the generals to command. The second ordered that whatever the field operations might take, enough troops should be left in and about Washington to leave the capital secure. This and other matters brought McClellan to the White House.

On Sunday, March 9, while McClellan sat in conference with Lincoln and Stanton, a message came with news that Johnston's army at Manassas had moved out of its entrenchments, broken from winter quarters, and moved southward, leaving as mementoes many "Quaker guns"—logs on wheels, painted to look like cannon.

McClellan, shocked into action, that very Sunday ordered his army to march. At three the next morning he telegraphed Stanton, "The troops are in motion." He arrived at Bull Run Creek, at Manassas, and found it as reported—empty. Then he marched his army back again to Washington. To those asking why he did not push on, find the enemy and attack, he let it be known he was giving his troops a practice maneuver.

Eight days later Browning wrote of seeing the President and "He told me he was becoming impatient and dissatisfied with McClellan's sluggishness of action."

Lincoln had ordered McDowell with 40,000 troops to stay in and near Washington. The capture of the national capital would probably bring Britain and France to recognize the Confederate Government, the blockade would be broken, arms and supplies would pour into the South. Lincoln wrote McClellan: "My explicit order that Washington should, by the judgment of *all* the commanders of Army corps, be left entirely secure, had been neglected. It was precisely this that drove me to detain McDowell."

Then came bickering. McClellan was to claim he must have more troops. He wrote his wife of "rascality" and "traitors" in Washington.

Other actions were staged elsewhere and with different results. Three days' fighting went on at Pea Ridge in the northwest corner of Arkansas between Missouri, Iowa, Illinois and Ohio regiments against Missouri, Arkansas and Texas regiments along with three Red Indian regiments. The Union forces lost 203 killed, 972 wounded, 174 missing, as against 800 to 1,000 killed, 200 to 300 missing, of the Confederates. The battle clinched Missouri deeper into the Union.

An action came as "a thrust into the vitals of the Confederacy." The sea dogs Commodore David Glasgow Farragut and Commodore David Dixon Porter, with battleships and mortar boats, along with Major General Ben Butler heading an army of land troops, ran and battered their way through the forts and batteries at New Orleans and captured the largest seaport and the most important metropolitan center of the South, a city of 168,000. An army of 10,000 Confederates left the city, their torches lighting 15,000 bales of cotton, a dozen large ships, several fine steamboats, unfinished gunboats and property worth millions of dollars.

On the Tennessee River near the Mississippi State line at Shiloh Church and Pittsburg Landing, General Albert Sidney Johnston had hurled 40,000 Confederate troops in attack on 36,000 under Grant. The Union lines were steadily forced back. Would night find them driven to the bank of the wide Tennessee River and no bridge to cross? Sherman had three horses shot under him, got a bullet in the hand, another through his hat; a third grazed his shoulder. Toward evening Grant sat his horse, watching the Confederates try to take a hill guarded by a battery and Union gunboats. Someone asked him if things looked gloomy. He answered: "Delay counts for everything with us. Tomorrow we shall attack them with fresh troops, and drive them, of course."

Darkness fell on the Sabbath slaughter. Rain came in torrents on the tentless soldiers of the two armies. In the gray of dawn the Union troops moved in attack and that day, reinforced by 20,000 under Buell and 6,000 under Lew Wallace, drove the enemy to retreat. Albert Sidney Johnston, counted one of the most brilliant of Confederate commanders, was killed the day before, it was learned. The Union army lost 13,047 in killed, wounded and missing, the Confederates 10,694.

The President issued a proclamation: "It has pleased Almighty God to vouchsafe signal victories to the land and naval forces engaged in suppressing an internal rebellion, and at the same time to avert from our country the dangers of foreign intervention and invasion." He recommended to the people that "at their next weekly assemblages in their accustomed places of public worship" they should "especially acknowledge and render thanks to our Heavenly Father for these inestimable blessings." He spoke of hope for peace, harmony and unity in his own country, and beyond that "the establishment of fraternal relations among all the countries of the earth."

In Richmond on February 22, 1862, Jefferson Davis had taken his inauguration oath for a six-year term of office. Heavy rain fell while President Davis under a canvas cover addressed a big crowd holding umbrellas: "After a series of successes and victories… we have recently met with serious disasters." He was referring to Fort Donelson. Pale, worn, resolved, and around him men also resolved, they would consecrate their toil, property, lives, to a nation of their own. Tears trickled down the faces of gray-headed men of the planter aristocracy. They joined in silence in the prayer of Davis spoken across the rain: "Acknowledging the Providence which has so visibly protected the Confederacy during its brief but eventful career, to Thee, O God! I trustingly commit myself, and prayerfully invoke Thy blessing on my country and its cause."

And in the White House the President was hit hard by a personal grief. The boys Tad and Willie, joined by two playmates from Cincinnati, Bud and Holly Taft, were often a comfort to him. Tad was dashing, valorous, often impudent; Willie more thoughtful and imaginative. All the main railroad stations from New York to Chicago were in Willie's memory and at his tongue's end. He could call them off, including Troy, Schenectady, Utica, Rome, including Ashtabula, Cleveland, Sandusky, Toledo. He spent hours drawing up timetables and would conduct an imaginary train from Chicago to New York with perfect precision. Also Willie spent hours curled up in a chair enjoying books, a grave, delicate boy. In his diary Attorney General Bates wrote that Willie was too much "idolized" by his parents. The boy had rare lights and the father and mother made much of him.

Willie Lincoln went riding on his pony in a chilly rain and fell sick with a cold and fever in February '62, at a time when a White House ball was planned. The President spoke of the ball to Miss Dorothea Dix, wanted to stop it, had it announced officially there would be no dancing. "But the Marine band at the foot of the steps filled the house with music while the boy lay dying above," wrote one woman. "A sadder face than that of the President I have rarely seen. He was receiving at the large door of the East Room, speaking to the people as they came, but feeling so deeply that he spoke of what he felt and thought, instead of welcoming the guests. To General Fremont he at once said that his son was very ill and he feared for the result . . . The ball was becoming a ghastly failure."

A few days later Willie lay still and cold. Elizabeth Keckley, the mulatto seamstress and Mrs. Lincoln's trusted companion, wrote, "The light faded from his eyes, and the death-dew gathered on his brow." She had been on watch but did not see the end, telling of it: "I was worn out with watching, and was not in the room when Willie died, but was immediately sent for. I assisted in washing and dressing him, and then laid him on the bed, when Mr. Lincoln came in." He lifted the cover from the face of his child, gazed at it long, and murmured, "It is hard, hard, hard to have him die!" The mother wept long hours, moaned and shook with grief.

They closed down the lids over the blue eyes of the boy, parted his brown hair, put flowers from his mother in his pale, crossed hands, and soldiers, Senators, Cabinet officers, foreign Ministers, came to the funeral. The mother, too far spent, could not come.

The body was later sent west to Illinois for burial. And the mother clutched at his memory and if his name was mentioned

Fifteen officers on the deck of the Monitor.

her voice shook and the tears came. "She could not bear to look upon his picture," said Mrs. Keckley. "And after his death she never crossed the threshold of the Guest's Room in which he died, or the Green Room in which he was embalmed."

On Sunday, March 9, 1862, news came that sent Secretary Welles hurrying to the President, who at once called the Cabinet. A U.S. 40-gun frigate, the *Merrimac,* had been fitted by the Confederates with a cast-iron ram, and covered with four-inch iron plates. On Saturday afternoon, she had met two Union war vessels, the *Congress* and the *Cumberland,* and shot and rammed their wooden hulls till they were helpless. Another Union war vessel, the *Minnesota,* also wooden, had been run aground. And the news was that the *Merrimac* would on Sunday morning be free to move on Washington or New York.

Welles told of one hope; the *Monitor,* a new type of sea-fighting craft, had arrived at Hampton Roads the night before. When Welles mentioned to Stanton that the *Monitor* carried only two guns, "his mingled look of incredulity and contempt cannot be described," wrote Welles. ". . . To me there was throughout the whole day something inexpressibly ludicrous in the wild, frantic talk, action, and rage of Stanton as he ran from room to room . . . swung his arms, scolded, and raved."

Crypt in Georgetown's Oak Hill Cemetery where Willie Lincoln was buried. Photo by Nancy Lodge.

View from above of Willie Lincoln's burial crypt in Oak Hill Cemetery. Photo by Nancy Lodge.

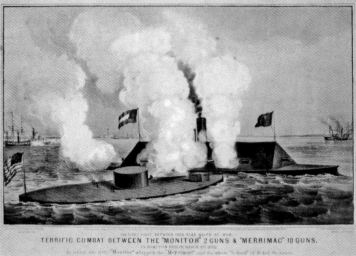

Terrific combat between the Monitor *and the* Merrimac, *March 9, 1862. Engraved by Currier & Ives.*

Towed by a tug out of New York Harbor three days before, the little *Monitor* met rough weather; water broke over the engines, down the blower pipes and smokestacks; hand pumps were rigged and worked. Then the wind and high waves went down, or the *Monitor* would have gone to sea bottom. Once again fighting rough sea in shoals the captain and crew wondered if the hawser running to the tug would hold. It did and they rode out two storms.

They were a tired crew on the *Monitor*, twice nearly sunk, no food but hard sea biscuit on a storm-soaked vessel, and no sleep in 48 hours. Their commander, Lieutenant John Worden, said no captain ever had a better crew; the crew swore their captain was the best that ever walked a deck. As the Confederate *Merrimac* came on toward the *Minnesota* next morning, the little *Monitor* made straight for her, a David against a Goliath, ten guns on the *Merrimac* against two on the *Monitor*. "A cheesebox on a raft," "a tin can on a shingle," that was the *Monitor*, equipped with a revolving steel tower or turret, so that she could shoot from any position; and her raftlike deck was so low that it would be difficult for the big *Merrimac* to ram her.

The tiny *Monitor* moved around the giant *Merrimac* like a fast bantamweight circling a ponderous heavyweight. The big one crashed its ten guns against the little one. And the little one did not move except to answer with its two guns. A deep thrill went round the hearts of the men handling the guns in the *Monitor* turret when the first heavy slugs of the *Merrimac* thundered their impact on the outside of the turret. Sometimes it was hard to start the turret revolving. They hoped it would not snarl. "Once the *Merrimac* tried to ram us," wrote S. Dana Greene, lieutenant commander, "but Worden avoided the direct impact by skillful use of the helm, and she struck a glancing blow which did no damage."

At ten yards' distance a shell from the *Merrimac* hit the sight-hole of the pilothouse, stunning Lieutenant Worden, filling his eyes with powder and blinding him, his face covered with blood. The *Monitor* drew off to care for its commander and to examine how badly the pilothouse was wrecked. The *Merrimac* drew off and steamed to Norfolk.

After six hours it was a drawn battle. Each side had made its mistakes. If the *Merrimac* had concentrated its entire fire on the *Monitor* pilothouse from the first, it would have destroyed the *Monitor*'s control. If the *Monitor* had shot at the *Merrimac*'s water line, where the armor was weak, it would have sunk the *Merrimac*. However, the two ships had taught the navies of the world a lesson. London and Paris declared that the era of wooden fighting craft was over. The Washington Government would now begin building a fleet of monitors. The blockade of Southern ports would go on.

News of the battle came with pleasure to John Ericsson, the Swede who designed the *Monitor*. He grew up among mines and

Battle between the Monitor *and the* Merrimac, *March 9, 1862.*

ironworks in Sweden, became a captain in the Army, resigned, invented an instrument for taking sea soundings, a hydrostatic weighing machine, artificial drafts that decreased smokestack size and economized fuel, a self-acting gunlock for naval cannon, a steam carriage in 1829 which ran 30 miles an hour. He came to the United States in 1839, and two years later furnished designs for a screw warship, "the first vessel having propelling machinery below water-line, out of reach of hostile shot." This granitic man of quiet pride had written to the President in August '61 that "steel-clad vessels cannot be arrested in their course by land batteries." He was 58 when in '61 he laid his plans before a naval board of three commodores.

Finally they gave Ericsson a contract with a clause saying that if the *Monitor* did not prove "invulnerable" he was to refund all Government money paid him.

Croakings were in his ears as he went to New York, drew his final plans, and saw the ship built in exactly 100 days. When she went into action the final Government payment on her had not been made. Now he could read a letter from the chief engineer of the *Monitor* saying: "Thousands have this day blessed you. I have heard whole crews cheer you."

On the day after the *Merrimac-Monitor* battle Lincoln wrote advising Welles the *Monitor* could be easily boarded and captured, her turret wedged, her machinery drowned by pouring water. He passed on the advice from Lieutenant Worden that "she should not go sky-larking up to Norfolk."

A naval lieutenant arrived at a Cabinet meeting to tell the President the wounded Worden was at his house. The President dismissed the Cabinet. Ushering Lincoln into an upstairs room at his house, the naval lieutenant said, "Jack, here is the President come to see you." The President stood gazing down on Worden in bed, the scorched eyes closed, the torn face bandaged. "You do me great honor," murmured Worden. No answer came. The lieutenant turned to see Lincoln in tears with nothing to say for the moment. When he did find words he said: "It is not so. It is you who honor me and your country, and I will promote you." And he made Worden a captain that very day.

Six regiments were put on shore, marched to Norfolk, found it evacuated by the Confederates, with smoking ruins of large stores of military supplies. The mayor of Norfolk formally surrendered the city to General Wool. The President had been "greatly alarmed for our safety" by the report of General Mansfield, wrote Chase, "and you can imagine his delight when we told him Norfolk was ours. Mr. Stanton came into the President's room and was equally delighted. He fairly hugged General Wool."

The President, with Stanton and Chase, next day rode through the streets of captured Norfolk and gazed on the ruined hulk of the *Merrimac*, which the Confederates had blown up rather than risk another fight with the *Monitor*, Then the party sailed back to Washington on the steamer *Baltimore*, Chase writing to his daughter Janet: "So ended a brilliant week's campaign by the President; for I think it quite certain that if he had not gone down, Norfolk would still have been in the possession of the enemy . . . The whole coast is now virtually ours."

McClellan's army after nine months of organization, practice, drill, first went under fire in April '62, fought a rear-guard action at Williamsburg, and moved to White House Landing, 20 miles from Richmond. Meanwhile McClellan renewed his calls on the War Department and the President for more men and guns. Also he continued, with some of his generals, an undiminished political activity.

The wounded Confederate commander Joseph E. Johnston was replaced by Robert E. Lee. Lee sent Stonewall Jackson to the Shenandoah Valley. Jackson with 17,000 men swept the valley region and in 14 days marched his army 170 miles, routed 12,500 Union troops, captured $250,000 worth of supplies and property, took 3,000 prisoners and 9,000 rifles, a raid which threatened Washington so seriously that Lincoln called off McDowell from co-operation with McClellan.

The enemy struck at his White House Landing base of supplies, where food, guns, powder, wagons, mules, arrived from Washington, and what came to be known as the Seven Days' battles were on. McClellan ordered a change of base to Harrison's Landing on the James River. On McClellan's retreat Lee put in every last man and gun he had and tried to crumple up McClellan and capture his army. In the finish, and after bloody fighting, McClellan still held Harrison's Landing and had lost only 16,000 men as against 20,000 Confederate losses.

A complex and weary McClellan, after the first of the Seven Days' battles, telegraphed to Secretary Stanton: "I have seen too many dead and wounded comrades to feel otherwise than that the government has not sustained this army. If you do not do so now the game is lost." Then McClellan used accusing words: "If I save this army now, I tell you plainly that I owe no thanks to you or any person in Washington. You have done your best to sacrifice this army." Of these words, McClellan wrote his wife: "Of course they will never forgive me for that. I knew it when I wrote it."

But Lincoln and Stanton did not see the final accusing words of the telegram till much later. For Colonel E. S. Sanford, supervisor and censor of telegraphic messages, found these words to be outrageous, infamous, treasonable, designed by McClellan "to

reach the public as a means of shifting the cause of defeat from his own to other shoulders." And Colonel Sanford took on himself the duty of cutting from the telegram what he regarded as treason. Lincoln replied to the mutilated telegram: "Save your Army at all events. Will send re-inforcements as fast as we can."

At Malvern Hill a Confederate colonel had shouted: "Come on, come on, my men! Do you want to live forever?" For all his losses of men and material McClellan had won a victory. His cannon mounted tier on tier at Malvern Hill had mowed down the repeated lines of Confederates ordered up by Lee. Moving from Yorktown toward Richmond, McClellan had killed more of the enemy forces than they had of his. And now, having broken the fiercest blow the enemy could bring against him, he shrank under the protection of his gunboats at Harrison's Landing. The collapse of this campaign staggered Lincoln, who remarked of it later, "I was as nearly inconsolable as I could be and live."

With Stanton, Lincoln started for Harrison's Landing, spent a day there, talked with McClellan, quizzed his generals, and found McClellan had 86,500 troops present for duty, 34,000 absent by authority, 3,700 absent without authority, his command including more than 120,000.

The habit of blaming others for mistakes, accidents, fate, had grown on McClellan. He wrote to his wife, "I am tired of serving fools. God help my country!" He saw "incompetents" in Washington doing "injustice" to him. This, that, was "infamous."

Lincoln had called General Halleck from the West to serve as General in Chief of all land forces. Halleck was to puzzle Lincoln. Forty-seven years old, New York born, a West Pointer, an engineer with artillery in the Mexican War, he had written a book, *Elements of Military Art and Science*. When the war opened he was head of the leading law firm of San Francisco and major general of the state militia. After Shiloh he took the field, replacing Grant, moved slowly onward with pick and shovel, entrenching, making sure that his 100,000 would bag the enemy 50,000. After six weeks he had arrived at Corinth when the enemy had slipped out and was 50 miles away again. He reported this to Washington as a victory.

Halleck was asking McClellan's generals whether they ought to stay before Richmond on the peninsula. Some said No, some Yes.

The Army of the Potomac, its sick and wounded, its cannon and horses, its farm hands, shopmen, college boys, store clerks, was brought back from the peninsula to old places on the Potomac River within sight of the Capitol. And McClellan was relieved of command in the field and told to report for orders at Alexandria.

On August 4, 1862, Lincoln issued a second call for 300,000 troops. This meant conscription by the states, "the draft." Sheriffs and commissioners took lists of all men between 18 and 45 in counties and cities. Names written on folded ballots were shaken in a revolving wheel or drum-shaped box. A blindfolded man drew the names of those who were to go to war for nine months, or inside of five days pay a substitute to go.

Men who did not want to go to war, by thousands, filed exemption claims—they were physically unfit to go; they were citizens of other countries; they held to a religious belief that war was a sin. In ten days, 14,000 claims were filed in New York City. Thousands were crossing into Canada or buying steamship tickets for Europe. One steamer was overhauled at sea and all men passengers were taken back to New York.

Resistance and evasion of the attempts of the state governments to draft soldiers spread so far that the President issued a proclamation that "all persons discouraging volunteer enlistments, resisting militia drafts, or guilty of any disloyal practice, affording aid and comfort to Rebels against the authority of the United States" would come under martial law—and the writ of habeas corpus would be useless in any jail where they were held.

Some decisions came easy, such as signing the Pacific Railway Bill July 1, 1862. Rails were to be laid from the western Iowa line to San Francisco Bay. The Union Pacific and the Central Pacific corporations were to build the road, getting ten sections of land per mile alongside the right of way, with graduated Government loans on a per-mile basis—$16,000 for level work, $32,000 for desert work (the Great Basin), and $48,000 for mountain work. As the bill stood now, it was under "military necessity" an offer to railroad financiers to push through a job that would tie the two coasts closer.

He signed the Homestead Bill May 20, 1862, giving a farm free to any man who wanted to put a plow to unbroken sod. Immense tracts of land were thrown open in the Western Territories. Anyone a citizen of the United States or taking out first papers declaring intention of citizenship, paying a registration fee of $10 and staying on the same piece of ground five years, could have title papers making him the owner of 160 acres. Tens of thousands of Britons, Irish, Germans, Scandinavians came, many exclaiming, "What a good new country where they give away farms!" As a war measure touching enlarged food supply, and as an act fulfilling a Republican party pledge, Lincoln found it easy to sign the bill.

CHAPTER 25

SECOND BULL RUN—
BLOODY ANTIETAM—CHAOS

Lincoln at Antietam (detail). Photo by Alexander Gardner.

SECOND BULL RUN—BLOODY ANTIETAM—CHAOS

Confederate General Jonathan Thomas "Stonewall" Jackson.

DURING that desperate, hammering summer of '62 Lincoln revolved often in his mind the curious failure of his 200,000 men in Virginia against half that number. Would he have to try one general, another and still another, and for how long?

Robert Edward Lee, 55 years old, had become the most portentous personality with whom Lincoln would have to contend in the months ahead. Lee had two rare gifts, patience with men and readiness with unforeseen circumstance. His training in

handling and understanding men had been long, hard, varied and thorough. The smooth reciprocal functioning of Lee with Davis was almost startling in contrast to Lincoln and McClellan. Militarily Lee and Davis were one head of the Army of Northern Virginia. Where Davis would often fail to read the enemy mind Lee supplied the deficiency. Neither jealousy, envy, nor ambition, in any ordinary sense, gnawed at the heart of Lee.

In Alexandria he read of Virginia's secession. He sent Secretary Cameron his resignation and wrote to Scott: "I shall carry to the grave the most grateful recollections of your kind consideration, and your name and fame will always be dear to me . . . Save in defence of my native State, I never desire to again draw my sword." He had written a son, "While I wish to do what is right, I am unwilling to do what is wrong, either at the bidding of the South or the North." Of his hope for preservation of the Union he wrote, "I will cling to it to the last." He felt and resented "the aggressions of the North," though "I am not pleased with the course of the 'Cotton States.'"

When offered high command of the Union armies, Lee had said, according to Old Man Blair, "If I owned the four million slaves of the South I would sacrifice them all to the Union," and then asked a question that Blair couldn't answer: "But how can I draw my sword against Virginia?" The very asking of the question included its answer.

Suddenly, when General Joseph Johnston was wounded, Lee had been sent forward to take in hand four different armies, weld them into a unit for action. In a four months' campaign, at times outnumbered two to one, he had stopped McClellan and earned a name as the savior of Richmond and the Confederacy. To a doubting inquirer one of Lee's generals had said his first name was "Audacity," that he would tower head and shoulders above all others in audacity. In a conference with generals just before the Seven Days' battles, one of them, busy with pencil and paper, was showing that McClellan with superior forces could sweep on to Richmond. "Stop, stop!" said Lee. "If you go to ciphering we are whipped beforehand."

Lee knew better than McClellan that war is a conflict of wills, and had imposed his will on McClellan to the extent that McClellan believed he was a loser when he was not, which was why he did not try to push through and take Richmond after Malvern Hill.

Lee's right-hand man Thomas Jonathan Jackson also was born for war. His valley campaign up and down the Shenandoah, in which he captured half of one Union army, beat off three other armies with which Lincoln was trying to trap him, and slipped through for a rapid march to join Lee, had become a shining chronicle of the Confederacy.

Lincoln from the White House undertook to direct continuously from day to day the field movements of several armies. Why Lincoln at such a distance should have undertaken what he did

was not clear. Lincoln, advising with McDowell about starting to destroy Jackson, heard McDowell say he could begin marching the next Sunday but he had been excoriated all over the country for fighting Bull Run on a Sabbath. An orphan boy who managed to get into West Point, Jackson had graduated far below the class leader, George B. McClellan. His Mexican War record bright, he became professor of natural philosophy and artillery tactics in the Virginia Military Institute. Tall, rawboned, with big hands and a peculiar stride, he would walk alone, raise his right hand high over his head and let it down.

He joined the Presbyterian church in Lexington, became a deacon, conducted a Sunday school for Negroes. He married Eleanor Junkin and a year later saw her and a newborn child to their double grave. Four years afterward he married Mary Anna Morrison, and their household ran like clockwork in its daily program. Of all Southern commanders who had the ear of Lee and of Davis none was more fiercely in favor of defending by taking the offensive, of striking deep into Northern territory. Of his chief he said: "Lee is a phenomenon. He is the only man I would follow blindfold."

A new combination named the Army of Virginia, formed by the three commands of McDowell, Banks and Fremont, was headed by General John Pope. Frémont, however, decided to resign rather than serve under Pope. The new commander was a dashing horseman, his valor in battle impetuous and undisputed. He had been one of Lincoln's military escort en route to inauguration. Kentucky-born, a graduate of Transylvania University, his father a judge whom Lincoln had met in Illinois, a West Pointer, a Mexican War officer promoted for gallantry on the field, an engineer, surveyor, explorer, an 1860 Republican, John Pope had been continuously an army man, soldiering his lifework. His victories had brought in 1,300 prisoners at Blackwater, Missouri, and some 6,000 at Island No. 10 on the Mississippi. He wrote letters from "Headquarters in the Saddle," issued an address to his new command: "I have come to you from the West, where we have always seen the back of our enemies." His overconfidence ran into bombast. For Pope was facing two great proved fighters, two strange captains of men, Lee and Jackson.

John Hay wrote in his diary of a horseback ride from Soldiers' Home to the White House with Lincoln, and of matters that

Lincoln and General McClellan meet at Antietam.
Photo by Alexander Gardner, 1862.

Group of soldiers by tent. Photo by O. Pierre Havens.

made public would have further torn the country: "We talked about Bull Run and Pope's prospect. The President was very outspoken in regard to McClellan's present conduct. He said that it really seemed to him McC. wanted Pope defeated. The President seemed to think him a little crazy. Envy, jealousy and spite are probably a better explanation of his present conduct. He is constantly sending despatches to the President and Halleck asking what is his real position and command. He acts as chief alarmist and grand marplot of the Army . . ."

Everything seemed to be going well on Saturday, August 30, as Lincoln and Hay saw it. "We went to bed expecting glad tidings at sunrise. But about eight o'clock the President came to my room as I was dressing and, calling me out, said 'Well, John, we are whipped again, I am afraid. The enemy reinforced on Pope and drove back his left wing and he has retired to Centreville where he says he will be able to hold his men. I don't like that expression. I don't like to hear him admit his men need holding.'"

On Sunday things began to look better. "The President was in a singularly defiant tone of mind. He often repeated, 'We must hurt this enemy before it gets away.'"On Monday when Hay spoke of the bad look of events, the President said: "No, Mr. Hay, we must whip these people now. Pope must fight them.

What with jealousy, spite, bickering, officialism, politics, pride, sloth, ignorance, large bodies of troops stayed quiet in scattered positions while Pope farther off was outguessed, flanked, surprised, hacked and harassed, and driven off from Bull Run Creek with slaughter. In combat and retreat he lost 14,000 out of 80,000; Lee lost 9,000 out of 54,000.

Stormy tides rocked Washington as the broken pieces of a defeated army straggled in. Outbound railroad trains were packed; thousands fled the national capital. The Federal Treasury building was barricaded with hundreds of barrels of cement. By order of the President clerks in the civil departments enrolled and began military drill. Stanton had important papers gathered into bundles to be carried away on horseback, if necessary.

Three thousand convalescent soldiers were moved from Washington to Philadelphia to make room for serious cases from Bull Run. Floors in the Capitol, in the Patent Office building, were cleared for torn and mutilated men.

Pope was relieved of command and assigned to the Northwest to curb Indian tribes. Welles noted that the President "spoke favorably" of Pope and clearly believed he had not had a fair chance. "Pope," said the President, "did well, but there was an army prejudice against him, and it was necessary he should leave.

Lincoln and officers meet at Antietam.
Photo by Alexander Gardner, 1862.

President Lincoln on Battlefield of Antietam.
Photo by Alexander Gardner.

Stanton, Chase, Bates and Smith of the Cabinet had signed a paper in Stanton's handwriting, a remonstrance to be handed the President against McClellan's being once more entrusted with command of the army. Chase argued with Welles to sign. Welles held off, saying that while he wished to get rid of McClellan, it was not exactly fair to the President to be circulating such a paper behind his back. Then this paper disappeared, and Chase came to Welles with a second one, in the handwriting of Bates and with the same four signers as before. Welles said this second one was more reasonable in tone, but he told Chase he could not join with them. At one Cabinet meeting Lincoln had all his counselors but one against him.

Before one Cabinet meeting Lincoln had gone with Halleck to McClellan and given him command of the Army again. But the actual words by which authority was once more handed over to him were not spoken by Lincoln. It was left to Halleck, Lincoln explaining to Welles, "I could not have done it, for I can never feel confident that he will do anything effectual."

McClellan wrote his wife: "I was surprised this morning, when at breakfast, by a visit from the President and Halleck, in which the former expressed the opinion that the troubles now impending could be overcome better by me than anyone else. Pope is ordered to fall back on Washington, and, as he reenters, everything is to come under my command again!"

Lincoln had, however, offered command in the field to Burnside, who would not take it, saying to the President, "I do not think that there is anyone who can do as much with that army as McClellan." Also, Lincoln had consented to the dismissal of three major generals, Porter, Franklin and Griffin, who were to have a court-martial on their conduct in the field. And with a heavy heart Lincoln agreed there should be a court of inquiry for McDowell.

"The President," said Chase, ". . . told me that the clamor against McDowell was so great that he [McDowell] could not lead his troops unless something was done to restore confidence; and proposed to me to suggest to him the asking for a Court of Inquiry." Both Chase and Stanton, along with Lincoln, had long ago become convinced that McDowell was a firstrate, loyal officer, never sulking nor talking loose nor taking a hand in military politics. McDowell went away "very sad," on a 15-day leave of absence, to return for the trial he asked.

The yellow corn stood ripe in the fields of Maryland. Lee and Jackson knew that corn could help feed their armies. They marched gray and butternut regiments across the Potomac, ragged and footsore men who could fight, as the world knew.

McClellan with an army marched toward Lee. He was feeling better. His three dismissed major generals had been cleared without court-martial and restored to him by the President. McClellan wrote his wife, "The feeling of the government towards me, I am sure, is kind and trusting." Not in a year had he sent his wife any such pleasant words about the Government. His friend, Lincoln, against a majority of the Cabinet, had again put him at the head of a great army in the field.

Telegrams tumbled into the White House telling of Bragg's Confederate army in Kentucky slipping past Buell's army, which had been set to watch him. Bragg was marching north toward Cincinnati and Louisville, both cities anxious. Also Kirby Smith's men in gray had marched into Kentucky, chased the state legislature out of Frankfort, and captured Lexington, the home town of Mary Todd Lincoln.

"Where is General Bragg?" Lincoln queried in telegrams to several generals in the field. He wired Buell and others, "What degree of certainty have you, that Bragg, with his command, is not now in the valley of the Shenandoah, Virginia?" He wired McClellan, who was calling for reinforcements, that he could have 21,000 under Porter and "I am sending you all that can be spared."

Stonewall Jackson smashed at the Union garrison in Harpers Ferry, trapped them, and took 11,000 prisoners. Four days later, September 17, McClellan's 90,000 troops met Lee's army, about half that of McClellan in troop numbers, at Antietam Creek. Around a cornfield and a little white Dunker church, around a stone bridge, and in a pasture lane worn by cowpaths, surged a human tornado. General Joseph Hooker rode in the worst of the

Confederate Brigadier Gen. James Longstreet fought at Battles of Bull Run.

storm, and said of it, "Every stalk of corn in the northern and greater part of the field was cut as closely as could have been done with a knife, and the slain lay in rows precisely as they had stood in their ranks a few moments before." Hooker fell from his saddle with a bleeding foot. An old man with his white hair in the wind, Major General J. K. F. Mansfield, fell dead from his saddle. General Sedgwick was three times wounded, in shoulder, leg, wrist. Four other Union generals fell off their horses with wounds. On the Confederate side, Colonel B. B. Gayle of Alabama was surrounded, drew his revolver, called to his men, "We are flanked, boys, but let's die in our tracks," and fell riddled with bullets. "Don't let your horses tread on me," a wounded man called from a huddle of corpses where officers were picking their way through.

On a golden autumn Sabbath morning three-mile lines of men had faced each other with guns. And when the shooting was over the losses were put at 12,000 on each side. Lee crossed the Potomac, back into the South again. But McClellan did not follow though his chances of wiping out Lee's army were estimated by Longstreet: "We were so badly crushed that at the close of the day ten thousand fresh troops could have come in and taken Lee's army and everything it had. But McClellan did not know it." He had two soldiers to the enemy's one, completely superior cannon, rifles, supplies. He had 93,000 men answering roll call as Lee was fading down the Shenandoah Valley with less than 40,000.

Lincoln, according to Kelley, was slow and deliberate as he said: "I am now stronger with the Army of the Potomac than McClellan. The supremacy of the civil power has been restored, and the Executive is again master of the situation. The troops know, that if I made a mistake in substituting Pope for McClellan, I was capable of rectifying it by again trusting him."

CHAPTER 26

THE INVOLVED SLAVERY ISSUE—
PRELIMINARY EMANCIPATION
PROCLAMATION

THE INVOLVED SLAVERY ISSUE—PRELIMINARY EMANCIPATION PROCLAMATION

SOME OF THE more isionary crusaders believed that with the slaveholders crushed, then would rise a nation of men and women all free, all Christian, "ultimately redeemed." First, however, must be the tragedy of sacrifice and vengeance. Touched with sorrow yet awful with warning, was Julia Ward Howe's "Battle Hymn of the Republic":

Mine eyes have seen the glory of the coming of the Lord;
He is trampling out the vintage where the grapes of wrath are stored;
He hath loosed the fateful lightning of His terrible swift sword;
His truth is marching on.

Published in February '62 her verses had now gone to singing millions.

Denunciation poured from abolitionists when the President dealt with a military order issued by his good friend Major General David Hunter, commanding at Port Royal, South Carolina. The General confiscated slaves and declared them free. Also, reasoning that martial law and slavery could not go together, the General declared all slaves in Georgia, Florida and South Carolina "forever free." Chase urged that these orders should stand, that nine-tenths of the country was for them.

Lincoln wrote to Chase, "No commanding general shall do such a thing, upon *my* responsibility, without consulting me." He again urged that the Federal Government co-operate with any Slave State in gradual compensated emancipation of the slaves. To the Border State people, "I do not. argue—I beseech you to make arguments for yourselves." Afraid that they were not reading the drift of events, he warned them: "You cannot, if you would, be blind to the signs of the times. I beg of you a calm and enlarged consideration of them, ranging, if it may be, far above personal and partizan politics."

Lincoln and the "Contrabands." (Freed slaves)

Border State Congressmen at the White House on Lincoln's invitation in July '62 heard him plead for graduated, compensated abolishment of slavery. "I intend no reproach or complaint," he said, "when I assure you that in my opinion, if you all had voted for the resolution . . . of last March, the war would now be substantially ended." He still believed the plan would be swift to end the war. With the slaves freed by purchase in the Border States, the other states farther south would see they could not long keep up the war. In time, as the war dragged on, slavery would be extinguished by mere friction, urged the President. The money spent for buying slaves and setting them free would shorten the war.

Lincoln in a letter dated August 22, 1862, told the country in simple and skillfully wrought sentences what the war was for, as he saw it. Widely reprinted, probably reaching nearly all persons in the country who could read, the letter said:

. . . I would save the Union. I would save it the shortest way under the Constitution. The sooner the national authority can be restored; the nearer the Union will be "the Union as it was." If there be those who would not save the Union, unless they could at the same time *save* slavery, I do not agree with them. If there be those who would not save the Union unless they could at the same time *destroy* slavery, I do not agree with them. *My paramount object in this struggle is to save the Union, and is not either to save or to destroy slavery.* [Italics added.] If I could save the Union without freeing *any* slave, I would do it, and if I could save it by freeing *all* the slaves I would do it; and if I could save it by freeing some and leaving others alone I would also do that. What I do about slavery, and the colored race, I do because I believe it helps to save the Union; and what I forbear, I forbear because I do *not* believe it would help to save the Union. I shall do *less* whenever I shall believe what I am doing hurts the cause, and I shall do *more* whenever I shall believe doing more will help the cause. I shall try to correct errors when shown to be errors; and I shall adopt new views so fast as they shall appear to be true views.

I have here stated my purpose according to my view of *official* duty; and I intend no modification of my oft-expressed *personal* wish that all men every where could be free.

On August 14, 1862, there came to the Executive Mansion the first committee of free Negroes to arrive by invitation of the President. Greetings and preliminaries over, the President explained that money had been put at his disposal by Congress for the purpose "of colonizing people of African descent," a cause he had long favored. One of those present wrote a memorandum of the words of the President.

"Why," Lincoln asked, "should the people of your race be colonized, and where? Why should they leave this country? . . . Your race suffers very greatly, many of them, by living among us, while ours suffers from your presence . . . Your race are suffering, in my judgment, the greatest wrong inflicted on any people. But even when you cease to be slaves, you are yet far removed from being placed on an equality with the white race . . ."

The principal difficulty in the way of colonization, the President suggested to the committee of Negroes, was that "the free colored man cannot see that his comfort would be advanced by it." The President had in view for them to colonize a tract in the Republic of New Granada. But there were contending factions in the government of New Granada; necessary assurances could not be had of security, and the plan was soon abandoned. The enthusiasm of the free Negroes over such colonization was slight, almost negligible.

Lincoln signed an act ending Negro slavery in the District of Columbia, the Federal Government to buy the slaves at prices not exceeding $200 each. And, the President wishing it, there was provision for steamship tickets to Liberia or Haiti for any freed slaves who cared to go to those Negro republics. This act of Congress and the President was one of many laws, decisions, new precedents, that by percussion and abrasion, by erosion and attrition, were opening gaps in the legal status of slavery, wearing down its props and bulwarks.

Congress revised the war regulations so as to forbid any officer of the Army or the Navy to use his forces to capture and return fugitive slaves. Another act provided that such officers could not hear evidence and try cases as to whether a runaway slave should be returned on the claim of an owner. A treaty was negotiated with Great Britain for suppression of the African slave trade. By another act of Congress all slaves in Territories of the United States were declared free. Further legislation provided for the education of Negro children, and Negroes were made admissible as mail-carriers.

These acts of Congress were capped by the Confiscation Act, which the President signed in July '62. Slaves owned by persons convicted of treason or rebellion should be made free, this act declared, and furthermore, slaves of rebels who escaped into Union army lines, or slaves whose masters had run away, or slaves found by the Union Army in places formerly occupied by rebel forces, should all be designated as prisoners of war and set free. Other bills provided that slaves entering Union Army lines could be put to work and earn their freedom; the President could enroll and employ Negroes for camp labor and military service, while the wives, mothers and children of such Negro slaves, if they were the property of armed "rebels," should be set free; the President was authorized "to employ as many persons of African descent as he may deem necessary and proper for the suppression of this rebellion, and for this purpose he may organize and use them in such manner as he may judge best for the public welfare."

On July 22, 1862, as the McClellan campaign for Richmond was fading in mist, mud and disaster, Lincoln called his Cabinet. And as he told it himself at a later time: "I felt that we . . . must change our tactics, or lose the game. I now determined upon the adoption of the emancipation policy . . . I prepared the original draft of the proclamation, and . . . I said to the Cabinet that I . . . had not called them together to ask their advice, but to lay the subject matter of a proclamation before them, suggestions as to which would be in order, after they had heard it read . . . Secretary Seward . . . said in substance, 'Mr. President, I approve of the proclamation, but I question the expediency of its issue at this juncture . . . It may be viewed as the last measure of an exhausted government, a cry for help . . .' His idea was that it would be considered our last *shriek*, on the retreat. 'Now,' continued Mr. Seward, 'while I approve the measure, I suggest, sir, that you postpone its issue, until you can give it to the country supported by military success . . .'

Lincoln drafting Emancipation Proclamation, 1862.

"I put the draft of the proclamation aside . . . Well, the next news we had was of Pope's disaster, at Bull Run. Things looked darker than ever. Finally, came the week of the battle of Antietam . . . The news came, I think, on Wednesday, that the advantage was on our side . . .I finished writing the second draft of the preliminary proclamation . . . called the Cabinet together to hear it, and it was published the following Monday."

Then Lincoln took a grave tone, with a solemn deliberation read the proclamation, commenting as he went along. It began with saying the war would go on for the Union, that the efforts would go on for buying and setting free the slaves of the Border States, and the colonizing of them; that on January 1, 1863, all slaves in states or parts of states in rebellion against the United States "shall be then, thenceforward, and forever free," and the Federal Government would "recognize the freedom of such persons." It was a preliminary proclamation.

Seward suggested adding the words "and maintain" after the word "recognize." Chase joined Seward in this, and it was done. Blair said he was for the principle involved, but the result of the proclamation would be to send the Border States into the arms of the secessionists; also it would give a club to hostile political elements in the North. Seward made another minor suggestion, that colonization should be only with the consent of the colonists; Negroes were to be sent out of the country only as they were willing to go. Lincoln put that in quickly.

Two days later, September 24, on a Monday morning, this preliminary Emancipation Proclamation was published, for the country and the world to read. Serenaders came with a brass band to have music over the proclamation. The President addressed them from a White House balcony: ". . . I can only trust in God I have made no mistake . . . It is now for the country and the world to pass judgment on it, and, may be, take action upon it." He was "environed with difficulties," he soberly wished the crowd to know. "Yet they are scarcely so great as the difficulties of those who, upon the battle field, are endeavoring to purchase with their blood and their lives the future happiness and prosperity of this country." He wanted those soldiers with him. He was privately wondering how many of them now were stronger for him.

On invitation of Curtin a gathering of governors of Northern States met that day in Altoona, Pennsylvania. Sixteen of them signed an address to the President, pledging loyalty to the Union, endorsing the new emancipation policy, and suggesting that he should call for 100,000 more troops to be organized into a reserve corps for emergencies. Five governors held off from signing. They were from the Slave States Kentucky, Missouri, Maryland and Delaware, and the odd Northern bailiwick of New Jersey. While also pledging loyalty to the Union and support of the President, these five governors could not endorse the Emancipation Proclamation.

Beyond the newspapers and politicians were the People and Lincoln's question was: What were they thinking? In many quarters the proclamation was called grand, historic, and its author an immortal. Lincoln wrote in a letter marked "Strictly private," ". . . while commendation in newspapers and by distinguished individuals is all that a vain man could wish, the stocks have declined, and troops come forward more slowly than ever."

The proclamation was aimed at Europe as well as North and South America.

The press and Premier Palmerston and the voices of the ruling class of England could not hope to change the basic instinct of the masses, now deeper in response to the Lincoln Government as against that of Davis at Richmond. In the inner circles of the ruling class it was admitted that now there would be increased difficulty for any European government to recognize the South.

A wave of fury swept the South. Lincoln was breaking the laws of civilized warfare, outraging private-property rights, inviting Negroes to kill, burn and rape, said statesmen, orators, newspapers. The Richmond *Enquirer* fumed, "What shall we call him? Coward, assassin, savage, murderer of women and babies? Or shall we consider them all as embodied in the word fiend, and call him Lincoln, the Fiend?"

Lincoln had warned nearly a year back that the contest might develop into "remorseless, revolutionary warfare." The awful responsibility of carrying on and finishing a war of conquest lay ahead.

CHAPTER 27

McClellan's "Slows"—Election Losses—Fredericksburg—'62 Message

McClellan's "Slows"—Election Losses— Fredericksburg—'62 Message

FROM DAY to day political questions interwove with military. At several Cabinet meetings the last week in September '62 came the matter of deporting freed Negroes.

Outside of Cabinet meetings Chase was telling Welles that Stanton felt useless and deemed it his duty to resign from the Cabinet. Welles said he was not surprised to hear it, that sooner or later either Stanton or some of the generals would have to go.

Towering over immediate issues stood the sphinx of McClellan's army—how to get it moving. On October 1 Lincoln, without notifying McClellan, started for the Army of the Potomac camps. McClellan got word of Lincoln's being on the way, rode to Harpers Ferry, and was pleased to find that no Cabinet members or politicians were with the President, "merely some western officers." "His ostensible purpose," McClellan wrote his wife, "is to see the troops and the battle-field; I incline to think that the real purpose of his visit is to push me into a premature advance into Virginia."

They rode horseback all of one afternoon around the camps. Mathew B. Brady photographed them together sitting in McClellan's tent, Lincoln's right arm resting against a flag draping a table where his tall silk hat stood upside down between two stubs of candles.

At Frederick, Maryland, the troops were drawn up. The President told them it was not proper for him in his present position to make speeches. He gave thanks to the soldiers for good services, energy shown, hardships endured and blood shed for the Union. He hoped their children, and their children's children for a thousand generations to come, would enjoy the benefits of a united country.

Repeatedly across months Lincoln remarked of McClellan, "He's got the slows." Like fact was the gossip that a Government official, getting a pass to see McClellan, remarked, "I'll report

when I come back if I find the army." "Oh, you will," said Lincoln. "It's there. That's just the difficulty."

By latter October, it seemed, McClellan's dealings at Washington were entirely with Lincoln. "All his official correspondence is with the President direct and no one else," wrote Welles. McClellan now slowly moved his army across the Potomac and put it about where Pope's army had lain before Second Bull Run. It was November. Lincoln told John Hay he would make a final judgment of McClellan. If he should permit Lee to cross the Blue Ridge and place himself between Richmond and the Army of the Potomac, Lincoln would remove McClellan from command. When Lee's army reached Culpeper Court House the test of McClellan was over.

The November elections of '62 nearly doubled the number of Democratic Congressmen, raising it from 44 to 75. In five states where Lincoln two years before had won the electoral vote, his party now lost; and the Democrats elected Horatio Seymour as governor of New York. The proadministration New York *Times* said the balloting registered "want of confidence" in the President.

Two men traveled in a driving snowstorm near midnight November 7 to find the tent of General McClellan near Rectortown. They stepped in and shook off the snow from their overcoats. They had interrupted him in the writing of a letter to his wife. One of the men was Adjutant General C. P. Buckingham of the War Department. The other was Major General Ambrose Everett Burnside. Buckingham handed McClellan a message relieving him of command of the Army of the Potomac and ordering him to turn it over to Burnside. A second message told McClellan to report to Trenton, New Jersey, for further orders. McClellan finished the letter to his wife: "Alas for my poor country! . . . Do not be at all worried—I am not."

A farewell letter from McClellan read to the army was cheered. Where McClellan showed himself among the soldiers

Abraham Lincoln.

he was cheered. He had a way with him, a magnetism, and a figure and manner. The man taking his place, Burnside, came near weeping as he told McClellan he had refused to accept command until ordered.

No case was ever made out that McClellan was not brave and able. Only politicians, personal enemies, loose talkers, called him coward or sloven. At Malvern Hill and Antietam he performed superbly—and then failed to clinch and use what he had won. If he had been the bold ambitious plotter that Stanton, Chase and others saw, he would have marched his army to Washington and seized the Government there, as he said many urged him to do. His defect was that while he could not have instigated such treason himself, he did allow approaches to such treason to be talked freely in his staff and army without rebuke or repression from him.

Burnside spent three days with McClellan going over the army organization and plans. He was 39, a log-cabin boy, born at Liberty, Indiana, one of nine sons. His father, a state senator, got him a cadetship at West Point, where he met McClellan, Stonewall Jackson and others who rose in the Army. Burnside's Rhode Island regiment was among the first troops to arrive in Washington, where Lincoln often visited his camp. His chief distinction was in leading a joint naval and military force that early in 1862 captured Roanoke Island with 2,600 prisoners and 32 guns. This won applause, an embellished sword from Rhode Island, and the thanks of the Massachusetts and Ohio Legislatures.

Now came Fredericksburg, a trap. Lee with 72,000 men was ready and waiting for Burnside with 113,000. For a month Burnside had been waiting for pontoons to cross the river. While the pontoons were on the way Lee made arrangements. Burnside's columns crossed over. They found hills spitting flame and metal, a sunken road swarming with riflemen waiting human prey. "A chicken can not live on that field when we open on it," a Confederate engineer had told General Longstreet of the plain facing Marye's Hill. Meagher led his Irish Brigade of 1,315 up the hill and left 545 in the frozen mud. Hancock's division lost 40 of each 100 of its men. Between the fog of morning and twilight of evening 7,000 killed and wounded Union soldiers fell. The wounded lay 48 hours in the freezing cold before they were cared for. Some burned to death in long, dry grass set afire by cannon. Total Confederate losses were 5,309; Union, 12,653.

U.S. Maj. General Ambrose Burnside. Photo by Mathew Brady.

The morale of the army was hard hit. The troops had shown all the courage asked for. But with such commanders above them, what could they do? They asked that. On review they were called to give a cheer for their general. They hooted. Some went above Burnside and blamed Lincoln. More officers resigned. More privates deserted.

Burnside gave out a letter to Halleck taking all blame on himself, praising officers and men for gallantry, courage, endurance. "For the failure in the attack I am responsible," he wrote.

The President's message to Congress December 1, 1862, opened with reports and comments on miscellaneous affairs and flowed on into discussions of the Union, slavery, the Negro. The argument for the Union mixed logic and sentiment: "A nation may be said to consist of its territory, its people, and its laws. The territory is the only part which is of certain durability." Laws change; people die; the land remains."

In previous messages Lincoln had not given so heavy an emphasis to the argument against secession in behalf of the Middle West from which he came. He pleaded: "Our strife pertains to ourselves—to the passing generations of men; and it can, without convulsion, be hushed forever with the passing of one generation." From this almost mystic appeal for the saving of the Union he passed to a concrete proposal, the Constitution of the United States to be amended to provide that every state which abolished slavery at any time before January 1, 1900, should be paid for its freed slaves in U.S. bonds at a rate of interest and in sums to be agreed upon for each slave. Congress would be given express power to set aside money and otherwise provide for colonizing free colored persons. "Without slavery the rebellion could never have existed; without slavery it could not continue."

Permanent constitutional results would be achieved. First, two-thirds of Congress, and afterwards three-fourths of the states, would have to concur in the plan. This would assure emancipation, end the struggle and save the Union for all time.

In his last paragraph he struck for motives to move men. "Fellow-citizens, we cannot escape history. We of this Congress and this administration, will be remembered in spite of ourselves. No personal significance or insignificance can spare one or another of us. The fiery trial through which we pass, will light us down, in honor or dishonor, to the latest generation."

He flung out sentences edging on irony. "We *say* we are for the Union. The world will not forget that we say this. We know how to save the Union. The world knows *we* do know how to save it. We—even we here —hold the power, and bear the responsibility . . . Other means may succeed; this could not fail. The way is plain, peaceful, generous, just—a way which, if followed, the world will forever applaud, and God must forever bless."

Thus ended the lesson. What came of it? No action at all except a faint groping toward compensated abolishment in the Slave State of Missouri. The Border States were too divided in viewpoint to act decisively. They were not yet cemented back into the Union. Lexington, Kentucky, on December 18 again fell into Confederate hands when Bedford Forrest's raiders drove off Illinois cavalry commanded by Colonel Robert G. Ingersoll of Peoria, Illinois.

This December message prepared the way for the Emancipation Proclamation to be issued January 1, 1863—*if* the President should decide to issue it. The question was in the air whether he would. Radical antislavery men were saying the President would not dare issue the proclamation. Certain Border State men were saying he would not dare confiscate and destroy $1,000,000,000 in property values. Army men were not lacking to pronounce the judgment that such a proclamation would bring wholesale desertions, that entire companies and regiments would throw down their arms.

C H A P T E R 28

THUNDER OVER THE CABINET— MURFREESBORO

William Seward, U.S. Secretary of State, 1861-1869.
Photo by Mathew Brady.

THUNDER OVER THE CABINET—MURFREESBORO

WHEN Chase told Senator Fessenden there was "a backstairs influence" controlling the President, he knew Fessenden understood no one else was meant but Seward. That Seward with his cigars, cynicism, wit and nonsense, was the most companionable human being in the Cabinet had no bearing.

The Republican Senators in secret caucus December 15, 1862, discussed a letter written by Seward to Minister Adams six months before. Senator Sumner had taken the letter to Lincoln and asked if he had approved it. Lincoln said he had never seen the letter before. The newspapers got hold of this and raked Seward. The radicals claimed one more proof that Seward was a backstairs influence paralyzing the President's best intentions. Seward's offending letter had these words: "It seems as if the extreme advocates of African slavery and its most vehement opponents were acting in concert together to precipitate a servile war—the former by making the most desperate attempts to overthrow the Federal Union, the latter by demanding an edict of universal emancipation as a lawful and necessary, if not, as they say, the only legitimate way of saving the Union."

The committee of Senators was to call on him at seven that night, Lincoln told Browning—and added, "Since I heard last night of the proceedings of the caucus I have been more distressed than by any event of my life." The committee came that December night of '62, Collamer, Wade, Grimes, Fessenden, Trumbull, Sumner, Harris, Pomeroy and Howard. "The President received us with his usual urbanity," Fessenden noted, though Browning had seen Lincoln only a few minutes earlier wearing a troubled face and saying he was "more distressed" than by any event of his life.

When the committee of Senators came to the White House that Friday night they did not know that Lincoln had arranged for them to meet the Cabinet, to sit face to face in a three-cornered session. The President told them he had invited the Cabinet, with the exception of Seward, to meet the committee for a free and friendly conversation in which all, including the President, should be on equal terms. He wished to know if the committee had any objection to talking over matters with the Cabinet. "Having had no opportunity for consultation, the committee had no objection," noted Fessenden.

The President opened by admitting that Cabinet meetings had not been very regular, excusing that fact for want of time. He believed most questions of importance had received reasonable consideration, was not aware of any divisions or want of unity.

After hours of threshing over the issues and getting better acquainted, the President asked the Senators to give him their opinions as to whether Seward ought to leave the Cabinet. Collamer said he did not know how his constituents felt and he would not go beyond the paper he had handed the President. Grimes, Trumbull, Sumner, said Seward should go. Harris said No, that Seward's removal would be a calamity to the Republican party of New York. Pomeroy said he had once studied law in Seward's office but his confidence in Seward was gone. Howard said he had not spoken during the evening and would not. Chase suggested, "The members of the Cabinet had better withdraw." They did so. It was midnight. Senators Collamer and Harris took their hats and also went away.

Lincoln and Welles agreed next morning that while Seward's resignation should not be accepted by the President, neither should Seward get up on his dignity and press for immediate acceptance. Welles said he would go over and see Seward. Lincoln "earnestly" desired him to do so. Lincoln had a messenger sent to notify Chase that the President wished to see him.

Seward was pleased at Welles' report of his interview with the President. He said that "if the President and country required of him any duty in this emergency he did not feel at liberty to refuse it . . ." Back at the White House, Welles met Chase and Stanton in the President's office. Welles told them he was decidedly against accepting Seward's resignation. Neither would give a

John Bright, Liberal British politician.

direct answer. The President came in, asked Welles if he "had seen the man." Welles said "Yes" and the man was agreed. The President turned to Chase. "I sent for you, for this matter is giving me great trouble."

Chase said he had been painfully affected by the meeting last evening, which was a total surprise to him. Then after some vague remarks he told the President he had written his resignation as Secretary of the Treasury. "Where is it?" asked Lincoln, his eyes lighting up. "I brought it with me," said Chase, taking the paper from his pocket. "I wrote it this morning." "Let me have it," said the President, reaching his long arm and fingers toward Chase, who held on to the paper and seemed to have something further to say before giving up the document. But the President was eager, did not notice Chase, took the letter, broke the seal and read it.

"This," said Lincoln, holding up the letter toward Welles with a triumphal laugh, "cuts the Gordian knot." His face of worry had changed to satisfaction. "I can dispose of this subject now without difficulty," he added as he turned on his chair. "I see my way clear."

The President sent polite notes to Seward and Chase that he could not let them quit and must ask them to take up again their duties. Seward replied that he had "cheerfully resumed" his functions. Chase held off. "I will sleep on it." Something rankled in Chase's bosom. He was afraid Lincoln had a sinister cunning that had outguessed and outwitted him. His pride was hurt. He wrote to the President: "Will you allow me to say that something you said or looked, when I handed you my resignation this morning, made on my mind the impression that having received the resignations both of Governor Seward and myself, you felt that you could relieve yourself from trouble by declining to accept either, and that this feeling was one of gratification?" However, after a Sunday of deep thinking Chase decided he would go back to his old place.

They were affairs seething and warm in human relationships. Here, working with Seward, Lincoln more often knew precisely what he was doing.

Seward informed him of how the Spanish, British and French governments were joining hands to collect money due from Mexico; so they gave diplomatic explanations. They announced they were not seeking new territory; they asked the United States to join their scheme. Slowly Seward and Lincoln had seen it become reasonably clear that Emperor Napoleon III of France was planning to beat the armies of Mexico, overthrow their republican government, and set up a royal throne, whereon would sit the Archduke Maximilian of Austria.

Across Europe ran two extremes of opinion, with many moderate views intermingled.

The liberal John Bright of England favored a united country in America, sent a letter to the Chamber of Commerce of New York. Bright wished it known that "there is no other country in which men have been so free and so prosperous as in yours, and that there is no other political constitution now in existence, in the preservation of which the human race is so deeply interested." The conservative London *Dispatch* phrased its view: "The real motives of the civil war are the continuance of the power of the North to tax the industry of the South, and the consolidation of a huge confederation to sweep every other power from the American continent, to enter into the politics of Europe with a Republican propaganda, and to bully the world."

An international world opinion favoring the North was Seward's steady objective. Often he brought to Lincoln's desk designs and schemes for approval on matters of broad policy. The President and his State Minister spent more and more time together, grew in respect and affection. "The President is the best of us," Seward had written to his wife. Often on Sunday mornings they had long talks, came nearer being cronies than any other two of the Cabinet.

Congress passed an act making West Virginia a state, seceding her from Virginia. Blair, Bates and Welles were against the act. Seward, Chase, Stanton, favored it, recommended that the President sign the bill. He did so, urging in a written opinion that her brave and good men regarded her admission into the Union as a matter of life and death. They had been true to the Union through severe trials. "We have so acted as to justify their hopes; and we can not fully retain their confidence, and co-operation if we seem to break faith with them."

Then Lincoln presented the quixotic phase of the matter. "The division of a State is dreaded as a precedent," he wrote. "But a measure made expedient by a war, is no precedent for times of peace. It is said that the admission of West-Virginia is secession, and tolerated only because it is our secession. Well, if we call it by that name, there is still difference enough between secession against the constitution, and secession in favor of the constitution." He did not like to do it but with a wry face he signed the bill.

On New Year's Eve, 1862, telegrams to the War Department reported one of the bloodiest battles of the war opening at Murfreesboro, Tennessee, along Stone's River, the Union army of Rosecrans fighting the Confederates under Bragg. The Confederates drove the right wing of the Union army back two miles, and Bragg sent a telegram of victory to Richmond on New Year's Eve: "God has given us a happy New Year." Lincoln went to bed that night with news of men marching in rain, sleeping on wet ground. fighting through mud, the South having made the gains of the day. Two days more of maneuvering and grappling went on between 41,000 under Rosecrans and 34,000 under Bragg. They fought in the rain and fog of raw winter days of short twilights. On the second day willing horses and cursing drivers couldn't get cannon moved over the soaked and slippery ground. One out of four men on the field was shot down, killed, wounded or taken prisoner; the Union army lost 12,906, the Confederates 11,739. Bragg retreated south.

And this huggermugger of smoke and steel, flame and blood, in Tennessee meant to the President far off in the White House one episode. The Union men of Tennessee would have easier going. The manpower of the South was cut down by so many figures. The war would never be ended by any one event, any single battle; the war might go on 20 or 30 years, ran the warning of Lincoln, Sherman and others.

Lincoln telegraphed Rosecrans: "God bless you, and all with you! Please tender to all, and accept for yourself, the Nation's gratitude for yours, and their, skill, endurance, and dauntless courage."

CHAPTER 29

FINAL EMANCIPATION
PROCLAMATION, '63

FINAL EMANCIPATION PROCLAMATION, '63

ON JANUARY 1, 1863, the day set for the second and final Emancipation Proclamation, many doubted the President would issue the edict. Rumors ran in Washington that Lincoln on January 1 would withdraw, not issue, the proclamation. His courage, they were saying and writing, required bolstering, "puffing," as Greeley put it. John Murray Forbes of Boston wrote to Sumner that perhaps "a mixed deputation of laymen and clergy" could "try and influence" Lincoln to issue the document.

Copies of the proclamation were handed Cabinet members December 30. Next morning at ten they went into session. Seward and Welles suggested minor changes. Chase argued that the slaves should be declared free in entire states, with no parts or fractions stipulated as not being included. Also Chase had brought along a complete draft of a proclamation he had written himself. He suggested to Lincoln a closing sentence to read: "And upon this act, sincerely believed to be an act of justice warranted by the Constitution, and an act of duty demanded by the circumstances of the country, I invoke the considerate judgment of mankind, and the gracious favor of Almighty God." Said Chase, "I thought this, or something like it, would be appropriate." Lincoln adopted this sentence; he left out one clause and added that "military necessity" dictated the action.

Thirteen parishes in Louisiana and counties in Virginia around Norfolk were specifically excepted by Lincoln in the proclamation. Tennessee and the nonseceded Border Slave States of Missouri, Kentucky, Maryland and Delaware were not mentioned in the proclamation. In all these areas the slaves were not to be declared free. Blair argued that people long after would read and wonder why the Louisiana parishes and Virginia counties were excepted; they were in the very heart and back of slavery, and unless there was some good reason, unknown to him, he hoped they would not be excepted. Seward remarked, "I think so, too; I think they should not be excepted."

On the morning of New Year's Day the high officers of the Government, the civil, military and naval departments, the diplomatic corps in gold braid and official hats, arrived at the White House for the annual presidential reception. The carriages drove in the half-oval roadway, the horses champed, the important guests were delivered at the door; the long porch of the White House, the sidewalk and part of the lawn filled up with bystanders and beholders. The President began handshaking and greeting and went on for three hours.

That afternoon Seward and his son Fred walked over to the White House carrying Lincoln's own draft of the Emancipation Proclamation. Lincoln had left it with them for the State Department duly to engross. To be a complete document, the President must sign it. They found Lincoln alone in his office. The broad sheet was spread out before him on a table. He dipped his pen in an inkstand, held the pen in the air over the paper, hesitated, looked around, and said: "I never, in my life, felt more certain that I was doing right, than I do in signing this paper. But I have been receiving calls and shaking hands since nine o'clock this morning, till my arm is stiff and numb. Now this signature is one that will be closely examined, and if they find my hand trembled they will say, 'he had some compunctions.' But anyway, it is going to be done."

And with that he slowly and carefully wrote the name of Abraham Lincoln at the bottom of the Emancipation Proclamation, a bold, clear signature, though "slightly tremulous," Lincoln remarked. The others laughed, for it was better than he or they expected from fingers squeezed and wrenched by thousands that day. Then Seward signed, the great seal was affixed, and the document went into the archives of the State Department. The document—the most exciting news matter telegraphed, mailed, published, heralded over the world that day and month, for all that it was dry and formal—read:

The Emancipation Proclamation of 1862-1863 freeing the slaves. Engraved by Stobridge Lith. Co.

BY THE PRESIDENT OF THE UNITED STATES OF AMERICA:

A PROCLAMATION.

Whereas, on the twentysecond day of September, in the year of our Lord one thousand eight hundred and sixty two, a proclamation was issued by the President of the United States, containing, among other things, the following, towit:

"That on the first day of January, in the year of our Lord one thousand eight hundred and sixty-three, all persons held as slaves within any State or designated part of a State, the people whereof shall then be in rebellion against the United States, shall be then, thenceforward, and forever free; and the Executive Government of the United States, including the military and naval authority thereof, will recognize and maintain the freedom of such persons, and will do no act or acts to repress such persons, or any of them, in any efforts they may make for their actual freedom.

"That the Executive will, on the first day of January aforesaid, by proclamation, designate the States and parts of States, if any, in which the people thereof, respectively, shall then be in rebellion against the United States; and the fact that any State, or the people thereof, shall on that day be, in good faith, represented in the Congress of the United States by members chosen thereto at elections wherein a majority of the qualified voters of such State shall have participated, shall, in the absence of strong countervailing testimony, be deemed conclusive

*Lincoln wriiting the Emancipation Proclamation after a painting by David Gilmour Blyth.
Engraved by Ehrgott, Forbriger & Co.*

evidence that such State, and the people thereof, are not then in rebellion against the United States."

Now, therefore I, Abraham Lincoln, President of the United States, by virtue of the power in me vested as Commander-in-Chief, of the Army and Navy of the United States in time of actual armed rebellion against authority and government of the United States, and as a fit and necessary war measure for suppressing said rebellion, do, on this first day of January, in the year of our Lord one thousand eight hundred and sixty three, and in accordance with my purpose so to do publicly proclaimed for the full period of one hundred days, from the day first above mentioned, order and designate as the States and parts of States wherein the people thereof respectively, are this day in rebellion against the United States, the following, towit:

Arkansas, Texas, Louisiana, (except the Parishes of St. Bernard, Plaquemines, Jefferson, St. Johns, St. Charles, St. James, Ascension, Assumption, Terrebonne, Lafourche, St. Mary, St. Martin, and Orleans, including the city of New-Orleans) Mississippi, Alabama, Florida, Georgia, South-Carolina, North-Carolina, and Virginia, (except the forty eight counties designated as West Virginia, and also the counties of Berkley, Accomac, Northampton, Elizabeth-City, York, Princess Ann, and Norfolk, including the cities of Norfolk & Portsmouth); and which excepted parts are, for the present, left precisely as if this proclamation were not issued.

And by virtue of the power, and for the purpose aforesaid, I do order and declare that all persons held as slaves within said designated States, and parts of States, are, and henceforward shall be free; and that the Executive government of the United States, including the military and naval authorities thereof, will recognize and maintain the freedom of said persons.

And I hereby enjoin upon the people so declared to be free to abstain from all violence, unless in necessary self-defence; and I recommend to them that, in all cases when allowed, they labor faithfully for reasonable wages.

And I further declare and make known, that such persons of suitable condition, will be received into the armed service of the United States to garrison forts, positions, stations, and other places, and to man vessels of all sorts in said service.

And upon this act, sincerely believed to be an act of justice, warranted by the Constitution, upon military necessity, I invoke the considerate judgment of mankind, and the gracious favor of Almighty God.

Emancipation Proclamation first read to Negro Slaves. By Joseph Boggs Beale.

Lincoln and slave family.

The infamous Hermitage at Savannah, Georgia. These cabins were used to raise slaves for market.

Salutes of a hundred guns were fired in Pittsburgh, Buffalo, Boston, after newspapers published the proclamation. At night in Tremont Temple, Boston, it was read before an abolitionist crowd including the Negro members of the Union Progressive Association.

Critics took much the same view as they did of the preliminary proclamation in September. The London *Times* and the antiadministration press in general agreed with the New York *Herald*: "While the Proclamation leaves slavery untouched where his decree can be enforced, he emancipates slaves where his decree cannot be enforced. Friends of human rights will be at a loss to understand this discrimination." The Richmond *Examiner* spoke for much of the South in declaring the proclamation to be "the most startling political crime, the most stupid political blunder, yet known in American history," aimed at "servile insurrection,"

with the result that "Southern people have now only to choose between victory and death."

Henry Adams in London wrote: "The Emancipation Proclamation has done more for us here than all our former victories and all our diplomacy. It is creating an almost convulsive reaction in our favor all over this country. The London *Times* furious and scolds like a drunken drab. Certain it is, however, that public opinion is very deeply stirred here and finds expression in meetings, addresses to President Lincoln, deputations to us, standing committees to agitate the subject and to affect opinion, and all the other symptoms of a great popular movement peculiarly unpleasant to the upper classes here because it rests on the spontaneous action of the laboring classes."

Around the world and into the masses of people whose tongues and imaginings create folk tales out of fact, there ran this item of the Strong Man who arose in his might and delivered an edict, spoke a few words fitly chosen, and thereupon the shackles and chains fell from the arms and ankles of men, women and children born to be chattels for toil and bondage.

The living issues coiled and tangled about Lincoln's feet were not, however, to be set smooth and straight by any one gesture, or a series of them, in behalf of freedom. His authority, worn often as a garment of thongs, was tied and knotted with responsibilities. Nailed with facts of inevitable fate was his leadership. The gestures of stretching forth his hand and bestowing freedom on chattel slaves while attempting to enforce his will by the violence of armies subjugating the masters of slaves on their home soil, the act of trying to hold a just balance between the opposed currents of freedom and authority, raised a riddle that gnawed in his thought many nights.

"A great day," wrote Longfellow that New Year's Day of '63. "The President's Proclamation for Emancipation of Slaves in the rebel States, goes into effect. A beautiful day, full of sunshine, ending in a tranquil moonlight night. May it be symbolical.

CHAPTER 30

HOOKER—CHANCELLORSVILLE—
CALAMITY

HOOKER—CHANCELLORSVILLE—CALAMITY

THE ARMY of the Potomac in early '63 had lost—on the peninsula, twice at Bull Run, and again in the slaughter at Fredericksburg. It had, however, kept enemy bayonets out of Washington and the Free States. And other Northern armies, with naval co-operation, had captured all the Confederate strongholds—except Forts Sumter and Morgan—on the seacoast from Fortress Monroe in Virginia to points in Texas. Rosecrans was marching close to the Alabama line, Grant was in Mississippi, Curtis in Arkansas, Banks in New Orleans.

After breakfast at staff headquarters next morning General Hooker talked with a newspaperman about how the commanding general was incompetent, the President and Government at Washington were imbecile and "played out," a dictator was needed and the sooner the better.

Burnside resigned, was persuaded to withdraw his resignation, was relieved of duty, and January 25, 1863, the President ordered Hooker to the command of the Army of the Potomac. Chase was pleased; so were members of the Committee on the Conduct of the War; so were many people attracted by his fighting quality and a touch of the dramatic and impetuous about Hooker. "Now there is Joe Hooker," Nicolay heard the President say. "He can fight. I think that is pretty well established—but whether he can 'keep tavern' for a large army is not so sure."

A handsome soldier, Hooker looked warlike for those to whom war is color, dash, valor. Blond of hair, with wavy ringlets, with a flushed and rosy face, 49 years old, he was tall, blue-eyed, had a martial air. A West Point graduate, brevetted captain for bravery at Monterey in the Mexican War, he was a farmer and superintendent of military roads on the West Coast when the war began.

Tad Lincoln dressed in his Zouave uniform, 1861.

At Williamsburg on the peninsula under McClellan he had 2,228 killed and wounded. He was nicknamed "Fighting Joe" Hooker. Shot in the foot at Antietam, he stayed in the saddle on the field with his men till the fighting was over. Often the words came from him "When I get to Richmond" or "After we have taken Richmond." Lincoln was near groaning as he said in confidence to Brooks: "That is the most depressing thing about Hooker. It seems to me that he is over-confident."

Early in April Hooker said that under his command was "a living army, and one well worthy of the republic." He also rated it "the finest army on the planet." He had 130,000 troops against Lee across the river with 60,000. The President kept in constant touch with the forging and welding of this new weapon for smiting the Confederacy, sending Hooker such communications as "Would like to have a letter from you as soon as convenient" and "How does it look now?" On April 3 he notified Hooker he would arrive at the Fredericksburg camp on Sunday and stay till Tuesday morning.

In an April snowfall, Lincoln with Tad, Mrs. Lincoln, and a few friends arrived at Aquia Creek water front, lined with transports and Government steamers unloading supplies for 130,000 men and 60,000 horses and mules. A crowd of army people cheered the arrival of the President. Lincoln insisted on going to the nearest hospital tent, stopping to speak with nearly every one of the sick and wounded, shaking hands with many, asking a question or two here and there, and leaving a kind word as he moved from cot to cot.

Tad said he must see "graybacks," Confederate soldiers. Two staff men took Tad and his father on a frosty morning down to the picket line opposite Fredericksburg. They saw hills and a city war-swept, mansions and plain homes in ruins, farms desolated. Smoke rose from enemy campfires just above a stone wall where Burnside's men by thousands had weltered in blood.

From a reviewing stand the President, Hooker and the staff watched 17,000 horsemen file past, the biggest army of men on horses ever seen in the world, said Hooker, bigger even than the famous cavalry body of Marshal Murat with Napoleon. Mud flew from the horses' feet on ground soft with melting snow.

These platoons of regulars, volunteers, conscripts, bounty men, were marching for adventure and glory; for the country and the flag; for a united nation from coast to coast; for the abolition of chattel slavery; or because they were drafted and there was no escape; or because they were paid a bounty of cash.

Mrs. Lincoln wore, wrote the New York *Herald* man, "a rich black dress with narrow flounces, a black cape with broad trimming of velvet around the border and a plain hat of the same hue composed her costume. A shade of weariness, doubtless the result of her labors in behalf of the sick and wounded in Washington, rested upon her countenance but the change seemed pleasant to her. The President wore a dark sack overcoat and a fur muffler."

In the Confederate army across the river horses were gaunt from lack of forage. Scurvy had begun to appear among troops lacking balanced rations. Cattle had arrived so thin that Lee asked to have them kept to fatten in the spring and salt meat issued instead. Through an unusually bleak and frigid winter some of Lee's troops had no blankets. Many wore coats and shoes in tatters.

On May 1 Hooker had brought most of his army across the Rappahannock River, to a crossroads named Chancellorsville. Hooker attacked, Lee counterattacked, and Hooker ordered his men to fall back. "Just as we reached the enemy we were recalled," wrote Meade, while General Couch, second to Hooker in command, said: "Hooker expected Lee to fall back without risking battle. Finding himself mistaken he assumed the defensive."

Early next morning Lee sent half his army under Stonewall Jackson on a march that took them till late in the afternoon, when they delivered a surprise attack that smashed the Union flank and rear. Next day Lee outguessed and outfought Hooker. With an army half the size of Hooker's, he so mangled and baffled the Union forces that Hooker called a council of his generals, of whom four voted to stay where they were and fight, two voted to retreat across the river. Hooker then ordered the retreat.

The white moon by night and the red sun by day had looked down on over 20,000 men who lay killed or wounded on the open farms and in the wilderness of trees, thickets and undergrowth, the figures giving Union losses at 11,000, Confederate at 10,000, not including 6,000 prisoners captured by Lee and 2,000 by Hooker.

Numbers, however, could not tell nor measure the vacancy nor the Southern heartache left by the death of Stonewall Jackson, shot by his own men, it was reported, as he was inspecting positions in the zone of fire. A cannon ball had broken a mansion pillar against which General Hooker leaned, knocked him down, left him senseless a half-hour, dazed for an hour or more, while the battle lines rocked and tore on the second day.

News of what happened to Hooker was slow reaching the White House. "I this P.M. met the President at the War Department," wrote Welles May 4. "He said he had a feverish anxiety to get facts; was constantly up and down, for nothing reliable came from the front." "In an hour or so, while the doctor and I sat talking, about 3 o'clock in the afternoon," wrote Noah Brooks, "the door opened and Lincoln came into the room. He held a telegram in his hand, and as he closed the door and came toward us I mechanically noticed that his face, usually sallow, was ashen in hue. The despatch was from General Butterfield, Hooker's chief of staff, addressed to the War Department, and was to the effect that the army had been withdrawn from the south side of the Rappahannock and was then 'safely encamped' in its former position. The appearance of the President, as I read aloud these fateful words, was piteous . . . broken . . . and so ghostlike. Clasping his hands behind his back, he walked up and down the room, saying 'My God! my God! What will the country say! What will the country say!'

The President wrote May 7 to Hooker as though a good fighter had been sent reeling, wasn't hurt, and might make a swift comeback. "An early movement would . . . help," he wrote, asking if Hooker had in mind a plan wholly or partially formed. "If you have, prossecute it without interference from me . . ."

Lee rested his army, received new divisions of freshly conscripted troops, slipped away into the Shenandoah Valley, and by June 29 had crossed the Potomac, marched over Maryland, and had an army of 75,000 on Pennsylvania soil. Hooker broke camp with his army and moved it northward in scattered formation.

At Frederick, Maryland, a man in civilian clothes, riding in a buggy, begging, buying and wheedling his way through straggling parties of soldiers and wagon trains, arrived at three o'clock the morning of June 28 and went to the tent of General George Gordon Meade, was let in after wrangling. He woke Meade from sleep, saying he had come to give him trouble. Meade said his conscience was clear; he was prepared for bad news.

A letter from General in Chief Halleck was put in Meade's hands: "You will receive with this the order of the President placing you in command of the Army of the Potomac . . . You will not be hampered by any minute instructions from headquarters. Your army is free to act as you may deem proper under the circumstances as they arise." Meade argued with General James A. Hardie, chief of staff of the Secretary of War, who had brought the order. He did not want the place. But every point he made had been anticipated. Meade was ordered as a soldier to accept, which he did, issuing notice that day: "By direction of the President of the United States, I hereby assume command of the Army of the Potomac."

Lincoln met his Cabinet the Sunday morning Meade took command. "The President . . . drew from his pocket a telegram from General Hooker asking to be relieved," noted Welles. "The President said he had, for several days as the conflict became imminent, observed in Hooker the same failings that were witnessed in McClellan after the Battle of Antietam—a want of alacrity to obey, and a greedy call for more troops . . ." Chase, in a long polite letter to the President that day, intimated that trickery had been on foot in the ousting of Hooker.

The next great battle, it seemed to many, would be a duel between Meade and Lee, somewhere in Pennsylvania, at Philadelphia, Chambersburg, Harrisburg, perhaps Gettysburg.

U.S. Brig. Gen. Joseph Hooker who fought at Chancellorsville.

C H A P T E R 31
WILL GRANT TAKE VICKSBURG?

Union General Ulysses S. Grant and Confederate General John C. Pemberton discussing the terms of the capitulation of Vicksburg.

WILL GRANT TAKE VICKSBURG?

Siege of Vicksburg, engraved by Currier & Ives, 1863.

ONE QUESTION weighed heavily on the Richmond Government in the spring of '63. Would Grant take Vicksburg? If so the Mississippi River would pass wholly into Union possession. Lincoln had talked about such a result to Commander D. D. Porter, pointing at a map and saying, as quoted by Porter: "See what a lot of land these fellows hold, of which Vicksburg is the key . . . Let us get Vicksburg and all that country is ours. The war can never be brought to a close until that key is in our pocket. I am acquainted with that region and know what I am talking about . . ."

From the fall of '62 till July 1 of '63 Grant performed with armies roundabout Vicksburg, a city of 5,000 people, 250 feet above the river, marching troops along the Yazoo River, the Yalobusha, the Tallahatchie.

The commander of Vicksburg, John C. Pemberton, was a favorite of President Davis. A West Pointer, Mexican War veteran, Indian fighter, Pennsylvania-born and raised, a descendant of three generations of Quakers, his Northern birth was held against him. After Grant's second storming attempt, Pemberton spoke to his troops: "You have heard that I was incompetent and a traitor; and that it was my intention to sell Vicksburg. Follow me and you will see the cost at which I will sell Vicksburg. When the last pound of beef, bacon and flour, the last grain of corn, the last cow and hog and horse and dog shall have been consumed, and the last man shall have perished in the trenches, then, and only then, will I sell Vicksburg."

For six months and more Grant, to many people in the North, seemed to be wandering around, stumbling and bungling on a job beyond him. So crazily intricate became the layout that in early June Sherman wrote home: "I don't believe I can give you an idea of matters here. You will read so much about Vicksburg and the people now gathered about it that you will get bewildered." In March he had written, "No place on earth is favored by nature with natural defense such as Vicksburg, and I do believe the whole thing will fail"; another plan would have to be worked on.

Sherman stuck on with the army, held by affection and admiration for Grant, writing to his Senator brother that Grant was honest, able, sensible and a hero, which sentiments reached Lincoln. He was redheaded, lean, scrawny, this Sherman, with a mind of far wider range than usual in the army. One of the 11 children of a lawyer who served as judge of the Supreme Court of Ohio, he was taken into the home of Thomas Ewing, lawyer and famous Whig, when his father died. An 1840 West Pointer, Sherman saw Indian fighting in Florida, studied law, was an adjutant general in California during the Mexican War, managed a bank in San Francisco, operated a New York office for a St. Louis firm, practiced law in Leavenworth, Kansas, and at the opening of the war was superintendent of the Louisiana State Military Academy at Alexandria. He had seen the United States and anxiety rode him about it; newspapers, politicians, the educated classes, were corrupt, blind, selfish, garrulous, to the point of tragedy.

A steady stream of letters in the mail, and persistent callers at the White House, brought Lincoln the advice that for the sake of the country he must get rid of Grant. The tone of many ran like that of a letter of Murat Halstead, editor of the Cincinnati *Commercial*, to Secretary Chase. "How is it that Grant, who was behind at Fort Henry, drunk at Donelson, surprised and whipped at Shiloh, and driven back from Oxford, Miss., is still in command? Governor Chase, these things are true. Our noble army of the Mississippi is being wasted by the foolish, drunken, stupid Grant. He cannot organize or control or fight an army. I have no personal feeling about it; but I know he is an ass. There is not among the whole list of retired major-generals a man who is not Grant's superior."

During June, Grant's army, earlier numbering only about 40,000, was reinforced to 70,000 and more. The plantations of Jefferson Davis and his brother Joseph had been captured and supplies from them lent aid to the Union cause. A world audience was looking on and wondering how many days or months the siege might last.

The marching of Lee with 80,000 Confederate troops up into Pennsylvania, with Meade and the Army of the Potomac trailing him for battle, hoping to stop him, was a bold movement, partly made on the chance that the danger to Northern cities would cause Lincoln and Halleck to draw off troops from Grant to fight Lee. In such event it was believed Pemberton might cut his way out of the seven miles of Union trenches encircling Vicksburg.

In hundreds of caves dug in the clay hillsides of the besieged city, women and children wondered how long till the end. One eyewitness told of seeing a woman faint as a shell burst a few feet from her. He saw three children knocked down by the dirt flung out from one explosion. "The little ones picked themselves up, and wiping the dust from their eyes, hastened on." Said another, "I saw one bright young bride whose arm shattered by a piece of shell had been amputated." Yet these were minor incidents to the thousands whose daily monotonous menu of mule and horse meat with parched corn had run out in latter June. Pemberton, as he had said he would, killed the last dog for food. Then he fed the men of his garrison on rats, cane shoots and bark. Some of the men standing in the firing trenches were wobbly on their legs. Pemberton was obeying instructions from President Davis to hold Vicksburg at all costs.

CHAPTER 32

DEEP SHADOWS—LINCOLN IN EARLY '63

DEEP SHADOWS—LINCOLN IN EARLY '63

IN THE months between Fredericksburg and Chancellorsville, events swirled round the peculiar pivot where Lincoln moved, and put him into further personal isolation.

The first combat of Negro troops against white had taken place in the Vicksburg area when 1,000 enlisted Union black men defended Milliken's Bend from an attack of some 2,000 Confederates. The fighting was mainly hand-to-hand. General Elias S. Dennis said, "White and black men were lying side by side, pierced by bayonets. Two men, one white and the other black, were found side by side, each with the other's bayonet through his body." As such news spread North it intensified agitation for and against the use of more Negro regiments. In the deepening bitterness General John M. Thayer and others heard Lincoln say his main anxiety was in the North. "The enemy behind us is more dangerous to the country than the enemy before us."

New York Peace Democrats took fresh vigor from their new governor, Horatio Seymour, 53, a man of inherited fortune who had served as mayor of Utica, speaker of the state assembly, lieutenant governor, delegate to national conventions. Seymour shaved his face, liked a muffler of whiskers under his jaws; ringlets of hair circled his bald pate. He called for an end to "the incompetents" at Washington who would never save the nation; he said compromise measures could have prevented the war. The Emancipation Proclamation, Seymour said on taking office, violated the Constitution; to free 4,000,000 Negro slaves, the North would require a military despotism. Seymour sent a brother to Washington to convey assurances of loyal support and to protest against arbitrary arrests.

On the last day before a new Congress with new Democratic members would take their seats, a Conscription Act was passed empowering the Government to divide the country into districts with provost marshals and enrollment boards authorized to raise troops by drafting all able-bodied citizens between 20 and 45.

The terror of secret and arbitrary arrests was softened somewhat by the Habeas Corpus bill of March 3, 1863. The Secretaries of State and of War were directed to furnish courts with names of all persons held as prisoners by authority of the Secretaries or the President. Congress made it clear that control over the habeas corpus writ rested with Congress, yet it directly authorized the President to suspend the writ. This was carefully done so that no appearance was presented of any conflict of authority between the President and Congress.

From house to house enrollers in the spring of '63 took the names of men and boys fit for the Army. Cripples, the deaf and dumb, the blind and other defectives were exempt. So were the only son of a widowed mother, the only son of aged and infirm parents, others having dependents. In a family where two or more sons of aged and infirm parents were drafted, the father if living, or if dead the mother, must say which son would stay home and which go to war. Also anyone having $300 cash, and willing to pay it as "bounty" to a substitute, was exempt and could stay at home and laugh at the war.

Western governors reported the secret Knights of the Golden Circle as disguising itself under various names, with oaths, passwords, rituals and rifles, aiming to encourage desertion, defeat the draft, and protect its members by force. In a few weeks 2,600 deserters had been arrested. Seventeen deserters fortified a log cabin and, provisioned by neighbors, defied siege. Two draft-enrollers were murdered in Indiana; women threw eggs, men rioted with clubs, guns, bricks. In a Pennsylvania county one enroller was forced to quit taking names, another was shot, the sawmill of another was burned. The Molly Maguires, an Irish miners' secret society in Pennsylvania, made resistance; coal operators refused to give the names of leaders to the Government in fear their breakers might be burned; Stanton sent troops to quell the disturbers.

Illinois had 2,001 deserters arrested in six months. In January the wholesale desertions and fraternizing with the enemy among troops of the 109th Illinois regiment began to look so much like a mutiny that the entire regiment was arrested, disarmed and put under guard at Holly Springs, Mississippi; these were recruits from southern Illinois, from a triangle of land wedged between the Slave States of Kentucky and Missouri.

The Sons of Liberty, the Circle of Hosts, the Union Relief Society, the Order of American Knights and other oath-bound secret societies of like aims progressed in size. They sometimes bought a storekeeper's stock entire of Colt revolvers, rifles and ammunition. Union men horsewhipped by masked committees in lonesome woodlands at night, Union men shot down in their own homes by Southern sympathizers, had their friends and kin who banded and took oaths. Violence met violence.

The seething of strife was not eased in the spring of '63 by Order No. 38 issued by General Burnside commanding the Department of the Ohio, with Cincinnati headquarters. Treason, of course, was forbidden, and giving aid and comfort to the enemy. Order No. 38 was positive: "The habit of declaring sympathy for the enemy will not be allowed in this department," thereby making Burnside and his officers the judges of what was "sympathy" and how many times "sympathy" had to be declared to become a habit. They would also decide whether treason hid and lurked in the words of any suspect, Order No. 38 admonishing, "It must be distinctly understood that treason, express or implied, will not be tolerated in this department."

Thousands of Negroes had been enlisted as soldiers in the first six months of 1863. Adjutant General Lorenzo Thomas of the War Department, in the lower Mississippi region in March, reported renewed faith in arming the blacks. He addressed 11,000 troops of two divisions, mentioning the rebels keeping at home all their slaves to raise subsistence for the armies in the field. "The administration has determined . . . to take their negroes and compel them to send back a portion of their whites to cultivate their deserted plantations. They must do this or their armies will starve."

A new status of the Negro was slowly taking form. In August '62 for the first time was sworn testimony taken from a Negro in a court of law in Virginia. Also Negro strikebreakers in New York were attacked by strikers, and in Chicago Negroes employed in meat-packing plants were assaulted by unem-ployed white men. The colored man was becoming an American citizen.

In an Indiana town, controlled by Copperheads, Sojourner Truth was introduced to speak at an antislavery meeting. A local physician and leading Copperhead rose and said word had spread over the community that the speaker of the evening was a man in woman's disguise; it was the wish of many present that the speaker of the evening should show her breasts to a committee of ladies. Sojourner Truth, tall, strong, unafraid, illiterate though having a natural grace of speech and body, stood silent a few moments. Then she loosed the clothing of her bosom, showed her breasts, and said in her own simple words and her deep contralto voice that these breasts she was showing had nursed black children, yes, but *more white children than black*. The audience sat spellbound.

There came to Lincoln the foremost of fugitive slaves. By authority of the President to Governor Andrew of Massachusetts to raise two regiments of colored men, this ex-slave had led in recruiting the 54th and 55th Massachusetts regiments, two of his own sons in the 54th. Hundreds of black men of the 54th, and their white colonel, had been killed assaulting a fort in South Carolina, the white colonel's body resting, as South Carolinians reported, "between layers of dead niggers." And Lincoln held his first conference on important business of state with a mulatto, Frederick Douglass. Born in Maryland of a black slave mother, his father a white man, Douglass had grown up as a plantation boy living through winters without shoes or stockings. He grew to a superb physical strength, worked in shipyards as a calker, and learned to read. In the red shirt and bandanna of a sailor, with papers loaned to him by a free Negro, he rode out of Baltimore on a railroad train. In New York he recognized on Broadway another escaped slave, who told him to stay away from all Negroes, as there were informers among them who would send him back where he came from for a few dollars' reward. Then Douglass met abolitionists who paid his way to New Bedford, where he worked at his trade of calker.

Antislavery men noticed he was a natural orator and sent him from city to city to tell of his life as a slave. He had sent word to a free black woman in Maryland, who came North, married him and they made a home in Rochester, New York, where in the cellar they once had 11 runaway Negroes.

Douglass read Lincoln as completely mistaken in his Negro colonization policy. "The colored race can never be respected anywhere till they are respected in America." According to Douglass, the President listened with patience and silence, was serious, even troubled. "Though I was not entirely satisfied with his views," noted Douglass, "I was so well satisfied with the man and with the educating tendency of the conflict, I determined to go on with the recruiting."

From Memphis early in '63 Charles A. Dana reported to the War Department "a mania for sudden fortunes made in cotton, raging in a vast population of Jews and Yankees." Under Federal permits they bought cotton low from Southern planters and sold high to New England textile works. Dana himself had put in $10,000, gone into partnership with a cotton expert, and was in line to make a fortune, yet he wrote to Stanton, "I should be false to my duty did I . . . fail to implore you to put an end to an evil so enormous, so insidious."

One public sale by an army quartermaster of 500 bales of cotton confiscated by Grant at Oxford and Holly Springs, Mississippi, brought over $1,500,000 cash, nearly paying the cost of Grant's supplies and stores burned by the enemy at Oxford.

A war prosperity was on, gold rising in price, paper money getting cheaper. Food prices had slowly gone up; clothes, house rent, coal, gas, cost more. This pressure on workingmen brought an agitation in New York that resulted in new trade-unions. The *World* reported a mass meeting in Cooper Union with the building crammed to capacity and hundreds waiting outside. Nearly all trades were represented, and resolutions were adopted unanimously pointing to wage rates inadequate to the cost of living and urging all trades to organize and send delegates to a central body.

The National Bank Act of February '63 was presented as a device to get money to run the war, while gaining stability in currency through co-operation with the bankers, bondholders and business interests having cash and resources. Therefore it stipulated gold payment of interest on bonds. Five or more persons, under the National Bank Act, could associate and form a bank having capital of $50,000 or more. On depositing in the U.S. Treasury interest-bearing bonds to the amount of one-third of the paid-in capital of the bank, the Government would engrave

money for them, National Bank certificates, to the amount of 90 per cent of the par value of the bonds deposited. The banks would use these new certificates for carrying on a regular banking business, receiving the full profit as though they were the bank's own notes. Also the banks would receive, from the Government, interest payment in gold on the bonds deposited in the Treasury.

Lincoln in his December '62 message to Congress advocated its passage.

Amid the snarling chaos of the winter of 1862-63 there were indications of a secret movement to impeach Lincoln. Stubbornly had he followed his own middle course, earning in both parties enemies who for different reasons wanted him out of the way. There were radical Republicans who wanted a man obedient to their wishes. There were reactionaries in both parties who hoped the confusion of an impeachment would slow down the war, bring back habeas corpus and other civil rights.

The talk of a Southern woman spy in the White House arrived at the point where Senate members of the Committee on the Conduct of the War set a secret morning session for attention to reports that Mrs. Lincoln was a disloyalist. One member of the committee told of what happened. "We had just been called to order by the Chairman, when the officer stationed at the committee room door came in with a half-frightened expression on his face. Before he had opportunity to make explanation, we understood the reason for his excitement, and were ourselves almost overwhelmed with astonishment. For at the foot of the Committee table, standing solitary, his hat in his hand, his form towering, Abraham Lincoln stood. The President had not been asked to come before the Committee, nor was it suspected that he had information that we were to investigate reports, which, if true, fastened treason upon his family in the White House."

At last the caller spoke slowly, with control, though with a depth of sorrow in the tone of voice: "I, Abraham Lincoln, President of the United States, appear of my own volition before this Committee of the Senate to say that I, of my own knowledge, know that it is untrue that any of my family hold treasonable communication with the enemy." Having attested this, he went away as silent and solitary as he had come. "We sat for some

African-American Union soldiers helped eventually to turn the tide of the war.

moments speechless. Then by tacit agreement, no word being spoken, the Committee dropped all consideration of the rumors that the wife of the President was betraying the Union. We were so greatly affected that the Committee adjourned for the day."

The author of *Uncle Tom's Cabin* came to the White House, and Lincoln, as she related it, strode toward her with two outreached hands and greeted her, "So you're the little woman who wrote the book that made this great war," and as they seated themselves at the fireplace, "I do love an open fire; I always had one to home." They talked of the years of plowshares beaten into swords. Mrs. Stowe felt about him "a dry, weary, patient pain, that many mistook for insensibility." He said of the war, "Whichever way it ends, I have the impression I shan't last long after it's over."

CHAPTER 33

THE MAN IN THE WHITE HOUSE

Mrs. Abraham Lincoln,
photographed at the Brady Studio.

THE MAN IN THE WHITE HOUSE

THE WHITE HOUSE or Executive Mansion gave a feeling of Time. The statue of Thomas Jefferson in front of the main portico stood with green mold and verdigris. The grounds during Lincoln's first year had a smooth outward serenity. Yet hidden in shrubbery were armed men and in a basement room troops with muskets and bayonets. Two riflemen in bushes stood ready to cover the movements of any person walking from the main gate to the building entry.

Company K of the 150th Pennsylvania Volunteers went on guard duty the first week in September and in a way became part of the White House family, taking care of Tad's goats and doing other chores. "He always called me Joe," said one private. The President asked about their sick, sometimes personally looked after passes and furloughs.

The main executive office and workroom on the second floor, 25 by 40 feet, had a large white marble fireplace, with brass andirons and a high brass fender, a few chairs, two hair-covered sofas, and a large oak table for Cabinet meetings. Lighting was by gas jets in glass globes, or when needed, by kerosene lamps. Tall windows opened on a sweep of lawn to the south, on the unfinished Washington Monument, the Smithsonian Institution, the Potomac River, Alexandria, and slopes alive with white tents, beef cattle, wagons, men of the army. Between the windows was a large armchair in which the President usually sat at a table for his writing. A pull at a bell cord would bring Nicolay or Hay from the next room. A tall desk with many pigeonholes stood nearby at the south wall. Among books were the *United States Statutes,* the Bible and Shakespeare's plays. At times the table had been littered with treatises on the art and science of war. Two or three frames held maps on which blue and red pins told where the armies were moving, fighting, camping.

The President was at his desk often before seven in the morning, after "sleep light and capricious," noted Hay. His White House bed, nine feet long, nearly nine feet high at the head board, had bunches of grapes and flying birds carved in its black walnut. Nearby was a marble-topped table with four stork-shaped legs; under its center was a bird's nest of black walnut filled with little wooden bird eggs.

"Late in the day," wrote Hay, "he usually drove out for an hour's airing; at six o'clock he dined. His breakfast was an egg and a cup of coffee; at luncheon he rarely took more than a biscuit and a glass of milk, a plate of fruit in its season; at dinner he ate sparingly of one or two courses. He drank little or no wine . . . and never used tobacco.

The military telegraph office at the War Department was for Lincoln both a refuge and a news source. The bonds were close between Lincoln and David Homer Bates, manager of the office, and the chief of staff, Thomas T. Eckert.

In this telegraph room Lincoln had first heard of the killing of Ellsworth, of the first and second Bull Run routs, of the Seven Days' battles and McClellan's cry for help at Harrison's Landing, of the *Monitor* crippling the *Merrimac,* of the Antietam shaded victory, of Burnside and Hooker failing at Fredericksburg and Chancellorsville, of blood "up to the bridles of horses," of Lee moving his army far up in Pennsylvania toward Gettysburg. Here he quoted from Petroleum V. Nasby: "Oil's well that ends well"; and after one of McClellan's peninsular defeats, from Orpheus C. Kerr: "Victory has once again perched upon the banners of the conquerors."

Mrs. Lincoln had, inevitably, become a topic. "I went to the reception at Mrs. Eames'," wrote Charles Francis Adams, Jr. "If the President caught it at dinner, his wife caught it at the reception. All manner of stories about her were flying around; she wanted to do the right thing, but not knowing how, was too weak and proud to ask; she was going to put the White House on an economical basis, and, to that end, was about to dismiss 'the help' as she called the servants. Numberless stories of this sort were current."

On New Year's Day, 1863, Browning rode in her carriage. "Mrs. Lincoln told me she had been, the night before, with Old Isaac Newton, out to Georgetown, to see a Mrs. Laury, a spiritualist and she had made wonderful revelations to her about her little son Willy who died last winter, and also about things on the earth. Among other things she revealed that the cabinet were all enemies of the President, working for themselves, and that they would have to be dismissed."

When she took her boys to Niagara Falls and returned, when she stopped at the Metropolitan Hotel in New York and shopped at the big stores, it was chronicled from day to day. *Leslie's Weekly* gave brief items: "Mrs. Lincoln held a brilliant levee at the White House on Saturday evening. She was superbly dressed."

Mrs. Lincoln visited hospitals, gave time and care to sick and wounded. She interceded with General McClellan, won pardon for a soldier ordered shot. McClellan in letters referred to her as "Mrs. President." From several dressmakers who applied she had chosen the comely mulatto woman, Mrs. Elizabeth Keckley, who once had been dressmaker to the wife of Jefferson Davis. The first spring and summer 15 new dresses were made, and as time passed Mrs. Lincoln felt a rare loyalty and spirit of service in Elizabeth Keckley, giving her trust and confidence not offered to others.

Away on frequent shopping trips to New York or Philadelphia, she had telegrams from her husband: "Do not come on the night train. It is too cold. Come in the morning." Or: "Your three despatches received. I am very well, and am glad to hear that you and Tad are so."

The secretaries could not always agree with her opinion that wages specified for an unfilled position in the White House might be handed to her directly. She questioned whether the Government or the secretaries should pay for the grain of the secretaries' horses in the White House stables. The two secretaries eventually were to find it more comfortable to move from the White House and lodge at Willard's.

The boy Tad meant more to Lincoln than anyone else. They were chums. "Often I sat by Tad's father reporting to him about some important matter that I had been ordered to inquire into," wrote Charles A. Dana, "and he would have this boy on his knee; and, while he would perfectly understand the report, the striking thing about him was his affection for the child." Tad usually slept with him, wrote John Play. Often late at night the boy came to the President's office: "He would lie around until he fell asleep, and Lincoln would shoulder him and take him off to bed."

"Tad" was short for Tadpole, a wriggler, nervous, active. With a defective palate, his occasional "papa dear" sounded more like "pappy day." He could burst into the President's office and call out what he wanted. Or again Tad would give three sharp raps and two slow thumps on the door, three dots and two dashes he had learned in the war telegraph office. "I've got to let him in," Lincoln would say, "because I promised never to go back on the code." Tad enjoyed strutting along with Captain Bennett inspecting the cavalry on White House guard duty.

Robert T. Lincoln, his press nickname "the Prince of Rails," away at Harvard, never saw his father, even during vacations, for more than ten minutes of talk at a time, so he said. Stepping up to his father at one reception and bowing with severe formality, "Good evening, Mr. Lincoln," his father handed Robert a gentle open-handed slap across the face.

Mrs. Lincoln's afternoon receptions and the President's public levees were held regularly during the winters. Usually twice a week, on Tuesday evenings at so-called dress receptions and on Saturday evenings at a less formal function, the President met all who came. "A majority of the visitors went in full dress," wrote Noah Brooks, "the ladies in laces, feathers, silks, and satins, without bonnets; and the gentlemen in evening dress . . . Here and there a day-laborer, looking as though he had just left his workbench, or a hardworking clerk with ink-stained linen, added to the popular character of the assembly."

The friendship of the President and Noah Brooks steadily deepened. Brooks wrote in one news letter: "It does appear to me that it is impossible to designate any man in public life whose character and antecedents would warrant us in the belief that we have anyone now living whose talents and abilities would fit him to administer this Government better than it has been conducted through the past stormy years by the honesty, patriotism, and far-sighted sagacity of Abraham Lincoln . . ." On the way to Soldiers' Home the Lincoln carriage passed through a city where one traveler had commented that everything worth looking at seemed unfinished. In March '63 the public grounds around the unfinished Washington Monument held droves of cattle, 10,000

Lincoln and family painted by S.B. Waugh and engraved by Wm. Sartain.

beeves on the hoof. Shed hospitals covered acres in the outlying suburbs; one of the better they named the Lincoln Hospital.

Into churches, museums, art galleries, public offices and private mansions had arrived from battlefields the wounded and dying. The passing months saw more and more of wooden-legged men, men with empty sleeves, on crutches, wearing slings and bandages.

From a population of 60,000 the city had gone above 200,000. Among the newcomers were contractors, freed Negroes, blockade-runners, traders, office seekers, elocutionists, gamblers, keepers of concert saloons with waiter girls, liquor dealers, candy-criers, umbrella-menders, embalmers, undertakers, manufacturers of artificial limbs, patent-medicine peddlers, receivers of stolen goods, pickpockets, burglars, sneak thieves.

Of the new arrivals of footloose women it was noted they ranged "from dashing courtesans who entertained in brownstone fronts to drunken creatures summarily ejected from army camps." The majority of the 'patrons' of the better class houses are men of nominal respectability, men high in public life, officers of the army and navy, Governors of States, lawyers, doctors, and the very best class of the city population. Some come under the influence of liquor, others in cool blood."

The high-class gambling houses, located mostly on Pennsylvania Avenue, were carpeted, gilded, frescoed, garnished with paintings and statuary for the players of faro and poker. At the four leading establishments, where introductions were necessary, could be found governors, members of Congress, department officials, clerks, contractors, paymasters. Colonel La Fayette C. Baker reported to Stanton in the summer of '63 that 163 gaming houses in full blast required attention.

Walt Whitman, author of *Leaves of Grass,* prophet of the Average Man, crier of America as the greatest country in the world—in the making—wrote to the New York *Times* in the summer of '63: "I see the President almost every day, as I happen to live where he passes to or from his lodgings out of town . . . He always has a company of twenty-five or thirty cavalry, with sabres drawn, and held upright over their shoulders .. . None of the artists have caught the deep, though subtle and indirect expression of this man's face. They have only caught the surface. There is something else there.

Lincoln and son Tad reading. Photo by Anthony Berger, Brady Studio, 1864.

Mary Todd Lincoln.

In Halleck's office one evening in the summer of '63 Lincoln discussed plans for a joint naval and land attack on Charleston, illustrating gradual approaches of artillery and infantry with three or four lead pencils and pen handles which he arranged in parallels and shifted according to his notions of the strategy. Gustavus Vasa Fox came in, agreed with Lincoln, but Halleck could not see it, and as Lincoln walked home that evening he spoke to Brooks of his discouragement with what he termed "General Halleck's habitual attitude of demur."

Did the President vacillate? Was he managed by others? Men and journals shifted in view. The New York *Herald* in May '63 approved Lincoln's reversal of a court-martial order for the hanging as traitors of citizens of loyal states captured wearing uniforms of Confederate officers. Lincoln had declared them to be merely prisoners of war.

In the President's discussions of peace, said the London *Spectator,* "He expresses ideas, which, however quaint, have nevertheless a kind of dreamy vastness not without its attraction. The thoughts of the man are too big for his mouth." He was saying that a nation can be divided but "the earth abideth forever," that a generation could be crushed but geography dictated the Union could not be sundered.

At home and abroad judgments came oftener that America had at last a President who was All-American. He embodied his country in that he had no precedents to guide his footsteps; he was not one more individual of a continuing tradition, with the dominant lines of the mold already cast for him by Chief Magistrates who had gone before.

Also around Lincoln gathered some of the hope that a democracy can choose a man, set him up high with power and honor, and the very act does something to the man himself, raises up new gifts, modulations, controls, outlooks, wisdoms, inside the man, so that he is something else again than he was before they sifted him out and anointed him to take an oath and solemnly sign himself for the hard and terrible, eye-filling and center-staged role of Head of the Nation.

CHAPTER 34

GETTYSBURG—VICKSBURG
SIEGE—DEEP TIDES, '63

U.S. General George G. Meade,
photographed at Brady Studio.

Gettysburg—Vicksburg Siege—Deep Tides, '63

Panorama of second day's battle, Gettysburg. Photo by Haines Photo Co.

THE Cincinnati *Gazette* correspondent with the Army of the Potomac chanced to hear Lincoln say, "I tell you I think a great deal of that fine fellow Meade." Meade's father was a merchant, shipowner, U.S. naval agent in Cadiz, Spain. Born in Cadiz in 1815, graduated from West Point, the son took a hand in fighting Seminole Indians, resigned from the Army, worked on War Department surveys, was brevetted first lieutenant for gallantry in the Mexican War, and for five years was a lighthouse-builder among Florida reefs. He married Margaretta, daughter of John Sergeant, noted Philadelphia lawyer, in 1840, and often when away on duty wrote her a letter every day.

After Meade's appointment as brigadier general of volunteers August 31, 1861, he had seen active and often front-line service in every battle of the Army of the Potomac—except for a short interval of recovery from a gunshot wound at New Market Road on the Peninsula.

The President on June 15, 1863, issued a call for 100,000 troops—from Pennsylvania 50,000, Maryland 10,000, West Virginia 10,000, Ohio 30,000—to serve for six months unless sooner discharged. The Secretary of War called for help from the governors of 13 states. Thirty regiments of Pennsylvania militia, besides artillery and cavalry, and 19 regiments from New York were mobilized at Harrisburg under General Couch from the Army of the Potomac.

From day to day through latter June the news overshadowing all else in the public prints was that of Lee's army. Far behind Lee now was Richmond and its small defensive force. He and his chief, Davis, had decided that "valuable results" might follow the taking of Harrisburg, Philadelphia, Baltimore, Washington; besides immense amounts of supplies, provisions, munitions, there would be European recognition. Men well informed believed that Lee had nearly 100,000 men and 250 cannon, so Simon Cameron at Harrisburg sent word to Lincoln.

The Springfield *Republican* urged Lincoln himself to take the field; he was as good a strategist as the Northern generals had proved, and his personal presence would arouse enthusiasm. Lincoln's instructions to Meade ran that not Richmond but Lee's army must be the objective. Meade followed Lee

Federal dead at Battle of Gettysburg.

with orders from Lincoln "to find and fight" the enemy. From day to day neither Meade nor Lee had been certain where the other was. Lee would rather have taken Harrisburg, its stores and supplies, and then battled Meade on the way to Philadelphia.

Lee rode his horse along roads winding through bright summer landscapes to find himself suddenly looking at the smoke of a battle he had not ordered or planned. Some of his own marching divisions had become entangled with enemy columns, traded shots, and a battle had begun that was to swirl around the little town of Gettysburg. Lee could draw away or carry on; he decided to carry on.

One factor was against Lee: he would have to tell his cannoneers to go slow and count their shells, while Meade's artillery could fire on and on from an endless supply. Also Lee was away from his Virginia, where he knew the ground and the people, while Meade's men were fighting for their homes, women, barns, cattle and fields against invaders and strangers, as Meade saw and felt it.

Lee hammered at the Union left wing the first day, the right wing the second day, Meade on that day sending word to Lincoln that the enemy was "repulsed at all points."

On the third day, July 3, 1863, Lee smashed at Meade's center. Under Longstreet's command, General George Edward Pickett, a tall arrow of a man, with mustache and goatee, with long ringlets of auburn hair flying as he galloped his horse, headed 15,000 men who had nearly a mile to go up a slow slope of land to reach the Union center. Before starting his men on their charge to the Union center, Pickett handed Longstreet a letter to a girl in Richmond he was to marry if he lived. Longstreet had ordered Pickett to go forward and Pickett had penciled on the back of the envelope, "If Old Peter's [Longstreet's] nod means death, good-bye, and God bless you, little one!" An officer held out a flask of whisky: "Take a drink with me; in an hour you'll be in hell or glory." And Pickett said No; he had promised "the little girl" he wouldn't.

Across the long rise of open ground, with the blue flag of Virginia floating ahead, over field and meadow Pickett's 15,000

The National Cemetery at Gettysburg, photographed in 1913. The monument stands where Lincoln was supposed to have delivered the Gettysburg Address.

marched steadily and smoothly, almost as if on a drill ground. Solid shot, grape and canister, from the Union artillery plowed through them, and later a wild rain of rifle bullets. Seven-eighths of a mile they marched in the open sunlight, every man a target for the Union marksmen behind stone fences and breastworks. They obeyed orders; Uncle Robert had said they would go anywhere and do anything. As men fell their places were filled, the ranks closed up. As officers tumbled off horses it was taken as expected in battle. Perhaps half who started reached the Union lines surmounting Cemetery Ridge. Then came cold steel, the bayonet, the clubbed musket. The strongest and last line of the enemy was reached. "The Confederate battle flag waved over his defences," said a Confederate major, "and the fighting over the wall became hand to hand, but more than half having already fallen, our line was too weak to rout the enemy."

Meade rode up white-faced to hear it was a repulse and cried, "Thank God!" Lee commented: "They deserved success as far as it can be deserved by human valor and fortitude. More may have been required of them than they were able to perform." To one of his colonels Lee said, "This has been a sad day for us, a sad day, but we cannot expect always to gain victories." As a heavy rainfall came on the night of July 4 Lee ordered a retreat toward the Potomac.

Meade was seen that day sitting in the open on a stone, his head in his hand, willing it should rain, thankful that his army had, as he phrased it, driven "the invaders from our soil." For three days and nights Meade wasn't out of his clothes, took only snatches of sleep, while he had spoken the controlling decisions to his corps commanders in the bloodiest battle of modern warfare up till that time. Tabulations ran that the Union army lost 23,000 killed, wounded and missing, the Confederate army 28,000. Pickett came out of it alive to write his Virginia girl, "Your soldier lives and mourns and but for you, he would rather, a million times rather, be back there with his dead to sleep for all time in an unknown grave."

Confederate bayonets had taken Union cannon and Union bayonets had retaken the cannon. Round Top, Little Round Top, Culp's Hill, rang with the yells of men shooting and men shot. Meadows of white daisies were pockmarked by horse hoofs. Dead and wounded lay scattered in rows, in little sudden piles. The first battle of the war fought outside a Slave State was over. Lee could have managed it better. So could Meade. The arguments began.

Meade issued an order thanking the Army of the Potomac for glorious results: "An enemy superior in numbers and flushed with the pride of a successful invasion, attempted to overcome and destroy this Army. Utterly baffled and defeated, he has now

withdrawn from the contest . . . The Commanding General looks to the Army for greater efforts to drive from our soil every vestige of the presence of the invader."

On the wall map in his office, Lincoln had watched the colored pins as they changed to indicate military positions. Zach Chandler came in, spoke of painful anxiety because the fate of the nation seemed to hang in the balance, noted "the restless solicitude of Mr. Lincoln, as he paced up and down the room, reading despatches, soliloquizing, and often stopping to trace positions on the map."

The President announced to the country July 4 that news had arrived up to 10 P.M. July 3 such as to cover with honor the Army of the Potomac, to promise great success to the cause of the Union, and to claim condolence for the many gallant fallen. "For this he especially desires that on this day He whose will, not ours, should ever be done be everywhere remembered and reverenced with profoundest gratitude."

While the Battle of Gettysburg was being fought the President had wondered what was happening to Grant. For months he had been haunted by the colossal Vicksburg affair. Grant was trying to starve out one Confederate army in Vicksburg while he held off other Confederate armies from reaching Vicksburg. Against

many representations and pleadings Lincoln had kept Grant in command and was hoping for great results. But the months passed.

Welles July 7 was just saying good afternoon to a distinguished delegation when a dispatch was handed to him with news from Admiral Porter at Vicksburg; that city, its defenses and Pemberton's army of some 30,000 troops had surrendered to Grant and the Union army. Welles excused himself and headed for the Executive Mansion; he found the President with Chase and others, pointing on a map to details of Grant's movements.

Welles gave the news of the Porter telegram. The President rose at once, said they would not discuss Vicksburg and the map any more, and, "I myself will telegraph this news to General Meade." He took his hat as if to go, suddenly stopped and looked down with a shining face at Welles, took him by the hand, put an arm around him and broke forth: "What can we do for the Secretary of the Navy for this glorious intelligence? He is always giving us good news. I cannot, in words, tell you my joy over this result. It is great, Mr. Welles, it is great!"

Over the North as the news spread were mass meetings and speeches, rejoicing, firing of guns, ringing of bells. In hundreds of cities large and small were celebrations with torchlight processions, songs, jubilation, refreshments. "The price of gold . . .

Poster for Frank G. Campbell's Military re-creation
of the Battle of Gettysburg.

fell ten or fifteen cents and the whole country is joyous," wrote Welles. A brass band and a big crowd serenaded the President at the White House. He spoke to the crowd: ". . . in a succession of battles in Pennsylvania, near to us, through three days, so rapidly fought that they might be called one great battle on the 1st, 2d and 3d of the month of July; and on the 4th the cohorts of those who opposed the declaration that all men are created equal, 'turned tail' and run. Gentlemen, this is a glorious theme, and the occasion for a speech, but I am not prepared to make one worthy of the occasion." He would praise those who had fought so bravely. "I dislike to mention the name of one single officer, lest I might do wrong to those I might forget."

The detailed facts arrived at Washington of Grant receiving 31,600 prisoners, 172 cannon, 60,000 muskets. Port Hudson, a little farther south on the Mississippi, had fallen to General Banks with 6,000 prisoners, 51 cannon, 5,000 muskets. The starved Confederates filed out of Vicksburg in silence, the Union soldiers obeying Grant's instructions "to be orderly and quiet as these prisoners pass, and to make no offensive remarks." They were paroled, Grant explaining they were largely from the Southwest. "I knew many of them were tired of the war and would get home just as soon as they could." The prisoners included Lieutenant General John C. Pemberton, a favorite of President Davis, 4 major generals, 15 brigadiers, 80 staff officers.

Meade was writing to Halleck July 8, "I think the decisive battle of the war will be fought in a few days," receiving from Halleck two days later the advice, "I think it will be best for you to postpone a general battle till you can concentrate all your forces and get up your reserves and reinforcements." On July 12 Meade reported to Halleck that he would attack next day "unless something intervenes to prevent it," recognizing that delay would strengthen the enemy and would not increase his own force. The war telegraph office operator Albert B. Chandler said that when this dispatch arrived from Meade, Lincoln paced the room wringing his hands and saying, "They will be ready to fight a magnificent battle when there is no enemy there to fight."

Next day Halleck wired Meade in words surely Lincoln rather than Halleck: "You are strong enough to attack and defeat the enemy before he can effect a crossing. Act upon your own judgment and make your generals execute your orders. Call no council of war. It is proverbial that councils of war never fight. Reinforcements are being pushed on as rapidly as possible. Do not let the enemy escape."

Robert Lincoln said he went into his father's room to find him "in tears, with head bowed upon his arms resting on the table at which he sat." To the question, "Why, what is the matter, father?" the answer came slowly, "My boy, I have just learned that at a council of war, of Meade and his Generals, it had been determined not to pursue Lee, and now the opportune chance of ending this bitter struggle is lost."

On the last day of the Battle of Gettysburg Alexander H. Stephens, Vice-President of the Confederate States, had with one companion started down the James River from Richmond in a small steamer, aiming to reach Washington as commissioners of the Confederate Government and hold a conference with the President of the United States. Their dispatch of July 4 requested permission to pass through the blockade. The final decision after much consultation was in a telegram sent by Lincoln to the blockading admiral: "The request of A. H. Stephens is inadmissible. The customary agents and channels are adequate for all needful communication and conference between the United States forces and the insurgents." Thus did Lincoln dismiss his old-time colleague.

There was issued a "Proclamation of Thanksgiving," July 15, 1863, by the President. "It has pleased Almighty God to hearken to the supplications and prayers of an afflicted people," ran the opening chords, "and to vouchsafe to the army and the navy of the United States victories on land and on the sea so signal and so effective as to furnish reasonable grounds for augmented confidence that the Union of these States will be maintained, their constitution preserved, and their peace and prosperity permanently restored . . . It is meet and right to recognize and confess the presence of the Almighty Father and the power of His Hand equally in these triumphs and in these sorrows:

"Now, therefore, be it known that I do set apart Thursday the 6th. day of August next, to be observed as a day for National Thanksgiving, Praise and Prayer, and I invite the People of the United States to assemble on that occasion in their customary places of worship, and in the forms approved by their own consciences, render the homage due to the Divine Majesty, for the wonderful things he has done in the Nation's behalf . . ."

On the date this proclamation was issued the dignity and majesty of the U.S. Government was being challenged, upset, smeared with insult and threatened with the disorders and violence of revolution, in the largest city in the United States.

During the three days of July 13, 14, 15, mobs or crowds in New York City met by prearrangement, with a specific design as to what points they would attack and carry, drove out the U.S. provost marshal from his office at 43d Street and Third Avenue, wrecked the wheel or revolving drum from which the names of drafted men were drawn, tore to pieces the books and papers, poured turpentine on the floor, set the building on fire, fought off police and firemen, and the draft office and six adjoining buildings burned. They wrecked and burned the U.S. draft office on Broadway two doors from 29th Street, looted stores nearby, and burned 12 buildings; they smashed windows and doors and sacked the home of Republican Mayor Opdyke and burned at midnight the home of U.S. Postmaster Abram Wakeman.

The mobs of the first day's riots aimed straight at a thing they hated: the Draft. It was a Monday, and on the previous Saturday 1,200 names had been picked by a blindfolded man out of the wheel. These 1,200 names had been published, and unless something happened to make the Government change its mind most of the men answering to these 1,200 names would be put into uniforms and sent to fight.

Drafted men, their relatives and friends, reinforced by thousands of sympathizers who favored some kind of direct action, gathered early the morning of July 13 in vacant lots with clubs, staves, cart rungs, pieces of iron, and moved as if by agreement to a lot near Central Park where they organized, began patrolling the city, and put the first sign of their wrath and vengeance on the draft offices wrecked and burned. The first acts of the three days' tornado had some semblance of an uprising of the people against a Government discriminating in its conscription between the rich and the poor. The second and third days, however, saw the events come under the sway of the city's criminal and gang elements, then numbering between 50,000 and 70,000, who swarmed out for loot and the work of getting the police defied and overrun.

A photo from the battlefield of Gettysburg. This is a dead Confederate sharpshooter at foot of Little Round Top in the area known as Devil's Den.

Besides the many mobs carrying banners inscribed "No Draft" and "No $300 Arrangements with Us," there had been many other mobs with varied and mixed motives. Class war was the cry behind the big placards of one division: "The Poor Man's Blood for the Rich Man's Money." In thousands of boys the savage was unleashed; they robbed houses and set them on fire; they beat to death with fists and clubs the young Negro cripple Abraham Franklin; they tore off the clothes of Jeremiah Robinson, who was trying to escape to a ferryboat wearing his wife's dress and hood, threw him to the pavement, kicked him in the face and ribs, killed him and threw the body into the river.

Robert Nugent, assistant provost marshal in charge of conscription, received the second day of the riots a telegram from his Washington chief, James B. Fry, directing him to suspend the draft. Governor Seymour and Mayor Opdyke clamored that he should publish this order. Nugent said he had no authority, but he finally consented to sign his name to a notice: "The draft has

been suspended in New York City and Brooklyn," which was published in newspapers. This had a marked quieting effect.

The storm in the streets began to slow down as though winds had changed. There was added quieting effect as infantry, cavalry, artillery, from the Army of the Potomac commenced arriving.

After 150 Regular Army soldiers with ball cartridges had faced a crowd of 2,000, fired in the air, and received a volley of stones in reply, and had then shot into the swarming and defiant mass, killing 12 and wounding more, the hullabaloo began to die down.

Lincoln did during those hectic summer weeks prepare an address to the country giving the facts and logic which dictated his actions in the draft. His mind had dwelt, evidently, on a law to

Confederate soldiers at Gettysburg battfield, in the "slaughter pen" which was also at the foot of Little Round Top.

U.S. General Henry W. Halleck.

enforce universal selective service, the Government taking all men physically fit, no man escaping by purchase or substitution. Such conscription was operating in several European monarchies and republics, but as Lincoln looked out across the American scene in 1863, he seemed to believe it could not then be put to work in the United States, even if he could find Congressmen to advocate it. Perhaps the opposition had more than a demagogue's idle phrase in the cry "The rich man's money against the poor man's blood."

New York City saw on August 19, 1863, no less than 10,000 troops from the Army of the Potomac assisted by the 1st Division New York State Guards. Governor Seymour proclaimed that citizens should obey the law of Congress as to conscription. New draft offices went into operation. Cavalry patrols rode up and down the streets.

Lincoln wrote a letter that James C. Conkling read at an immense mass meeting in Springfield, Illinois: "There are those who are dissatisfied with me. To such I would say: You desire peace; and you blame me that we do not have it." One way to peace was to suppress the rebellion by force of arms. "This, I am trying to do. Are you for it? If you are, so far we are agreed. If you are not for it, a second way is, to give up the Union. I am against this. Are you for it? If you are, you should say so plainly. If you are not for *force*, nor yet for *dissolution*, there only remains some imaginable *compromise*."

He promised that if any peace proposition came from those who controlled the Confederate Army, "It shall not be rejected, and kept a secret from you." There was another issue. "You are dissatisfied with me about the negro . . . I suggested compensated emancipation; to which you replied you wished not to be taxed to buy negroes. But I had not asked you to be taxed to buy negroes, except in such way, as to save you from greater taxation to save the Union exclusively by other means."

He launched into the finish of what was really a paper aimed at the masses of people in America and Europe: "The signs look better. The Father of Waters again goes unvexed to the sea . . . And while those who have cleared the great river may well be proud, even that is not all. It is hard to say that anything has been more bravely, and well done, than at Antietam, Murfreesboro, Gettysburg, and on many fields of lesser note. Nor must Uncle Sam's Web-feet be forgotten. At all the watery margins they have been present. Not only on the deep sea, the broad bay, and the rapid river, but also up the narrow muddy bayou, and wherever the ground was a little damp, they have been, and made their tracks. Thanks to all. For the great republic—for the principle it lives by, and keeps alive—for man's vast future,—thanks to all."

"Peace does not appear so distant as it did. I hope it will come soon, and come to stay; and so come as to be worth the keeping in all future time. It will then have been proved that, among free men, there can be no successful appeal from the ballot to the bullet; and that they who take such appeal are sure to lose their case, and pay the cost. And then, there will be some black men who can remember that, with silent tongue, and clenched teeth, and steady eye, and well-poised bayonet, they have helped mankind on to this great consummation; while, I fear, there will be some white ones, unable to forget that, with malignant heart, and deceitful speech, they strove to hinder it. Still, let us not be over-sanguine of a speedy final triumph. Let us be quite sober. Let us diligently apply the means, never doubting that a just God, in his own good time, will give us the rightful result."

No previous letter, address or state paper of Lincoln's received such warmhearted comment. Many newspapers joined with the New York *Times* seeing it as having hard sense, a temper defying malice. "Even the Copperhead gnaws upon it as vainly as a viper upon a file. The most consummate rhetorician never used language more pat to the purpose and still there is not a word not familiar to the plainest plowman . . . Abraham Lincoln is today the most popular man in the Republic . . ."

In September '63 the Boston publisher Benjamin B. Russell issued a collection of *The Letters of President Lincoln on Questions of National Policy*, with a preface, as though the letters were literature and unique reading matter. The sheaf frilled 22 pages, and sold at eight cents a copy, two copies 15 cents.

By the carefully wrought appeal in simple words aimed to reach millions of readers and by the face-to-face contact with thousands who came to the White House, Lincoln was holding to the single purpose of adding momentum to what there was of popular will for war. The late summer and early fall of '63 seemed to mark a deepening of loyalties to Lincoln and his vision of where to go and how.

BATTLE OF CHICKAMAUGA.

CHAPTER 35

LINCOLN AT STORM CENTER

The Battle of Chickamauga, September 19 & 20, 1863.

LINCOLN AT STORM CENTER

Gen. Meade's headquarters, near Brandy Station, April 12, 1864.

AFTER the drawn battle at Murfreesboro in January '63, General Rosecrans kept the Army of the Cumberland at that same place in Tennessee for six months, fortifying, drilling, setting no troops into motion. Late in June '63 Rosecrans marched his forces through rough and broken country, and by September 9 had, without a battle, maneuvered the Confederate army under Bragg out of Chattanooga and put his own troops into that strategic center. While on this operation, Rosecrans wrote to Lincoln early in August reciting conditions: bad roads, bad weather, cavalry weakness, long hauls for bridge material.

Rosecrans, 44 years old, was born in Kingston, Ohio. Graduating fifth in the class of 1842 at West Point, he served four years as professor of natural philosophy and of engineering at the National Academy. He had organized a kerosene manufacturing company just before the war began, quit coal oil and money-making, and served with credit under McClellan in West Virginia;

he came through hard fighting at Corinth and Murfreesboro, rated as an able commanding officer, not lacking piety.

The Richmond War Department had arranged for Longstreet with 20,000 troops from the Army of Northern Virginia to be sent by railroad down across the Carolinas and up into far northern Georgia to the help of Bragg. This gave Bragg 70,000 troops as against Rosecrans' 57,000. The two armies grappled at Chickamauga Creek near Crawfish Spring September 19, 1863.

Late that Sunday afternoon Dana at Chattanooga wired: "My report today is of deplorable importance. Chickamauga is as fatal a name in our history as Bull Run." The right and center were shattered. The left wing, under the Union Virginian General George H. Thomas, held. Till sunset, till darkness and night, his 25,000 men held solid on a horseshoe of a rocky hillock against twice their number. One brigade ran out of ammunition and met

Longstreet's veterans with the bayonet. Next day Thomas began moving in good order to Chattanooga, Bragg failing to make another attack.

A heavy day's work had been done that Sunday, with Union killed, wounded and missing reckoned at 16,000, Confederate at 18,000, a larger affair in blood loss than Antietam.

Enough news of the battle reached Lincoln that Sunday night so he could not sleep. Welles noted on Monday: "The President came to me this afternoon with the latest news. He was feeling badly. Tells me a dispatch was sent to him at the Soldiers' Home shortly after he got asleep, and so disturbed him that he had no more rest, but arose and came to the city and passed the remainder of the night awake and watchful."

At 2:30 A.M. September 24, Meade was ordered by telegraph to prepare two army corps, under General Hooker, ready for transport, with five days' cooked provisions, with baggage, artillery, ammunition, horses, to follow. To Mrs. Lincoln at the Fifth Avenue Hotel in New York, the President September 24 telegraphed as to Chickamauga that the Union army was worsted mainly in yielding ground. "According to rebel accounts . . . they lost six killed, and eight wounded. Of the killed, one Major Genl. and five Brigadiers, including your brother-in-law, Helm." Now Lincoln wrote for his wife's stepmother at Lexington, Kentucky: "Allow Mrs. Robert S. Todd, widow, to go south and bring her daughter, Mrs. General B. Hardin Helm, with her children, north to Kentucky."

Then in three weeks, early in September, Burnside and the Army of the Ohio had crossed the Tennessee line, entered Kingston, and marched into Knoxville to be met by cheering crowds. Flags long hidden were flashed out into sunlight, officers and soldiers welcomed into homes.

Though repeatedly ordered to join Rosecrans, Burnside delayed, and September 25 Lincoln wrote him: ". . . On the 19th you telegraph once from Knoxville, and twice from Greenville, acknowledging receipt of order, and saying you will hurry support to Rosecrans. On the 20th you telegraph again from Knoxville, saying you will do all you can, and are hurrying troops to Rosecrans. On the 21st. you telegraph from Morristown, saying you will hurry support to Rosecrans; and now your despatch of

the 23rd comes in from Carter's Station, still farther away from Rosecrans."

The Confederates had a hold on the Tennessee River by which they blocked water transport of food and supplies for Rosecrans' army; and the long rough wagon route that met rail connections with Nashville was threatened. The Dana reports ran gloomier that second week in October; Rosecrans was "dawdling" while catastrophe hung close, starvation or disorderly retreat. And on October 16: "The incapacity of the commander is astonishing, and it often seems difficult to believe him of sound mind. His imbecility appears to be contagious."

The same day Halleck wrote to Grant at Cairo, Illinois: "You will receive herewith the orders of the President of the United States placing you in command of the Departments of the Ohio, Cumberland and Tennessee." Thus Lincoln put Grant at the head of all military operations west of the Alleghenies. "It is left optional with you to supersede General G. H. Thomas or not."

Now Thomas was joined with Sherman and other tried commanders, with Grant as chief of the West, with forces massed at Chattanooga near the Alabama and Georgia state lines, wedging toward the Deep South as if hoping to cut it in two.

But Lee had again outguessed Meade, as Meade humbly and frankly confessed to his wife in a note from Warrenton, Virginia, four days later: "Lee has retired across the Rappahannock, after completely destroying the railroad on which I depend for my supplies. His object is to prevent my advance, and in the meantime send more troops to Bragg. This was a deep game, and I am free to admit that in the playing of it he has got the advantage of me."

From the Southern press and home strategists, Lee was receiving the same sort of criticism as that heaped on Meade in the North. Like Meade, he was too slow and too prudent, ran many an editorial. They were both Christian gentlemen, Meade and Lee, clean, reverent and pious, each strict in the observance of Episcopal forms, praying regularly to the same God while they led their hosts seeking to mangle and eviscerate each other.

In promoting Admiral Dahlgren, Lincoln gave his approval to aggressive tactics at Charleston, whatever the increased cost.

During six days in August a fleet of monitors and gunboats bombarded Charleston; an army of 18,000 troops waited while 12 batteries of heavy rifled cannon opened fire at a two-mile distance; in one 40-minute period they dropped 120,000 pounds of projectiles into the defending forts. A storming column of Negro soldiers led by the white Colonel Robert Gould Shaw, of an old and distinguished Boston family, captured Fort Wagner. Shaw, "the blue-eyed child of fortune," crying, "Onward, boys!" fell dead from bullets, and became an enshrined memory and a symbol to the antislavery forces of the North.

Lincoln read the news telegraphed by the commanding general, August 24: "Fort Sumter is today a shapeless and harmless mass of ruins." As later news trickled in it turned out that the much-hated city still serenely held her own. And though Fort Sumter seemed to be a ruin, it kept a garrison. For many months Charleston was let alone.

On September 15 was issued a proclamation as finally drafted by Seward. Solemnly it was made known by the President that "the privilege of the writ of *habeas corpus* is suspended throughout the United States" and this suspension would continue till modified or revoked by a later proclamation. A sonorous pronouncement it would be when read by a provost marshal, in support of the marshal's saying in effect to the judge, "I'm going to take this drafted man away with me and put him in the army and your court can't stop me because I have the United States Army and Navy backing me."

While the President in early October was dealing with habeas corpus, with the committee of radicals from Missouri and Kansas, with Burnside in Tennessee, Rosecrans at Chattanooga and Meade in Virginia, besides many routine matters, Seward took on the work of writing a Thanksgiving proclamation, which the President signed. Over the signature of A. Lincoln came the pronouncement, "I do therefore invite my fellow citizens in every part of the United States, and also those who are at sea and those who are sojourning in foreign lands, to set apart and observe the last Thursday of November next, as a day of Thanksgiving and Praise to our beneficent Father who dwelleth in the Heavens."

Both Lee and Davis, after the July defeats, issued appeals to soldiers to come back to the army. Davis offered pardon to officers and men absent without leave who would return in 20 days. Wives, mothers, sisters, daughters of the Confederacy were beseeched by the Richmond head of their Government, "If all now absent return to the ranks you will equal in numbers the invaders."

Thousands of Confederate deserters in the mountains of Alabama fought off cavalry sent to arrest them. The Confederate Bureau of Ordnance asked for the church bells of Georgia to be melted and remolded for war. One gold dollar bought ten paper Confederate dollars. A Louisiana father, beginning to doubt the Southern orators, was writing his son in the Confederate Army, "This war was got up drunk but they will have to settle it sober."

In a call for 300,000 more troops October 16, 1863, Lincoln said the new men were wanted to follow up and clinch the winning streak of Union armies that summer. The document stipulated that quotas would be *required* from the various states. In reality it was another executive order for a draft. Between provost marshals and various state officials, particularly Governor Seymour of New York, there began discussions and quarrels as to methods of drafting. The war, the draft, habeas corpus suspension, had been denounced at five overflow meetings in and around Cooper Union in New York City June 3, 1863, at a Peace Convention.

On October 13, Election Day in Ohio and Pennsylvania, Welles called at the White House, and noted, "The President says he feels nervous." The wires that night clicked off news that the Ohio Copperhead ticket had the votes of 185,000 citizens and 2,200 soldiers of Ohio. However, John Brough of the Union party was elected governor by a majority of 61,910 in the citizen vote and 39,179 in the soldier ballots, a total of over 101,000. Pennsylvania returns gave Governor Curtin re-election by a 41,000 majority. A letter from General McClellan endorsing Curtin's opponent had had little effect.

Welles on October 14 found Lincoln relieved of the gloom of the day before.

In all the Northern States except New Jersey, the Union party ticket swept the field. A Chicago newspaper exulted: "Everywhere it has been a slaughter of Copperheads. Springfield, Ill., went Union by 138, a gain of 440 since 1862."

CHAPTER 36

LINCOLN SPEAKS AT GETTYSBURG

LINCOLN SPEAKS AT GETTYSBURG

David Wills house (historic photo).

David Wills house (contemporary photo).

APRINTED invitation notified Lincoln that on Thursday, November 19, 1863, exercises would be held for the dedication of a National Soldiers' Cemetery at Gettysburg.

The duties of orator of the day had fallen on Edward Everett. Born in 1794, he had been U.S. Senator, governor of Massachusetts, member of Congress, Secretary of State under Fillmore, Minister to Great Britain, Phi Beta Kappa poet at Harvard, professor of Greek at Harvard, president of Harvard. His wife was Charlotte Gray Brooks, daughter of Peter Chardon Brooks, first of American marine and life-insurance millionaires. Serene stars had watched over their home life and children until Everett's wife was sent to a private retreat, incurably insane.

The Union of States was a holy concept to Everett, and the slavery issue secondary, though when president of Harvard from 1846 to 1849 he refused to draw the color line, saying in the case of a Negro applicant, Beverly Williams, that "If this boy passes the examinations, he will be admitted." Suave, handsomely venerable in his 69th year, Everett was a natural choice of the

Copy Portrait of Abraham Lincoln.

Pennsylvania commissioners. He notified them that he would appear for the Gettysburg dedication November 19.

Lincoln meanwhile, in reply to the printed invitation, sent word to the commissioners that he would be present at the ceremonies. The commissioners then considered whether the President should be asked to deliver an address. Clark E. Carr of Galesburg, Illinois, representing his state on the Board of Commissioners, noted that the decision of the board to invite Lincoln to speak was "an afterthought."

Lamon noted that Lincoln wrote part of his intended Gettysburg address in Washington, covered a sheet of foolscap paper with a memorandum of it, and before taking it out of his hat and reading it to Lamon he said it was not at all satisfactory to him. He had been too busy to give it the time he would like to.

The Gettysburg speech was shaping at the same time that Lincoln was preparing his annual message to Congress, assembling it in less than three weeks. In that message he would point to "actual commencement of work upon the Pacific railroad," his own act of fixing an initial point being the most tangible part of the commencement.

Andrew G. Curtin, Governor of Pennsylvania, headed the Gettysburg cemetery dedication.

When Lincoln boarded the train for Gettysburg November 18, his best chum in the world, Tad, lay sick abed and the doctors not sure what ailed him. The mother still mourned for Willie and was hysterical about Tad. But the President felt imperative duty called him to Gettysburg.

Flags and red, white and blue bunting decorated the four-car special train. Aboard were three Cabinet members, Seward, Usher and Blair, Nicolay and Hay, Army and Navy representatives, newspapermen, the French and Italian Ministers and attaches. The rear third of the last coach had a drawing room, where from time to time the President talked with nearly everyone aboard as they came and went. Approaching Hanover Junction, he arose and said, "Gentlemen, this is all very pleasant, but the people will expect me to say something to them tomorrow, and I must give the matter some thought." He then returned to the rear room of the car.

Edward Everett, orator at Gettysburg ceremony.

Gettysburg arrived afoot and horseback—members of the U.S. Government, the Army and Navy, governors of states, mayors of cities, a regiment of troops, hospital corps, telegraph company representatives, Knights Templar, Masonic Fraternity, Odd Fellows and other benevolent associations, the press, fire departments, citizens of Pennsylvania and other states. At ten o'clock Lincoln in a black suit, high silk hat and white gloves came out of the Wills residence, mounted a horse, and held a reception on horseback. At 11 the parade began to move. Clark E. Carr, just behind the President, believed he noticed that the President sat erect and looked majestic to begin with and then got to thinking so that his body leaned forward, his arms hung limp, his head bent far down.

A long telegram from Stanton at ten o'clock had been handed him. Burnside seemed safe though threatened at Knoxville, Grant was starting a big battle at Chattanooga, and "Mrs. Lincoln reports your son's health as a great deal better and he will be out today."

At sundown the train pulled into Gettysburg and Lincoln was driven to the Wills residence. A sleepy little country town of 3,500 was overflowing with human pulses again.

At dinner in the Wills home that evening Lincoln met Edward Everett, Governor Curtin and others. About 11 o'clock, he gathered his sheets of paper and went next door for a half-hour with his Secretary of State. Whether Seward made slight or material alterations in the text was known only to Lincoln and Seward. It was midnight or later that Lincoln went to sleep. He slept better for having a telegram from Stanton reporting there was no real war news and "On inquiry Mrs. Lincoln informs me that your son is better this evening."

Fifteen thousand, some said 30,000 or 50,000, people were on Cemetery Hill for the exercises next day when the procession from

The march was over in 15 minutes. But Mr. Everett, the orator of the day, had not arrived. Bands played till noon. Mr. Everett arrived. On the platform sat Governors Curtin of Pennsylvania, Bradford of Maryland, Morton of Indiana, Seymour of New York, Parker of New Jersey, Dennison of Ohio, with ex-Governor Tod and Governor-elect Brough of Ohio, Edward Everett and his daughter, Major Generals Schenck, Stahel, Doubleday and Couch, Brigadier General Gibbon and Provost Marshal General Fry, foreign Ministers, members of Congress, Colonel Ward Hill Lamon, Secretary Usher, and the President of the United States with Secretary Seward and Postmaster General Blair immediately at his left.

The U.S. House chaplain, the Reverend Thomas H. Stockton, offered a prayer while the thousands stood with uncovered heads. Benjamin B. French, officer in charge of buildings in Washington, introduced the Honorable Edward Everett, who

Only known photo of Lincoln at Gettysburg (seated, center).

rose, bowed low to Lincoln, saying, "Mr. President." Lincoln responded, "Mr. Everett."

The orator of the day then stood in silence before a crowd that stretched to limits that would test his voice. Beyond and around were the wheat fields, the meadows, the peach orchards, long slopes of land, and five and seven miles further the contemplative blue ridge of a low mountain range. His eyes could sweep all this as he faced the audience. He had taken note of it in his prepared address. "Overlooking these broad fields now reposing from the labors of the waning year, the mighty Alleghanies dimly towering before us, the graves of our brethren beneath our feet, it is with hesitation that I raise my poor voice to break the eloquent silence of God and Nature . . . As my eye ranges over the fields whose sods were so lately moistened by the blood of gallant and loyal men, I feel, as never before, how truly it was said of old that it is sweet and becoming to die for one's country."

He gave an outline of how the war began, traversed decisive features of the three days' battles at Gettysburg, discussed the doctrine of state sovereignty and denounced it, drew parallels from European history, and came to his peroration quoting Pericles on dead patriots: "The whole earth is the sepulchre of illustrious men." He had spoken for one hour and 57 minutes,

some said a trifle over two hours, repeating almost word for word an address that occupied nearly two newspaper pages.

Everett came to his closing sentence without a faltering voice: "Down to the latest period of recorded time, in the glorious annals of our common country there will be no brighter page than that which relates the battles of Gettysburg." It was the effort of his life and embodied the perfections of the school of oratory in which he had spent his career.

The Baltimore Glee Club sang an ode written for the occasion by Benjamin B. French. Having read Everett's address, Lincoln knew when the moment drew near for him to speak. He took out his own manuscript from a coat pocket, put on his steel-bowed glasses, stirred in his chair, looked over the manuscript, and put it back in his pocket. The Baltimore Glee Club finished. Ward Hill Lamon rose and spoke the words "The President of the United States," who rose, and holding in one hand the two sheets of paper at which he occasionally glanced, delivered the address in his high-pitched and clear-carrying voice. The Cincinnati *Commercial* reporter wrote, "The President rises slowly, draws from his pocket a paper, and, when commotion subsides, in a sharp, unmusical treble voice, reads the brief and pithy remarks." Hay wrote in his diary, "The President, in a firm, free way, with more

Close-up of Lincoln at Gettysburg.

Lincoln's address at the dedication of the Gettysburg National Cemetery, Nov. 19, 1863. Engraved by Sherwood Lith. Co.

grace than is his wont, said his half dozen words of consecration." Charles Hale of the Boston *Advertiser*, also officially representing Governor Andrew of Massachusetts, had notebook and pencil in hand, took down the slow-spoken words of the President:

Fourscore and seven years ago, our fathers brought forth upon this continent a new nation, conceived in liberty and dedicated to the proposition that all men are created equal.

Now we are engaged in a great civil war, testing whether that nation—or any nation, so conceived and so dedicated—can long endure.

We are met on a great battle-field of that war. We are met to dedicate a portion of it as the final resting place of those who have given their lives that that nation might live.

It is altogether fitting and proper that we should do this.

But, in a larger sense, we cannot dedicate, we cannot consecrate, we cannot hallow, this ground. The brave men, living and dead, who struggled here, have consecrated it, far above our power to add or to detract.

The world will very little note nor long remember what we say here; but it can never forget what they did here.

It is for us, the living, rather, to be dedicated, here, to the unfinished work that they have thus far so nobly carried on. It is rather for us to be here dedicated to the great task remaining before us; that from these honored dead we take increased devotion to that cause for which they here gave the last full measure of devotion; that we here highly resolve that these dead shall not have died in vain; that the nation shall, under God, have a new birth of freedom, and that government of the people, by the people, for the people, shall not perish from the earth.

In the written copy of his speech from which he read Lincoln used the phrase "our poor power." In other copies of the speech which he wrote out later he again used the phrase "our poor power." So it was evident that he meant to use the word "poor" when speaking to his audience, but he omitted it. Also in the copy held in his hands while facing the audience he had not written the words "under God," though he did speak those words and include them in later copies which he wrote. Therefore the words "under God" were decided upon after he wrote the text the night before at the Wills residence.

The New York *Tribune* and many other newspapers indicated "(Applause.)" at five places in the address and "(Long continued applause.)" at the end. The applause, however, according to most of the responsible witnesses, was formal, a tribute to the occasion. Ten sentences had been spoken in less than three minutes. A photographer had made ready to record a great historic moment, had bustled about with his dry plates, his black box on a tripod, and before he had his head under the hood for an exposure, the President had said "by the people, for the people" and the nick of time was past for a photograph.

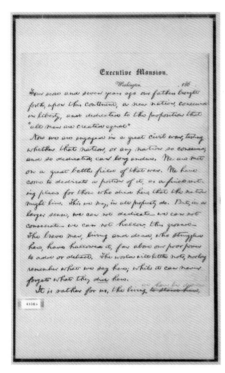

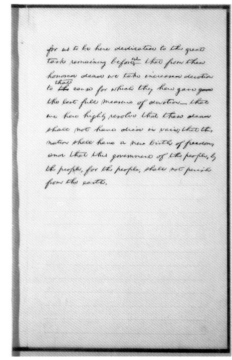

The Chicago *Tribune* had a reporter who telegraphed (unless some editor who read the address added his own independent opinion) a sentence: "The dedicatory remarks of President Lincoln will live among the annals of man." "The Lounger" in *Harper's Weekly* inquired why the ceremony at Gettysburg was one of the most striking events of the war. "The President and the Cabinet were there, with famous soldiers and civilians. The oration by Mr. Everett was smooth and cold . . . The few words of the President were from the heart to the heart. They can not be read, even, without kindling emotion. 'The world will little note nor long remember what we say here, but it can never forget what they did here.' It was as simple and felicitous and earnest a word as was ever spoken."

Everett's opinion was written to Lincoln the next day: "I should be glad if I could flatter myself that I came as near to the central idea of the occasion in two hours as you did in two minutes." Lincoln's immediate reply was: "In our respective parts yesterday, you could not have been excused to make a short address, nor I a long one. I am pleased to know that, in your judgment, the little I did say was not entirely a failure."

At Everett's request Lincoln wrote with pen and ink a copy of his Gettysburg Address, and the manuscript was auctioned at a Sanitary Fair in New York for the benefit of soldiers. On request of George Bancroft, the historian, he wrote another copy for a Soldiers' and Sailors' Fair at Baltimore. He wrote still another to be lithographed as a facsimile in a publication, *Autographed Leaves of Our Country's Authors.* For Mr. Wills, his host at Gettysburg, he wrote another. The first draft, written in Washington, and the second one, held while delivering it, went into Hay's hands to be eventually presented to the Library of Congress.

He had stood that day, the world's foremost spokesman of popular government, saying that democracy was yet worth fighting for. What he meant by "a new birth of freedom" for the nation could have a thousand interpretations. For the first time since he became President he had on a dramatic occasion declaimed, howsoever it might be read, Jefferson's proposition which had been a slogan of the Revolutionary War—"All men are created equal"—leaving no other inference than that he regarded the Negro slave as a man. His outwardly smooth sentences were inside of them gnarled and tough with the enigmas of the American experiment.

Lincoln's speech at Gettysburg.

CHAPTER 37

EPIC '63 DRAWS TO A CLOSE

*Abraham Lincoln portrait lithographed
by Chr. Kimmel & Forster, 1865.*

EPIC '63 DRAWS TO A CLOSE

A WEEK after Lincoln's return from Gettysburg, Hay wrote to Nicolay: "The President is sick in bed. Bilious." Still later came definite information. The President had varioloid, a mild form of smallpox. Owen Lovejoy sent in his name, waited in the reception room, saw a door open just enough to frame Lincoln in a dressing gown saying, "Lovejoy, are you afraid?" "No, I have had the smallpox." And walking in, he heard Lincoln: "Lovejoy, there is one good thing about this. I now have something I can give everybody." Press items told of office seekers suddenly fleeing the White House on hearing what ailed the President.

An epic of action around Chattanooga came to its high point and Lincoln on a sickbed could read a Grant telegram: "Lookout Mountain top, all the rifle-pits in Chattanooga Valley, and Missionary Ridge entire, have been carried and now held by us," and a dispatch from Thomas: "Missionary Ridge was carried simultaneously at six different points . . . Among the prisoners are many who were paroled at Vicksburg." For the first time in a large-scale combat, Confederate soldiers had been routed, had run away. They had valor, as they had shown at Chickamauga. What explained their panic? The usual answer was Bragg, upright, moral, irascible, disputatious, censorious, dyspeptic, nervous, so harsh with his corrections and criticisms that the discipline of his army had gone to pieces. Grant had studied Bragg, knew him as Lee knew McClellan, and gauged his plans accordingly. Bragg had cornered Grant, put his army within gunshot range overlooking the Union army, making retreat for Grant "almost certain annihilation," said Grant. Then the rank and file of Grant's army had thrown orders to the wind and taken mountains away from an army holding the top ridges with cannon and rifle pits.

Anger at Jeff Davis, and mistrust of him, arose among some of his best aides because of his not knowing Bragg was second-rate. And Jeff Davis answered by appointing his friend Bragg Chief of Staff of the Confederate armies, with headquarters in Richmond Newspapers of the North spread the story before their readers the last Thursday of November, the Day of Thanksgiving proclaimed by the President weeks earlier.

Now Sherman could be released with an army to march on Knoxville and relieve Longstreet's siege of Burnside there—which Sherman did in a clean, fast operation. Now Grant and Sherman could lay their plans to move farther south—on Atlanta—perhaps drive a wedge and split the Confederacy that lay east of the Mississippi.

The President's annual message to Congress began with "renewed, and profoundest gratitude to God" for another year "of health, and of sufficiently abundant harvests." Efforts to stir up foreign wars had failed. The treaty between the United States and Great Britain for suppression of the slave trade was working. The national banking law passed by Congress had proved a valuable support to public credit. The troops were being paid punctually. And the people? The President saluted them. "By no people were the burdens incident to a great war ever more cheerfully borne."

Looking to the present and future, the President had thought fit to issue a Proclamation of Amnesty and Reconstruction, a copy of it being transmitted to Congress. To those who wanted it the Union Government would give amnesty, forget what had been. Reconstruction, the bringing together again of the departed brothers into the Union, would begin with amnesty. This was the theory and the hope, not explicitly formulated, that underlay the proclamation and the oath Lincoln discussed for Congress in his message. He cited his constitutional pardoning power: through the rebellion many persons were guilty of treason; the President was authorized to extend pardon and amnesty on conditions he deemed expedient. Full pardon would be granted with restoration of property, except as to slaves and where rights of third parties intervened, and on condition that every such person took an oath:

. . . in presence of Almighty God, that I will henceforth faithfully support, protect and defend the Constitution of the United States, and the union of the States thereunder; and that I will, in like manner, abide by and faithfully support all acts of

Congress . . . and . . . abide by and faithfully support all proclamations of the President made during the existing rebellion having reference to slaves . . . So help me God.

The proclamation had no reference to states that had kept loyal governments, never seceded—meaning Missouri, Kentucky, Maryland, Delaware. The intention of the proclamation was to give a mode by which national authority and loyal state governments might be re-established. The President's message reasoned for the amnesty proclamation. "The form of an oath is given, but no man is coerced to take it. The man is only promised a pardon in case he voluntarily takes the oath . . ."

The Executive set at rest all talk that the Emancipation Proclamation would be revoked. "While I remain in my present position I shall not attempt to retract or modify the emancipation proclamation; nor shall I return to slavery any person who is free by the terms of that proclamation, or by any of the acts of Congress." Before this sentence the silence in the hall was "profound," noted Noah Brooks, but with its reading "an irresistible burst of applause" swept the main floor and galleries.

Movements for emancipation in states not included in the Emancipation Proclamation were "matters of profound gratulation." He still favored gradual emancipation by Federal purchase of slaves. "While I do not repeat in detail what I have heretofore so earnestly urged upon this subject, my general views and feelings remain unchanged."

This month of December '63 seemed to mark the beginning of a period in which, North and South, extremists more often referred to Confederate leaders ending on the gallows. Hanging with rigor, system, ceremonial, lay in the imaginings of the more fiery Republican radicals.

The new Congress in December '63, by the New York *Tribune Almanac,* had in the House 102 Republicans and unconditional Unionists, 75 Democrats, 9 Border State men; in the Senate 36 Republicans and unconditional Unionists, 9 Democrats and 5 conditional Unionists.

Day after day the question of the Negro and his destiny crossed the events of each hour. The trend of feeling against slavery went on deepening. Francis George Shaw of Boston wrote to the President, "My only son, Colonel Robert Gould Shaw of the 54th Regiment Massachusetts Volunteers (colored troops) was killed on the parapet of Fort Wagner in South Carolina, and now lies buried in its ditch among his brave and devoted followers." The father urged the President to take immediate measures for protection to colored troops. "If our son's services and death shall contribute in any degree towards securing to our colored troops that equal justice which is a holy right of every loyal defender of our beloved country, we shall esteem our great loss a blessing."

That the year of '63 was coming to an end with not one Negro slave revolt, not one scene of killing and plunder, as a result of the Emancipation Proclamation, made the going easier for Lincoln.

The year of 1863 saw glimmering of the last hopes of the Richmond Government for European recognition. The despair of Jefferson Davis as to overseas help, as to ships or money from England was set forth in his December message to the Confederate Congress. Davis dwelt at such length and so bitterly on the point that he was rebuked by some of the Southern newspapers for overemphasis of it.

Meanwhile the war, the Emancipation Proclamation, the messages of Lincoln, the antislavery propaganda, had sharpened the instinct against slavery among masses of people in all countries. For all the quaffing of toasts to the British Queen and her people, Lincoln and Seward saw that their only dependable wellwisher in Europe, except republican Switzerland, was the land of absolutist monarchy, Russia, the farthest of European extremes from "government of the people, by the people, for the people."

Seward arranged secret understandings with Russia so momentous that he must have consulted with Lincoln about them. In America perhaps only Seward and Lincoln knew what conditional assurances were given the Russian government as to the purchase of the peninsula of Alaska. Not to Nicolay nor Hay nor Noah Brooks, nor to others to whom the President sometimes revealed secrets of state, did he give any inklings. And not even to his bosom friend Thurlow Weed did Seward give clues. Estimates ran that it was worth from $1,400,000 to $10,000,000. The United States was to buy it as soon as convenient, the purchase price to include certain naval expenses of the Russian government—some such understanding was worked out between the Washington and St. Petersburg governments.

Early in October '63 one Russian fleet lay in San Francisco harbor, another at New York with five first-class war vessels. Stalwart Muscovites in gay uniforms, outlandish whiskers, in excellent Russian, indifferent French and worse English, added merriment wherever they went. They sat for Brady photographs. They visited Meade's headquarters in Virginia, fell from the upper decks of cavalry horses, ate heartily, carried their liquor well.

New Year's Day of 1864 came, and Benjamin Perley Poore noted at the morning reception in the White House: "Mr. Lincoln was in excellent spirits, giving each passer-by a cordial greeting and a warm shake of the hand, while for some there was a quiet joke." Mrs. Lincoln stood at his right hand, wearing purple silk trimmed with black velvet and lace, a lace necktie fastened with a pearl pin, a white plume topping her headdress. Noah Brooks' eye took in Mrs. Lincoln lacking mourning garb for the first time in the more than twenty months since Willie Lincoln died.

While the President had lain abed with varioloid, an immense crowd had streamed down Pennsylvania Avenue to the Capitol grounds looking skyward toward the Capitol dome. The bronze legs and torso of the massive heroic figure of a helmeted woman representing Armed Freedom, after years of lying helpless and forlorn on the ground below, had been lifted to the top of the dome. And on this day, precisely at noon, the last section of this 19 ½-foot high bronze statue, consisting of the head and shoulders of the incomplete goddess, left the mass of material at the foot of the dome and moved serenely upward, drawn by a slender wire cable.

From a chaos of timbered scaffolding the head and shoulders emerged and swung lightly and calmly into place joined to her torso. A workman drove a ringing sledge hammer three times. The Union banner ran up a flagstaff. Artillery roared a salute.

Lincoln said, "If people see the Capitol going on, it is a sign we intend the Union shall go on."

MRS. LINCOLN.

Entered, according to Act of Congress, in the year 1865, by Wm. H. Mumler, in the Clerk's Office of the District Court for the District of Massachusetts. 23d Washington Street, Boston.

Mrs. Lincoln.

CHAPTER 38

GRANT GIVEN HIGH COMMAND, '64

GRANT GIVEN HIGH COMMAND, '64

AS A FORMER Douglas Democrat now for the war and the Union, Grant was accepted and endorsed by an element that could never see Lincoln as their leader. The powerful New York *Herald* spoke for a miscellany of interests when through the winter of '63 and '64 it kept up a cry for Grant for President, "Grant, the People's Candidate." Many other newspapers joined in.

Lincoln had never seen Grant. He knew Grant only from what he read and what he heard in talk about his best fighter. To Congressman Washburne, Lincoln said: "About all I know of Grant I have got from you. I have never seen him. Who else besides you knows anything about Grant?" Washburne: "I know very little about him. He is my townsman but I never saw very much of him. The only man who really knows Grant is Jones. He has summered and wintered with him." Washburne referred to a Galena man, J. Russell Jones, a U.S. marshal at Chicago who had visited with Grant in Mississippi.

Lincoln wired Jones to come on to Washington. Jones picked up his mail on the way to the depot and opened it on the train. In it was a letter from Grant answering one Jones had written urging the General to pay no attention to the newspapers trying to run him for President. Grant was saying that he had as big a job as one man could ask, that he was out to suppress the "rebellion," and everything that reached him trying to push him into politics went into the wastebasket. Arriving in Washington, Jones sent word he would be glad to call when convenient and the President set eight o'clock that evening. Then as Jones told it: "The President gave directions to say to all that he was engaged for the evening . . . opened the conversation by saying that he was anxious to see somebody from the West with whom he could talk upon the general situation . . . Mr. Lincoln made no allusion whatever to Grant.

Abraham Lincoln. Photo by Alexander Gardner, Nov. 8, 1863.

I had been there but a few minutes, however, when I fancied he would like to talk about Grant. 'Mr. President, if you will excuse me for interrupting you, I want to ask you kindly to read a letter that I got from my box as I was on my way to the train.' Whereupon I gave him Grant's letter. He read it with evident interest. When he came to the part where Grant said that it would be impossible for him to think of the presidency as long as there was a possibility of retaining Mr. Lincoln in the office, he read no further, but arose and, approaching me, put his hand on my shoulder and said: 'My son, you will never know how gratifying that is to me. No man knows, when that presidential grub gets to gnawing at him, just how deep it will get until he has tried it; and I didn't know but what there was one gnawing at Grant.' The fact was that this was just what Mr. Lincoln wanted to know."

Among the first acts of Congress that winter was the voting of a medal of thanks to Grant for his victories. Bills in House and Senate to revive the rank of lieutenant general of the armies of the United States on February 26 passed both houses. On February 29 the President signed the bill, named Grant for the newly created office and the Senate confirmed it.

Grant traveled toward Washington with his 14-year-old boy Fred, and his chief of staff John Rawlins. Crowds and cheers met Grant as the train moved on to Washington. There on the evening of March 8 he walked into Willard's and asked for a room. The clerk said he had only a top-floor room. Grant said that would do—and signed the register. The clerk took a look at the name and then jumped fast to assign Grant the best in the house.

Grant walked into the dining room and was ordering food when word passed among the guests, "It's Grant," and questions: "Where is he?" "Which is he?" Someone stood on a chair and called for three cheers for Grant. Three cheers rang out. The diners pounded on tables, waved napkins, threatened the glassware, yelled the name of Grant, Grant, Grant!

Abraham Lincoln. Photo by Alexander Gardner, Nov. 8, 1863.

After a few minutes, as Noah Brooks noted it, "General Grant, looking very much astonished and perhaps annoyed, rose to his feet, awkwardly rubbed his mustache with his napkin, bowed, resumed his seat and attempted to finish his dinner." The diners then seemed slowly to get the idea that Grant had come to the dining room for a meal. And they let him eat in peace.

Soon Grant was on his way with Senator Cameron to report to the President at the White House, in a tarnished uniform with a major general's stars on the shoulder straps.

It was the night of the President's weekly reception. A buzz and a murmur ran round the big East Room, reaching the President with news that Grant would soon step into the room. As the General entered, a hush fell on the crowd. They moved back and made a pathway. Lincoln saw him coming, put out his long bony hand for the shorter and smaller one of Grant's. "I'm

glad to see you, General." The two men stood a moment with struck hands.

Lincoln introduced the General to Seward, who escorted him toward Mrs. Lincoln in the East Room. The buzz of talk became a hullabaloo. "It was the only real mob I ever saw in the White House," wrote Noah Brooks "For once at least the President of the United States was not the chief figure in the picture. The little scared-looking man who stood on a crimson-covered sofa was the idol of the hour. He remained on view for a short time, then he was quietly smuggled out by friendly hands."

Grant returned when the crowd was gone and met Lincoln with Stanton and Nicolay in a small drawing room. And Lincoln did nearly all the talking—all of it on the point that the next day, when he was to hand formally to Grant the new commission, each of them should say little, but what they did say should

Ulysses S. Grant. Photo by Matthew Brady.

be pat to the occasion. Grant put in his inside coat pocket a copy of the President's speech and, saying good night, left the room with Stanton. Next day at one o'clock the Cabinet, Halleck, Grant's son Fred, Rawlins, Owen Lovejoy and Nicolay assembled to hear two little speeches that were telegraphed to the wide world.

Lincoln, facing Grant, read four sentences: "General Grant, The nation's appreciation of what you have done, and it's reliance upon you for what remains to do, in the existing great struggle, are now presented with this commission, constituting you Lieutenant General in the Army of the United States. With this high honor devolves upon you also, a corresponding responsibility. As the country herein trusts you, so, under God, it will sustain you. I scarcely need to add that with what I here speak for the nation goes my own hearty personal concurrence."

Grant held a half-sheet of note paper, on it a hurried lead-pencil scrawl. "His embarrassment was evident and extreme," noted Nicolay. "He found his own writing very difficult to read." The speech, however, fitted Grant as he read, facing Lincoln, his three-sentence response: "Mr. President: I accept this commission with gratitude for the high honor confered. With the aid of the noble armies that have fought in so many fields for our common country, it will be my earnest endeavor not to disappoint your expectations. I feel the full weight of the responsibilities now devolving on me and know that if they are met it will be due to those armies, and above all to the favor of that Providence which leads both Nations and men."

The news of Lincoln and Grant meeting, their two simple little speeches, was at once a universal press and sidewalk topic. The North brightened a little. The South saw Northern morale changed, at least slightly, for the better.

Grant rode by rail to the Army of the Potomac headquarters at Brandy Station, talked with Meade, felt out the spirit of the officers and men, said nothing much. Of intrigue and wire-pulling in Washington he had heard and seen not a little in this week. Senators Wade and Chandler had been to the President and called for removal of Meade from command of the Army of the Potomac. Grant found Meade sincere, generous, open-minded, and told Meade he had no thought of a substitute for him.

After four days in Washington Grant told Lincoln he would go west, be gone about nine days, then return and direct operations from eastern headquarters. Of his four-day stay in Washington he said to Lincoln, "This has been rather the warmest campaign I have witnessed during the war."

Before starting west, Grant ordered Sherman in command of all Western armies, He rode to Nashville, talked with Sherman on a campaign plan, huge but simple. As Sherman put it: Grant "was to go for Lee and I was to go for Joe Johnston." That was all. The two of them believed they would start a never-ending hammering, a pressure of irresistible pincers—and close out the war. Returning to Washington, Grant found himself hailed as the most popular man in the United States.

Phil Sheridan arrived in Washington early in April. Grant had appointed him to head the combined cavalry of the Army of the Potomac. Five feet five inches high, less than 130 pounds in weight—a total stranger to Washington and service in the east—young-looking, 33 years old, cool and guarded he was, refusing to tell anybody how to win the war. Halleck took him to Stanton and it was a meeting with no compliments. Halleck took him to the White House. Lincoln offered Sheridan both his hands, said he hoped Sheridan would fulfill Grant's expectations, and added that the cavalry of the Army of the Potomac had not gone so far as it might have.

At Culpeper Court House with Grant next day Sheridan again felt at home. A black-haired Irish Catholic boy who went from Perry County, Ohio, to West Point, Sheridan had followed soldiering ever since. As a fighter leading men against odds he had proved his wild and stubborn ways at Murfreesboro, Chickamauga and Chattanooga.

Grant was to hit Lee so hard in Virginia that Lee could send no help to Johnston in Georgia. Sherman was to hit Johnston so heavily in Georgia that Johnston would never shift troops to Lee in Virginia. So they hoped and planned. Grant's orders to his scattered subcommanders were relayed through Haileck at Washington. Burnside was taking his orders from Grant.

The Burnside corps had mobilized at Annapolis, its veterans of Roanoke, the Peninsula, Antietam, Fredericksburg, Chancellorsville and Knoxville being joined by new recruits that included several Negro regiments. They passed in review before the President standing on the balcony of Willard's. The black troops cheered, laughed, threw their caps in the air, marching past the signer of the Emancipation Proclamation. A rain blew up and soaked the marchers. Bystanders urged Lincoln to go in out of the rain. "If they can stand it, I guess I can," he answered as burnt and shot-riddled flags swept by on Pennsylvania Avenue.

CHAPTER 39

WILL HIS PARTY RENOMINATE LINCOLN?

WILL HIS PARTY RENOMINATE LINCOLN?

Owen Lovejoy, U.S. Representative from Illinois. Photo by Mathew Brady, 1865.

EARLY in '64 several newspapers agreed with the Detroit *Free Press* man at Washington: "Not a single Senator can be named as favorable to Lincoln's renomination for President." Any Senator who might want Lincoln for a second term was not making himself heard. On this the Republican party organs were mainly silent.

In the House only one Congressman was definitely committed to Lincoln. A Pennsylvania editor visiting Washington said to Thaddeus Stevens, "Introduce me to some member of Congress friendly to Mr. Lincoln's renomination." "Come with me," said Stevens. He took the editor to Isaac N. Arnold and said: "Here is a man who wants to find a Lincoln member of Congress. You are the only one I know, and I have come over to introduce my friend to you." "Thank you," said Arnold. "I know a good many such and I will present your friend to them, and I wish you, Mr. Stevens, were with us." Thus the scrupulous Arnold recorded the incident.

The only remarks then favoring Lincoln's renomination for President delivered in either Senate or House came from Arnold in the first week of the year and in March. " . . . I ask the ardent and impatient friends of freedom to put implicit faith in Abraham

Lincoln. If you deem him slow, or if you think he has made mistakes, remember how often time has vindicated his wisdom. The masses of the people everywhere trust and love him . . . You have a Chief Magistrate . . . sagacious, firm, upright, and true. Somewhat rude and rough, it may be, but under this rough exterior you have the real and true hero . . . Taking the last five years, and Mr. Lincoln has exerted a greater influence upon the popular heart and in forming public opinion than any other man."

Thus Isaac N. Arnold, 49 years old, once a country schoolteacher in New York State, city clerk of Chicago in 1837, practicing attorney of Cook County, put into the *Congressional Globe* an estimate of Lincoln as a hero. Not then nor in many months after did any member of the House or Senate stand up and deliver any similar estimate.

Of Owen Lovejoy in early '64 it should be noted that he was a sick man for months. Lincoln had one note from him saying: "I am gaining very slowly. It is hard work drawing the sled uphill." And Lincoln had repeatedly visited Lovejoy's bedside, once telling the veteran abolitionist: "This war is eating my life out. I have a strong impression that I shall not live to see the end."

In early February Lyman Trumbull wrote to H. G. McPike of Alton, Illinois: "The feeling for Mr. Lincoln's re-election *seems* to be very general, but much of it I discover is only on the surface. You would be surprised, in talking with public men we meet here, to find how few, when you come to get at their real sentiment, are for Mr. Lincoln's reëlection. There is a distrust and fear that he is too undecided and inefficient to put down the rebellion. You need not be surprised if a reaction sets in before the nomination, in favor of some man supposed to possess more energy and less inclination to trust our brave boys in the hands and under the leadership of generals who have no heart in the war. The opposition to Mr. L. may not show itself at all, but if it ever breaks out there will be more of it than now appears."

The Republicans had five candidates for President whom the New York *World* set down "in the order of their availability and probable chances": Abraham Lincoln, Salmon P. Chase, John C. Frémont, Nathaniel P. Banks, Benjamin F. Butler. To defeat Lincoln would be simply to nominate Chase, deduced the *World*. "Only the adherents of Chase have any interest in thwarting Lincoln."

Early in '64 the New York *World* presented General McClellan as the one man of worth, dignity and patriotism for nomination by the Democratic party to overwhelm Lincoln. In this effort the *World* served financial, industrial and transportation interests represented in politics by Erastus Corning and Dean Richmond of the New York Central Railroad; by William Henry Aspinwall of the New York-to-San Francisco steamship lines and the Panama Isthmus 49-mile railway which up to 1859 had netted him a fortune of $6,000,000; and more directly and dominantly by August Belmont, politically and financially the most eminent Jew in America.

Born in a rich landholding family in Rhenish Prussia in 1816, Belmont at 14 had worked without pay as office boy, swept and dusted the rooms of the powerful banking firm of Rothschild Brothers in Frankfort while learning finance. In the panic year 1837 he set up in New York his own banking house of August Belmont & Company, his great asset being the agency for the Rothschilds in America. Becoming a U.S. citizen, Belmont served on foreign missions, was U.S. Minister to Holland, championed Stephen A. Douglas at the 1860 Baltimore convention, saw himself chosen chairman of the national Democratic committee. After an interview with Lincoln and Seward, Belmont had gone to Europe and quietly warned financial circles that the Southern Confederacy was not a good business risk, wreaking practical damage to the South under cover.

An old question bothered Senators and Congressmen and found its way into editorials. The *World* on February 11, 1864, headed one: "Ought a President to Re-elect Himself?" In a sentence in Lincoln's '61 inaugural address, said the one-term advocates who were becoming vocal, it could be seen that the President had pledged himself to one term and no more. That sentence ran, "I now enter upon the same task [as fifteen previous Executives] for the brief constitutional term of four years, under great and peculiar difficulty." Entirely aside from this point, Chase held it had now become an American tradition that the President should not serve a second term; for 30 years no President had served two terms, and the custom was established.

Lincoln held no mood fixed and frozen. His eye caught light and shadow, color and mass, in the flow and heave of a reality he termed Public Opinion. His moods ranged with those of the

People in a democracy that in spite of war kept a wide measure of freedom in personal expression.

Without a doubt, too, Lincoln felt a loyalty due from him to people who trusted him, who saw logic and sense in what he was doing, who were afraid to try some other man as President. It was to them Lincoln's Government and Lincoln's Army that held the boys and men from so many homes. Father Abraham was not merely a nickname. He cared. They trusted him as he trusted them. There was this kinship between him and a certain legion of loyalists. He seemed to reason that if they wanted him to go on as President they would have their way—and if they didn't want him, he could stand that if they could.

While the army had its quota always of deserters, stragglers and malingerers, the mass of sentiment there plainly favored "Old Abe." Thousands of soldier letters written home told this. Letters of protest and murmuring were few in comparison. A veteran on furlough spoke in Chicago on whether the soldiers wanted Lincoln re-elected. He cocked his eyes with a reckless glint: "Why, of course they do. We all re-enlisted to see this thing through, and Old Abe must re-enlist too. He mustered us in and we'll be damned if he shan't stay where he is until he has mustered us out. We'll never give up till every rebel acknowledges he is the Constitutional President . . . I don't give a cuss for this country if the beaten side has a right to bolt after an election; it would not be fit to live in."

Francis Bicknell Carpenter, portrait painter, wished to give his public a momentous historic setting for Lincoln. A rich lawyer friend assured Carpenter six months' income for work on his vision, and Speaker Colfax and Congressman Lovejoy recommended him to the President. Carpenter at a White House reception heard Lincoln with a twinkle of the eye, playfully, "Do you think, Mr. Carpenter, that you can make a handsome picture of *me?*" In his office he said, "Well, Mr. Carpenter, we will turn you loose in here, and try to give you a good chance to work out your idea." In the painting the Cabinet members were to be seated and standing around the President seated at a table, in their midst at the exact center of the design that world-famous parchment, the Emancipation Proclamation. This was the idea Carpenter outlined.

On the evening of the day Lincoln reviewed Burnside's corps, Governor Curtin came with a friend to the President's office. And in their talk Curtin referred to the volunteer citizen soldier as "worthy of profound respect." Lincoln gave quiet assent, Carpenter noting a "peculiar dreaminess" creep over his face, as if he could not find words should he try to speak his heart about volunteers his heart knew.

Carpenter in February called on Lovejoy, saw him sit up and take nourishment, saying he was better, not knowing he had only three months to live.

On his death Lincoln said to Carpenter, "Lovejoy was the best friend I had in Congress."

Several Copperhead editors made peculiar comment when Lovejoy died. They saluted him as a true man holding mistaken ideas. Underlying these salutations it could be seen that these Copperhead editors divided anti-slavery men into genuine heroes and counterfeit, true crusaders and bogus.

And to the end Lovejoy, his once magnificent physical frame nearly used up, burned with a loyalty to the President. According to Carpenter, his words ran: "I tell you, Mr. Lincoln is at heart as strong an antislavery man as any of them, but he is compelled to *feel* his way . . . His mind acts slowly, but when he moves, it is *forward*. You will never find him receding from a position once taken. It is of no use talking, or getting up conventions against him. He is going to be the candidate and is sure to be reëlected. 'It was foreordained from the foundation of the world.'"

CHAPTER 40

CHASE THIRSTS TO RUN
FOR PRESIDENT

Chase Thirsts to Run for President

Hon. Henry Jarvis Raymond of New York, founder & editor of the New York Times.

IN CHASE'S department were more than 10,000 job-holders high and low, and according to Nicolay and Hay, the President let Chase have his way as to all of these except in rare cases, seldom interfering. The two secretaries saw Chase trying to undermine Lincoln. "He regarded himself as the friend of Mr. Lincoln; to him and to others he made strong protestations of friendly feeling, which he undoubtedly thought were sincere; but he held so poor an opinion of the President's intellect and character in comparison with his own, that he could not believe the people so blind as deliberately to prefer the President to himself."

"Chase looks and acts as if he meant to be the next President," Richard Henry Dana had written from Washington to Charles Francis Adams at London in March '63. A few days after a visit with Lincoln in December, Thurlow Weed wrote from Albany to John Bigelow in Paris: "Mr. Chase's report is very able, and his huge banking machine will make him strong. But how pitiable it is to know that his eye is single—not to the welfare of his country but to the presidency! Mr. Lincoln says he is 'trying to keep that maggot out of his head,' but he cannot."

Perhaps no one else wrote more shifting and contradictory opinions than did Chase of Lincoln. To the wealthiest man in the Senate, his son-in-law, Chase wrote November 26, 1863, that he could never be driven into any hostile or unfriendly position as to Mr. Lincoln. "His course toward me has always been so fair and kind." He dwelt at length on his "respect and affection" for Mr. Lincoln. Yet in the same letter he made the point that no President should have a second term, and "I think a man of different qualities from those of the President will be needed for the next four years."

A short, thickset man wearing side whiskers and the latest cut of clothes, carrying a monocle in the English manner and sporting a gold-headed walking stick, came to see Lincoln while the Chase movement was under way. And Lincoln gave this man plenty of time and talked much with him. He was Henry Jarvis Raymond, editor and owner of the most distinctly pro-Lincoln daily organ in New York City, the *Times*, the one morning newspaper that tried to hurl back the daily javelins of Greeley, Bennett, Brooks, Fernando Wood. A Congressman-elect from New York State had pressed Lincoln for official action in an important matter, according to Carpenter, and the answer from Lincoln was: "You must see Raymond about this. He is my *Lieutenant-General* in politics. Whatever he says is right in the premises, shall be done."

Raymond was 44 years old. Born in Lima, New York, a University of Vermont graduate, teacher in a young ladies' seminary, he was once editor of a literary weekly. He founded the New York *Times* in 1851 and edited it for a public that wanted more trustworthy reporting of the day's news than was to be had in the brilliant and slimy *Herald* or in the quirks and shifts of the *Tribune*.

A delegate to the Whig national convention of 1850, later lieutenant governor of New York, Raymond had helped organize the Republican party in 1856, stumped for Frémont, in 1858 independently swung away to support of Stephen A. Douglas for President, but in 1860 swung back to Lincoln. He was close to Weed and Seward; the triumvirate of Seward-Weed-Raymond was often satirized and excoriated. And now Raymond worked on the most comprehensive and formidable biography of Lincoln that had ever been attempted, to be published late in the spring.

Republican and Democratic papers enjoyed reprinting facetious charges of the New York *Herald* that Mr. Chase was "putting his own portrait upon the greenbacks of *small* denominations, which everybody sees, while he sticks Mr. Lincoln's comical phiz upon the *large* bills, in order that he may make himself generally known to the public."

The Union League Club of Philadelphia came out strong for Lincoln's renomination, the National Union Club of Philadelphia chiming in. In New York City the National Conference Committee of the Union Lincoln Association issued an address "To the Loyal Citizens of the United States" declaring that in electing an "occupant for the presidential chair" the people should choose "a true leader," one "tried and not found wanting," naming Abraham Lincoln.

Among Union members of the Pennsylvania Legislature early in January a paper was passed around. An address to the President, it was, saying that the voters of Pennsylvania had endorsed his policies generously at the recent election and "We are only responding to their demand when we thus publicly announce our unshaken preference for your reëlection to the Presidency in 1864." Signed by every Union member of senate and assembly, this paper was sent to Lincoln January 14 by Simon Cameron with the message, "You are now fairly launched on our second voyage . . . Providence has decreed your reelection, and no combination of the wicked can prevent it."

A New Hampshire State convention of the Union party had already met January 6 to nominate a state ticket, and before the chairman knew exactly what he was doing with so many Treasury Department employees present, the delegates had sent up rockets and declared for Lincoln's renomination. The Union Central Committee of New York unanimously took like action, and in sending the news to Lincoln, Senator Morgan said, "It is going to be difficult to restrain the boys, and there is not much use in try-ing to do so." With only one dissenting voice both houses of the Kansas Legislature endorsed renomination of the President. The Union members of the legislature of New Jersey joined in saying, without disparagement of other true men, "You are the choice of the people."

California legislators, almost unanimously, declared, "While we revere and honor other noble patriots who have performed their parts, the people will look to Abraham Lincoln as the instrument selected by Providence to lead their country in safety through its perils." In much the same tone the legislatures of Maryland, Michigan, Wisconsin, Rhode Island, declared themselves, as also state conventions in Minnesota, Iowa, Indiana, New Hampshire, Connecticut. When February '64 ended, 14 states had by official action gone on record speaking their preference for Lincoln for a second term.

While the Chase band wagon was trying at once to make a noise and be quiet, the mass sentiment favoring Lincoln was exploded and reverberated through the state legislatures. Pomeroy and his committee decided in February on a bold play. A circular was prepared—for private and confidential distribu-tion. It was said to be a joint product of Sumner, Stevens, Henry Winter Davis and Wade, though signed by Pomeroy only. Printed copies were mailed over the country and marked "private and confidential." From men inside the President's own party went this appeal to Union men that they must counteract the President's attempt to re-elect himself through using the official machinery of the Government.

While the circular was still being mailed out, and read as strictly private and confidential, many copies fell into the hands of Lincoln workers and soon began coming to the White House. On the day the *National Intelligencer* burst into print with the cir-cular, Chase wrote a sick-at-heart letter to Lincoln saying it was probable he had already seen a letter printed in the *Intelligencer*. Until he saw it in print, "I had no knowledge of the existence of this letter." Lincoln studied this letter with its careful excuses, its blurred justifications, its embarrassed self-portraiture. Next day, February 23, he wrote a one-sentence note to Chase: "Yours of yesterday in relation to the paper issued by Senator Pomeroy was duly received; and I write this note merely to say I will answer a little more fully when I can find the leisure to do so." Lincoln waited six more days.

Chase could study the letter, a self-portrait in exchange for the one received from Chase: "I would have taken time to answer yours of the 22nd. sooner, only that I did not suppose any evil could result from the delay . . . on consideration, I find there is really very little to say. My knowledge of Mr. Pomeroy's letter having been made *pub-lic* came to me only the day you wrote; but I had, in spite of myself, known of it's *existence* several days before. I have not yet read it, and I think I shall not. I was not shocked, or surprised by the appearance of the letter, because I had had knowledge of Mr. Pomeroy's Committee, and of secret issues which I supposed came from it, and of secret agents who I supposed were sent out by it, for several weeks. I have known just as little of these things as my own friends have allowed me to know. They bring the documents to me, but I do not read them— they tell me what they think fit to tell me, but I do not inquire for more . . . Whether you shall remain at the head of the Treasury Department is a question which I will not allow myself to consider from any stand-point other than my judgment of the pub-lic service; and, in that view, I do not perceive occasion for a change."

Still Chase hoped on. Ohio might come his way. His home state might say Yes. Surely the Buckeyes would want their old gov-ernor for a White House figure. But the Ohio legislative mem-bers plopped one and all for Lincoln.

The National Union party convention which would renomi-nate Lincoln—or not—was to meet in Baltimore June 7, accord-ing to a call of its national committee in February. This would be too soon, said Greeley, Bryant and others. Raymond, *Harper's Weekly* and others asked, "Why not?" The ground swell of mass sentiment was for Lincoln, and an early convention would be good strategy. One or two inexplicable disasters might send the mass sentiment dwindling.

CHAPTER 41

SPRING OF '64—
BLOOD AND ANGER

SPRING OF '64—BLOOD AND ANGER

NEVADA'S miners, prospectors, gamblers, gold- and silver-hunters, with 26,000 voters, wanted to have a state and be in the Union. She liked the idea of her little desert population sending a Congressman and two Senators to Washington. Two out of three voters were Republican.

The President called on Assistant Secretary of War Charles A. Dana, who wrote of what followed. Lincoln told Dana the administration had decided the Constitution should be amended to prohibit slavery; this was not only a change in national policy but a most important military measure equivalent to new armies in the field, worth at least a million men, tending to paralyze and break the continuity of enemy ideas. To pass such an amendment would require approval by three-fourths of the states. Nevada might be of critical importance as a state. Dana quoted Lincoln, "It is easier to admit Nevada than to raise another million soldiers."

The Senate bill of February 24, 1864, authorized a Nevada convention the first Monday in July, to declare on behalf of the people that they adopt the Constitution of the United States and to frame a state government. In the House through March this bill was held up by lack of votes.

Lincoln walked over to Dana's office, said: "Dana, I am very anxious about this vote. It has got to be taken next week. The time is very short. It is going to be a great deal closer than I wish it was . . . There are three [members of Congress] that you can deal with better than anybody else, perhaps, as you know them all. I wish you would send for them." Lincoln told Dana who they were. Dana considered it unnecessary to tell their names to anyone not immediately concerned. One was from New Jersey and two from New York. "What will they be likely to want?" asked Dana. The President said, ". . . It makes no difference what they want. Here is the alternative: that we carry this vote, or be compelled to raise another million, and I don't know how many more, men, and fight no one knows how long. It is a question of three votes or new armies." "Well, sir, what shall I say to these gentlemen?" "I don't know, but whatever promise you make to them I will perform."

Dana sent for the men and saw them one by one. So the extra votes needed to pass the Nevada bill through the House were gotten. And the Yeas and Nays on the vote in Senate and House were not indexed or recorded in the *Congressional Globe*, whether through clerical inattention or by official arrangement.

Hay had talked with the President in December about reconstruction in Florida, the possibility of getting one-tenth of the voters in the state to swear Union allegiance and be recorded as U.S. citizens in an oath book. To General Q. A. Gillmore, in whose department Florida lay, Lincoln wrote January 13 that he had commissioned Hay a major in the army and Hay with oath books and blank certificates would arrive and explain to General Gillmore the President's general views on the subject of reconstructing a loyal state government in Florida.

Hay sailed to Gillmore's headquarters on the South Carolina coast, assured the General it was not the President's intention to do anything to embarrass his military operations. At Jacksonville, Florida, Hay read the President's proclamation of amnesty to a lineup of prisoners, explained that if they signed the oath book, certificates to that effect would be issued to them and they would be allowed to go home. Otherwise they would be sent North as prisoners of war for exchange. "There is to be neither force nor persuasion used in the matter. You decide for *yr* selves." They signed, nearly half making their mark. They were tired of the war.

Then came shocking news. General Truman Seymour, a Regular Army officer in charge of some 5,500 men, sought out a Confederate force of about the same size at Olustee River in a picked position, welcoming battle. The Union loss was 1,800, the Confederate half that. Seymour's orders from Gillmore had been to wait. But he had plunged and his army was routed.

With Union bayonets in disgrace for the moment, Hay had a harder time enrolling loyal Unionists. He went to Fernandina, where he got a few more names, noted: "Some refused to sign, on the ground that they were not repentant rebels." On March 3 he wrote, "I am sure that we cannot now get the President's 10th." His hopes vanished that the required 10 per cent of voters to form a state government could be enrolled.

That wholesale and regimented oath-taking might easily become ridiculous was in Lincoln's mind when he issued the Amnesty Proclamation in December; he had warned that it was only a method, a mode, for re-establishing national authority. He heard in January '64 from General Banks, commanding the Department of the Gulf, that there were loyal Union people in Louisiana who wished to avoid taking the oath prescribed. The President replied: ". . . it is not even a modification of anything I have heretofore said when I tell you that you are at liberty to adopt any rule which shall admit to vote any unquestionably loyal free-state men and none others. And yet I do wish they would all take the oath."

Far down in that changing patchwork of military and civil governments, Louisiana, Lincoln tried to guide General Nathaniel Prentiss Banks, a Democrat, three times governor of Massachusetts. Banks on January 11 proclaimed an election to be held February 22. Free white male voters who had taken the oath of allegiance cast over 11,000 ballots, of which the Banks candidate Michael Hahn received 6,183, J. Q. A. Fellows, a proslavery conservative, 2,996, and B. F. Flanders, 2,232.

In his Louisiana domain Governor Michael Hahn estimated that in three-fourths of the state allegiance lay mainly with the Confederate governor and the legislature in session at the capitol in Shreveport. Hahn was 34 years old.

To Hahn, Lincoln wrote a letter marked "Private": "I congratulate you on having fixed your name in history as the first-free-state Governor of Louisiana. Now you are about to have a Convention which, among other things, will probably define the elective franchise. With this the President included a one-sentence letter, perhaps equally important, notifying Hahn that until further orders he would be military governor of Louisiana. Thus if his civil authority given him by election was questioned, he could call out the troops and riot squads.

Banks headed in March the Red River expedition of some 40,000 men. And the forces mishandled by Banks were beaten and sent reeling so that Banks was glad to get his army safe in Alexandria, 80 miles back eastward from the town where 20 days earlier he had written John Hay he was anxious lest the enemy might not give him battle.

In May, Banks was relieved of his command and resigned his army commission. "The President gave me too much to do more than any other major-general in the army," he wrote, as fact and not complaint.

Lincoln and Banks agreed that, if only for its effect on politics and war morale in the North, the ballot should be given to at least a part of the free Negro population. Governor Hahn hoped to work out Lincoln's suggestion that Negroes who had fought for the Union, and possibly those who could read and write, should be the first Negro voters.

Grant suggested General E. R. S. Canby to supersede Banks and it was so ordered. But Lincoln and Banks remained friends and Banks was staying on in New Orleans advising with the Louisiana constitutional convention and reporting to Lincoln.

After General Frederick Steele's column of 13,000 Union troops had marched into Little Rock, the capital of Arkansas, September 13, 1863, a large part of the state came under Union control. Eight regiments of Arkansas citizens had been enlisted under the Union flag. And early in January the President sent oath books and blank certificates to General Steele, for use in reorganizing a state government. Word came to Lincoln of a series of Union meetings with speeches and resolutions and election of delegates to a convention of 44 members who claimed to represent 22 of the 54 counties of the State of Arkansas.

This convention on January 22, 1864, declared secession null and void, slavery abolished immediately and unconditionally, and the Confederate debt repudiated. An address to the voters of Arkansas adopted January 2 3 frankly acknowledged "that while we could not properly claim to be the people of Arkansas in convention assembled," yet as representatives of a considerable portion of the state, and understanding the sentiment of citizens desiring a government under U.S. authority, they had determined to present a state constitution for the voters to ballot on. They appointed and inaugurated for provisional governor one Isaac Murphy, 62 years old, born near Pittsburgh, Pennsylvania, schoolteacher, lawyer, California gold-hunter, civil engineer and public-land surveyor. As a member in May '61 of the state convention which decided that Arkansas would secede, Murphy was the one delegate voting against secession. He became a staff officer of General Steele and his son Frank a major in the 1st Arkansas U.S. Infantry.

General Steele proclaimed an election for March 14 as scheduled by the convention, the polls to be kept open three days. The returns gave 12,179 votes for the new constitution and 226 against it; for Isaac Murphy, with no opposition candidate for governor, 12,430 ballots were cast by oath-of-allegiance voters in 40 counties. With brass bands, flags and formalities the new state government was sworn in and took office April 11. Its two U.S. Senators-elect and its three Congressmen-elect went to Washington, presented their credentials, heard the wrangling and the squabbling in Senate and House over how the occupied Southern States should be reconstructed, and came back home to tell their people that not yet, though maybe after a while, they might be admitted to seats.

Meanwhile in this April of 1864, came news of an affair, the central figure of which was Confederate Major General Nathan Bedford Forrest, born for war. Fifteen horses had been killed under him. At Murfreesboro, Shiloh, Chickamauga, he was in the vortex. No other commanding officer North or South, it was believed, had sat his horse and personally sabered to death so many of the enemy. His record for swift movement and fast fighting was compared to that of Stonewall Jackson.

At Fort Pillow, on the Mississippi 40 miles north of Memphis, Forrest with 6,000 troops drove the 600 defenders from outworks into the fort. While his white flags of truce were in the air he served notice that he would storm the fort. The Union commanders claimed that while thus negotiating under flags of truce Forrest moved his troops into better positions, violating the laws of civilized warfare. Forrest's regiments rushed the fort, took it, and put to death over half the garrison, Forrest claiming the fort flag had not been hauled down in token of surrender and in accord with civilized military law. Of the 262 Negro soldiers in the garrison nearly all were killed, wounded in escape, or buried alive.

Confederate General Nathan Bedford Forrest, 1863.

The news shocked the North. Press, pulpit and politicians of antislavery trend cried the affair as a fiendish atrocity demanding retaliation.

Whether one side tricked the other under a flag of truce was left in doubt; perhaps neither side could have cleared up the point. But a historian would have to record that a certain moment arrived when Forrest's men were no longer fighting a battle in a war between civilized nations; they were sharing in a race riot, a mass lynching, and the event became an orgy of unleashed primitive human animals riding a storm of anger and vengeance.

A telegram of Forrest to Richmond reported driving the enemy into Fort Pillow and demanding surrender, "which was declined." Then: "I stormed the fort, and after a contest of thirty minutes captured the entire garrison, killing 500 and taking 100 prisoners . . . I sustained a loss of 20 killed and 60 wounded." Forrest at Paducah and at Columbus in weeks immediately preceding had indicated that if he must storm the works "no quarter" would be shown the Negro troops. His view was made clearer a few weeks later when he wrote to a Union general, "I regard captured negroes as I do other captured property, and not as captured soldiers."

Six days after the Fort Pillow massacre Lincoln spoke at a Sanitary Fair, reminded his Baltimore audience that in looking out on so many people assembled to serve the Union soldiers, the fact was that three years earlier the same soldiers could not so much as pass through Baltimore. "We all declare for liberty; but in using the same *word* we do not all mean the same *thing*. With some the word liberty may mean for each man to do as he pleases with himself, and the product of his labor; while with others the same word may mean for some men to do as they please with other men, and the product of other men's labor . . . The shepherd drives the wolf from the sheep's throat, for which the sheep thanks the shepherd as a *liberator*, while the wolf denounces him for the same act as the destroyer of liberty, especially as the sheep was a black one. Plainly the sheep and the wolf are not agreed upon a definition of the word liberty; and precisely the same difference prevails to-day among us human creatures, even in the North, and all professing to love liberty . . . "

CHAPTER 42

GRANT'S OFFENSIVE, '64—FREE PRESS—
LINCOLN VISITS THE ARMY

Grant's Offensive, '64—Free Press—Lincoln Visits the Army

ACROSS the Rapidan River and into the Wilderness of Spotsylvania, Grant with some 120,000 men had vanished at midnight May 4. On a piece of ground ranging 10 to 12 miles across in any direction Grant was to meet Lee's army. Grant had two men to Lee's one. Lee, as Grant came on, could choose where he wanted to fight Grant. For Grant's men, crossing a river, seeking their opponent and going to him, it would be at times a groping in the dark.

Lincoln sat scanning flimsies in the telegraph room, and during Thursday, May 5, and past midnight of Friday, May 6, had no news of Grant. A locomotive ordered by Lincoln brought a cub reporter, Henry E. Wing, from 30 miles away for a two-o'clock-in-the-morning interview. As Wing told it to Lincoln, Grant had given orders for a daybreak offensive against the enemy and had said to him on leaving, "If you do see the President, see him alone and tell him that General Grant says there will be no turning back." Until four that Saturday morning the man and the youth talked, Lincoln squeezing from Wing every last point as to what he had seen and heard.

While Lincoln tried to sleep, Grant sat by a campfire, his hat slouched low, the collar of his blue overcoat hiding most of his face. He smoked a cigar, slowly chewed it, sat motionless except for an occasional shift of one leg over the other. Grant had lost 14,000 men, killed, wounded or missing, in 48 hours of fighting. Ambulances streaming north choked the roadways. Lee had lost more than he could spare as Grant hour on hour ordered up assaulting columns. After such desperate fighting it was customary to rest an army. Grant could decide to hold back—or go on.

As hours passed after midnight, slouched and grizzled, outwardly calm as bronze and steel but underneath shaken in turmoil, Grant did his thinking and made his decision. He would move on. His reasoning included his proposition, "Accident often decides the fate of battle." He could name the simple accidents that had operated against him and against Lee that day. He reasoned too that there would be an advantage in doing what the other fellow did not want him to do. He would move on, toward Richmond, by the left, toward Spotsylvania Court House. And Lee was at Spotsylvania, again in Grant's path. Till dawn of May 13 the combat went on at Spotsylvania. For ten days the Army of the Potomac had marched and fought continuously, losing 26,815 killed and wounded, 4,183 missing. The Confederates gave out no records of losses, though on the basis of prisoners taken by Grant, it was plain that Lee's army was being mercilessly slashed of irreplaceable manpower.

Now emerged Phil Sheridan. His cavalry swept round the flank of Lee's army, tore up ten miles of railway, released 400 Union prisoners, struck the reserve stores of Lee's supplies, destroyed 504,000 rations of bread and 904,000 of meat, and in combat six miles from Richmond killed the dauntless and priceless cavalry officer, J. E. B. Stuart, 31 years old, Lee's most irreplaceable general officer, "the eyes of the army."

By the left again Grant moved, to Cold Harbor, almost in sight of the steeples of Richmond. There he ordered a frontal assault that in 22 minutes lost 3,000 men. The night of June 3 saw 7,000 Union soldiers dead or ready for hospitals, as against Confederate losses of 1,200 to 1,500. "I have always regretted that the last assault at Cold Harbor was ever made," wrote Grant later. It was 30 days since he had crossed the Rapidan and forced

*Confederate General
J.E.B. Stuart, killed in 1864.*

Lee into a succession of battles. Never before had the Army of Northern Virginia been pressed from point to point and day to day of fighting by an Army of the Potomac that never rested or quit. A new mental and psychic factor was entering the war.

Suddenly Grant made a complete shift in his style of fighting. While Lee waited for direct combat and bloody frontal assaults, Grant moved—by night—in so shrouded a secrecy that only a few high officers knew where the army was going. Lee's skirmishers next day brought him word that the long trenches in front of Cold Harbor were empty. Grant was gone. A long march, and the wide James River crossed, brought Grant's army to the Petersburg defenses of Richmond. In four days of assaults 10,000 Union troops were now lost as against half that number of the enemy. On June 19 Grant sent word to Washington that he would order no more assaults. For a time he would rest his army. From the Wilderness through Cold Harbor he had lost 54,000 men, nearly as many as the entire force under Lee, but reinforcements had brought his army to about the same number he had when he crossed the Rapidan in early May.

While the bloody assaults at Petersburg were under way Grant had a telegram from Lincoln June 15, 1864: "Have just read your despatch of 1 P.M. yesterday. I begin to see it. You will succeed. God bless you all." This implied salutations on the grand strategy. For Grant was directing several armies. Sigel in the Shenandoah had failed him. Butler on the James River had dallied and lost big chances. But Sheridan had performed, while Sherman was steadily approaching Atlanta. Long toils were ahead. Could Sherman and Grant press through and join their armies? If so, the war would be over. "I begin to see it," Lincoln wired Grant.

Down the Potomac and around to the James River Lincoln and Tad rode on a white river steamer and June 21 Lincoln stepped from upper deck to gangway, wrung the hand of his General in Chief, spoke appreciation. Lincoln chatted at Grant's headquarters and rode to the Butler and Meade commands. Astride a horse he wore a tall black silk hat, black trousers and frock coat. Wrote Horace Porter, "By the time he had reached the troops he was completely covered with dust, and the black color of his clothes had changed to Confederate gray . . . his trousers gradually worked up above his ankles, and gave him the appearance of a country farmer riding into town wearing his Sunday clothes. However, the troops were so lost in admiration of the man that the humorous aspect did not seem to strike them. The soldiers rapidly passed the word along the line that 'Uncle Abe' had joined them, and cheers broke forth from all the commands, and enthusiastic shouts and even words of familiar greeting met him on all sides."

After a while Grant suggested they should ride on and see the colored troops. Lincoln said, "Oh, yes. I want to take a look at those boys. I read with the greatest delight the account in Mr. Dana's despatch of how gallantly they behaved. He said they took six out of the sixteen guns captured that day. I was opposed on nearly every side when I first favored the raising of colored regiments; but they have proved their efficiency, and I am glad they have kept pace with the white troops in the recent assaults . . ."

At the 18th corps camp Lincoln met a torrent of black men who circled roundabout him. Tears ran down some faces.

Little "Tad" Lincoln astride a horse.

Cheers, laughter, songs, mixed and rang in the air. "God bress Massa Linkum!" "De Lawd save Fader Abraham!" They waved their hands, brandished their arms, kissed the hands of their mystic hero, crowded around fondling his horse, bridle and saddle. "The President," noted Porter, "rode with bared head; the tears had started to his eyes and his voice was broken."

Lincoln next morning cruised upriver, amid the gunboats, met Admiral Lee and General Butler, saw breastworks and parapets and heard army men explain them. Some particularly strong positions recently seized and fortified were pointed out and brought Lincoln's remark to Butler, "When Grant once gets possession of a place, he holds on to it as if he had inherited it." He sailed back to Washington with new-made friends in the army, not the least of them the General in Chief. Their bonds drawing closer would need yet to be stronger.

CHAPTER 43

THE LINCOLN-JOHNSON TICKET OF THE NATIONAL UNION PARTY

THE LINCOLN-JOHNSON TICKET OF THE NATIONAL UNION PARTY

JUSTICE DAVID DAVIS and Thurlow Weed as between two practical party managers wanted more action from Lincoln toward clinching the nomination for President. Swett wrote to Orme, "Lincoln out of 150 delegates elected previous to May 25, figures them all up for him." The National Union convention was ten days away. And so far no delegates had been picked for anyone but Lincoln.

John Charles Fremont and followers in Cleveland, Ohio, May 31, 1864, organized a party. They met eight days before the National Union convention at Baltimore in order to notify that convention it must not nominate Lincoln. Their platform: the constitutional prohibition of slavery, free speech and a free press, a one-term Presidency, reconstruction of states to be left entirely with Congress. They nominated for President Major General John C. Frémont and for Vice-President Brigadier General John Cochrane. They named their new party Radical Democracy.

June 7 the Baltimore convention of the National Union party met. The name National Union was adopted as a gesture of respect or even reverence for Democrats fighting in the Union armies and those who had continuously supported the Lincoln administration. June 7 Grant was still burying his dead four days after the bloody repulse at Cold Harbor. June 7 the gold speculators in New York were crazy and wild-eyed over the betting that gold, now higher than ever, would go higher yet. June 7 and potatoes were quoted at $160 a bushel in Richmond, cabbage at $10 a head.

Next morning the convention voted 440 to 4 in favor of seating the Missouri radicals who had obstructed and harassed Lincoln and by a series of roll calls sifted what it wanted. Only the delegates from South Carolina were thrown out entirely. The Virginia and Florida delegations were admitted to seats with no right to vote. Arkansas and Louisiana were given seats and the right to vote. By 310 to 151 the convention gave Tennessee delegates seats with the right to vote.

Nominations were in order. Cameron had sent to the clerk's desk a written resolution with a demand that it be read. The convention heard a call for the unanimous renomination of Abraham Lincoln of Illinois and Hannibal Hamlin of Maine.

"A frightful clamor shook the hall," wrote Brooks. "Almost every delegate was on his feet objecting or hurrahing . . . For a few minutes pandemonium reigned, and in the midst of it Cameron stood with his arms folded, grimly smiling, regarding with composure the storm that he had raised. After the turmoil had spent itself . . . Raymond of New York, in an incisive, clear-cut speech, advocated nomination by a call of States . . ." Raymond's resolution passed.

The roll call began. Maine announced 16 votes for Lincoln. New Hampshire, coming next, tried a little speechmaking but was choked off with cries of "No speeches!" From then on each state announced its vote without oratory. One by one the undivided delegations threw in their ballots for Lincoln. Only one snag broke the smooth and orderly unanimity. The Missouri delegation announced it was under positive instructions to cast its 22 votes for Ulysses S. Grant. "This caused a sensation," wrote Brooks, "and growls of disapproval arose from all parts of the convention." Before the result of the balloting was announced Hume of Missouri moved that the nomination of Lincoln be declared unanimous. This under the rules could not be done until the secretary read the results: 484 votes for Lincoln, 22 for Grant. Missouri then changed its vote, and the secretary gave the grand total of 506 for Lincoln.

A storm of cheers was let loose, lasting many minutes, dying down and then flaring up again. "Men hurrahed, embraced one another," noted Brooks, "threw up their hats, danced in the aisles or on the platform, jumped on the benches, waved flags, yelled, and committed every possible extravagance . . . One of the most comical sights I beheld was that of Horace Maynard and Henry J. Raymond alternately hugging each other and shaking hands."

Campaign banner for John C. Fremont and John Cochrane for the radical Democrats party. Engraved by Currier & Ives, ca. 1864.

A Grand National Union Banner depicting Lincoln & Johnson. Lithographed by Currier & Ives, 1864.

The hilarity over, they settled down to nominations for Vice-President. On roll call Maine was solid for Hamlin. The number of votes Johnson had picked up in other New England States was surprising. Connecticut plopped solid its 12 for Johnson. Massachusetts split with 17 for Dickinson, 3 for Hamlin, 2 for Butler. The chairman was solemn, the convention too, as the New York tally was read: Johnson 32, Dickinson 28, Hamlin 6. Delegates pondered. Louisiana split evenly between Dickinson and Johnson. Arkansas threw its 10 votes to Johnson and Tennessee its 15. The Missouri radicals gladly pinned a rose on Ben Butler with 20 votes, though 2 put in for Johnson. The final total was shocking and almost unbelievable to the Hamlin men: Johnson 200, Dickinson 108, Hamlin 150.

Kentucky now announced that its complimentary vote of 21 for its General Rousseau and 1 for Tod would be thrown to Johnson. Oregon and Kansas followed for Johnson. A wave of applause came with Cameron handing Pennsylvania's 52 to Johnson. As New Jersey swung into line Senator Morrill of Maine, Hamlin's manager, who the night before had been publicly and privately confident of Hamlin's chances, changed the vote of Maine in favor of the Tennessee tailor. The convention secretary announced: Johnson 494, Dickinson 17, Hamlin 9.

"Of Andrew Johnson it is enough to say that there is no man in the country, unless it be Mr. Lincoln himself, whom the rebels more cordially hate," said *Harper's Weekly* in June. "He fought them in the Senate, when they counted upon his aid, and he has fought them steadily ever since." Greeley in the *Tribune* saw as "happy" the nomination of Johnson, who had "never wavered or faltered" in the Union cause, a man who would be hanged at noon on the day the Confederates captured him. From various points now was voiced one thought or instinct that had lain behind the framing of the Lincoln-Johnson ticket: it would nationalize the Republican party; no longer would Lincoln stand as the head of a sectional party.

The plan so odious and stenchladen to the radicals, known as "Lincoln's ten-per-cent plan," had only to be announced for Johnson to leap to embrace it. In a speech six months earlier Johnson had said: "Abraham Lincoln is an honest man and is going to put down this infernal rebellion. He is for a free government and I stand by him . . ."

Of medium height, a little swarthy of skin, with fine shoulders and a deep chest, Johnson carried a massive head. His deep-set and darkly piercing eyes looked at men without fear. Weapons and threats had no effect on him. If an idea or an impulse of depth moved him, he acted on it and stood by it. Physically he trusted the revolver in his right hip pocket and spiritually he had an ego that rested on a bulwark he called his conscience. He wore clean linen, was almost dainty about his collar and his shirt front, had small hands and feet; but the blandishments of the social set couldn't sway him.

From his beginnings in politics Johnson had voiced the poor whites as against the exclusive and propertied aristocracy which for 30 years had ruled the South and unduly controlled at Washington. Sometimes he was brave unto stubborn folly. He could wear his hate of the aristocrats and his passion for democracy till it was a pose and an overdone attitude. He could be so overly zealous to stand square and clear on a human issue that important half-lights of it were lost to him. Perhaps only such a man could have been the first to so manage a seceded state that it could give some color of promise to "Lincoln's ten-per-cent plan."

Many messages of congratulation rolled in to Lincoln on his renomination but none from Johnson. Many telegrams and letters came to Johnson but none from Lincoln. Each said publicly that the ticket was a good one. But neither sent word to the other that it was pleasant they were running mates.

Horace White, from a wire in the convention hall had sent Lincoln the first message of congratulation on renomination. This with the news from Nicolay arrived at the War Department telegraph office. When Major Eckert congratulated him, his face lighted elusively. "What! Am I renominated?" Operator Tinker showed him Nicolay's telegram. "Send it right over to the Madam. She will be more interested than I am."

To a committee the next day notifying him of his nomination, the President answered: "I will neither conceal my gratification, nor restrain the expression of my gratitude . . ." The same day he said to a National Union League delegation: "I have not permitted myself, gentlemen, to conclude that I am the best man in the country; but I am reminded, in this connection, of a story of an old Dutch farmer, who remarked to a companion once that 'it was not best to swap horses when crossing streams.' "

The convention platform and the President's public addresses had projected above all other immediate issues the need of a Constitutional amendment to prohibit slavery. But one week after the convention adjourned, when the House of Representatives took up a joint resolution to that effect, 64 members voted Nay, and it failed for lack of a two-thirds majority. The Nay votes were all Democratic and forecast a campaign issue.

Party lines were shaken. Two men, one a Republican and the other a Democrat, were heading a National Union ticket. The great American game of politics was in chaos.

From a photograph by Gardner of Lincoln seated, with Nicolay and Hay standing, *Harper's Weekly* made a drawing which it presented to its readers the week after the Baltimore convention. "In this earnest care-worn face," it commented, "saddened by a solemn sense of the great responsibility which in God's providence has devolved upon him, we see the man who said to his neighbors, as he left his home three years ago, that he was called to a graver task than any chief magistrate since Washington. Through an infinite perplexity of events the faith of the President has never faltered . . . Look thoughtfully at this rugged face. In its candor, its sagacity, its calmness, its steadiness and strength, there is especially conspicuous the distinctive American. Turn then to the portrait of General Grant . . . and there you see another purely American face, the same homely honesty, capacity and tenacity. Children of the people both of them . . . these two men illustrate at once the character of American civilization. There is but one prayer in the great multitude of American hearts today, God bless President Lincoln and General Grant!"

CHAPTER 44

WASHINGTON ON THE DEFENSIVE—PEACE BABBLINGS

WASHINGTON ON THE DEFENSIVE—PEACE BABBLINGS

J UNE 27, 1864, Chase sent the President the nomination of Maunsell B. Field for Assistant Treasurer at New York. Lincoln next day wrote Chase: "I cannot, without much embarrassment, make this appointment, principally because of Senator Morgan's very firm opposition to it," and naming three men Morgan had mentioned to Chase. "It will really oblige me if you will make choice among these three . . ."

Chase wrote asking an interview and the President the same day replied reciting inexorable political considerations, and, "When I received your note this forenoon suggesting a verbal conversation . . . I hesitated, because the difficulty does not, in the main part, lie within the range of a conversation between you and me. As the proverb goes, no man knows so well where the shoe pinches as he who wears it . . ."

The tone of this was a little new to Chase. Once more he resigned. This made four times.

And now Lincoln wrote to Chase that his resignation was accepted. "Of all I have said in commendation of your ability and fidelity, I have nothing to unsay; and yet you and I have reached a point of mutual embarrassment in our official relations which it seems cannot be overcome, or longer sustained, consistently with the public service." In his diary Chase wrote: "So my official life closes. I have laid broad foundations . . . I am too earnest, too anti-slavery, and, say, too radical, to make the President willing to have me connected with the Administration, just as my opinion is that he is not earnest enough, not anti-slavery enough, not radical enough."

Early next morning the President wrote out a nomination for William Pitt Fessenden, Senator from Maine, to fill the vacancy. The Senate took about one minute to confirm the nomination unanimously.

Telegrams and letters of approval beyond precedent had poured in on Fessenden. The New York and Boston clearing-houses, bankers and merchants in all quarters, it seemed, urged his acceptance of the President's nomination when it was reported

he would refuse. At the first report that Fessenden was to be Secretary of the Treasury, Government bonds advanced, pork declined $10 a barrel, and all provisions went to lower prices.

Fessenden was sworn in. The press held forth in compliments such as never before, except in the case of Grant, over a major Lincoln appointment.

Starting as a young lawyer in Portland, Maine, Fessenden had become a Whig Congressman, later a Senator, helped found the Republican party, watched the tariff, fisheries and shipping interests of his state, clashed with Welles over Maine's share of favors and patronage, and was now to undergo the trials of an executive. The national debt was $1,700,000,000, the Treasury almost empty, the war costing $2,000,000 a day.

In the deep gloom months of July and August '64, the barometric indicator, gold, was to say that Lincoln and the Union Government were failing. Thirty-nine dollars of gold would buy $100 of greenbacks. This was the bottom gold price of the Union Government's paper promises to pay. One interpretation was that the holders of gold in those months had less hope than ever of the Union Government winning its war.

On July 4 of this gloomy summer Congress adjourned. Among the bills piled on the President's desk for signature was one that would slash the slender supports on which the "Lincoln ten-per-cent plan" rested. Since December '63, when the President had launched his plan, much had happened to it. Then Hay wrote in his diary that all factions in Congress seemed to agree, and on the reading of the President's message, "Men acted as if the millennium had come. Chandler was delighted, Sumner was beaming." Border State men said they were satisfied.

Then slowly had come deepening suspicions of the President's motives, more open claims that the states in secession had committed suicide and that the President was impossible in his plan for a loyal 10 per cent to be authorized to reorganize the governments of those states. Henry Winter Davis led this opposition in the House, and Ben Wade in the Senate. Davis was tall, slender, with wavy hair and a curly mustache, a musical voice, mental caliber, oratorical and theatrical style. Born in a Maryland slaveholding family, he had come to hate slavery as fiercely as any New Englander. In politics first a Whig, then an American or Know-Nothing, he became a Republican. That Monty Blair of Maryland should be named Postmaster General was a stench in his nostrils. He led in Maryland a faction that hated Blair.

Davis brought in a bill intended to block the restoration efforts already started by the President in Louisiana and Tennessee; the measure aimed to stop the spread of the President's policy in other Southern States. In the House Davis was the one radical most often reminded by Thaddeus Stevens that he was going too far and ought to take what he could get now. The one speaker who could draw in more members from the cloakrooms than any other was Davis. He spoke his guess and vision for the Negro with cadence: "The folly of our ancestors and the wisdom of the Almighty, in its inscrutable purpose, having allowed them to come here and planted them here, they have a right to remain here to the latest syllable of recorded time."

By 73 to 59 the Davis bill passed the House May 4, 1864. In the Senate its course had been guided by Wade, who said: "The Executive ought not to be permitted to handle this great question to his own liking." That a state should have self-government originated by one-tenth of the population seemed to Wade absurd, anti-republican, anomalous and entirely subversive.

Into this confusion and perplexity four days after Congress adjourned the President stepped with an amazing document. He issued a proclamation reciting that Congress had passed a bill to guarantee republican form of government to certain states, and "the said bill was presented to the President of the United States for his approval less than one hour before the *sine die* adjournment of said session, and was not signed by him." Never before had an Executive assumed to reject those provisions in a legislative measure he disliked and to adopt those acceptable to him. And he went straight to the people proclaiming what he did. He had neither signed the bill nor vetoed it. "He put it in his pocket." Madison and others had used this pocket veto. He was "fully satisfied" with part of the bill but as to other parts he was

"unprepared." The key of the matter was in his saying he could not be "inflexibly committed to any single plan of restoration." Over the heads of Congress and its embittered and warring factions, he put his case to the country and the people.

The main landscape of the country was too somber for people to care that Wade and Davis had lost their heads or that Davis by his false stride was to fail of nomination and lose his seat in Congress to a Unionist colonel who had come near death from wounds in the Wilderness. In the three days immediately preceding his proclamation concerning the Wade-Davis bill the President issued, with detailed reasons, a proclamation suspending the writ of habeas corpus in Kentucky, and another proclamation, by direction of Congress, appointing the first Thursday of August as a day of national humiliation and prayer.

Once more General Robert E. Lee played a bold defensive game and struck fear into the heart of the Union cause. He gave Jubal A. Early and John C. Breckinridge an army of 20,000 men. Sheltered by the Blue Ridge Mountains, they marched up the Shenandoah Valley, slipped through a pass, headed for Washington. Early's men collected $20,000 cash at Hagerstown, tore up 24 miles of Baltimore & Ohio Railroad tracks, wrecked and burned mills, workshops, factories, at Baltimore burned the home of Governor Bradford, reached Silver Spring and in sight of the Capitol dome seized private papers, valuables, whisky, in the home of Postmaster General Blair, and then set the house afire. "Baltimore is in great peril," telegraphed a mayor's committee to Lincoln, asking for troops. Lincoln wired: "I have not a single soldier but whom is being disposed by the Military for the best protection of all. By latest accounts the enemy is moving on Washington. They can not fly to either place. Let us be vigilant but keep cool. I hope neither Baltimore or Washington will be sacked."

Lew Wallace, department commander at Baltimore, had marched troops out to Monocacy, fought a battle and, heavily outnumbered, was routed. His defeat delayed Early's army one day. That one day, it was generally admitted, saved Washington from the shame of capture.

Raw troops and soldiers just out of hospital made up the 20,000 men scraped together for manning the forts around Washington against Early, who had cut all wires north and July 11

U.S. Capitol, Washington, DC under construction. Photo by Andrew J. Russell, 1863.

WASHINGTON ON THE DEFENSIVE—PEACE BABBLINGS

marched his men on the Seventh Street Road that would lead him straight to the offices, arsenals, gold and silver, of the U.S. Government. Early halted his men just a little over two miles from Soldiers' Home, where Lincoln the night before had gone to bed when a squad from the War Department arrived with word from Stanton that he must get back to the city in a hurry. The President dressed and rode to the Executive Mansion.

Next day Lincoln saw through a spyglass transport steamers at Alexandria coming to unload two magnificent divisions of veteran troops fresh from Grant at City Point. The President met them at the wharf, touched his hat to them; they cheered and he waved his hand and smiled and they sent up more and more cheers. No mail, no telegrams, arrived from the outer world that day of July 12 in Washington.

From where Lincoln stood on a Fort Stevens rampart that afternoon he could see the swaying skirmish lines and later the marching brigade of General Daniel D. Bidwell, a police justice from Buffalo, New York, who had enlisted in '61 as a private, advanced in rank, and with his men had heard the bullets sing from Antietam through Gettysburg and the Wilderness. While Lincoln stood watching this bloody drama a bullet whizzed five feet from him and struck Surgeon Crawford of the 102d Pennsylvania in the ankle. Within three feet of the President an officer fell with a death wound. Those who were there said he was cool and thoughtful, seemed unconscious of danger, and looked like a Commander in Chief. "Amid the whizzing bullets," wrote Nicolay and Hay, the President held to his place "with . . . grave and passive countenance," till finally "General Wright peremptorily represented to him the needless risk he was running." Official records gave the Union losses at 380 killed and 319 wounded.

Next morning Early's army was gone. Again on July 14 Washington had mail and telegrams. Somewhere toward the Shenandoah Valley marched Early's army with its plunder-laden wagons, audacity on its banners, money in its strongboxes, shoes on feet that had started north barefoot. Early got away for the same reason, it was said, that he arrived. "Nobody stopped him."

Grant journeyed from south of Richmond to Monocacy north of Washington, August 6, 1864, for personal communication with Sheridan; his telegrams through the War Department were too often translated into something else.

Halleck had written to Sherman that the President wished to give him appointment as a major general in the Regular Army. "I wish you to say to the President," wrote Sherman, "that I would prefer he should not nominate me or anyone." He had all the rank he needed.

With the Armies of the Cumberland, Tennessee and Ohio joined into a force of 99,000, Sherman began his campaign from Chattanooga aimed at the capture of Atlanta. Between him and Atlanta was a Confederate army of 41,000, soon reinforced to 62,000, commanded by the master strategist General Joseph E. Johnston.

Carrying scars of wounds from Florida Indian wars, from Cerro Gordo and Chapultepec in the Mexican War, from Seven Pines in the Peninsular campaign near Richmond, now 57 years old, a West Pointer, a Virginian who had never owned slaves, a clean sportsman of a fighter, a silent, cautious Fabian—little Joe Johnston, familiar with the red hills of Georgia, seemed the one marshal in gray best able to stop or delay Sherman.

Sherman piled in his men on the fortified lines of Johnston hoping to break through and win victory and Atlanta. Sherman lost 3,000 as against the Confederate's 800. "One or two more such assaults would use up this army," said Old Pap Thomas. Not least of Johnston's hopes was the one that he could hold off any Sherman victory until the November elections in the North.

In 11 days Hood fought and lost three battles at a cost of 10,841 men to Sherman's 9,719.

Sherman had at last reached the Atlanta area. But would he take Atlanta? The North hoped. And the North despaired. Why did it take so long? Why had the whole war gone on so long? From Lincoln the last week of July Sherman had a long telegram which closed: "My profoundest thanks to you and your whole Army for the present campaign so far."

Only a certain procedure of guns, men, blood and iron, could bring peace, it seemed.

"Peace," said *Leslie's Weekly* August 6, 1864, "must come through the powerful negotiations of Gens. Grant and Sherman."

CHAPTER 45

"The Darkest Month of the War"— August '64

"THE DARKEST MONTH OF THE WAR"—AUGUST '64

SPEAKING in February '64, Senator Henry S. Lane of Indiana said the operation of the $300 clause in the conscription act had not been in favor of the poor man. "The poor man had to go at all events; he could not raise the $300; but it has operated, perhaps, beneficially upon the middle classes, and has exempted the rich entirely, for they could all pay the $300 exemption." What did it matter that $12,000,000 had been paid into the Government Treasury for draft exemptions? The measure was not intended to raise revenue. "We need men more than money. If we could print soldiers as fast as we print greenbacks, there would be something in this argument; but it cannot be done."

Congress had kept to itself certain strict powers. The President could be a dictator in enforcement of the draft law, but he was limited to *advising* Congress what the draft law should say. And so, June 8, 1864, Executive Document No. 97 went to Congress with the signature of Abraham Lincoln: "I have the honor to submit, for the consideration of Congress, a letter and inclosure from the Secretary of War, with my concurrence in the recommendation therein made." The letter enclosed, signed by Stanton and addressed "To the President," recommended "a repeal of the clause in the enrollment act commonly known as the $300 clause."

Attached to Stanton's recommendation was a report signed by Provost Marshal General Fry on the operation of the enrollment act as amended by Congress February 24, 1864. "I invite your attention," noted Fry, "to the small proportion of soldiers being obtained under the existing law. I see no reason to believe that the Army can be materially strengthened by draft so long as the $300 clause is in force."

On a clear-cut issue between Lincoln and Congress he was refused by overwhelming votes what he asked for in an essential point for carrying on the war. The refusal of Congress extended to Grant and Sherman, who favored a policy of no money

Portrait of Abraham Lincoln. Photo by Mathew Brady, Jan. 8, 1864.

payments and no substitutes entangling and retarding the draft. Grant and Sherman stressed the point that money payments brought a poorer brand of soldiers. Lincoln was speaking both as an executive in office and as a political candidate with re-election at stake in four months. He was willing to take his chances on whatever disorder might result from a new principle in the draft. And in face of political unrest and a vast gloom savage with suspicion and recrimination, Lincoln two weeks after the draft act was passed by Congress July 4, 1864, proclaimed a call for a half-million volunteers.

With the $300 clause done away with, any man drafted must either go into the Army himself or pay someone else to go for him. Such a substitute had to be either an alien, a veteran of two years' service, or a boy under 20. Hustlers, in the business of finding substitutes and selling them to those who wished to buy, came forward. "Wanted. Irishmen, Englishmen, Scotchmen, Germans, Frenchmen, to enlist as volunteers." Thus one amid columns of similar ads, paid for at regular rates, in the New York *Herald*. Only four days after the President's proclamation one New York *Herald* ad made the appeal: "It is clearly to the interest of every man liable to military duty to procure an alien substitute at once and save dollars, cents and worry. The price of substitutes will soon reach $1,200, because of the great bounties that will be offered by cities, towns and States."

"Six hundred dollars cash paid for substitutes," ran one ad in newspapers of Cincinnati, where on August 20 prices went to $1,200 and $1,500 for substitutes, for men to replace the fallen or the vanished in the ranks of Grant and Sherman. "A nice farm of eighty acres worth $600" was offered by one lacking cash and seeking a substitute.

What Congress did, after many conferences between Senate and House, was to provide that pay equal to that of the white soldiers should be given to all regularly enlisted "persons of color who were free" April 19, 1861. This resulted in an ingenious oath being used in many of the Negro regiments. Drawn up by Colonel E. N. Hallowell of the Massachusetts 54th, it required men to swear that they "owed no man unrequited labor on or before the 19th day of April, 1861." Thus they might be swearing to the truth and the fact, though they would be evading the category in which the U.S. Constitution still held them as chattels and property. Here and there, said Massachusetts colonels, were black men whose pride put them above a trick oath for evading a Constitution which still held them as chattels and property.

When a man enlisted as a substitute, pocketed the cash bounty, jumped elsewhere to enlist again and pocket another cash bounty, he was known as a "bounty-jumper." Newspapers carried a stream of items about fugitive and captured bounty-jumpers. One sentenced to four years in the Albany penitentiary confessed to having jumped the bounty 32 times.

In the war chronicle of the summer of '64, with its plodding in blood and muck, were two bright spots for the Union cause. On a Sunday morning in June, outside the international line off the coast of France at Cherbourg, two ships met and battled. The one flying the Confederate flag had cruised thousands of miles in the South Atlantic and Indian Oceans since August '63, had captured 62 merchantmen, and burned most of them at sea. She was the hated and feared *Alabama*, British-built, her seamen and gunners mainly British.

The *Kearsarge* had long trailed the *Alabama* and at last penned her in Cherbourg Harbor. Three hundred and seventy shells from the *Alabama* left the *Kearsarge* practically undamaged, with only the loss of a smokestack, while nearly every one of the 173 projectiles from the *Kearsarge* found its target and tore open the sides of the *Alabama* till she began sinking. Forty were killed on the *Alabama* under the Confederate flag; on the *Kearsarge* the losses were three men wounded, of whom one died.

In August, the Confederacy lost its most essential port on the Gulf of Mexico. Lashed to a flagship mast and leading his fleet into Mobile Bay, Admiral Farragut prayed, "O God, who created man and gave him reason, direct me what to do. Shall I go on?" His order, "Damn the torpedoes! Full speed ahead!" became a Unionist slogan. His fleet captured the ram *Tennessee*, rated one of the most powerful vessels of war afloat in any waters, and with land forces reduced the three forts guarding Mobile. Lincoln termed it a "brilliant achievement."

Across weeks of August '64, a movement, necessarily secret, among Republican party leaders operated with the aim of replacing Lincoln with another nominee for President. The name of Grant was most favored to replace that of Lincoln. A call was prepared for a convention to be held in Cincinnati September 28.

Events had brought new and definite viewpoints to the President. To Judge Joseph T. Mills and ex-Governor A. W. Randall of Wisconsin at Soldiers' Home Lincoln unburdened himself. "There are now between 1 & 200 thousand black men in the service of the Union . . . There have been men who have proposed to me to return to slavery the black warriors of Port Hudson and Olustee to their masters to conciliate the South. I should be damned in time and eternity for so doing. The world shall know that I will keep my faith to friends and enemies, come what will. My enemies say I am now carrying on this war for the sole purpose of abolition. It is & will be carried on so long as I am President for the sole purpose of restoring the Union. But no human power can subdue this rebellion without using the Emancipation lever as I have done . . . My enemies condemn my emancipation policy. Let them prove by the history of this war, that we can restore the Union without it."

Raymond waited in New York. From the President came no reply. In Washington the President was viewing the national situation. He was a candidate for re-election with as yet no opponent. It would be a week or more before the Democrats at Chicago would name a man to run against him; yet the signs were that he was already beaten by whoever might be named.

Two days later Raymond and the national executive committee of the Republican party, not having heard from the President that he would publicly proffer peace to the Richmond Government, arrived at the White House. They were, according to Nicolay and Hay, "in obvious depression and panic." Raymond was in a final and confidential session with the President and three Cabinet members when Welles entered. "I went in as usual unannounced," wrote Welles in his diary. "I found Messrs. Seward, Fessenden, and Stanton with Raymond . . . in consultation with the President. The President was making some statement as to a document of his, and said he supposed his style was peculiar and had its earmarks, so that it could not be mistaken. He kept on talking as if there had been no addition to the company, and as if I had been expected and belonged there.

Returning to New York, Raymond threw amazement into the Republican anti-Lincoln ranks with his positive statements in the *Times* that peace negotiation stories had no bottom; "the President stands firm against every solicitation to postpone the draft"; and as to rumors of this and that about the Government, "You may rest assured . . . its sole and undivided purpose is to prosecute the war until the rebellion is quelled."

John Eaton, with a pass signed by the President was authorized to "visit Gen. Grant at City Point, Va." Grant held strictly to army matters in the talk of the two men that ran past midnight. Eaton was interested, but was trying to find some entering wedge on political affairs. Finally he mentioned to Grant a conversation on a railroad train with army men who had asked Eaton if he thought Grant could be induced to run as a citizen's candidate for President. "The question is," said Eaton to Grant, "not whether you wish to run, but whether you could be compelled to run in answer to the demand of the people for a candidate who should save the Union."

Grant's instant reply amazed Eaton. The General brought his clenched fists down hard on the strap arms of his camp chair, "They can't do it! They can't compel me to do it." "Have you said this to the President?" "No, I have not thought it worth while to assure the President of my opinion. I consider it as important to the cause that he should be elected as that the army should be successful in the field."

Eaton, back at Washington, entering Lincoln's office heard the eager question, "Well, what did you find?" "You were right." And the President "fairly glowed with satisfaction," noted Eaton, as he heard Lincoln say, "I told you that they could not get him to run until he had closed out the rebellion."

Grant's letter for publication dated at City Point, August 16, 1864, took no sides with any Republican or Democratic party faction, was neither pro nor anti-Lincoln. And in its closing paragraph it endorsed by inference the President's emancipation policy. The old Steve Douglas Democrat, Grant, was saying by implication that the slavery issue had progressed to where the complications were inexorable: there was nothing else to do but free the slaves and make a peace that kept the slaves free. Regarding the war and the draft he wished to give the impression that the Confederacy was becoming a hollow shell sucked of its vitality.

Lincoln knew that no words, explanations, persuasions, letters, speeches, could save his cause. Only bayonets triumphant and red-dripping with Confederate defeat could bring anything like magic or potency to anything he might have to say. While decisive events waited he would manage a course as best he could, saying: "The pilots on our western rivers steer from point to point, as they call it—setting the course of the boat no farther than they can see. And that is all I propose to do in the great problems that are set before us."

A summer for sure it had been of steering from point to point, from Sherman's drive toward Atlanta and Grant's lunges at Richmond to the arrival of Early at the gates of Washington and the sinking of the *Alabama* and the capture of Mobile; from the smooth unanimous nomination of Lincoln at Baltimore to the clawing scorn of the Wade-Davis Manifesto; from the peace missions of Greeley at Niagara and Jaquess-Gilmore at Richmond to the secret Republican party manipulations hoping to replace Lincoln at the head of the ticket; from draft legislation authorizing conscripts to buy substitutes to the attempt to detach 50,000 men from Grant's army to enforce the draft in Northern cities, oath-bound secret societies threatening to take over the Government at Washington and one committee of Republican party leaders begging the President not to make his call for a draft of a half-million men until after the November election. He had given reply: "What is the Presidency worth to me if I have no country?"

Midsummer, Lincoln had told a Boston *Journal* man: "I have faith in the people. They will not consent to disunion. The danger is, in their being misled. Let them know the truth and the country is safe." He looked haggard and careworn to the correspondent, who said, "You are wearing yourself out with work." "I can't work less. But it isn't that. Work never troubled me. Things look badly, and I can't avoid anxiety . . . I feel a presentiment that I shall not outlast the rebellion. When it is over, my work will be done."

In the progress of the war Lincoln had constantly drawn closer to the churches. He replied to one delegation in May '64: "It is no fault in others that the Methodist Church sends more soldiers to the field, more nurses to the hospital, and more prayers to heaven than any. God bless the Methodist Church. Bless all the churches." And replying to a Baptist delegation later in the same day: "I have had great cause of gratitude for the support so unanimously given by all Christian denominations of the country."

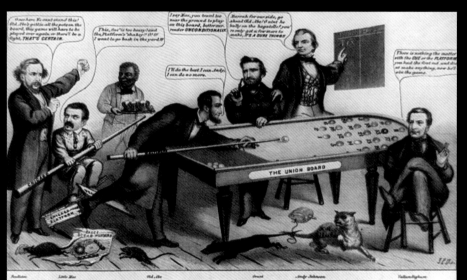

CHAPTER 46

THE FIERCE FALL CAMPAIGN OF '64

The contest for the presidency in 1864 is depicted as a game of bagatelle (a game similar to pool) between Republican candidate Abraham Lincoln and Democrat George B. McClellan.

THE FIERCE FALL CAMPAIGN OF '64

Battle of Five Forks, VA, Apr. 1, 1865. Engraved by Kurz & Allison, 1886.

BEFORE leaving for Chicago to report the Democratic national convention, Noah Brooks heard Lincoln: "They must nominate a Peace Democrat on a war platform, or a War Democrat on a peace platform; and I personally can't say that I care much which they do."

In the same Wigwam in Chicago where Lincoln had been nominated in 1860, the convention met August 29, a boiling kettle of partisans that included Peace Democrats, War Democrats, Whigs, Know-Nothings, Conservatives, states' rights extremists who endorsed secession, millionaires in broadcloth, run-down politicians in paper collars, men who had braved mobs and suffered for the rights of free speech and a free press, and a remnant of Confederate loyalists who could not be open about their efforts. The delegates were called to order by August Belmont.

The platform then adopted declared for the Union, the Constitution, civil liberty, and "care, protection, and regard" for the soldiers of the country. The measures of immediate action on taking power, directly pledged in the platform, were: (1) the armies would be ordered to cease hostilities and go home; (2) the Southern States would then be asked to join a convention to restore the Union; (3) free speech and a free press would be allowed and no matter what the opposition to the Government there would be no arbitrary arrests, while habeas corpus and trial by jury would return.

General Sheridan's ride. Engraved by L. Prang & Co. after a work by Thure de Thulstrup.

On the final showdown George B. McClellan had 202 ½ votes as against little more than one-tenth of that number for one T. H. Seymour of Connecticut. Vallandigham amid cheers moved that the nomination of McClellan for President be made unanimous, which was done with further cheers. Senator George H. Pendleton of Ohio, on his record entirely satisfactory to the peace men, was named for Vice-President. The politicians went home fairly well satisfied. Was not victory in the air? In that week did not everyone know that the leading prophets and weather vanes of the Republican party were conceding defeat?

Then fate stepped in. Like a moving hour hand on a clock of doom came news flung world wide, news setting crowds of Northern loyalists to dancing with mirth and howling with glee, news centering about one little dispatch from Sherman September 3. Lincoln read a flimsy saying: "So Atlanta is ours and fairly won . . . Since May 5th we have been in one constant battle or skirmish, and need rest."

The dull ache of defeat and failure in many hearts took a change. In all news sheets the first item, the one story overwhelming all others, was around Sherman's words: "Atlanta is ours and fairly won." A strategic crossroads, supply depot and transportation center of a pivotal Cotton State in the Deep South was gone. Vicksburg, New Orleans and the Mississippi River gone, Kentucky, Tennessee and Nashville gone, Mobile gone.

THE FIERCE FALL CAMPAIGN OF '64

Lee and his army penned between Grant and Richmond for how long? Bells rang again, guns boomed.

The President requested thanksgiving to be offered in all places of worship the following Sunday and announced: "The national thanks are herewith tendered by the President to Major General William T. Sherman, and the gallant officers and soldiers of his command before Atlanta . . . The marches, battles, sieges . . . must render it famous in the annals of war . . ."

Now in this September of '64 Phil Sheridan was heard from. For the first time in the war the Shenandoah Valley saw a destroyer with a system. Whatever would nourish man or provide fodder for beast was to be taken or burned or spoiled. When Grant's order should be met, then a crow would have to carry its own rations flying over the valley. At Harrisonburg from Gibbs Hill, residents counted 20 barns in the same hour lighting the dark night of the valley as the flames roared upward.

Four days' fighting at Winchester and Fisher's Hill followed Grant's order "Go in!" and Sheridan's telegram to Grant the night of September 19 had first place in all news sheets of the country: "I attacked the forces of General Early . . . completely defeated him, and driving him through Winchester, captured about 2,500 prisoners, 5 pieces of artillery, 9 army flags, and most of their wounded." To his army next day Sheridan read a telegram signed "A. Lincoln": "Have just heard of your great victory. God bless you all, officers and men. Strongly inclined to come up and see you."

A *Harper's Weekly* writer had noticed a man at a news bulletin board reading one of Sheridan's dispatches to Grant and commenting, "A few more such victories and Abe Lincoln will be elected in November." They were what Lincoln had wanted. No campaign speeches could equal them. The least he could do was appoint Sheridan a brigadier general in the Regular Army and place him in permanent command of the Middle Division, which he did.

On September 22 a letter was published of Frémont dropping his third party and coming out for Lincoln. And next day Lincoln asked Blair to leave the Cabinet and Blair did. Whether Lincoln made a deal for Frémont's return to the fold on condition of

Blair's being ushered out of the Cabinet was anybody's guess. It came as a necessary piece of work for Lincoln to write in his letter to Blair: "You very well know that this proceeds from no dissatisfaction of mine with you personally or officially. Your uniform kindness has been unsurpassed by that of any friend . . ."

Some newspapers made much of a remark dropped by Simon Cameron that in the event of re-election the President would call around him fresh and earnest men. Hay referred to this. Lincoln said: "They need not be especially savage about a change. There are now only 3 left of the original Cabinet."

For campaign purposes both parties now made use of the long letter McClellan had handed to Lincoln at Harrison's Landing more than two years before. The Democrats offered it as a modest self-portrayal of a Christian gentleman, a soldier and a statesman. The Republicans picked at it in editorials and squibs, the more radical editors saying its ego and covert insolence should have brought instant removal of a general stepping so completely out of the military field into politics.

On one point the Republicans and Democrats seemed to agree: that on July 7, 1862, when he dated that letter, and for some time before, McClellan had the definite notion in his head that he might make a good President and had carefully studied what he would announce as his policies if he were a candidate. Whether or not Fernando Wood had seduced McClellan into politics, as some believed, it was now in McClellan's favor that Wood announced in view of McClellan's repudiation of the Chicago platform he, Wood, could not support McClellan for President.

Marshaled solidly behind McClellan were powerful forces, the banking and transportation interests linked with August Belmont, Dean Richmond, Aspinwall, the industrialist churchman seen pre-eminently in Cyrus H. McCormick of Chicago, an array of respectably wealthy, intellectual or aristocratic types embodied in Horatio Seymour of New York and Robert C. Winthrop of Boston. Marching along were two-fisted and riotous elements, joined by those to whom the race issue was uppermost, fearful the Emancipation Proclamation might bring political and social equality. The recoil over McClellan's repudiation of the peace platform came in some of the most vocal sections of the party. The *Metropolitan Record* and the *Daily News* in New York announced they could not go along with McClellan. The Crisis at Columbus, Ohio, held that "fraudulent sale is not binding in law" and the "sell-out" in Chicago was treachery.

The vote for the platform at Chicago was far more unanimous than the vote for the candidate, in which connection Schurz would speak from experience: "There is no American who does not know that a President's policy is not made by him alone, but by those who have made him." In closing Schurz let the American Eagle scream. In 50 years the country would have 100,000,000 people, in another century 500,000,000, and the purpose of the North was a free republic "*so strong that its pleasure will be consulted before any power on earth will undertake to disturb the peace of the world.*"

Three speeches of Lincoln to Ohio regiments, "three months' men" going home, gave his attempt to tell in a few simple words what the shooting and crying, the war, was about. "A free government where every man has a right to be equal with every other man" was endangered. "Nowhere in the world is presented a government of so much liberty and equality. To the humblest and poorest amongst us are held out the highest privileges and positions. The present moment finds me at the White House, yet there is as good a chance for your children as there was for my father's. I happen, temporarily, to occupy this White House. I am a living witness that any one of your children may look to come here as my father's child has."

On October 11 the stump speakers and the tub thumpers paused slightly, the torchlights and the transparencies halted a moment, and there was less fury in the pamphlets blown loose as wild geese across the autumn sky. The electorate went to the polls that day in Pennsylvania, Ohio and Indiana. At eight o'clock in the evening the President with Hay walked over to the War Department.

The telegraph keys clicked. Governor Morton and the entire Republican ticket in Indiana were elected by 20,000 majority, with a gain of four Congressmen. Pennsylvania's Congressmen, equally divided between two parties, changed to 15 Republicans against 9 Democrats. The Union ticket carried Ohio by 54,000 and the 14 Democrats and 5 Republicans of '62 shifted now to 17 Republicans and 2 Democrats in Congress. The defamatory Peace Democrat "Sunset" Cox lost his seat to Samuel Shellabarger. Not least was the news from Maryland and her

adoption of a new state constitution abolishing slavery; the majority was slim, the soldier vote giving emancipation its day.

On October 12 Roger Brooke Taney died and the President must name a new Chief Justice. Spheres of influence formed and sought to have Lincoln name Montgomery Blair, Bates, Fessenden, Salmon P. Chase or some other one. And Lincoln was to hear them and to wait and to consider carefully and hold his patience.

When Smith had retired as Secretary of the Interior, Browning had hoped the President would agree with Mrs. Lincoln that he should have the place. When Browning brought to the President the matter of the vacant Chief Justiceship, he was not without faint hope he might be the man. Known as a familiar of the President, for him doors swung open when he sent his card in at the departments. He rode with the President and navy heads "to the navy yards to witness the throwing of rockets and signals from 6- and 12-pound guns. He worked in his office till night "then went and saw the President about fees in the Phillips cases, about Adml Wilke's case, and about appointment of Eben Moore to Montano."

A call signed by eminent and influential Democrats of the past endorsed the Lincoln-Johnson ticket. The call asked what kind of a Democratic party it was that excluded John A. Dix, Alexander T. Stewart, Theodore Roosevelt, Sr., R. B. Roosevelt, Peter Cooper, John A. Logan, John M. Palmer and many others who till now had had no political home except the Democratic party. "If these men are not Democrats, who are?"

The draft meanwhile proceeded. The relentless dragnet moved. Grant and Sherman wanted men. "Leading Republicans all over the country," noted Nicolay and Hay, "fearing the effect of the draft upon the elections, begged the President to withdraw the call or suspend operations under it." Cameron advised against it in Pennsylvania. Chase telegraphed from Ohio urging a three weeks' suspension. To an Ohio committee earnestly requesting suspension until after the November elections, Lincoln quietly answered, "What is the Presidency worth to me if I have no country?"

Twice came Governor Morton of Indiana, whose soldiers could not vote in the field, applying for the return of all Indiana soldiers possible on Election Day. And at Lincoln's refusal to go over the heads of his generals and order the soldiers home to vote, it was suggested that if Indiana went Democratic she could give no more help to the Government. Lincoln met this point: "It is better that we should both be beaten than that the forces in front of the enemy should be weakened and perhaps defeated on account of the absence of these men." Morton suggested that no Indiana troops be kept in hospitals outside his state and that all troops unfit for service be sent home. On these points Lincoln got action. And Stanton had Lincoln's approval in ordering home from Sherman's army for campaigning in Indiana six prominent Hoosier officers, along with Major Generals Logan and Frank Blair to stump Indiana and nearby states. In fact, Logan later wrote to Sherman that "when I left on leave after the Atlanta campaign, to canvass for Mr. Lincoln, I did it at the special and private request of the President. This I kept to myself and never made it public."

"There was a constant succession of telegrams from all parts of the country," wrote Dana of the War Office, "requesting that leave of absence be extended to this or that officer, in order that his district at home might have the benefit of his vote and political influence. Furloughs were asked for private soldiers whose presence in close districts was deemed of especial importance, and there was a widespread demand that men on detached service and convalescents in hospitals be sent home. All the power and influence of the War Department, then something enormous from the vast expenditure and extensive relations of the war, was employed to secure the re-election of Mr. Lincoln. The political struggle was most intense, and the interest taken in it, both in the White House and in the War Department, was almost painful."

Again Sheridan, his men and horses, were heard from. When the hour cried for it Sheridan had the genius of a daredevil who could make other men in the mass want to be daredevils. At ten o'clock the night of October 19 Sheridan telegraphed Grant:

"My army at Cedar Creek was attacked this morning before daylight, and . . . in fact, most of the line . . . driven in confusion with the loss of twenty pieces of artillery. I hastened from Winchester, where I was on my return from Washington, and found the armies between Middletown and Newtown, having been driven back about four miles. I here took the affair in hand . . . formed a compact line of battle, just in time to repulse an attack of the enemy, which was handsomely done at about 1 P.M. At 3 P.M., after some changes of the cavalry from the left to the right flank, I attacked, with great vigor, driving and routing the enemy, capturing, according to the last report, forty-three pieces of artillery, and very many prisoners . . . Affairs at times looked badly, but by the gallantry of our brave officers and men disaster has been converted into a splendid victory."

Lincoln telegraphed Sheridan October 22: "With great pleasure I tender to you and your brave army, the thanks of the Nation, and my own personal admiration and gratitude, for the month's operations in the Shenandoah Valley; and especially for the splendid work of October 19, 1864."

Twenty days before the November elections Sheridan gave the North one of the most dramatic victories of the war, following a methodical devastation of the Shenandoah Valley, with the result soon to come that his own army and the shattered forces of Early would be transferred to operations before Richmond. From innumerable platforms of the North were recited the verses of "Sheridan's Ride" by Thomas Buchanan Read. As a campaign tract it was fetching. As he heard this piece many and many a time Sheridan said he believed that what people liked best in the poem was the horse.

Soon now, on November 8, the American electorate would choose between Lincoln and the Baltimore platform and McClellan and the Chicago platform as revised by McClellan. That day of ballots would fix a momentous decision in the life of the American people.

CHAPTER 47

THE MAN WHO HAD
BECOME THE ISSUE

THE MAN WHO HAD BECOME THE ISSUE

THE MAN Lincoln, his person and mind, had come to be the pivotal issue of the 1864 campaign. Some would vote for him with no particular faith, others in a loyalty that had seldom or never swerved. In the chaos of the times he was to these folk a beacon light that in moments almost flickered out into a black despair, yet returned to shine without wavering. His life in the White House, his decisions, speeches and messages issued from there, went out over the country for interpretations, for thanks, curses, doubts. Those interpretations would be told of in the November 8 ballot boxes.

Seven biographies published in '64 presented Lincoln favorably for various audiences of readers. Several small paper-covered books issued by the opposition were chiefly humorous and satirical. Immense editions were sold of an issue of the monthly *Beadle Dime Library* by O. J. Victor and another "popular life" by the Reverend William M. Thayer of Boston. Each emphasized the opportunity before any American poor boy who wished "to climb the heights."

Leslie's Weekly enumerated "sweet scented compliments" paid by the opposition press to the President of the United States, namely: ape, gorilla, fool, filthy storyteller, despot, liar, thief, braggart, buffoon, usurper, monster, tortoise, ignoramus, old scoundrel, perjurer, robber, swindler, tyrant, fiend, butcher, land pirate.

The effect of this savage verbal warfare? In October '64 *Harper's Weekly* appraised it: "The personal character of the President is the rock upon which the Opposition is wrecked. It dashes against him and his administration, hissing and venomous, but falls back again baffled . . . the popular confidence in the unswerving fidelity and purity of purpose of the President has smiled the storm to scorn."

One October evening in '64 a torchlight procession of hundreds of Negroes marched to the White House lawn, carrying banners and transparencies, a brass band blaring, loud and repeated cheers bringing the President. He looked out from the portico on jubilant black faces, heard in the half-lighted darkness their moving hoarse voices, and began, "I have to guess, my friends, the object of this call which has taken me quite by surprise this evening." The tall, gaunt, slave-born black woman Sojourner Truth arrived at the Executive Mansion from Battle Creek, Michigan, "a long and halting journey," she said. The President gave Sojourner his hand, bowed. "I am pleased to see you." Then Sojourner released her speech poem: "Mr. President, when you first took your seat I feared you would be torn to pieces, for I likened you unto Daniel, who was thrown into the lions' den; and if the lions did not tear you to pieces, I knew that it would be God that had saved you; and I said if He spared me I would see you before the four years expired, and He has done so, and now I am here to see you for myself." He took the little book she brought out, and as Sojourner phrased it, "The same hand that signed the death-warrant of slavery wrote as follows":

For Aunty Sojourner Truth,

Oct. 29, 1864.   A. Lincoln

In the Executive Mansion for the first two years no colored persons were employed. "But," wrote Brooks, "the President has succeeded in getting about him a corps of attaches of Hibernian descent." Brooks wrote that the Irish coachman "did not consider it his business to run errands. This coming to the President's ears he ordered up the carriage next morning at six o'clock and sent a member of his household in the equipage to the Avenue where he bought a paper and rode back, with the mortified coachee on the box."

To the White House often had come the master photographer Mathew B. Brady. Since February '60, at the time of the Cooper Union speech, Brady had by autumn of '64 photographed Lincoln more than 30 times. From his profitable portrait gallery on Broadway and Tenth, New York, Brady had come to the war with his camera. Out in the camps, on the march and on battlefields Brady and his assistants made both single and stereoscopic wetplate exposures and were achieving a camera record comprising thousands of convincing likenesses of scenes and people. Lincoln wrote and signed a heavy card with the large scrawl "Pass Brady," which took Brady nearly everywhere he cared to go.

Abraham Lincoln. Brady's National Portrait Gallery, ca. 1863.

Tad Lincoln, 1865.

Collections of *cartes de visite*, photographs of fine clarity and definition of line, mounted on small cards usually 2 ½ by 3 ½ inches, were in many thousands of homes. Brady and Gardner photographs of Lincoln were often on show there. Frequently the illustrated weeklies, *Harper's* and *Leslie's*, and occasionally the daily newspapers, published large drawings from photographs, so that Lincoln's face and figure had become familiar to those who read, and of course to some who enjoyed pictures though they couldn't read.

Carpenter's painting, "The First Reading of the Emancipation Proclamation by President Lincoln to His Cabinet" was nearly finished. In his six months' stay he and Lincoln had passed many pleasant hours. Thirty-four years old, slender and delicate, with bushy black hair, devout in religion and strict in manners, Carpenter had a loyalty to the President and a belief that his painting would be a help. "I must go in and take one more look at the picture before you leave us," said Lincoln one July day. Carpenter spoke of the unvarying kindness the President had always shown him. Lincoln listened, kept gazing on the picture, and turned to say, "Carpenter, I believe I am about as glad over the success of this work as you are." By permission of the President the painting, when finished, was placed in the East Room, open to the public for two days, and was viewed by several thousand visitors.

Readers saw with interest press items of Mrs. Lincoln paying a complimentary visit to General Scott at West Point and receiving a salute of 15 guns; of her going to Harvard in June to attend the graduation of Robert; of her buying a set of earrings and a pin for $3,000 and a shawl for $5,000 on successive shopping trips to New York City; of her sister Martha Todd White of Selma, Alabama, receiving a pass signed by the President giving her

passage, with baggage, through the Union Army lines, resulting in rumors and accusations that she had been accorded special privileges and had smuggled contraband goods, including, *Leslie's Weekly* alleged mistakenly, "a rebel uniform, the buttons of which were gold, worth $40,000."

One evening Robert W. McBride, serving as corporal of the guard, picketed his horse in the rear of the White House and was standing in the driveway of the front portico. As he stood there he saw the President come out alone and walk to the edge of the portico where the steps began. There under a lighted gas jet the President stood, alone. His hands behind him, he stood there in a reverie. Then he came down the steps, and hardly seeming to notice the corporal, nevertheless gravely lifted his hat as a return salute and walked toward the War Department, alone. In about a half-hour he came back, alone.

Stanton's anxiety over the President's safety continued. He gave one standing order. Although the President might come to the War Office at midnight alone, as happened often, he should never be permitted to return alone, but must be escorted by a file of four soldiers and a noncommissioned officer.

Four police officers in November '64 were detailed by the chief of police of the District of Columbia, to serve as special guards for the President. They were John F. Parker, Alfonso Dunn, Alexander Smith and Thomas Pendel. On Pendel's later being appointed doorkeeper, that vacancy was filled by William H. Crook. Noted Crook, "The night guards were expected to protect the President on his expeditions to and from the War Department, or while he was at any place of amusement, and to patrol the corridor outside his room while he slept."

Of an odd affair about mid-August '64, nothing should be said, ran Lincoln's advice to John W. Nichols, a guard since the summer of '62. Nichols, on duty at the large gate entrance to the Soldiers' Home grounds, one night about eleven heard a rifle shot in the direction of the city and soon after heard the hoofbeats of a horse coming nearer and nearer. In two or three minutes a horse came dashing up. On it Nichols saw the President, bareheaded, and Nichols helped to quiet a favorite saddle horse. The President was now saying: "He came pretty near getting away with me, didn't he? He got the bit in his teeth before I could draw rein." To Nichols' query about his hat the President answered that somebody had fired a gun off down at the foot of the hill, and that his horse had become scared and had jerked his hat off.

Alone often, yet again with varied companions, Tad or Mrs. Lincoln, or Hay, Brooks, Sumner and others, the President went to the drama, visiting Grover's Theatre perhaps a hundred times since coming to Washington. When there was opera at Grover's, Mrs. Lincoln invariably attended with the President. "Mr. Grover, I really enjoy a minstrel show," Lincoln suggested once. And when Grover later announced Hooley's Minstrels soon to come Lincoln laughed. "Well, that was thoughtful of you."

Once in '64 Tad quietly slipped away from a box at Grover's. And soon the father saw his boy on stage with a chorus singing "The Battle Cry of Freedom," Tad half lost in a Union Army blue uniform blouse.

Often in subdued corners was talk of Colonel La Fayette C. Baker, chief of the Detective Bureau, a czar of various underworlds. He had 1,000 to 2,000 men operating under his orders, their webs and tentacles flung out among the just and the unjust, his bureau under Stanton. Baker's grandfather, named Remember Baker, was a Revolutionary War captain under Ethan Allen, and his father, named Green Mountain Boy Baker, was a Michigan farmer whose boy went east, then west, to become one of the most active members of the Vigilante Committee that overrode the openly lawless of San Francisco.

Register of the Treasury Lucius E. Chittenden pictured Baker as "cruel and rapacious"; his detectives were put on the rolls "without recommendation, investigation, or any inquiry." Usually the suspect arrested was handcuffed, and brought to Baker's office, then in the basement of the Treasury building. There the suspect was "subjected to a brow-beating examination, in which Baker was said to rival in impudence some heads of the criminal bar," this examination being repeated as often as he, Baker, chose. "Men were kept in his rooms for weeks, without warrant, affidavit, or other semblance of authority. If the accused took any measures for his own protection, he was hurried to the Old Capitol Prison, where he was beyond the reach of the civil authorities.

The phrase "lame duck" entered political lingo. A Western Senator on introducing his successor to Lincoln put in his request for himself to be Commissioner of Indian Affairs. Lincoln cut him short, it was said, and later explained: "I hate to have old friends like the Senator go away. And another thing I usually find out is that a Senator or Representative out of business is a sort of *lame duck*. He has to be provided for."

Had the people and events of those tornado years shaped Lincoln more and more into a man paradoxically harder than ever, yet also more delicate and tenuous in human judgments and affairs? Was there more often a phantom touch in what he did? Did certain men and women who studied him either close up or from far away feel that a strange shade and a ghost, having often a healing power, moving toward wider and surer human solidarity, lived and spoke in the White House? For such as there were of these, who knew an intimacy with Lincoln even when he was at his loneliest, who were ready to uphold him when they had no inkling of where his next decision might bring the George William Curtis, the writer, tried in *Harper's Weekly* of September 24, 1864, could see a ship torn and worn with a long voyage, met by head winds and baffling currents. "A feeling of disappointment and despondency takes possession of the passengers and the crew, and each one attributes to the officer of the ship the inevitable and necessary delays and discouragements . . ." Then the long-wished-for land heaves into view. "Certainty takes the place of disappointed hopes, and they feel with mortification and regret how unjust they have been to the officer whose every hour and thought has been devoted to their welfare, and who has at length brought them with safety, and with a prosperous voyage, to the end of their journey."

Beyond parties or partisan success were other motives to which G.W.C. would appeal in this popular pictorial weekly magazine going to nearly all towns of the North and camps of the Union Army. Though no loyal heart could envision Mr. Lincoln replaced "by some other, any other, man," his influence could not end with his discontinuance of power. "There is a fame which no station or absence of station can add to or diminish. His work, like that of the most obscure soldier who lies buried under the sod of Gettysburg or Antietam, has been done . . . Faithful and consecrated to the service of his country, his memory, though it were nameless as that of any private in our armies or any nurse in our hospitals, will, like theirs, be sweet in the heart of every true American . . ."

CHAPTER 48

ELECTION DAY,
NOVEMBER 8, 1864

Lincoln standing (portrait).

ELECTION DAY, NOVEMBER 8, 1864

O F NOVEMBER 8, 1864, the day of the national election, John Hay wrote that the White House was "still and almost deserted." The sky hung gray. Rain fell. About noon Brooks called on the President "and to my surprise found him entirely alone, as if by common consent everybody had avoided the White House." Lincoln had no ease, saying to Brooks: "I am just enough of a politician to know that there was not much doubt about the result of the Baltimore convention; but about this thing I am very far from being certain. I wish I were certain."

At seven o'clock that evening Lincoln with Hay stepped out of the White House into a night of wild rain and storm. They splashed across the grounds to the War Department telegraph office. At a side door a wet and steaming sentinel huddled in a rubber coat. As Lincoln entered the second-floor telegraph office a dispatch was put in his hands from Forney at Philadelphia claiming 10,000 majority there. "Forney," said Lincoln, "is a little excitable." To Mrs. Lincoln he sent over early reports, saying, "She is more anxious than I."

The wires worked badly because of the rain-and-wind storm. In a long lull about ten, wrote Brooks, "The President amused the little company in the War Office with entertaining reminiscences and anecdotes." In and out moved Eckert, handing telegrams to Stanton, the President then studying them and commenting.

As the evening wore on the wires worked badly from Illinois and from states west of the Mississippi. The returns in, however, were running close to the tabulation Lincoln had made weeks before of his own estimates. Toward midnight, noted Brooks, "It was certain that Lincoln had been reflected, and the few gentlemen left in the office congratulated him very warmly on the result. Lincoln took the matter very calmly, showing not the least elation or excitement, but said that he would admit that he was glad to be relieved of all suspense, grateful that the verdict of the people was likely to be so full, clear, and unmistakable that there could be no dispute." At a midnight supper, Hay noted, "The President went

awkwardly and hospitably to work shovelling out the fried oysters." It was two in the morning when he started to leave the War Office, at the door meeting serenaders with a brass band, with cheers calling for a speech. The rain, the storm, was over.

The President told them, "I earnestly believe that the consequences of this day's work, if it be as you assure me and as now seems probable, will be to the lasting advantage, if not to the very salvation, of the country . . . I do not impugn the motives of any one opposed to me. It is no pleasure to me to triumph over any one; but I give thanks to the Almighty for this evidence of the people's resolution to stand by free government and the rights of humanity."

A day of great fate was over. There was no going behind the returns. Complete tabulations yet to come were a mere formality. At thousands of polling places some 4,000,000 men had marked ballots. A nation had made a decision.

The American electorate, "the People," spoke on whether a colossal, heavy, weary war should go on, under the same leadership as it had begun, on whether the same guiding mind and personality should keep the central control and power. On a day of rain and wind that wrecked telegraph systems, the people said Yes to Lincoln.

The election returns when analyzed admonished humility. In the Electoral College vote, all the Northern States except Kentucky, Delaware and New Jersey went to Lincoln. But it was not so sweeping a triumph in the total of popular ballots. They gave Lincoln a majority of slightly more than 400,000. The votes for Lincoln from coast to coast, 2,203,831, represented 55.09 per cent of all that were cast, said *Appleton's Annual Cyclopaedia* for 1864. McClellan had 44.91 per cent of the total: between New York and San Francisco were 1,797,019 male voters opposed to Lincoln, his administration and his policies. In New York City McClellan carried by 78,746 against Lincoln's 36,673; in the Empire State Lincoln won with 50.47 per cent of the vote as against McClellan's 49.53 per cent. It was formidable that 212 of the Electoral College votes should go to Lincoln, with McClellan getting only 21. But a study of three states with the largest electoral votes, New York, Pennsylvania and Ohio, showed Lincoln receiving 930,269 to

843,862 for McClellan, a difference of only 86,407 votes, but giving Lincoln 80 in the Electoral College. Had these three key states by their narrow margin gone for McClellan and been joined by two or three other states, McClellan would have been elected.

Grant wired from City Point, "The victory is worth more to the country than a battle won." General Frank Blair wrote to Hay from Georgia, where he headed an army corps under Sherman, "The vote in this army today is almost unanimous for Lincoln. Give Uncle Abe my compliments."

And highlighted in the background of Lincoln's victory was the fact that hundreds of thousands of soldiers whose ballots would have been given to the President had no chance to vote, either because of required marching and fighting, or because their home-state legislatures had refused them the right of voting in the field. And in the foul rooms of Libby Prison at Richmond the votes were 276 for Lincoln, 95 for McClellan.

On the night of November 10 a procession with banners, lanterns, transparencies marched to the White House, surged around the main entrance and filled the front grounds. The newly elected President stepped out of a window opening on the north portico and the crowd uproar was many minutes going down. Lincoln made ready to read his script to the people. Hay stood alongside with a candle to light the written page. "Not very graceful," he smiled to Hay, "but I am growing old enough not to care much for the manner of doing things."

"It has long been a grave question," Lincoln began, under the night stars, "whether any government, not *too* strong for the liberties of its people, can be strong *enough* to maintain its own existence, in great emergencies. On this point the present rebellion brought our republic to a severe test . . . the election was a necessity. We can not have free government without elections; and if the rebellion could force us to forego, or postpone a national election, it might fairly claim to have already conquered and ruined us . . . Human-nature will not change. In any future great national trial, compared with the men of this, we shall have as weak, and as strong; as silly and as wise; as bad and good . . . Gold is good in its place; but living, brave, patriotic men, are better than gold."

He voiced the human spirit he would prefer to have breathing across the future. "So long as I have been here I have not willingly planted a thorn in any man's bosom. While I am deeply sensible to the high compliment of a re-election; and duly grateful, as I trust, to Almighty God for having directed my countrymen to a right conclusion, as I think, for their own good, it adds nothing to my satisfaction that any other man may be disappointed or pained by the result . . . And now, let me close by asking three hearty cheers for our brave soldiers and seamen and their gallant and skilful commanders." The applause and cheers roared. Then slowly the faces, lights and voices dwindled. The White House lawn took on its accustomed night shadows of trees, fences, buildings, and silence.

The outlook Lincoln had voiced was toward conciliation—no retaliation, no reprisals, no thorns knowingly planted in the bosoms of others. On November 11 at the Cabinet meeting the President took from his desk the folded and pasted memorandum that Cabinet members had signed August 23 without knowing what it said. He read it with its now odd-sounding statement of probability "that this Administration will not be re-elected."

On Election Day McClellan resigned as a major general in the Regular Army. To fill this vacancy Lincoln signed a commission for General Philip H. Sheridan. McClellan began on his plans for a trip to Europe, which would keep him away from the American scene and its war for many months.

The Charleston *Mercury* on November 22 printed Lincoln's speech of November 10, in full.

The *Spectator* of London, November 26, saw the North had pronounced by a majority that "though its land be covered with hospitals and its cities filled with bankrupts, though every family weep for its sons and the course of material civilization be thrown back centuries, it is ready to fight manfully on rather than freedom should be proved a chimera . . . Had the North shrunk, or even faltered, had she refused the necessary sacrifices or accepted the evil compromise, the cause of liberty would have received a heavy, perhaps a deadly wound."

Grant's telegram to Lincoln held true. The November election counted for more than a great battle won. It answered many questions. Would the war go on? Yes, more brutally than before. Would conscription go on? Yes, and with less outspoken opposition. Those claiming free speech and a free press? They would be less noisy and foul, though not giving up old habits. Some were a little stunned and helpless.

CHAPTER 49
LINCOLN NAMES A CHIEF JUSTICE

Portrait of Salmon P. Chase, who was Secretary of the Treasury between the years 1861-1864.

LINCOLN NAMES A CHIEF JUSTICE

WHO WOULD be named as Chief Justice? In the press, in political circles, across tea cups and over whisky toddies, there was guess and gossip. Of the eminent New York attorney William M. Evarts, Justice Swayne, Justice David Davis, there was public mention. Attorney General Bates modestly and privately mentioned in his diary that his appointment would be a fitting close to his career. Fessenden said for himself he could not consent. Browning wrote: "Called on the President and urged on him the appointment of Mr. Stanton as chief Justice. He said nothing in reply to what I urged except to admit Mr. Stanton's ability, and fine qualifications."

Across November the President heard a series of delegations and individual callers and gave them no committals. Union League Club men from Philadelphia spoke for Chase, and read a signed memorial. The President replied: "Will you do me the favor to leave that paper with me? I want it in order that, if I appoint Mr. Chase, I may show the friends of the other persons for whom the office is solicited by how powerful an influence and by what strong personal recommendations the claims of Mr. Chase were supported." The Union Leaguers, pleased and satisfied at this, then noticed the President had not finished. He had merely paused. Now he went on. "And I want the paper also in order that, if I should appoint any other person, I may show his friends how powerful an influence and what strong personal recommendations I was obliged to disregard in appointing him." The Philadelphians walked out knowing no more than when they came.

Chase personally seemed to have high hopes at first. Later he was not so sure what the President would do. Days passed into weeks. The deliberation of the President seemed ominous to Chase. Behind the scenes it seemed that Lincoln had only one distinct doubt and this he spoke to one after another of those who came to the front for Chase.

From active enemies of Chase in Ohio came spoken and written protests against his appointment. From Treasury Department officials, from the Blair and other groups, came many descriptions of Chase as too partisan, too ignorant of men, too much of a grumbler and a marplot. Nicolay and Hay noted the President heard with respect any points of merit they had against Chase but when they tried to remind him of how and when Chase had sought to undermine him, "he sternly checked them." The secretaries believed Lincoln intended from the first to appoint Chase. To Nicolay he said, using boyhood Kentucky lingo, "I shall be very 'shut pan' about this matter."

Congress had assembled. On December 6, at whatever risk and not unaware there were risks, guided by joined motives of statecraft and political balances, the President named Chase for Chief Justice.

As the author of the National Bank Act, as an acquaintance of August Belmont who proposed in the summer of '64 the conditions under which he [Chase] would join the Democratic party, as a man of "a certain solid weight of character," Chase was not offensive to a large section of conservatives. The appointment, once made, met with little opposition, and, noted Nicolay and Hay, was "received with the greatest satisfaction throughout the Union."

The somber and dignified old Supreme Court was filled to its limits December 15 with people who came to see Chase sworn in. The new Chief Justice read the oath of office in a clear but tremulous voice. Then, laying down the paper, he lifted his right hand, looked upward to the noble dome, and with deep feeling, "So help me God." Over the room was a breathless hush. The Chief Justice took his seat.

Chief Justice Salmon P. Chase.

CHAPTER 50

The "Lost Army" — The South in Fire and Blood — War Prisons

Maj. General William T. Sherman, who burned Atlanta.

THE "LOST ARMY"—THE SOUTH IN FIRE AND BLOOD—WAR PRISONS

Panorama of Atlanta before being burnt by Sherman, photographed by George N. Barnard, Oct. 1864.

IN LATE '64, observers in America and Europe hung breathless and wondering over the audacity and fate of a general and an army that had vanished. To his wife the head of this adventure wrote that he would come out of it reputed a great general or just plain crazy. Sherman had not seen the newborn baby who had arrived at his home in June. The baby would die while he was gone, while millions were wondering where he was, and he would accept this as war.

"If you can whip Lee," Sherman had written in September to Grant as between family men, "and I can march to the Atlantic, I think Uncle Abe will give us a twenty days' leave of absence to see the young folks." This he was writing in Georgia, where he had taken Atlanta. Nearby was Hood's army, which Jefferson Davis was saying had every advantage of being on home ground, so that it would yet cut Sherman's communications and destroy Sherman. To Grant, Sherman offered his plan. He would divide his army, give Thomas 60,000 with which to take care of Hood's 41,000, and then himself start on a thousand-mile march which was to end by joining Grant in Virginia, pausing at Savannah-by-the-Sea.

Thousands of people abroad and in the South would reason, wrote Sherman, "If the North can march an army right through the South it is proof positive that the North can prevail in this contest . . . Mr. Lincoln's election, which is assured, coupled with the conclusion thus reached, makes a logical whole."

Grant wired Lincoln: "Sherman's proposition is the best that can be adopted . . . Such an army as Sherman has, and with such a commander, is hard to corner or capture." This seemed to be a day of acid test for Lincoln on whether he would get behind his two best proven generals. Within three hours after Grant's telegram arrived, Stanton telegraphed Sherman complete approval.

Sherman had not intended to burn as much of Atlanta as did burn. His chief engineer under orders wrecked all railroads in and about Atlanta, heated the rails red hot and twisted them around trees. Then smokestacks were pulled down, furnace arches broken, steam machinery smashed, holes punched in all boilers, all devices of industrial production wrecked against possible use. Before this work had begun, firebugs had set in flame a score of buildings, General Slocum offering a reward of $500 for the detection of any soldier involved. Atlanta buildings, 1,800, went up in smoke.

Sherman rode into the city with an aide near sunset November 15. Roses still bloomed in a few gardens of fine houses and Atlanta was a quiet city, not soothed but calm with a hint of heavy fate. The night held little quiet as an engineer corps fired more fallen buildings, as flames spread to a wrecked arsenal and shell explosions rattled the windows of hundreds of homes where no sleepers lay to be awakened. A fire department of soldiers struggled several hours of the night, managing to hold the fire mainly to the downtown and industrial districts, as intended. When Sherman rode out of the city at seven the next morning, a third, perhaps more, of Atlanta lay in ashes.

Toward the east and southward, toward Savannah and the Atlantic Ocean, toward a path that was to twist upward in the Carolinas, Sherman turned his horse. Toward the east by the Decatur road Sherman paused on a hill and took a last look at smoking Atlanta. On the horizons around him a bright sun slanted down on the shining rifles of 55,000 picked men, veterans of proved capacity for action, for marching, for legwork, for many disease immunities, survivors of hard campaigns. Each man carried 40 rounds of cartridges, and in wagons were enough

more to make 200 rounds per man. The sun slanted too on 65 cannon, each drawn by four teams of horses. Six-mule wagons, 2,500 of them, hauled supplies and forage. And 600 ambulances, two horses to each, were prepared for battle service. Between Sherman and his friend Grant at Richmond lay a thousand miles of cities and towns, lands, swamps and rivers, alive with a bitterly hostile people hating with a deepening despair.

This army had 218 regiments, all but 33 from Western States, 52 from Ohio, 50 from Illinois, 27 from Indiana, 13 from Wisconsin, 10 from Michigan, 15 from Iowa, 3 from Minnesota, 10 from Missouri, 4 from Kentucky. From New York were 16 regiments, from Pennsylvania 10, from New Jersey 3, from Massachusetts and Connecticut 2 each. They would be heard from—sometime. The word of Sherman to Grant, to the War Department and the President, was that communications were cut off from central Georgia and his next message he hoped to send from somewhere on the Atlantic Coast.

Starting November 15, marching in four columns sweeping a path 20 to 40 or more miles wide, this army began a systematic campaign of destruction. "The State of Georgia alone," Jefferson

THE "LOST ARMY"—THE SOUTH IN FIRE AND BLOOD—WAR PRISONS

Davis had said in a recent speech in Augusta, "produces food enough not only for her own people and the army within but feeds too the Army of Virginia." On this storehouse and granary of the Confederacy worked the destroyers. What the army could not eat or carry away it burned, spoiled, ruined.

Now they had their war, was Sherman's thought, the war they had asked for. Until now the Border States had taken the punishment. Now it had come to the doorsills of the Deep South. Now sometimes you couldn't see the roses and the magnolia trees for the depot and warehouse smoke, for the dust of marching columns and rumbling wagons.

His conscience worried Sherman less than his sense of timing. He and Grant would join their armies some day, if their timing was right. Then the war would end. He traveled light. The saddlebags which his orderly carried held "a change of underclothing, my maps, a flask of whiskey, and a bunch of cigars." He could live as plainly as rank-and-file soldiers; they had seen him sleep in his blanket on cold ground. He watched over details till midnight and past, was out early in the morning, made up lost sleep sometimes with 10- and 15-minute naps on the ground during the day. When his troops had orders to do things that at first seemed impossible they said, "Well, *he* can't make a mistake."

Of the railroad-wrecking, wrote Sherman, "I gave it my personal attention." Bonfires were made of crossties, the iron rails laid on and when red hot carried to telegraph poles or trees and twisted around to make what were nicknamed "Sherman hairpins," though sometimes called "Lincoln gimlets." Of again they were "Jeff Davis neckties." A month of this and 265 miles of railway were *unbuilt*.

Each brigade commander had authority to detail a forage company, usually about 50 men headed by one or two commissioned officers. Before daylight this party would leave, knowing where to rejoin their command on the march later in the day. On foot five or six miles from the brigade route, they visited every plantation and farm within range. On a farm wagon or a family carriage they loaded bacon, corn meal, turkeys, ducks, chickens, "everything that could be used as food or forage," to use Sherman's words. They regained the main road, usually in advance of their wagon train, and delivered to the brigade commissary the day's supplies gathered.

How many hundreds or thousands of stragglers, skulkers and deserters from the Confederate Army there were at this time in Georgia could not get into official records; in Georgia and all the Southern and Border States were roving bands of bushwhackers and guerrillas, lawless, desperate, living on the country. In more than one case deserters said they had heard that if Lincoln was elected in November the war would be over, that it was common talk that with Lincoln President again the South would quit fighting. Many rumors of the Confederacy being on its last legs encouraged desertion. Union commanders circulated Lincoln's proclamation offering amnesty. Across picket posts, through printed circulars, by means open and secret, the report spread that deserters into the Union lines would meet good treatment. That the earlier Confederate unity was breaking, that cracks and seams had come in their governmental structure, was known to the Georgians, who saw their state legislature joined with those of Mississippi and North Carolina in refusals to take as constitutional the act of their Congress at Richmond in suspending the writ of habeas corpus. And timed with Sherman's march from Atlanta toward the sea ran the rumor that President Davis was to be impeached. It was not a harmonious Confederate Georgia over which Sherman was laying devastation. Daily as Sherman's troops swung along on the march came remarks from sidewalks, from roadsides. Most often there was silence. But General Hazen noted that the most typical expression from the Georgians was: "Why don't you go over to South Carolina and serve them this way? They started it."

Arriving next day at the state capital, Milledgeville, Sherman found Governor Joseph Brown, the state officials, and the members of the legislature gone, the Governor's mansion stripped of carpets, curtains, furniture, food. Here Federal troops used stacks of Confederate paper money for a breakfast fire. Here Federal officers held a mock session in the state legislative chamber, repealed the Ordinance of Secession, voted the state back into the Union, made sarcastic speeches, and appointed a committee officially to kick the buttocks of Governor Brown and President Davis. And while Sherman in Milledgeville read these and other items, thousands of bales of cotton got the torch, many cotton gins and presses were wrecked, and as Sherman reported, "I burned the railroad buildings and the arsenals; the statehouse and Governor's Mansion I left unharmed."

Sherman's men as seasoned soldiers more often gave misleading than correct information when they were asked what would be the route of the army. As less and less could be gleaned from Southern newspapers, the Union army marching in Georgia, the "lost army," became a world mystery, for speculation and surmise in the North and in Europe. "If Sherman has really left his army in the air and started off without a base to march from Georgia to South Carolina," said the experts of the *Army and Navy Gazette* in England, "he has done either one of the most brilliant or one of the most foolish things ever performed by a military leader."

Sherman's brother, the Ohio Senator, came in anxiety over published Southern reports of his brother in retreat and disaster. Could anyone tell him the facts? Lincoln said: "Oh, no, I know the hole he went in at, but I can't tell you what hole he will come out of."

An army for 32 days to the outside world "lost sight of," as Sherman phrased it, now had behind it 300 miles of naked smokestacks, burned culverts, shattered trestleworks, wailing humanity. Of the railroads every rail was twisted beyond use, every tie, bridge, tank, woodshed and depot building burned. Thirty miles ran the devastation on either side of the line from Atlanta, estimated Sherman. Kilpatrick's 5,000 horsemen had ravaged beyond the reach of foot troops. For the economy of powder they had sabered hogs, knocked horses between the ears with axes, killing more than a hundred horses on one plantation with a fine mansion, and shooting every bloodhound, mastiff or other dog that looked as though it could track runaway Negroes in swamps and forest. Over many square miles of this area now was left not a chicken, not a pig, not a horse nor cow nor sheep, not a smokehouse ham nor side of bacon, not a standing corncrib with a forgotten bushel, not a mule to plow land with, not a piece of railroad track, nor cars nor locomotives nor a bunker of coal.

On December 10 General Howard's right wing stood ten miles from Savannah. To Washington Howard sent a telegram notifying the Government that the march had won through. By scouts overland to Port Royal, South Carolina, and wire relays, this good-news message reached Washington the evening of December 14. Next day Halleck passed on to Lincoln Howard's dispatch: "We have met with perfect success thus far, troops in fine spirit and General Sherman near by."

Over the North flashed this news. Across streets in town, over roads and fields in the country, went the jubilant cry that Sherman had got to Savannah. From Boston to Council Bluffs and points west there were cheers and prayers of thanks.

On December 13 Sherman with staff officers climbed to the top of a rice mill, looked toward the sea for the fleet, looked toward a forest edge where the 15th corps was ready to move on Fort McAllister. The fort overlooked a river needed for supply transport between Sherman and the fleet—if the fleet had arrived as planned. For hours Sherman and his aides kept their lookout. It was near sundown when a smokestack took clearer form, at last could be seen, and later a flag wigwagged the words, "Who are you?" "General Sherman," said the rice-mill flag. "Is Fort McAlister taken yet?" asked the ship. "Not yet, but it will be in a minute."

As though this was a signal, Sherman's old Shiloh division under General William B. Hazen broke from cover, sharpshooters running out to fling themselves flat on the ground and pick off enemy gunners, the whole line soon charging through a hail of shot, shell and rifle bullets, rushing the defenses, soon dancing on the parapets of Fort McAllister.

By the light of a pale moon this December 13 Sherman rode a fast yawl downstream, boarded the Union ship, the *Dandelion*, and before midnight was writing dispatches to be read five days later by Stanton, Halleck and Lincoln—and parts of them passed on to a world starving for news and sure fact.

Savannah fell, its garrison of 9,000 under General Hardee moving out and away toward the north the night of December 20. Sherman wrote Lincoln a message: "I beg to present you as a Christmas gift, the city of Savannah, with one hundred and fifty guns and plenty of ammunition, also about twenty-five thousand bales of cotton." The day after Christmas Lincoln wrote a letter to Sherman and sent it South: "When you were about leaving Atlanta for the Atlantic coast, I was *anxious*, if not fearful; but feeling that you were the better judge, and remembering that 'nothing risked, nothing gained' I did not interfere. Now, the undertaking being a success, the honor is all yours; for I believe none of us went farther than to acquiesce . . . Please make my grateful acknowledgments to your whole army, officers and men."

The campaigning in Tennessee was strange and involved, with none of the dramatic simplicity of Sherman's march, General Schofield writing Sherman that they in Tennessee had the work while he in Georgia had the fun. Schofield on leaving Sherman and trying to connect his force of 29,000 with Thomas at Nashville had to right a battle with Hood's 41,000 Confederate troops at Franklin, Hood in desperate frontal attacks thrown back with losses of 6,000 as against 2,300 on the Union side. Schofield drew off. Hood followed. Schofield joined Thomas at Nashville. There Hood camped with his army, now reduced to 26,000, intending as he said in a report of December 11 "to force the enemy to take the initiative."

On December 8 Grant had wired Halleck: "If Thomas has not struck yet, he ought to be ordered to hand over his command to Schofield. There is no better man to repel an attack than Thomas but I fear he is too cautious to ever take the initiative."

Grant on this December 8 tried a further telegram to Thomas: "Why not attack at once? By all means avoid the contingency of a foot-race to see which, you or Hood, can beat to the Ohio." Thomas still delayed. In cavalry Hood outnumbered him four to one; he was getting remounts and hoped to have a force of 6,000. He wired Grant that in troop concentration and transport "I have made every effort possible." Grant, receiving this December 9, wired Halleck that as Thomas had not yet attacked, "Please telegraph orders relieving him at once, and placing Schofield in command." The order was made out. Before telegraphing it to Nashville Halleck asked Grant if he still wished it to be forwarded. Grant replied, "You will suspend the order until it is seen whether he will do anything."

Grant on December 13 ordered Logan to Nashville to replace Thomas in command. Logan started. Then Grant for the first

Portrait of Jefferson Davis, President of the Confederate States of America.

time since he had become lieutenant general himself started on a trip back west, for Tennessee, to take personal charge there. Grant had reached Washington. Logan was at Louisville, Kentucky, less than a day's travel from Nashville. To both of them came news that Thomas had launched his troops at Hood's army.

No rout of the war had been so complete. One factor was the cavalry for which Thomas had delayed action. Hood's army as a unit vanished. Parts of it, to the number of 15,000 men, held intact through the generalship of Forrest, who saved them for other Confederate commands. The Confederate losses in killed and wounded at least equaled the Union casualties of 3,000—and 4,462 Confederate prisoners were taken.

Sherman took pride in his friend "Old Tom" and was to write of this battle that it was the only one of the war "which annihilated an army."

A famous metaphor was coined: the Rock of Chickamauga became the Sledge of Nashville. Congratulations came from many, including Grant, Sherman, Stanton, Sheridan, Lincoln's of December 16 reading: "Please accept for yourself, officers, and men, the nation's thanks for your good work of yesterday. You made a magnificent beginning. A grand consummation is within your easy reach. Do not let it slip." To a commission naming Thomas for the vacant major generalship in the Regular Army Grant and Lincoln joined their signatures.

Lee's distressing need for men ran back in part to an order of Grant in April that not another Confederate prisoner of war should be paroled or exchanged until certain conditions were met that Grant probably knew would never be met. Cruel it was, he admitted, but necessary. "Every man we hold, when released on parole or otherwise, becomes an active soldier against us at once either directly or indirectly . . . If we hold those caught they amount to no more than dead men." At the particular time in late summer when the Confederate Government proposed to exchange prisoners man for man, said Grant, it "would insure Sherman's defeat" and "compromise safety" at Richmond.

Many were the influences brought to bear on Lincoln to reverse or modify this policy of Grant. Arguments based on political power and made in the name of reason, cries and prayers for the sake of humanity, rang in his ears. But Lincoln stood by his general. He let Grant have his way. And at this time there raged over the North a propaganda of horror with proposals of vengeance for the inhuman handling of Union soldiers in Southern prisons. They were starved. And they died of starvation. This was fact. They festered in rags and became living skeletons, chilled and shivering. This, for many, was fact. Atrocities monstrous and almost beyond belief were told of in Northern newspapers and pulpits and on political platforms. These too had some basis of fact. But the South had its answers. And these too held facts. The so-called laws of war were being violated, as in former wars, as an incident of humanity in the mass being violated—on both sides. Over this Lincoln troubled his mind and heart and was to refer to it in his second inaugural address.

A 27-acre piece of marshland in southwestern Georgia, fenced and stockaded for Union prisoners, bare of trees and hiding places, was Andersonville. A man going there died a dirty and lingering death; or killed himself by stepping over a line where guards at once put a bullet through him for attempted escape; or lost his mind; or by slim chance issued forth to freedom somehow with a woebegone look and a wild-animal stare in his eyes. When a few of these hunted ones had crept into Sherman's camp one night at Milledgeville, the sight of them brought mutterings of revenge.

The place named Andersonville won distinction as the one spot on the North American map where war was more hideous to look at than any other spot that could be named. In its close-packed and swarming population was less food and more scurvy and starvation; less soap and more filth, scabs and lice; less medicine and more gangrene, fever, diarrhea, ulcers, sores, hemorrhages, bleeding gums and swollen lips symptomatic of scurvy, than anywhere else in America.

The bloodiest battle of the war had not taken such a toll of death as Andersonville from June to September 1864, with its record of 8,589 dying. This reduced the peak population of 32,000 and enlarged the average space of six square feet per man. Vice-President Stephens suggested that Jefferson Davis visit Andersonville, that the Confederate President make a solemn speech to the prisoners and let them go home and tell the North the South was fighting only for independence.

A grumbling and muttering had begun that the President took no action in this field, assertions, wrote Carpenter, that he showed "a criminal indifference to the sufferings of our prisoners at Libby, Andersonville, and other places." There was the record, said these critics: nowhere in any public address or message of the President could you find any allusion to the Union soldiers murdered by foul treatment in Southern prisons. Purposely Lincoln avoided discussion of it. The issue had not become sharp till this fourth year of the war.

The Southern summer heat was bad for men from the North, and the Northern zero winter weather not so good for those from the South. Official statistics ran that 12 of every 100 Confederate prisoners died in the North, and 15 of every 100 Union captives in the South. Medical men agreed that the Southern troops were undernourished because of their own armies' inferior food supply, and therefore less resistant to disease.

Want and hunger threatened the life arteries of the Confederacy less than its own internal strife. The November message of President Davis to the Confederate Congress spoke desperately of conspiracies, of traitors and spies inside their own house. What any state capital announced was more important and authoritative to the people of that state than any proclamations from the Richmond Government. This faith in states' rights as much as want or military defeat was a gnawing and devitalizing factor in the Confederacy.

The Richmond *Whig* had spoken for an element with deep-rooted instincts about states' rights when it suggested dropping the name of Confederate States and substituting The Allied Nations or The Allied Republics. "We are sorry to see the word 'national' sometimes used with reference to Confederate affairs. We think it should be henceforth a forbidden word. This Confederacy is not a nation, but a league of nations."

ABRAHAM LINCOLN

NOVELTY SLIDE CO

CHAPTER 51

The Bitter Year of '64 Comes to a Close

The Bitter Year of '64 Comes to a Close

As CONFEDERATE money sank in value from month to month pathos and pity touched deeper the Confederate cause.

Now in the North and in Europe it was taken as full of portent that President Davis recommended to his Congress that slaves be drafted for the Confederate armies. This plan would throw 400,000 able-bodied and armed black men against the Northern armies. Slavery would not be abolished, but the enlisted Negroes would be given freedom. Factions in the Confederate Congress with polite contempt offered other plans to fill the thinning armies.

As with each year the South had dwindled in man power, in money and economic resources, in commerce and industry, in the comforts or necessities of life, the North had gained. In steel, oil, railroads, munitions, textiles and other industries, scores of large fortunes were already made, many others on their way. The fast and luxurious living in most of the large cities still contrasted with sacrifices on the march, in camp and on the battlefields. Travelers from Europe commented in surprise at seeing seaboard cities of a North at war with so few signs of war and such throngs of spenders and pleasure hunters as in no European cities. From Great Britain, especially Ireland, and from Germany and the Scandinavian countries, fresh populations poured in.

Westward across the plains and to the West Coast poured an endless migration, some of it to escape the draft. From March 1 to August 10, 1864, 9,300 teams and wagons passed Fort Kearney, Nebraska. One fast traveler on the road from St. Joseph, Missouri, to Fort Kearney passed 400 wagons in one day. At Council Bluffs in April and May a line of teams three miles long waited their turn to cross a ferry whose capacity was 200 in its operation day and night. By the middle of June it was estimated 75,000 men, 30,000 horses and mules, 75,000 cattle, had made the crossing. With each year farmers of the Midwest and Northwest bought more planters, reapers, threshers for putting in crops and harvesting; these labor-saving farm machines made more men available for Grant and Sherman.

In the fourth December of the war, Lincoln sent his message to Congress. The tone continuously traveled with high assumption that the United States was a going concern, that the Union of States was fated to become a great World Power.

The President read the message to his Cabinet December 3. The briefs of several Cabinet members were kept in the message "pretty much in their own words," noted Welles.

Foreign affairs were in a "reasonably satisfactory" condition. The Republic of Liberia should be given a gunboat at moderate cost, paying the United States for it in installments. Such a beginning of a navy would "stimulate a generous ambition" in this young Negro nation. An international telegraph system, the Atlantic cable, and co-operation toward "world-encircling communication" were approved. Thus far the message was chiefly Seward. Lincoln's hand became evident in a paragraph on the slave trade and those who did a business of shipping and selling black folk. "For myself, I have no doubt of the power and duty of the Executive, under the law of nations, to exclude enemies of the human race from an asylum in the United States."

The Treasury Department had taken in over $1,000,000,000 in cash and disbursed nearly as much for the Army and Navy. "Taxation should be still further increased." The paragraph completely endorsing the national banking system probably represented the views of Secretary Fessenden, with Lincoln in agreement.

The Navy now could show 671 vessels. Across the past year its actual increases over and above all losses by shipwreck and battle were 83 vessels, 167 guns and 42,427 tons. During the year 324 ships had been captured, making a total of 1,379 since the war commenced. Sales of condemned prize property had brought more than $14,000,000.

The Army and Navy could read of "liberal provisions" made by Congress for pensions. During the year ending June 30, 16,770 invalid soldiers and 271 invalid seamen had been added to the rolls. Of widows, orphans and dependent mothers, a total of 22,198 were on the army pension rolls and 248 on the navy rolls. Homesteaders had entered more than 4,000,000 acres of public land. Open to settlement were 133,000,000 acres of surveyed land. The Union Pacific railway had "assurance of success."

The President pointed to "the most important branch of national resources—that of living men." The North in spite of war losses had 145,551 more voters at the polls in November '64 than four years before. The fact stood out "that we have *more men now* than we had when the war *began;* that we are not exhausted, nor in process of exhaustion; that we are *gaining* strength, and may, if need be, maintain the contest indefinitely."

As to slavery, the President was brief but more decisive than in any other part of the message: "I repeat the declaration made a year ago that 'while I remain in my present position I shall not attempt to retract or modify the emancipation proclamation, nor shall I return to slavery any person who is free by the terms of that proclamation, or by any of the Acts of Congress.' If the people should, by whatever mode or means, make it an Executive duty to re-enslave such persons, another, and not I, must be their instrument to perform it."

Dry with a cool Lincolnian finality, touched with a faint preposterous irony, was the closing one-sentence paragraph: "In stating a single condition of peace, I mean simply to say that the war will cease on the part of the government, whenever it shall have ceased on the part of those who began it."

Far and wide went this document. By Union armies it was spread into Confederate areas where Confederate newspapers had not reprinted it from Northern journals. In Europe it was studied and discussed in state chambers and on the streets. Over the Northern States it was examined for every shading of fear and hope and promise. *Harper's Weekly* judged it a "calm, simple, concise statement of public affairs," and could understand a Northern opposition, "in common with the rebels," finding the message very "unconciliatory."

Lincoln's anonymous friend in the *Spectator* of London found his latest message "drier, shrewder, and more tenacious than ever." The peace terms offered by Mr. Lincoln were "precisely the terms every monarchy in Europe always offers to rebels."

Dry, informative, again casual as a locomotive, came the President's proclamation of December 19 calling for 300,000 more troops.

Had the November election given a mandate to Congress or to the President? Was it the duty of Congress now to challenge the Executive and cut down his powers? A test vote came in mid-December. Henry Winter Davis demanded a vote on his resolution that Congress had "a constitutional right to an authoritative voice" in foreign affairs, and, "it is the constitutional duty of the President to respect that policy . . . in diplomatic negotiations." Without debate or inquiry the House voted on a motion of Representative Farnsworth to lay the Winter Davis resolution on the table. This passed with 69 Yeas, 63 Nays, not voting 50.

Thad Stevens saw an opposition trying to save from destruction "the darling institution of the Democratic party, the institution of human bondage." Compromise on this was sought. They condemned the "President's determination to insist on the abandonment of slavery." When the President's own leading friends besought him to compromise, he refused to sue for peace. "There never was a day since Abraham Lincoln was elected President that he stood so high . . . in the estimation of the people as at this moment." The guiding fear of Stevens was that the war by compromise evasions might end without slavery uprooted.

A speech of the President in December reached the public in an unusual way. He sent for Noah Brooks "to hear a story." He had the story partly written. With a sheet five or six inches wide on one knee, his legs crossed, sunk comfortably in his armchair, he asked Brooks to wait till he finished. Soon he gave it to Brooks, who saw at the top of the sheet an underscored heading, followed by a paragraph. It read:

THE PRESIDENT'S LAST, SHORTEST, AND BEST SPEECH.

On Thursday of last week two ladies from Tennessee came before the President asking the release of their husbands held as prisoners of war at Johnson's Island. They were put off till Friday, when they came again; and were again put off to Saturday. At each of the interviews one of the ladies urged that her husband was a religious man. On Saturday the President ordered the release of the prisoners, and then said to this lady "You say your husband is a religious man; tell him when you meet him, that I say I am not much of a judge of religion, but that, in my opinion, the religion that sets men to rebel and fight against their government, because, as they think, that government does not sufficiently help *some* men to eat their bread on the sweat of *other* men's faces, is not the sort of religion upon which people can get to heaven!"

He remarked to Brooks that he wanted it copied and printed in the Washington *Chronicle*, adding, "Don't wait to send it to California in your correspondence. I've a childish desire to see it in print right away." So Brooks took it to the *Chronicle* and it was widely reprinted. "Lincoln," noted Brooks, "showed a surprising amount of gratification over this trifle."

Now here was the fourth New Year's Eve looking back on Grant named to head all the Union armies, plunging into the Wilderness and on through Spotsylvania, Cold Harbor, Petersburg, with overwhelming troops and resources battering Lee pitilessly while Early's gray horsemen reached the gates of Washington with their smoke to be seen from White House windows, while Sherman took Atlanta and marched to the sea and took Savannah, while Sheridan scattered Early's army from the Shenandoah and Thomas became the sledge that broke Hood's army into the first Confederate rout of the war, while the Navy sank the *Alabama*, took Mobile and tightened its throttling grip on all Southern ports—a fateful year that had seen the President of the United States win a party renomination against the almost unanimous disapproval of his party members in the House and Senate, winning a national election in November that looked dark and all lost in August, winning in a fairly conducted contest, amid good order, so that the longer one gazed at the November ballots, the more they seemed to say momentously that the Union would be held together and the underlying cause of the war, the propertied institution of slavery, outlawed forever. Not so bitter as the other three was the taste of this New Year's Eve. Across the horizons of the New Year of 1865, however, were signs of the storm to take new phases. Heavy labors lay ahead, and much mist of human confusion.

CHAPTER 52

"FOREVER FREE"—THE THIRTEENTH
AMENDMENT

"Forever Free"—The Thirteenth Amendment

MORE than 1,300,000 slaves had been freed "by the Lincoln Administration or by the events of the war," indicated a statistical table in the Philadelphia *North American* in November '64. Of slaves when the war began one out of three now was free—under the Emancipation Proclamation of "military necessity." The Federal Constitution, however, still held these slaves to be property, except in Missouri and Maryland, two states which had legalized emancipation.

To make all Negroes free under the law and the Constitution, Lincoln in his December message pointed to the last session of Congress. Then "a proposed amendment of the Constitution abolishing slavery throughout the United States, passed the Senate, but failed for lack of the requisite two-thirds vote in the House of Representatives."

The Senate was safe; 13 Democrats there had joined the four who voted with the Republicans the year before. But the House looked doubtful. For more than a year Lincoln had foreseen a narrow margin. Toward this day he planned when he instigated the admission into the Union of Nevada with her added votes, when he called in Charles A. Dana and arranged for patronage gifts that would have raised a high and noisy scandal if known to the opposition.

Sumner had introduced bills to curb what he termed a usurped power of taxation in New Jersey. Railroad interests affected were seeking to get Sumner to drop these bills, for the time, in exchange for Democratic Representatives of New Jersey voting for the Constitutional amendment to abolish slavery. Nicolay's memorandum indicated the desperate tactics being used to gather a few more needed votes.

This was January 18. On the 31st at noon the galleries of the House are filled to overflowing, in the air a subdued hum of excitement. After formal preliminaries, the joint resolution for a Constitutional amendment to outlaw "slavery or involuntary servitude," except for crimes, is up for final decision.

On two roll calls the House refuses to table, refuses to reconsider. The hour of the final vote comes nearer. The galleries fill till standing room is gone. Crowded to the doors are the corridors and lobbies, faces beyond races wondering if the two-thirds vote will be there. The Senate seems to have come over in a body. Grave spectators are four Associate Justices of the Supreme Court and the highly tensed Chief Justice Chase.

The Yeas and Nays are ordered. Alley, Allison, Ames, Anderson and so on. These are all Republicans, their Yeas expected. Comes the name of James E. English, a Connecticut Democrat. He shouts "Aye!" A long roll of applause bursts from the gallery and Republican House members. With each Democrat shooting his vocal Aye at the calling of his name there is a tumult of handclapping, cheers, laughter, the noise-making of pent-up emotion let loose. Eleven Democrats answer Aye. The roll call reaches the W's and Y's; the Wood brothers, Ben and Fernando of New York City, vote for slavery and Yeaman of Kentucky for freedom.

Swift pencils add up the lists. The clerk whispers to the Speaker who announces that the question is decided in the affirmative—Yeas 119, Nays 56, not voting 8. And, said the *Congressional Globe:* " . . . the two thirds required by the Constitution of the United States having voted in favor thereof, the joint resolution was passed."

A mass of still faces break shining and lighting. Emotions explode into a storm of cheers. Men in tears throw their arms around each other. The crowds stand up, many mounting their seats, to shout their glee. Man after man goes handshaking and backslapping. A cloud of women's handkerchiefs wave and float. Ten minutes go by before this hurricane of feeling lets down.

Outside is thunder. The air is torn. Someone has ordered three batteries of regular artillery on Capitol Hill to cry joy with a salute of 100 guns.

HARPER'S WEEKLY.
A JOURNAL OF CIVILIZATION.

Vol. IX.—No. 425.] NEW YORK, SATURDAY, FEBRUARY 18, 1865. [SINGLE COPIES TEN CENTS. $4.00 PER YEAR IN ADVANCE.

SCENE IN THE HOUSE ON THE PASSAGE OF THE PROPOSITION TO AMEND THE CONSTITUTION, January 31, 1865.

Harper's Weekly commemorated scene in the House on the passage of the proposition to amend the Constitution, January 31, 1865.

Victory came by the margin of three men voting Yea. Eight Democrats stayed away from this House session. Something was due these eight Democrats, absent, noted Nicolay and Hay, "not altogether by accident."

News coming next day that Illinois had ratified the amendment, starting the line-up of three-fourths of the states necessary to amend the Constitution, Lincoln smiled. "This ends the job. I feel proud that Illinois is a little ahead." To the White House that night came a crowd with a brass band, serenaders shouting for the President. At a window they saw standing in half-lights and shadows the solemn central figure of the drama of emancipation. He remarked, "There is a task yet before us— to go forward and consummate by the votes of the States that which Congress so nobly began yesterday. (Applause and cries—'They will do it.')"

CHAPTER 53

HEAVY SMOKE—DARK SMOKE

U.S. General Thomas Eckert. Photo by Mathew Brady, 1865.

HEAVY SMOKE—DARK SMOKE

Those blaming Jefferson Davis for Southern failure were in part hunting a scapegoat. He personified the Southern planter class in its pride, its aristocratic feudal outlook, its lack of touch with an almost world-wide abhorrence of slavery as distinguished from what was called "nigger-loving." The war years rolled on and Davis failed to become either an idol or a name and a figure of faith—like Robert E. Lee. Yet Lee had never been such a spokesman of the Confederate cause as Davis. On the death of his wife's mother in 1862 Lee emancipated the slaves to which his family fell heir. As the pressure became fiercer in early '65 Lee consented, in perfect accord with Davis, to take chief command of all the Confederate armies. As a first move he appointed General Joseph E. Johnston to head an army, made from various fragments, to block the path of Sherman from Savannah up across the Carolinas. This reflected Lee's judgment that Davis had been mistaken in his abrupt dismissal of Johnston.

Late on the night of January 15, after three days' bombardment, Fort Fisher fell. Wilmington, the last open port of the Confederacy, was closed to incoming supplies and outgoing cotton. To no one was it more galling news than to Major General Benjamin F. Butler. Political and military circles were amazed at the news from Washington January 13; it was "now specifically stated that on January 6 Lieutenant General Grant indicated to President Lincoln his earnest wish that Major General Butler be forthwith relieved of his command," and next day the President directed the Adjutant General to issue the order deposing Butler and ordering him to report at Lowell, Massachusetts, his home.

Amid hue and cry and guess and gossip, Grant and Lincoln got rid of the one man in the Union armies who stood foremost as a potential dictator. He was the one commander who, under conceivable circumstances, which Hay had in mind, would not have hesitated at marching an army to Washington, taking over the Government, and issuing regulations to the country.

In the summer of '64 Grant and Lincoln could have told the country during those gloom months that Richmond stood untaken because Butler had miserably blundered. Such an explanation, however true, would have brought scorn and blame on Grant and Lincoln for letting Butler blunder, for keeping in command of the Army of the James a politician "who could strut sitting down." Pertinent was the question of why Grant did not let Butler out in the summer of '64. The reason was plain, tacitly understood between Grant and Lincoln. Butler had a national political following. Shifting, as the war rolled on, from his former loyalty to the proslavery wing of the Democratic party, he turned radical on the slavery issue, radical enough so that Wendell Phillips publicly and repeatedly wished Butler were President instead of Lincoln.

In late January the outcry about Northern men languishing in Southern prisons reached the point where Grant decided to relent. In October '64 he had asked Lee whether the Confederate Government would deliver in exchange colored troops "the same as white soldiers," Lee rejoining that "negroes belonging to our citizens are not considered subjects of exchange." On January 24, 1865, however, when the Confederate Government again offered to exchange man for man, Grant accepted the offer without mention of color.

Three days after Savannah fell Old Man Blair was on hand and Lincoln wrote one sentence on a card: "Allow the bearer, F. P. Blair, Senr. to pass our lines, go South and return." Blair took a naval boat from City Point to Richmond. At the Confederate White House Blair dined with Davis, fraternized with old cronies of days agone in the Democratic party, noticed with surprise how many able-bodied men were walking the streets, men he would have expected to be in Lee's army.

On January 12, closeted with the Confederate President for a secret interview. Out of their suave and guarded confabulations came one thin result; Davis suggested he was willing to send men to some conference and the men he would appoint could be relied on by Mr. Lincoln. A letter written by Davis for Blair to

Alexander Stephens, the Vice-President of the CSA, was asked by Confederate President Jefferson Davis to head a secret delegation to speak with President Lincoln at Fort Monroe.

carry back to Lincoln read in closing: " . . . notwithstanding the rejection of our former offers, I would, if you could promise that a commissioner, minister, or other agent would be received, appoint one immediately, and renew the effort to enter into conference, with a view to secure peace to the two countries."

For Blair at the White House Lincoln wrote a one-sentence letter to Davis via Blair: "Your having shown me Mr. Davis' letter to you of the 12th. Inst., you may say to him that I have constantly been, am now, and shall continue, ready to receive any agent whom he, or any other influential person now resisting the national authority, may informally send to me, with the view of securing peace to the people of our one common country."

Thus the Davis letter ending with the words "the two countries" had Lincoln's letter in reply ending with the phrase "our one common country." And where Davis had referred to Lincoln as President of "etc." Lincoln now alluded to "Mr." Davis as though whatever Davis might be President of he was definitely a "Mr." The score was about even.

Now for the first time since the Confederate capital had been moved to Richmond, Davis asked his Vice-President to meet him in conference. Stephens suggested the names of three commissioners. Davis agreed with one of the names, John A. Campbell,

Assistant Secretary of War and former U.S. Supreme Court Justice, added R. M. T. Hunter, Senator and ex-Secretary of State, and Stephens himself.

With his fellow commissioners Stephens came to the Union Army lines the evening of January 29, claiming an understanding with General Grant to pass them on their way to Washington. On this being telegraphed to Washington, Lincoln at once sent Major Eckert of the war telegraph office with written directions to let the commissioners in with safe-conduct if they would say in writing they were ready to talk peace on the basis of the President's note of January 18, peace for "our one common country." Before Eckert arrived with this message the commissioners applied by a written note to General Grant for permission "to proceed to Washington to hold a conference with President Lincoln upon the subject of the existing war, and with a view of ascertaining upon what terms it may be terminated."

On receiving their note Grant at once telegraphed it to Stanton and Lincoln. Lincoln sent Seward to meet the commissioners at Fortress Monroe with written instructions that he was to make known to them three things as indispensable to peace: "1. The restoration of the national authority throughout all the States. 2. No receding, by the Executive of the United States on the Slavery question, from the position assumed thereon, in the late Annual Message to Congress, and in preceding documents.

3. No cessation of hostilities short of an end of the war, and the disbanding of all forces hostile to the government."

Seward started February 1, while Lincoln telegraphed Grant to let the war go on while peace was talked. "Let nothing which is transpiring, change, hinder, or delay your military movements, or plans." Grant promised in reply there would be no armistice, that troops were "kept in readiness to move at the shortest notice."

Lincoln next morning walked over to the War Office, read Major Eckert's report, was framing a telegram to call Seward back, when Grant's long telegram was put in his hands. "This despatch," wrote Lincoln later, "changed my purpose." He at once wired Grant: "Say to the gentlemen I will meet them personally at Fortress Monroe, as soon as I can get there."

The President went in a hurry and with secrecy. Even the trustworthy Nicolay was not told. The news leaked from several sources. Welles in his diary grumbled over it. "None of the Cabinet were advised of this move, and without exception, I think, it struck them unfavorably." Meantime down the Potomac on a naval vessel Lincoln journeyed.

"On the night of the 2nd. [of February]," ran Lincoln's account, "I reached Hampton Roads. On the morning of the 3rd., the three gentlemen, Messrs Stephens, Hunter and Campbell, came aboard of our Steamer and had an interview with the Secretary of State and myself of several hours duration. No question of preliminaries to the meeting was then and there made or mentioned. No other person was present; no papers were exchanged, or produced; and it was, in advance, agreed that the conversation was to be informal, and verbal merely." The instructions the President had written for Seward were insisted on. Five astute men of politics and law talked four hours in a steamboat saloon. What went on in the minds of the five men, the tangled cross-purposes underlying their words, no onlooker could have caught and reported.

The opening query of the conference had come from Stephens to Lincoln: "Well, Mr. President, is there no way of putting an end to the present trouble . . . existing between the different States and sections of *the country?*" In this Stephens did not go so far as Lincoln's term "our one common country," but he did with intention and meaning, as his first stroke at the conference, abandon the Davis phrase "two countries."

It was news to the Confederate commissioners that the U.S.

Congress on January 31 had passed the 13th Amendment to the Constitution and when this should also pass three-fourths of the state legislatures, it would outlaw and abolish slavery.

A hush fell over the conference when Lincoln felt required to contradict gravely and directly remarks made by the Confederate commissioners. His words were measured and sounded like doom: the conduct of certain rebel leaders had been such that they had plainly forfeited all right to immunity from punishment for the highest crime known to law. He had come to the brink of saying they should be strung up for treason, should hang high and lonesome as traitors.

After a quiet pause Hunter gave Lincoln a steady, searching look, and then very deliberately: "Mr. President, if we understand you correctly, you think that we of the Confederacy have committed treason; that we are traitors to your government; that we have forfeited our rights, and are proper subjects for the hangman. Is not that about what your words imply?" "Yes," rejoined Lincoln. "You have stated the proposition better than I did. That is about the size of it!" Another somewhat painful pause, then Hunter with a pleasant smile: "Well, Mr. Lincoln, we have about concluded that we shall not be hanged as long as you are President—if we behave ourselves."

Now came the friendly handshakings ending the Hampton Roads conference, a world of nations and people watching, a horde of journalists and politicians puzzling. The Confederate commissioners were put in a rowboat and taken to their steamer. Then a rowboat with a Negro at the oars headed for their steamer; he reached their deck with a basket of champagne and a note with the compliments of Mr. Seward. The commissioners waved their handkerchiefs in acknowledgment.

Next day, February 4, the Cabinet heard from Lincoln and Seward that the conference had no results. So the war would go on. The majestic and incalculably dynamic gesture Lincoln asked for, was out. A policy of nonretaliation, of "molding society for durability in the Union," as he hoped in the December message, would have to come slowly. His confidential advisers were thinking of Washington and Congress and politics; he was thinking of the great everyday masses of people North and South. The Cabinet was correct in feeling that the present controlling Southern politicians would hoot his proposed proclamation. But beyond might be a mass of Southern people moving and acting when those politicians were discredited as prophets and bankrupt as statesmen.

When the Confederate commissioners came back with their report, Richmond was turned upside down humanly. Jefferson Davis spoke; death or humiliation he would prefer "sooner than we should ever be united again." With curled lips of scorn he referred to the archantagonist "His Majesty Abraham the First" and prophesied that the Confederacy would yet "compel the Yankees, in less than twelve months, to petition us for peace on our own terms."

In the House session February 8, Stevens put through a resolution, much like one of Sumner's in the Senate, requesting the President to report on Hampton Roads. Many Senate and House members nursed a sullen mistrust of Lincoln's latest errand. With more than a few it was a baffled and inarticulate hate of the President. When Lincoln had followed Seward to Hampton Roads and the completely unexpected news of it went forth over Washington, undercurrents of excitement and frustration raged and whirled, wrote Noah Brooks.

On February 10 the tension began to let down. The House had been dealing with a variety of bills when the clerk announced a message from the President. All other business was suspended. The clerk began reading. Documents, letters, dispatches, poured forth in a long stream. It seemed almost as though Lincoln had awaited this hour. The pass written for Blair to Richmond, the letter of Davis to Blair which Blair carried to Lincoln, the reply of Lincoln to Blair meant for Blair to carry to Richmond and show to Davis, the rise of the phrases "our one common country" and "the two countries," the documents passing between the Confederate commissioners showing up at Grant's army lines and what passed between them and Grant, the further transactions between Eckert and the commissioners, the Lincoln letter of instructions to Seward with its three "indispensable" points, the dispatch to Grant to keep the war going no matter what he heard about peace, Grant's reply that he would sure keep the war going, the Eckert telegram in cipher to Lincoln which for the moment wrecked all chance of a conference, the long telegram of Grant to Stanton with Lincoln's brief comment that "this despatch . . . changed my purpose," the meeting at Hampton Roads and the reading of the commissioners' instruction from Davis that they were there "for the purpose of securing

peace to the two countries," the negotiations ending with no result. The foregoing, "containing as is believed all the information sought," was respectfully submitted.

Pressmen from their gallery noted "absolute silence" from first to last during the reading of this message. Looking over the hall at the hundreds seated or standing, one might say, wrote Noah Brooks, they "had been suddenly turned to stone." Soon House members began exchanging smiles and glances of meaning. The President had never for a moment lost footing, had gone into a winding labyrinth where anything could happen and had come out without a flaw. "When the reading was over," and the full name of "Abraham Lincoln" signed to the communication was read by the clerk with a certain grandiloquence, Brooks heard "an instant and irrepressible storm of applause, begun by members on the floor, and taken up by the people in the gallery."

Washburne moved that 20,000 extra copies of the message be printed. "The entire loyal people of this country" would approve the "wisdom and discretion in the President of the United States" shown in this matter. Thad Stevens spoke. "The President has thought it was best to make the effort . . . I believe even those who thought his mission was unwise will accord to him sagacity and patriotism, and applaud his action."

To the Senate the President sent no such marshaled array of documents as he gave the House. To that graver and more sedate body, empowered to ratify treaties and conduct foreign affairs, went a copy of a long note written by the Secretary of State to Minister Adams at London, reciting the Hampton Roads negotiations.

An old order was passing. Now in the Supreme Court chambers for the first time a Negro was admitted to practice before that high tribunal: John S. Rock, an attorney of ability and good name in the city of Boston. The race issue writhed and snarled again in debates over the proposed Bureau for the Relief of Freedmen and Refugees. The bill gave the President power to appoint commissioners to control the bureau, with authority to distribute "abandoned lands" among the Negroes, to pay out money and supplies.

Overshadowing all other discussions across February were those on bills for recognizing as "legitimate" the government set up in Louisiana a year earlier under the guidance of Lincoln and the military commander of the department, General Banks. The election of state officers ordered by Banks for February 22, 1864, covered an area of about one-third of the state. The voters were 11,411 white men, each having taken the oath required by the President, and they made a total of more than one-fifth of the entire vote of the State of Louisiana in 1860. They had elected three Congressmen and a governor, Michael Hahn. At a later election they had chosen delegates to a constitutional convention which met in New Orleans in April. This convention abolished slavery in Louisiana "forever" by a vote of 72 to 13. It gave the ballot to white males only, yet it empowered the legislature to give the ballot to Negro soldiers of service in the Union Army and to Negroes who could read and write, meeting the qualifications Lincoln had suggested in his letter to Governor Hahn.

The new state governments the President had guided were "shadows" and not "realities," according to the opposition. For himself he wished to regard them as "important," as "earnestly struggling," as admittedly "short of complete success."

In late February it was seen that most of the Democrats would vote against recognizing the new Louisiana state government. It was again the familiar Lincoln "military despotism," said Garrett Davis of Kentucky, a horse thief Government which had illegally run off with some of the best horseflesh in Kentucky, impressed for Union Army cavalry. The outspoken fear of other Democrats was that a military rule directed by a Republican administration in Washington would favor the Negroes. On the other hand the outspoken fear of the five Republican Senators who joined the Democratic opposition was that under the new state government of Louisiana, if it should be recognized, the whites would control and refuse the ballot to the Negroes. Therefore these five Republicans sought to put a rider on the bill which would insure the Negro the right to vote in Louisiana, this to be a precedent imperative on all other reorganized states.

The Senate February 27 postponed the measure by a vote of 34 to 12 "to to-morrow." This "to-morrow" never came. The session closed March 4 without a vote. Trumbull spoke his belief that there would have been a clear majority for the resolution had it not been fought by Sumner. In the last days of the session Sumner piled his desk high with documents, books, papers, notes, gave the word he was going to filibuster. He would stand and speak and read till the session officially ended. Thus he would kill three bills—a tax, a tariff and an appropriation bill. The Senate gave in. Sumner had his way. Louisiana was out. Lincoln's foremost immediate project was lost, for the time. Another Congress, further events, would pass on Louisiana.

Out of Savannah February 1 Sherman had moved, his plan of campaign a secret. A dispatch had come to Stanton and Lincoln that his route was inland. Before starting Sherman had said this march would be ten times as difficult, ten times more important, than the one from Atlanta to the sea.

In two columns with outriding cavalry Sherman's 60,000 men moved over the soil of the state that had led off in secession. Continuous winter rains had swollen all streams. Country not under water was mud and quagmire. They marched day on day with rain about two days out of three. They crossed five large navigable rivers, swollen torrents. At times every private in the army served as a pioneer, split saplings and carried fence rails for corduroy roads, laid pontoons, cleared entanglements. They waded streams, no time to bridge. Some forces worked for hours waist-deep in icy flood-waters. One captured Confederate trooper, seeing these exploits, told the 104th Illinois, "If your army goes to hell, it will corduroy the road." General Joseph E. Johnston said later, "I made up my mind there had been no such army since the days of Julius Caesar."

Foragers stripped the country of many farm buildings, farm animals, fences, much property, and food of all kinds. The railroads were torn up, and weather permitting, bridges burned, cotton bales set blazing, vacant dwellings and barns fired. Looters and bummers stole jewelry, watches and silverware, smashed pianos and shattered mirrors, though the extent and the manner of these outrages became an issue of veracity as between Northern and Southern witnesses.

In bloody actions of February 5, 6 and 7 Grant had so struck at Lee that by no chance could Lee send any men toward Sherman. In Washington February 22 by order of the President there was a night illumination of the high domed building on the top of Capitol Hill—lights and singing bright windows in celebration of victories resulting in Columbia, Charleston, Wilmington, and a fresh wide area coming again under the U.S. flag.

CHAPTER 54

THE SECOND INAUGURAL

THE SECOND INAUGURAL

ON MARCH 4, 1865, hours before noon, Lincoln in a Senate wing room considered and signed bills. A parade on Pennsylvania Avenue from the White House to the Capitol moved in a light drizzle of rain and cold, gusty winds. A muddy paste coated the sidewalks lined with spectators. On one wagon platform printers from the Typographical Society, a labor union, ran a hand press and scattered programs of the day's events. A battalion of Negro troops in Union Army blue marched, and the Negro Grand Lodge of Odd Fellows.

Toward noon flocks of women streamed around the Capitol, "crinoline smashed, skirts bedaubed, velvet and laces streaked with mud." Invited notables trod to their reserved seats. Noah Brooks wrote of Mrs. Lincoln, attended by Senator Anthony, seated in the Diplomatic Gallery, and a buzz when the Justices of the Supreme Court entered in their black robes. A few stray governors came in, then the Diplomatic Corps, in gold lace, feathers and white pantaloons. One ambassador had to unbutton himself to get his feet on the floor. Members of the House moved in at noon, then the Cabinet.

In the middle of the front row sat Lincoln; as the clock struck twelve his eyes turned with those of others to the entrance of Andrew Johnson, Vice-President-elect, escorted by Senator Doolittle. Johnson after introduction rose with no papers, saying impromptu to the Senators, to the Supreme Court, that their power came from the mass of the people, and further, "You, Mr. Secretary Seward, Mr. Secretary Stanton, the Secretary of the Navy [he couldn't quite dig up the name of Welles], and the others who are your associates—you know that you have my respect and my confidence—derive not your greatness and your power alone from President Lincoln." He was in a mood. "Humble as I am, plebeian as I may be deemed, permit me in the presence of this brilliant assemblage to enunciate the truth that courts and

Andrew Johnson, Lincoln's Vice-President who succeeded him after the assassination.

cabinets, the President and his advisers, derive their power and their greatness from the people."

By now Hamlin had pulled at Johnson's coattails while the Senate clerk, John W. Forney, with whom Johnson had been drinking the evening before, whispered loud, hoping to catch Johnson's eye and flag him down. Johnson swept on into thanking God that Tennessee had never been out of the Union, and declaring flatly, "No State can go out of this Union; and moreover, Congress cannot eject a State from the Union."

Far more sorry than funny was this performance—the sour note of the day. His face flushed, his voice hoarse, Johnson looked worn and sick. For weeks that winter he had been in bed with typhoid fever and general exhaustion from heavy labors amid terrific excitement. He had written to Lincoln inquiring whether by any precedents he could stay in Nashville and take his oath of office. Lincoln had wired: "It is our unanimous conclusion that it is unsafe for you not to be here on the fourth of March. Be sure to reach here by that time." In Hamlin's room in the Senate building he poured one tumbler of whisky and drank it down, and according to Hamlin, just before going into the overheated Senate chamber, drank another, saying, "I need all the strength for the occasion I can have."

As Johnson got well into his speech several Republican Senators bent their heads, unable to look at him. Sumner covered his face with his hands. Seward, wrote Noah Brooks, was "bland and serene as a summer day" and Stanton seemed "petrified." Speed "sat with eyes closed." Senators "turned and twisted" in their chairs. When Johnson had repeated inaudibly the oath of office, he turned, took the Bible in his hand, "and facing the audience, said, with a loud, theatrical voice and gesture, 'I kiss this Book in the face of my nation of the United States.'"

The procession to the Capitol portico formed and moved. The drizzle of rain had stopped. "A tremendous shout, prolonged

Lincoln delivering the 2nd inaugural address on the steps of the Capitol. Photo by Alexander Gardner, March 4, 1865.

and loud, arose from the surging ocean of humanity," wrote Noah Brooks. The President with invited notables took the platform. Then the sergeant at arms of the Senate arose and with raised hands got the crowd still. And Abraham Lincoln, rising tall, gaunt and outstanding, stepped forward to read his inaugural address. Applause roared, again and again was repeated, and finally died far away on the outer fringe of the throng.

In a silence almost profound the audience now listened. Seldom had a President been so short-spoken about the issues of so grave an hour. He read his carefully and deliberately prepared address:

[Fellow Countrymen:] At this second appearing to take the oath of the presidential office, there is less occasion for an extended address than there was at the first. Then a statement, somewhat in detail, of a course to be pursued, seemed fitting and proper. Now, at the expiration of four years, during which public declarations have been constantly called forth on every point and phase of the great contest which still

absorbs the attention, and engrosses the energies of the nation, little that is new could be presented. The progress of our arms, upon which all else chiefly depends, is as well known to the public as to myself; and it is, I trust, reasonably satisfactory and encouraging to all. With high hope for the future, no prediction in regard to it is ventured.

On the occasion corresponding to this four years ago, all thoughts were anxiously directed to an impending civil-war. All dreaded it—all sought to avert it. While the inaugural address was being delivered from this place, devoted altogether to *saving* the Union without war, insurgent agents were in the city seeking to *destroy* it without war—seeking to dissol[v]e the Union, and divide effects, by negotiation. Both parties deprecated war; but one of them would *make* war rather than let the nation survive; and the other would *accept* war rather than let it perish. And the war came.

One eighth of the whole population were colored slaves, not distributed generally over the Union, but localized in the Southern part of it. These slaves constituted a peculiar and powerful interest. All knew that this interest was, somehow, the cause of the war. To strengthen,

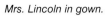
Mrs. Lincoln in gown.

perpetuate, and extend this interest was the object for which the insurgents would rend the Union, even by war; while the government claimed no right to do more than to restrict the territorial enlargement of it. Neither party expected for the war, the magnitude, or the duration, which it has already attained. Neither anticipated that the *cause* of the conflict might cease with, or even before, the conflict itself should cease. Each looked for an easier triumph, and a result less fundamental and astounding. Both read the same Bible, and pray to the same God; and each invokes His aid against the other. It may seem strange that any men should dare to ask a just God's assistance in wringing their bread from the sweat of other men's faces; but let us judge not that we be not judged. The prayers of both could not be answered; that of neither has been answered fully. The Almighty has His own purposes. "Woe unto the world because of offences! for it must needs be that offences come; but woe to that man by whom the offence cometh!" If we shall suppose that American Slavery is one of those offences which, in the providence of God, must needs come, but which, having continued through His appointed time, He now wills to remove, and that He gives to both North and South, this terrible war, as the woe due to those by whom the offence came, shall we discern therein any departure from those divine attributes which the believers in a Living God always ascribe to Him? Fondly do we hope—fervently do we pray—that this mighty scourge of war may speedily pass away. Yet, if God wills that it continue, until all the wealth piled by the bond-man's two hundred and fifty years of unrequited toil shall be sunk, and until every drop of blood drawn with the lash shall be paid by another drawn with the sword, as was said three thousand years ago, so still it must be said "the judgments of the Lord, are true and righteous altogether"

With malice toward none; with charity for all; with firmness in the right, as God gives us to see the right, let us strive on to finish the work we are in; to bind up the nation's wounds; to care for him who shall have borne the battle, and for his widow, and his orphan—to do all which may achieve and cherish a just, and a lasting peace, among ourselves, and with all nations.

A subdued handclapping and occasional cheers punctuated the address. Reporters noticed at the final paragraph many moist eyes and here and there tears coursing down faces unashamed.

The clerk of the Supreme Court brought the Bible. Then Lincoln, laying his right hand on an open page of the Book, repeated the oath of office after Chief Justice Chase, bent forward, kissed the Book and arose to full height again.

Presenting the Book to Mrs. Lincoln afterward, the Chief Justice pointed to the pencil-marked verses kissed by the President, in the fifth chapter of Isaiah:

None shall be weary nor stumble among them; none shall slumber nor sleep; neither shall the girdle of their loins be loosed, nor the latchet of their shoes be broken:
Whose arrows are sharp, and all their bows bent, their horses' hoofs shall be counted like flint, their wheels like a whirlwind.

Like the Gettysburg Address, and more particularly the House Divided speech, the second inaugural took on varied meanings. To some it was a howl for vengeance, to others a benediction and a plea—with deep music.

In the evening the White House was open for a reception. "The platform in front of the entrance, the walks and drives back of the Avenue, were packed with people," noted Lieutenant Ashmun of the guards. Occasionally a lady fainted or became terrified and would have to be taken out over the heads of the close-packed crowd. From 8 until 11 Lincoln spent in almost continuous handshaking. Newsmen wrote that he shook hands with more than 6,000 persons.

The crowds vanished and in the still midnight the White House looked to the guard Crook, "as if a regiment of rebel troops had been quartered there, with permission to forage." Mementoes were wanted. "A great piece of red brocade, a yard square almost, was cut from the window-hangings of the East Room. Flowers from the floral designs in the lace curtains were cut out. Some arrests were made, after the reception, of persons concerned in the disgraceful business." The President, noted Crook, was "distressed greatly." Usually he was so calm about things. Crook noted his saying, "Why should they do it? How can they?"

Lincoln's last reception.

Brady's Gallery
352 Penn:ᵃ Ave. Wash.

Mr Pres, Dear Sir

I have
repeated Calls every hour,
in the day for your Photograph
And would regard it as
a great favour if you
Could give me a Sitting
to day So that I may
be able to exhibit a
large picture on the 4th,
If you Cannot Call today
Please Call at your
earliest Convenience and
very Much oblige

Yours truly
M. B. Brady

C H A P T E R 55

Endless Executive Routine

*Mathew Brady letter asking Lincoln
to sit for a photograph, March 2, 1865.*

Endless Executive Routine

WHERE others had made little or no headway at calming Missouri, General Grenville M. Dodge as military commander was to try his hand. More than any other state Missouri was seeing civil war, neighbors arrayed against neighbors, with roving guerrillas and bushwhackers, barnburners, midnight shootings, Lincoln writing to Dodge January 15 of "so much irregular violence in Northern Missouri as to be . . . almost depopulating it." He suggested that Dodge consider "an appeal to the people there to go to their homes, and let one another alone," possible withdrawal of troops where they seemed an irritation. In suggesting steps he believed practical, Lincoln voiced a faith in humanity not easy to apply in Missouri at that hour.

The old and tried friend of true steel loyalty, Isaac N. Arnold, while giving all he had for Lincoln in Washington, had lost his seat in Congress, but was staying on in Washington to write a biography of Lincoln and a history of the overthrow of slavery. Lincoln offered him a choice of two good offices and Arnold was thinking it over.

In a period of less than seven weeks Lincoln had guided the delicate legislative passage of the 13th Amendment; had conducted the elaborate finesse of the Hampton Roads conference; had gone through the broils of the failure to secure recognition for Louisiana; had kept in touch with Grant and Sherman, naval affairs, the draft sending fresh replacements to the armies; had attended to a regular grist of courts-martial, arbitrary arrests, habeas corpus, pardons; had chosen two new Cabinet members; had written his second inaugural and taken oath for a second term; had passed on hundreds of applications for office. And on Tuesday, March 14, for the first time he held a Cabinet meeting as he lay in bed, worn and haggard from emotional stress and overwork.

The patience of the American people the President thought something matchless and touching; he was never weary of commending it, noted Brooks, "I have seen him shed tears when speaking of the cheerful sacrifice of the light and strength of so many happy homes throughout the land."

During four years the President had spoken many confidences and eased his mind freely to Brooks; their friendship had deepened. At no time in delicate moments of tangled affairs had Brooks mistaken his place. So the quiet understanding was that probably the following summer he was to be appointed private secretary to the President, Nicolay and Hay taking places in the Paris legation. Brooks had the required gravity—and humor—with loyalty, affection and sympathy, even though he had no special admiration for Nicolay and Hay.

At the inaugural ball, March 6, the President with Speaker Colfax entered the long marble hall of the Patent Office. The leading lady of the grand march was Mrs. Lincoln, and her escort Senator Sumner. It meant at least they were on speaking terms, that the President and his parliamentary foe, divided on principles, had not parted as personal friends. Mrs. Lincoln had a warm personal regard for Sumner. She sent him little notes, flowers from the White House conservatory and seemed to admire him in about the degree she hated Seward.

Indications were that Mrs. Lincoln chiefly shaped the military status of young Robert. In the White House Mrs. Lincoln's sister, Emilie Todd Helm, recorded a call from General Sickles and Senator Harris at the White House: "Senator Harris turned to Mrs. Lincoln abruptly and said: 'Why isn't Robert in the army? He is old enough and strong enough to serve his country. He should have gone to the front some time ago.' Sister Mary's face turned white as death and I saw that she was making a desperate effort at self-control. She bit her lip, but answered quietly, 'Robert is making his preparations now to enter the Army, Senator Harris; he is not a shirker as you seem to imply for he has been anxious to go for a long time. If fault there be, it is mine, I have insisted that he should stay in college a little longer as I think an educated man can serve his country with more intelligent purpose than an ignoramus.'"

The Lincoln bedroom in the White House.

The mother had had her wish. Her boy had stayed on at Harvard and graduated. It was probably by agreement with Mrs. Lincoln, that Lincoln on January 19, 1865, wrote to Grant: "Please read and answer this letter as though I was not President, but only a friend. My son, now in his twenty second year, having graduated at Harvard, wishes to see something of the war before it ends. I do not wish to put him in the ranks, nor yet to give him a commission, to which those who have already served long, are better entitled, and better qualified to hold. Could he, without embarrassment to you, or detriment to the service, go into your Military family with some nominal rank, I, and not the public, furnishing his necessary means? If no, say so without the least hesitation, because I am as anxious, and as deeply interested, that you shall not be encumbered as you can be yourself."

Harriet Beecher Stowe in old age.   *Robert Lincoln, 1860.*

Grant replied that he would be glad to have the son "in my military family in the manner you propose." What then followed in this delicate arrangement was reported by Grant's staff member Colonel Horace Porter: "The President replied that he would consent to this upon one condition: that his son should serve as a volunteer aide without pay or emoluments; but Grant dissuaded him from adhering to that determination, saying that it was due to the young man that he should be regularly commissioned, and put on an equal footing with other officers of the same grade. So it was finally settled that Robert should receive the rank of captain and

assistant adjutant-general; on February 23 he was attached to the staff of the general-in-chief. The new acquisition to the company at headquarters soon became exceedingly popular. He had inherited many of the genial traits of his father, and entered heartily into all the social pastimes at headquarters. He was always ready to perform his share of hard work, and never expected to be treated differently from any other officer on account of his being the son of the Chief Executive of the nation."

Press reports of February gave the President's income tax payment for the year at $1,279.13. Around the query "How much is Mr. Lincoln worth in money?" there seemed to be little curiosity. His salary of $25,000 a year was the largest steady income he had ever had. It was paid each month in Treasury Department warrants, with the income tax deducted. These payments Lincoln had invested in more than $75,000 worth of U.S. securities, of which more than $50,000 were "registered bonds bearing 6 per cent interest, payable in coin."

On March 11 went forth the President's proclamation that any and all deserters, wherever they might be and no matter what had happened to carry their feet away from the army, on return to their regiments or companies "shall be pardoned."

Harriet Beecher Stowe one winter evening had asked if he did not feel a great relief over the prospect of the war soon coming to a close. And Lincoln had answered, she said, in a sad way: "No, Mrs. Stowe, I shall never live to see peace. This war is killing me."

CHAPTER 56

LINCOLN VISITS GRANT'S ARMY— GRANT BREAKS LEE'S LINE

Lincoln Visits Grant's Army — Grant Breaks Lee's Line

Congressman Ashley, just from Grant's headquarters, reported to Lincoln of Grant saying, "For every three men of ours dead, five of theirs; for every three of our cattle dead, five of theirs." And picking up some paper from a table and crushing it in his hand, "Tell the President I have got them like that!" Ashley said, "It made the cold chills run over me."

Sheridan had driven Early's army out of the Shenandoah Valley and reported in late March 780 barns burned, 420,000 bushels of wheat taken, also 700,000 rounds of ammunition, 2,557 horses, 7,152 head of beef cattle. So often now the wagons of Lee went out for food and came back empty. In comparison the Union army had nearly all needs in supplies running over.

After long bickering, with the Confederate Senate reversing itself and by a majority of one voting to arm the slaves for defense, President Davis signed the bill. At last the Negro slave was to be put in the Confederate Army to fight for his master. This was their one final hope for more soldiers.

Up across North Carolina marched Sherman to Fayetteville, then to Goldsboro, where he paused for rest. Behind them toward Savannah lay 425 miles of foraged and ravaged country. Since July '63 his men had come on their feet no less than 2,500 miles, fording ordinary streams and flooded rivers, through rains and hot sun. Many were ragged, their trousers half gone from tussling through underbrush. More than half had thrown away their worn-out shoes, some walking barefoot, others with feet wrapped in blanket pieces. They leaped and shouted as they slid into new issues of shoes, uniforms, overcoats, at Goldsboro. The troops were mainly from the West, the Midwest and the Northwest.

Lincoln was to leave Washington to see Grant and have a breakaway from many pressures at Washington. And he might go over with Grant what terms should end the war. Early in March he had written an order through Stanton indicating Grant was to have no conference with General Lee unless on purely military affairs: ". . . you are not to decide, discuss, or confer upon any political questions. Such questions the President holds in his own hands, and will submit them to no military conferences or conventions."

The President was to sail from Washington on the *Bat*, a fast, comfortable, well-armed dispatch boat. Then came later orders for Captain Barnes to report at the White House, where, noted the Captain, "Mr. Lincoln received me with great cordiality, but with a certain kind of embarrassment, and a look of sadness which rather embarrassed me. After a few casual remarks he said that Mrs. Lincoln had decided that she would accompany him to City Point—could the *Bat* accommodate her and her maidservant?"

Barnes was ushered into Mrs. Lincoln's presence, noting that "she received me very graciously, standing with arms folded." Her wishes: "I am going with the President to City Point, and I want you to arrange your ship to take me, my maid and my officer [or guard], as well as the President." Barnes was bothered. He went to Fox. They agreed the *Bat* couldn't be fixed over. Together they went to the White House. There "in very funny terms the President translated our difficulties." Fox promised another and better boat. On the unarmed and less safe though more spacious *River Queen*, with the *Bat* as convoy, the Lincoln family made the trip, Tad sleeping in a stateroom with the guard Crook.

Grant came aboard at City Point. Any hour he expected the enemy, because of their forces dwindling through desertion, to make a desperate attempt to crash the Union lines and force a path toward joining Johnston in North Carolina.

Ulysses S. Grant and his Generals on horseback.
Lithographed by E. Boell, 1865.

In a jolting coach over the military railroad from City Point toward the front Lincoln rode past scenery where in the first daylight hours that morning men had been mowed down by fort guns and men had fought hand to hand with bayonet and clubbed musket. Confederate troops under General John B. Gordon had taken Fort Stedman and pressed on with the aim of destroying a railroad and Union supply stores. The Union troops had rallied, had driven the enemy back and retaken Fort Stedman—and Lincoln's breakfast hour, as he wired Stanton, saw the fight "ending about where it began." Lincoln saw close up the results of desperate combat on more than a small scale. Reports gave Union losses at 500 killed and wounded, 500 captured; Confederate losses 800 killed and wounded, 1,800 captured.

While the President journeyed to the front via railway, Mrs. Lincoln was joined by Mrs. Grant, who was living with her family on the ship *Mary Martin*. The two women rode in an ambulance over a muddy, rough corduroy road. They were to join the President and Meade's staff in reviewing Crawford's division. As they alighted at the reviewing ground General Meade walked up, paid his respects to Mrs. Lincoln, escorted her away, later returning her with diplomatic skill, Mrs. Lincoln informing Badeau, "General Meade is a gentleman, sir. He says it was not the President who gave Mrs. Griffin the permit, but the Secretary of War." Thus ran Badeau's account.

On the soil where Union countercharges began Lincoln saw the dead in blue and gray and butternut lying huddled and silent, here and there the wounded gasping and groaning. He saw a collection of prisoners taken that morning, a ragged and dusty crew, and remarked "on their sad condition," noted Barnes. "They had fought desperately and were glad to be at rest. Mr. Lincoln was quiet and observant, making few comments." On the train a "worn and haggard" Lincoln saw the loading of the Union wounded. "He remarked that he had seen enough of the horrors of war, that he hoped this was the beginning of the end." Wrote the guard Crook of this day, "I saw him [Lincoln] ride over the battlefields at Petersburg, the man with the hole in his forehead and the man with both arms shot away lying, accusing, before his eyes."

Beyond the immediate scene Lincoln gazed on that day other fighting had gone on. The Union troops advanced along the whole of Lee's right, taking entrenched picket lines. The Union estimate put their own losses at 2,080 as against 4,800 to 5,000 Confederate. Lee next day was writing Davis, "I fear now it will be impossible to prevent a junction between Grant and Sherman."

Next day Barnes "found Mr. Lincoln quite recovered," lamenting the loss of life, confident the war was ending, pleased at news that Sheridan from the Shenandoah Valley had moved in a big swing around Lee's army to the north and arrived safe at Harrison's Landing to join Grant that day.

The *River Queen* moved down the James River and from her deck Lincoln saw the bank lined with men shouting, laughing, swimming, watering their horses—Sheridan's men washing off the dust and grit of the Shenandoah Valley. They spotted the President and sent him cheers. The *River Queen* passed through a naval flotilla. The crews cheered the Commander in Chief, saw his tall frame in a long-tailed black frock coat, a cravat of black silk carelessly tied, a black silk hat. Barnes noted, "As he passed each vessel he waved his high hat, as if saluting friends in his native town, and seemed as happy as a school boy."

Up the James steamed the *River Queen* to Aiken's Landing for a field review of part of the Army of the James. Sheridan came aboard. The President ended his long-held handshake. "General Sheridan, when this peculiar war began I thought a cavalryman should be at least six feet four high, but"—still gazing down on the short General—"I have changed my mind—five feet four will do in a pinch."

Ord on one side, Grant on the other, escorted the President over a rough corduroy road two miles to the reviewing ground. An ambulance followed bringing Mrs. Lincoln and Mrs. Grant in care of Colonel Horace Porter and Adam Badeau.

Meantime the President, with a squadron of 20 or more officers and orderlies, rode through woods and swamp. Standing at "parade rest" the division had waited for hours. The troops cheered the Commander in Chief. The review over, shellfire began on the enemy picket line in sight, heavy skirmishing lines moved forward, took the picket-line trenches, swelled the day's total of prisoners to 2,700, repulsed two fierce counterattacks, ending the day with Union losses of about 2,000 to 4,000 Confederate.

On the return trip of the *River Queen*, "the President seemed to recover his spirits," according to Horace Porter, who thought perhaps the strength and fighting quality he witnessed that afternoon in the Army of the James "had served to cheer him up." Whatever his mood, whatever the trouble he might be disguising, he told Colonel Porter one of his favorite funny stories, repeating the same story later to Grant.

Of what happened that evening of March 26 when the *River Queen* returned to her moorings at City Point Badeau wrote: "That night the President and Mrs. Lincoln entertained General and Mrs. Grant and the General's staff at dinner on the steamer, and before us all Mrs. Lincoln berated General Ord to the President, and urged that he should be removed. He was unfit for his place, she said, to say nothing of his wife. General Grant sat next and defended his officer bravely."

Amid the scenes created by the disordered brain of a tragically afflicted woman, young Captain Barnes felt himself drawn to the one person he saw as writhing inwardly more than any other, writing, "I came to feel an affection for him that none other inspired." The melancholy of Lincoln he believed related in part to the torments Mrs. Lincoln was under. "I had the greatest sympathy for her and for Mr. Lincoln, who I am sure felt deep anxiety for her," Barnes noted. "His manner towards her was always that of the most affectionate solicitude, so marked, so gentle and unaffected that no one could see them together without being impressed by it." Though a common undertone phrase for her was "crazy woman," Barnes' more humanly decent description ran: "She was at no time well; the mental strain upon her was great, betrayed by extreme nervousness approaching hysteria, causing misapprehensions, extreme sensitiveness as to slights or want of politeness or consideration."

Four years now since Fort Sumter at Charleston had crumbled. Now that captured fort was under repair, and Stanton, Admiral Dahlgren, William Lloyd Garrison, Henry Ward Beecher and Nicolay to represent the President, were preparing to go down and hold a flag-raising ceremony of speeches and prayers, with the Union banner again floating from that citadel where the war had begun.

A steamer put Sherman ashore at City Point late in the afternoon of March 27. Grant was there waiting. They walked to Grant's cabin. Sherman had talked nearly an hour when Grant interrupted. "I'm sorry but the President is aboard the *River Queen.*" They took Admiral Porter and soon the three found Lincoln alone in the after cabin. Sherman and Lincoln after nearly four years again faced each other. The conversation ranged from laughter to solemnity.

Next morning, March 28, on the *River Queen* came a conference of the three pivotal Northern men of the war, with Admiral Porter present. Both Grant and Sherman supposed that one or the other of them would have to fight one more bloody battle, and that it would be the *last.* "Mr. Lincoln exclaimed, more than once," wrote Sherman, "that there had been blood enough shed, and asked us if another battle could not be avoided." The generals told Lincoln they could not control that event.

Sherman came now to a momentous point. He wrote of it later: "I inquired of the President if he was all ready for the end of the war. What was to be done with the rebel armies when defeated? And what should be done with the political leaders, such as Jeff. Davis, etc.? Should we allow them to escape, etc.? He said he was all ready; all he wanted of us was to defeat the opposing armies, and to get the men composing the Confederate armies back to their homes, at work on their farms and in their shops. As to Jeff. Davis, he was hardly at liberty to speak his mind fully, but intimated that he ought to clear out, 'escape the country,' only it would not do for him to say so openly."

Sherman was eager to hear any specific recommendations that might have occurred to the mind of the President. Of the answers Sherman later wrote: "Mr. Lincoln was full and frank in his conversation, assuring me that in his mind he was all ready for the civil reorganization of affairs at the South as soon as the war was over; and he distinctly authorized me to assure Governor Vance and the people of North Carolina that, as soon as the rebel armies laid down their arms, and resumed their civil pursuits, they would at once be guaranteed all their rights as citizens of a common country; and that to avoid anarchy the State governments then in existence, with their civil functionaries, would be recognized by him as the government *de facto* till Congress could provide others . . . His earnest desire seemed to be to end the war speedily, without more bloodshed or devastation, and to restore all the men of both sections to their homes . . . When at rest or listening, his legs and arms seemed to hang almost lifeless, and his face was care-worn and haggard; but, the moment he began to talk, his face lightened up, his tall form, as it were, unfolded, and he was the very impersonation of good-humor and fellowship."

The three Northern pivotal men were parting, Sherman to remember Lincoln in a most simple manner: "Sherman, do you know why I took a shine to Grant and you?" "I don't know, Mr. Lincoln, you have been extremely kind to me, far more than my deserts." "Well, you never found fault with me."

Lincoln and Sherman had done most of the talking, Grant not mentioning a matter he later brought before Lincoln. "I told him that I had been very anxious to have the Eastern armies vanquish their old enemy. If the Western armies should be even upon the field, operating against Richmond and Lee, the credit would be given to them for the capture, by politicians and noncombatants from the section of country which those troops hailed from. Western members [of Congress] might be throwing it up to the members of the East that they were not able to capture an army, or to accomplish much but had to wait until the Western armies had conquered all the territory south and west of them, and then come on to help them capture the only army they had been engaged with. Mr. Lincoln said he saw that now, but had never thought of it before, because his anxiety was so great that he did not care where the aid came from so the work was done."

At 8:30 the morning of March 29, 1865, Lincoln went ashore from the *River Queen* to Grant's shanty. They were putting the horses aboard the railroad train that was to take Grant and his staff to the Petersburg front.

The train was ready to start. They all raised their hats in respect to the President. His hat went off to them and his voice was broken and he couldn't hide it as he called to them: "Good-by, gentlemen. God bless you all! Remember, your success is my success." The whistle sounded. The train moved. Grant was off to a campaign all hoped would be his last and the last of the war.

Fair weather of several days on the evening of March 29 gave way to torrents from the sky. Fields became beds of quicksand. Troops waded in mud above their ankles. Horses sank to their bellies and had to be pulled out with halters. Wagon wheels sank to the hubs and in some cases above the axles to the wagon box. Roads became sheets of water. Marching on such terrain was only worse than trying to sleep in wet blankets on soaked ground. On March 30 men's tempers showed. Rawlins gloomed and Grant held that soon as the weather cleared up the roads the men would be gay again.

Sheridan went on dashing where the fire was most furious, waving his battle flag, praying, swearing, shaking his fist, yelling threats and blessings. With fixed bayonets and a final rousing cheer, the Union columns under General Ayres overran the enemy earthworks, swept everything before them, killed or captured in their immediate front every man whose legs had not saved him.

Lincoln while this battle raged did his best at picturing it from a dispatch sent by Grant. He wired Seward that "Sheridan, aided by Warren, had at 2. P.M. pushed the enemy back so as to retake the five forks, and bring his own Head Quarters up . . ." The next two days Lincoln sent to Stanton a series of Grant's dispatches, relayed as Grant wrote them, and these the Secretary of War gave to the press. Thus millions of readers in the North had what they took as authentic information about the crumbling of Lee's lines foreshadowing the fall of Richmond.

At a lesser price than predicted Lee's army was cut off from Richmond, and on the night of April 2 his troops, ordered out of Petersburg and other points on the line, were reconcentrating to march west. Lincoln boarded a railroad car at City Point and rode to Petersburg, where Grant and his staff were waiting, ready to go. Grant wrote of their meeting, "About the first thing that Mr. Lincoln said to me was: 'Do you know, general, that I have had a sort of sneaking idea for some days that you intended to do something like this.'" At City Point Lincoln wired Stanton at 5 P.M. this April 3: ". . . staid with Gen. Grant an hour & a half and returned here. It is certain now that Richmond is in our hands, and I think I will go there to-morrow."

CHAPTER 57
RICHMOND FALLS—APPOMATTOX

RICHMOND FALLS—APPOMATTOX

O
N THE Sabbath day of April 2, 1865, in the Davis family pew of St. Paul's Episcopal Church, seated erect and calm under the chancel, was Jefferson Davis. An adjutant, mud on his boots, a hard-riding man, came up the aisle in a swift military stride and handed a paper to Davis, who read the words Lee had long delayed: "I advise that all preparation be made for leaving Richmond tonight. I will advise you later, according to circumstances." Davis arose, walked to the War Department, telegraphed to Lee that a move from Richmond that night would "involve the loss of many valuables, both for the want of time to pack and of transportation." Lee in the field on receiving this message, according to one of his staff men, tore it into bits, saying, "I am sure I gave him sufficient notice," and replied calmly by telegraph to Davis that it was "absolutely necessary" to abandon the position that night.

By railroad at 11 that Sabbath night, Davis with his Cabinet and other officials left their capital city, their Executive Mansion, their arsenals and stores, arriving safely in Danville the next afternoon. Word spread in Richmond that Lee's army had taken its last man and gun out of Petersburg and Richmond would fall next. On railroad trains, on wagons, carts, buggies, gigs, on horses piled with bundles and belongings, the Government and many citizens in flight had a moving day.

Burning and dynamiting of bridges, arsenals and warehouses went on through the night. Heavy smoke clouds rose from cotton warehouses. Just after daylight April 3 a crowd of thousands of men, women and children swarmed at the doors of a commissary depot. Many of them had not tasted a full, nourishing meal in months. Behind those depot doors they had heard and heard correctly were barrels of ham, bacon, whisky, flour, sugar, coffee. Why these had not gone to General Lee's half-starved army weeks before was for responsible officials to answer. Rampaging

Lincoln's visit to Richmond. By Joseph Boggs Beale.

humans broke through those depot doors, so long guarded. Raging, laughing, snarling, the crowd surged in.

General Godfrey Weitzel received the surrender of Richmond that morning of April 3 at the city hall. By midafternoon his troops had stopped the rioting and main disorders.

In Washington, wrote David Homer Bates, "Lincoln's despatch from City Point gave us in the War Department the first news of the capture of Petersburg and Richmond." Shortly after that message, came the first one in four years wired from Richmond, General Weitzel saying: "We took Richmond at 8:15 this morning." The news spread fast. Press extras sent the excitement higher. Thousands crowded around the War Office; Stanton spoke gratitude to Almighty God for deliverance.

From City Point the *Malvern* with Lincoln aboard steamed toward Richmond. Dead horses floated by, broken ordnance, wrecked boats. Nearing Richmond, the *Malvern* went aground. Admiral Porter ordered a 12-oared barge to carry the President ashore. Lincoln, Tad and Crook sat amid the oarsmen. At a place called Rockett's the little barge landed the President. Twelve armed sailors formed an escort. At his left the President had Porter and Captain Penrose, at his right Crook holding Tad by the hand. This procession began its march. Barnes saw a lone cavalryman at a street corner and sent him galloping to Weitzel's headquarters with the news of who was coming. Wrote Crook: "Every window was crowded with heads. But it was a silent crowd. There was something oppressive in those thousands of watchers without a sound, either of welcome or hatred. I think we would have welcomed a yell of defiance. I stole a look sideways at Mr. Lincoln. His face . . . had the calm . . . of a brave man . . . ready for whatever may come."

Nearly two miles along dusty streets on a warm April day this little presidential party marched to the center of Richmond. Not a soldier, citizen, horse or wagon had met them. The President

Lieut.-General Ulysses S. Grant photographed
by Frederick Gutekunst, ca. 1865.

had stopped a moment to gaze at Libby Prison, according to Porter, and on someone calling, "Pull it down," he replied, "No, leave it as a monument."

The cavalry escort arrived and led them to the Confederate Executive Mansion, a two-story house fronted with tall Colonial pillars, now the headquarters of General Weitzel and the temporary government. Dusty and sweating from his walk amid sights of burned buildings, wreckage on the streets and terror in the air, Lincoln sank into a chair at a long table, "pale and haggard, utterly worn out," noted Barnes, his first words, "I wonder if I could get a glass of water." It interested him to know this was the chair in which Jefferson Davis had sat and over this table had handled high documents.

With a cavalry escort and with Weitzel, Porter and others, Lincoln rode in a carriage over the city, seeing some of the 700 burned dwellings and stores, Libby Prison, Castle Thunder, thousands of homeless whites and Negroes. Into the disordered building where the now fugitive Confederate Congress had held its sessions, Lincoln was ushered. And if he was reminded of any anecdote no one made a record of it—though it was said his eyes often had a dreaminess.

Porter and Crook heaved sighs of relief on getting the President aboard the *Malvern*, which had now been brought upriver. Any one of many kinds of fools could have taken a pot shot at Lincoln that day.

At noon April 6 Mrs. Lincoln arrived at City Point in a party of important persons, including Senator Sumner. And on this day Lincoln telegraphed Grant that Seward had been thrown from his carriage, seriously injured, and this with other matters would take him to Washington soon.

Grant wired Lincoln a message from Sheridan reporting captures of several thousand prisoners, including Custis Lee, the son of General Robert E. Lee, and Generals Ewell, Kershaw, Button, Corse and Debray, Sheridan closing his dispatch, "If the thing is pressed I think that Lee will surrender." Lincoln wired Grant: "Gen. Sheridan says 'If the thing is pressed I think that Lee will surrender.' Let the *thing* be pressed."

The roofs of Washington came into view. Sumner in a carriage with the President and Mrs. Lincoln, drove to the White House. Then straight to the home of Seward the President drove. Four days before on a sunny spring afternoon Seward in his customary daily drive, in company with his son and daughter, had watched his fast young horses prance and go, had enjoyed it. Suddenly the horses took fright and plunged into a wild runaway. Seward stood up, tried for a leap to the pavement, was thrown in the air, and when a crowd gathered he was unconscious. Taken home, physicians found the right shoulder badly dislocated, the jaw broken on both sides, his slow and partial return to consciousness coming with agonizing pain.

The gaslights in the house were turned low as Lincoln entered, the rooms quiet, everyone moving softly and speaking in whispers. On a bed in the center of his second-floor room lay the

Confederate General Robert E. Lee.

Secretary of State, swathed in bandages. Young Frederick Seward guided the President, who sat down on the side of the bed near the left arm of the sick and broken man. Lincoln leaned across the bed, rested on an elbow so as to bring his face nearer to the face of his friend, and told of many things he had seen and heard on the trip to City Point. Seward listened, his mind eager. "They were left together for a half hour or more," wrote the son Frederick.

In ten days of latter March and early April Lee had lost 19,000 men to Grant as prisoners. In a series of desperate fights the total of Lee's killed and wounded ran highand of effective troops he had none to spare. The race westward on parallel lines was clocked with running battles. The one day's stop at Amelia Court House instead of expected food supplies for Lee's men saw nothing at all. The rank and file of the army must march on slim rations, mainly of parched corn. At Sayler's Creek enough of the Union army had overtaken Lee to force a combat that resulted in Lee's saying to one of his officers, "General, that half of our army is destroyed." The cannon of Lee were on short rations as well as the foot soldiers and cavalry horses. The artillerists knew that in a straight frontal battle they wouldn't have shells to last through.

While Lincoln journeyed toward Washington the night of April 8, Grant in the rear of the Army of the Potomac pressing Lee's rear guard, stopped at a farmhouse with a sick headache.

Abraham Lincoln. Photo by Alexander Gardner, April 1865 after Appomattox.

He spent the night bathing his feet in hot water and mustard, putting mustard plasters on his wrists and the back of his neck, moving restlessly on a sitting-room sofa trying to snatch a little sleep. His mind had concentrated intensely on notes he had written to Lee and Lee's answers. Each of these great and adroit commanders was making deep guesses about what was going on in the mind of the other. Grant however believed he knew the mind and feeling of Lincoln beyond instructions. Their many talks at City Point made him sure of what he could offer Lee that would be as though from the President. He sent Lee another note to the effect that while he had "no authority to treat on the subject of peace," he would however state "that I am equally anxious for peace with yourself, and the whole North entertains the same feeling." Lee read the note as an invitation for him to meet Grant and discuss terms of surrender, this in line with Grant's hope "that all our difficulties may be settled without the loss of another life."

On Palm Sunday morning, April 9, 1865, across the path of Lee's army and blocking its way stood the cavalry of Phil Sheridan. At five o'clock that morning General Lee on high ground studied the landscape and what it held. Eight o'clock came. Also came word that Sheridan's cavalry had fallen slowly back and widened out. Behind the cavalry, and screened by woodland, waited heavy bodies of infantry in blue, the troops of Ord and Griffin, who had made an almost incredible march of 30 miles the night and day before, coming up at daybreak to support Sheridan and invite battle. To the left, to the rear, were other Union lines.

Lee's staff officers heard him say, "There is nothing left me to do but to go and see General Grant, and I would rather die a thousand deaths." "Oh, General," protested one, "what will history say of the surrender of the army in the field?" "Yes, I know they will say hard things of us! They will not understand how we were overwhelmed by numbers. But that is not the question, Colonel: The question is, is it right to surrender this army. If it is right, then I will take all the responsibility."

Lee sent a note asking Grant for an interview "with reference to the surrender of this army." Grant at once wrote Lee to name the place for their meeting. Grant riding toward the front said to Colonel Horace Porter, "The pain in my head seemed to leave me the moment I got Lee's letter."

At the McLean house on the edge of Appomattox village, 95 miles west of Richmond, the two great captains of men faced each other in a little room and Lee gave over his army to Grant. Lee tall and erect, Grant short and stoop-shouldered; Lee 58 years old with silver hair, near the evening of life, Grant 42 with black hair and unspent strength of youth yet in him; Lee in a clean and dazzling military outfit, Grant in a rough-worn and dusty blouse telling his high rank only by the three stars on the shoulders, apologizing to Lee that he had come direct from the field and hadn't had time to change his uniform.

Lee inside was writhing over the bitter ordeal, and Grant later admitted he was embarrassed, though both wore grave, inscrutable faces and no one could have read the mixed feelings masked by the two commanders. "I met you once before, General Lee," began Grant in even voice, "while we were serving in Mexico . . . I have always remembered your appearance, and I think I should have recognized you anywhere." "Yes, I know I met you on that occasion, and I have often thought of it and tried to recollect how you looked, but I have never been able to recall a single feature."

Talk about Mexico ran into memories of that war when they both wore blue. Grant just about forgot why they were there, it seemed. Lee brought him to the point. "I suppose, General Grant, that the object of our present meeting is fully understood. I asked to see you to ascertain upon what terms you would receive the surrender of my army."

Grant went on as between two good neighbors. "The terms I propose are those stated substantially in my letter of yesterday that is, the officers and men surrendered to be paroled and disqualified from taking up arms again until properly exchanged, and all arms, ammunition and supplies to be delivered up as captured property." "Those," said Lee, "are about the conditions I expected would be proposed."

Grant, seated at a table, put it in writing, his staff aides and corps commanders standing by; Lee was seated with his aide Colonel Charles Marshall standing behind his chair. Grant rose,

Battle of Appomattox Court House and containing the house of Wilmer McLean, where the surrender of the Confederate Army under Robert E. Lee to Union commander Ulysses S. Grant took place on April 9, 1865, effectively ending the American Civil War.

stepped over to Lee and handed him the paper scrawled in pencil. Lee took out spectacles, pulled a handkerchief and wiped the glasses, crossed his legs, read slowly and carefully the strangest and most consequential paper that had ever met his eyes. And with his first touch of warmth he said to Grant, "This will have a very happy effect on my army."

Grant asked for any further suggestions. Lee had one. In his army the cavalrymen and artillerists owned their horses; he wanted these men to have their mounts for spring plowing on their farms. Grant said: "I take it that most of the men in the ranks are small farmers, and as the country has been so raided by the two armies, it is doubtful whether they will be able to put in a crop to carry themselves and their families through the next winter without the aid of the horses they are now riding." So without changing the written terms he would instruct officers receiving paroles "to let all the men who claim to own a horse or mule take the animals home with them to work their little farms." Lee showed relief. "This will have the best possible effect upon the men. It will be very gratifying and will do much toward conciliating our people."

Lee shook hands with some of Grant's generals who offered theirs, bowed, then turned to Grant saying that a thousand Union prisoners had been living the last few days on parched corn only; they required attention, and of provisions "I have, indeed, nothing for my own men." This was discussed briefly and Grant directed that 25,000 rations be sent to Lee's men.

Lee wrote an acceptance of Grant's terms, signed it, and the documents of surrendering an army were completed. There remained only such formalities as roll call and stacking of arms. Union gunners made ready to fire a salute of grand national triumph, but Grant forbade any signs of rejoicing over a broken enemy he hoped hereafter would no longer be an enemy.

Lee rode among his men who crowded around him crying, "We'll fight 'em yet" and explained, with tears and in a choked voice, that they had fought the war together, he had done his best, and it was over. Many were dazed. Some wept. Others cursed and babbled. The army could die but never surrender, they had hoped. Yet they still worshiped Lee. They touched his hands, his uniform; they petted his horse Traveller, smoothing his flanks with their hands. One man, throwing down his musket, cried to the blue heaven: "Blow, Gabriel, blow! My God, let him blow, I am ready to die!"

For Grant it was one more odd day. Three times now he had bagged a whole army, at Fort Donelson, at Vicksburg, at Appomattox. He had kept his pledge to Lincoln that he would do his best to avoid a final bloody battle.

Next day it rained. The paroles numbered 28,231. Grant and Lee sat their horses between lines for a farewell talk. Grant said that not a man in the South had so great an influence with soldiers and people as General Lee, that if Lee would now advise the surrender of the other armies his advice would be followed. Lee said he could not do this without first consulting Davis. And with no misunderstandings Grant and Lee said good-by.

From Appomattox Grant telegraphed Stanton at 4:30 P.M. April 9: "General Lee surrendered the Army of Northern Virginia this afternoon on terms proposed by myself."

The war was over. It would have various dying flares in a sunset sky. The costs and sacrifices could never be forgotten. There would be hates and rankling memories. The war nevertheless had spent itself and had gone now into a realm of memory and hallucination, a national ordeal and fever over and past.

The area in front of the White House filled with an enormous crowd. Brass bands had their music interrupted by guns. Tad showed at the well-known window from which the President always spoke; the crowd roared as he waved a captured Confederate flag. Hats went in the air with volleys of yells as the President came out to look at a throng where hatless men were now throwing into the air other men's hats and wild emotion poured out in screams that rose and curved in rockets.

Over the North that day of April 10 everything done before in victory celebrations was done again, but longer, oftener and with complete and final enthusiasm. To the prowar celebrants were joined the antiwar people, peace men and women who had always said the war was a cruel and costly failure; they too were glad now. So many, even many of the loyal ones, had been heartsick about the way it dragged for four years beyond all first expectations. Great God, but Lincoln must be thankful today. Hurrah for the Union! Hurrah for Lincoln! Hurrah for Grant and Sherman, the grand right and left arms of Lincoln! Get out the flags. Hang out every rag in the house that looks like a flag. Hang out red, white and blue bunting. Make a show. Great Jehovah, but we're glad the war's over!

CHAPTER 58

"Not in Sorrow, but in Gladness of Heart"

"Not in Sorrow, but in Gladness of Heart"

APRIL 11 the President issued a proclamation closing Southern ports. Any ship or vessel from beyond the United States trying to enter these ports with articles subject to duties, "the same, together with its tackle, apparel, furniture and cargo, shall be forfeited to the United States."

Also of this date was a proclamation barring from all U.S. ports the war vessels of any foreign country whose ports refused equal privileges and immunities to U.S. war vessels. The home war fading, the Union could risk challenging other countries.

The President spent his best working hours this day on his speech for the evening. He was seizing the initiative to set in motion his own reconstruction program. Not until next December would Congress meet, not unless he called a special session. He intended to speak to the country so plainly that before Congress met, he could hope the majority of the people would be with him.

A "carefully written paper" rather than a speech the President held in waiting for the crowd. With bands of music and banners of freedom, with shouting and hoorah, an immense throng poured into the area in front of the White House. Many were the surging calls and cries for the President. "There was something terrible," thought Noah Brooks, "in the enthusiasm with which the beloved Chief Magistrate was received. Cheers upon cheers, wave after wave of applause, rolled up, the President patiently standing quiet until it was all over."

He began to read his speech holding a candle in his left hand and the manuscript in the right. "Speedily becoming embarrassed with the difficulty of managing the candle and the speech," wrote Brooks, "he made a comical motion with his left foot and elbow, which I construed to mean that I should hold his candle for him, which I did." Then, "We meet this evening, not in sorrow, but in gladness of heart . . . A call for a national thanksgiving is being prepared, and will be duly promulgated . . . To Gen. Grant, his skilful officers, and brave men, all belongs. The gallant Navy stood ready, but was not in reach to take active part."

This to the crowd was in somewhat the expected tone. Then the key changed. The crowd was "perhaps surprised," thought Brooks. The President read on, dropped to the floor each written page when read, and became aware that Tad was picking them up as they dropped. He could hear Tad, unseen to the crowd, calling for "another" and "another" of the fluttering sheets. He read on: "By these recent successes the re-inauguration of the national authority—reconstruction—which has had a large share of thought from the first, is pressed much more closely upon our attention. It is fraught with great difficulty. Unlike the case of a war between independent nations, there is no authorized organ for us to treat with. No one man has authority to give up the rebellion for any other man. We must simply begin with, and mould from, disorganized and discordant elements."

Those of the crowd who had come for hoorah wondered how much more of it there would be. It was a little heavy, it seemed. Others knew he was talking not to the thousands on the White House lawn but to the whole American and European world.

He came to his closing words. "Important principles may, and must, be inflexible. In the present 'situation' as the phrase goes, it may be my duty to make some new announcement to the people of the South. I am considering, and shall not fail to act, when satisfied that action will be proper."

As he stood for a moment taking the plaudits of the crowd, he smiled to the candle-bearer Brooks. "That was a pretty fair speech, I think, but you threw some light on it."

There were applause and cheers, with no such uproar as had begun the evening. The speech had been too long, too closely reasoned, to please a big crowd. He would hear from the country about the speech. What he heard would help guide him further. His powers were vast. Before Congress met in December he might put through a series of decisions and actions that would channel and canal future policy for years, in accord with his outspoken designs of this evening.

Stereoscopic view of Hon. Abraham Lincoln by the American & Foreign Portrait Gallery, Feb. 1865.

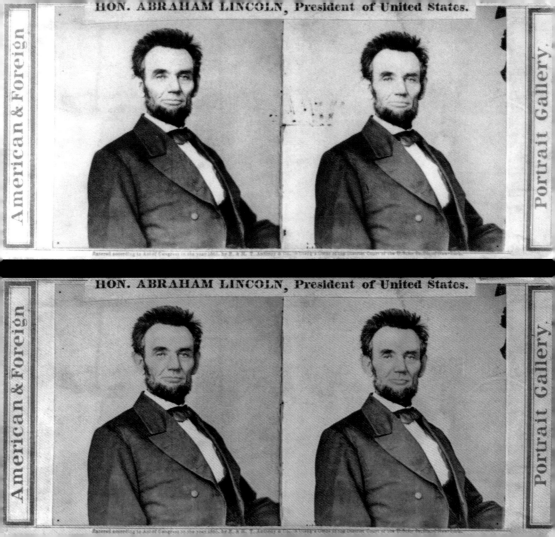

CHAPTER 59

NEGOTIATIONS—
AN OMINOUS DREAM

Ward H. Lamon escorted the newly elected president to Washington in the spring of 1861 and served as the marshal of the District of Columbia and Lincoln's personal bodyguard during the Civil War.

Negotiations—An Ominous Dream

Seward was among those who mainly favored the President's policy of good will, of being generous and taking chances on double-dealing. Through different processes of thought, "we frequently arrived at the same conclusion," Seward described their joint operations; on the large questions "no knife sharp enough to divide us."

Among those high in the Government persistently vocal for punishing the defeated Confederates was Vice-President Johnson. To Dana in Richmond he insisted "their sins had been enormous," and if they were let back into the Union without punishment the effect would be bad, raising dangers in the future.

To Grant it came that Vice-President Johnson in Washington, in Richmond, had an "ever-ready" remark: "Treason is a crime and must be made odious." To Southern men who went to Johnson for assurances that they might begin some sort of rebuilding, he offered vehement denunciations. To Grant this was a sorry performance, Grant believing that the Lincoln view had behind it "the great majority of the Northern people, and the soldiers unanimously," the Lincoln view favoring "a speedy reconstruction on terms that would be the least humiliating to the people who had rebelled against their government." Sherman's ideas about peace terms and reconstruction, it would be too easy to say, were identical with those of Grant. The Union general who more than any other favored a war strategy of punishment and destruction of the South decidedly favored a mild and kindly peace policy. In the balances of early April the three high commanders and a million soldiers were, to use Grant's word, "unanimous" for ending the war on practically any terms that would bring a restored Union with slavery gone.

The two men who most often warned Lincoln about his personal safety were Stanton and Lamon. To Lamon he had laughing retorts. The envelope on which he had written "Assassination," wherein he filed threat letters, numbered 80 items in latter March. He told Seward, "I know I am in danger; but I am not going to worry over threats like these."

According to Lamon's study, Lincoln held that any dream had a meaning if you could be wise enough to find it. Of the dream that came to Lincoln this second week of April '65, Lamon wrote that it was "the most startling incident" that had ever come to the man, of "deadly import," "amazingly real." Lincoln said "About ten days ago I retired very late. I had been up waiting for important dispatches from the front. I could not have been long in bed when I fell into a slumber, for I was weary. I soon began to dream. There seemed to be a death-like stillness about me. Then I heard subdued sobs, as if a number of people were weeping. I thought I left my bed and wandered downstairs. There the silence was broken by the same pitiful sobbing, but the mourners were invisible. I went from room to room; no living person was in sight, but the same mournful sounds of distress met me as I passed along. It was light in all the rooms; every object was familiar to me; but where were all the people who were grieving as if their hearts would break? I was puzzled and alarmed. What could be the meaning of all this? Determined to find the cause of a state of things so mysterious and so shocking, I kept on until I arrived at the East Room, which I entered. There I met with a sickening surprise. Before me was a catafalque, on which rested a corpse wrapped in funeral vestments. Around it were stationed soldiers who were acting as guards; and there was a throng of people, some gazing mournfully upon the corpse, whose face was covered, others weeping pitifully. 'Who is dead in the White House?' I demanded of one of the soldiers. 'The President,' was his answer; 'he was killed by an assassin!' Then came a loud burst of grief from the crowd, which awoke me from my dream. I slept no more that night; and although it was only a dream, I have been strangely annoyed by it ever since."

The dream had shaken its dreamer to the depths, noted Lamon. As he had given the secret of it to others he was "grave, gloomy, and at times visibly pale, but perfectly calm." To Lamon afterward, in a reference to it Lincoln quoted from *Hamlet*, "To sleep; perchance to dream! ay, *there's the rub!*"—stressing the last three words.

CHAPTER 60

THE CALENDAR SAYS
GOOD FRIDAY

THE CALENDAR SAYS GOOD FRIDAY

FROM mid-April '61 to mid-April '65 some 3,000,000 men North and South had seen war service—the young, the strong, the physically fit, carrying the heavy load and taking the agony. The fallen of them had seen Antietam, Murfreesboro, Fredericksburg, Chancellorsville, the Wilderness, Spotsylvania, Cold Harbor, each a shambles, a human slaughterhouse. In the burned and blackened Shenandoah Valley were enough embers of barns and men to satisfy any prophet of doom. From Malvern Hill and Gettysburg down to Chickamauga, Chattanooga, Island Number 10, Vicksburg, the Red River and beyond, the burying grounds deep and shallow held the consecrated dead.

Killed in action or dead from wounds and disease were some 620,000 Americans, 360,000 from the North, 260,000 from the South—planted in the tomb of the earth, spectral and shadowy. They were phantoms never absent from Lincoln's thoughts. Possibly from that vanished host, rather than from the visible and living, Lincoln took his main direction and moved as though the word "reconciliation" could have supreme beauty if he could put it to work.

In Greensboro, North Carolina, at a rather ordinary house, in an upstairs room having a bed, a few small chairs, a table with pen and ink, Jefferson Davis, with four remaining Cabinet members and two veteran generals, held a final meeting over the affairs of the Confederate States of America, its government, its armies and prospects. They agreed a letter should be written to Sherman asking for terms. Johnston asked Davis to write it—which he did. They parted.

As Davis packed his kit for moving farther south he knew there were not a few in the North who wished to see him hang on a sour-apple tree. One report credited Lincoln with saying: "This talk about Mr. Davis tires me. I hope he will mount a fleet horse, reach the shores of the Gulf of Mexico, and ride so far into its waters that we shall never see him again."

Lincoln sat for a photograph by Alexander Gardner—and for the first time when facing a camera in the four years of his administration permitted a smile to wreath his face. Until this camera register in the second week of April '65, he had most often been grave and somber. Now he smiled. The hurricane was spent, the high storm winds gone down. Rough weather and choppy seas were ahead—but the worst was over and could not come again. He hoped for good will and mutual trust and let that hope shine on his face.

On the calendar it was Holy Week and April 14th was Good Friday. Some were to say they had never before this week seen such a shine of beneficence, such a kindling glow, on Lincoln's face. He was down to lean flesh and bone, 30 pounds underweight, his cheeks haggard, yet the inside of him moved to a music of peace on earth and good will to men. He let it come out in the photograph Gardner made this Holy Week.

The schedule for this day as outlined beforehand was: office business till eight; breakfast and then interviews till the Cabinet meeting at 11; luncheon, more interviews, a late afternoon drive with Mrs. Lincoln; an informal meeting with old Illinois friends; during the day and evening one or more trips to the War Department; another interview, then to the theater with Mrs. Lincoln and a small party. Such was the prepared docket for this Good Friday.

In Washington General Grant had arrived from the front, heard shouts of welcome, and in trying to walk from his hotel to the War Department had to call on the police to help make a path through the curious, cheering throngs.

Lincoln was disinclined to go to the theater party planned by Mrs. Lincoln. A third-rate drama, *Our American Cousin*, which the star Laura Keene had carried to popularity, was showing at Ford's Theatre. But Mrs. Lincoln had set her heart

The last photograph of Lincoln the day after Lee's surrender at Appomattox. Photo by Alexander Gardner, April 10, 1865.

on it, and on his suggestion she invited General and Mrs. Grant. And General Grant accepted, the newspapers were announcing.

Grant however had changed his mind. Mrs. Grant, in all probability, had told the General that the more she thought about it, the more it seemed impossible that she could endure an evening with the unfortunate woman she had last seen in such outbursts of temper and rages of jealousy at City Point. The General himself, anyone who knew him would testify, could see no fun in such a social evening.

Grant sat that morning in his first session with a President and a Cabinet. Welles wrote in his diary the President's comment on re-establishing law and order and new state governments in the South. Changing Welles' report from the third person to the first, Lincoln said: "I think it providential that this great rebellion is crushed just as Congress has adjourned and there are none of the disturbing elements of that body to hinder and embarrass us. If we are wise and discreet we shall reanimate the States and get their governments in successful operation, with order prevailing and the Union reestablished before Congress comes together in December . . . I hope there will be no persecution, no bloody work after the war is over. No one need expect me to take any part in hanging or killing those men, even the worst of them. Frighten them out of the country, open the gates, let down the bars, scare them off"—throwing up his hands as if scaring sheep. "Enough lives have been sacrificed."

THE CALENDAR SAYS GOOD FRIDAY

Grant said he was hourly expecting to hear from Sherman. Young Frederick Seward attended this Cabinet meeting as Acting Secretary of State in place of his father, who still lay abed with a broken jaw. Young Seward's account of the session added details that escaped Welles. Curiosity was spoken about the "rebel" leaders. Would they escape? Would they be caught and tried, and if so, what would be the penalties? "All those present thought that, for the sake of general amity and good will, it was desirable to have as few judicial proceedings as possible." "I suppose, Mr. President," said Postmaster General Dennison, "you would not be sorry to have them escape out of the country?" "Well," came a slow answer, "I should not be sorry to have them out of the country; but I should be for following them up pretty close, to make sure of their going."

As to various details of any new state government, Seward heard the President: "We can't undertake to run State governments in all these Southern States. Their people must do that—though I reckon that at first some of them may do it badly."

So the Cabinet session of Friday, April 14, came to an end with the expectation that on Tuesday, April 18, they would again meet and resume discussion of how to bind up the nation's wounds.

A long afternoon carriage drive made an interlude. Mrs. Lincoln told Crook and others later of her query whether some friends should be invited for this drive, Lincoln saying No, he wanted "just ourselves." As the carriage rolled along he talked about the next four years in Washington, how he hoped afterward perhaps for a trip abroad, then a return to Springfield, perhaps law practice and a prairie farm on the banks of the Sangamon. Mrs. Lincoln spoke too of a happiness moving him, a happiness so strange and unusual that she could not read it, and it troubled her. She quoted him as saying, "I never felt so happy in my life," and a fear crossed her as she replied, "Don't you remember feeling just so before our little boy died?"

Walking over to the War Department late this afternoon of April 14, Lincoln did one thing perhaps for the first time. Always others had brought up the matter of possible harm to come to him—and he had laughed them off or promised to take care. In this instance it was Lincoln who first mentioned it, according to Crook's account. They passed some drunken men, profane, violent, irresponsible. And Lincoln turned, saying, "Crook, do you know, I believe there are men who want to take my life?" And after a pause, half to himself, "And I have no doubt they will do it."

Lincoln's tone was so calm and sure that Crook found himself saying, "Why do you think so, Mr. President?" "Other men have been assassinated"—this still in the manner of half talking to himself. "I hope you are mistaken, Mr. President," offered Crook. And after a few paces in silence, Lincoln in a more ordinary tone: "I have perfect confidence in those who are around me—in every one of you men. I know no one could do it and escape alive. But if it is to be done, it is impossible to prevent it."

After a short conference in Stanton's office Lincoln came out, Crook noticing that the "depression" or "intense seriousness" had passed. "He talked to me as usual." Of the theater party planned for the evening he said: "It has been advertised that we will be there, and I cannot disappoint the people. Otherwise I would not go. I do not want to go." This surprised Crook, who knew well the ease and enjoyment Lincoln usually found at the theater. So Crook meditated, "It seems unusual to hear him say he does not want to go tonight." At the White House door he stood facing his guard a moment and then, "Good-bye, Crook." This puzzled Crook somewhat. Until then it had always been "Good-night, Crook."

After dinner the President was unusually cheerful, thought Brooks, "never more hopeful and buoyant concerning the condition of the country, full of fun and anecdotes," though he had no enthusiasm about the play for the evening, felt "inclined to give up the whole thing." The party stepped out on the White House portico, Lincoln going toward the carriage, saying, "Grant thinks we can reduce the cost of the army establishment at least a half million a day, which, with the reduction of expenditures of the navy, will soon bring down our national debt to something like decent proportions, and bring our national paper up to a par, or nearly so, with gold—at least so they think."

CHAPTER 61

Blood on the Moon

Blood on the Moon

Ford's Theater as it appears today.

IN THE carriage into which the President and his wife stepped were Henry Reed Rathbone, assigned by Stanton to accompany the President, and his fiancée, Miss Clara Harris. He was 28 years old, of a well-to-do clan of Rathbones in Albany, New York, a major of volunteers since November '62, a trusted War Office attaché. His sweetheart was the daughter of Judge Ira Harris of Albany, since 1861 U.S. Senator from New York.

The guard with Lincoln this evening was John F. Parker, one of the four officers detailed from the Metropolitan Police Force of the city for White House duty in staying close to the President and keeping a sharp eye on anyone who might have designs on the life and person of the President. Of these four guards only one, it afterward appeared, had a questionable record—and he was John F. Parker. On this evening he was 35 years old lacking one month; born in Frederick County, Virginia, he had worked at the carpenter's trade in Washington, enlisted in the Army as a three-month man, in '61 joining the Metropolitan Police as a patrolman. At his home on 750 L Street he had a wife and three children.

In March and April of '63 Parker was on trial on various charges: of being found asleep on a streetcar when he should have been patrolling his beat; of conduct unbecoming an officer through five weeks of residence in a house of prostitution, where it was alleged he had been drunk, had been put to bed, had fired a revolver through a window; the board found he was "at a house of ill fame with no other excuse than that he was sent for by the Keeper (Miss Annie Wilson)," although there was "no evidence that there was any robbery there or disturbance of the peace or quiet of that neighborhood." The list of trials, the repeated similar charges against Parker, the board's findings in the evidence showed conclusively that he was of loose habits rather than a steady reliable man.

How Parker found his way into the White House to begin with was not clear in the records. On April 3, however, when he was drafted for army service, Mrs. Lincoln on Executive Mansion stationery had written to the District of Columbia Provost Marshal, James R. O'Beirne, a certificate "that John F. Parker . . . has been detailed for duty at the Executive Mansion by order of [signed] Mrs. Lincoln."

The carriage left the White House with its four occupants, coachman Francis Burns holding the reins, and alongside him the footman and valet Charles Forbes.

At Ford's Theatre, Burns pulled up his horses. Forbes swung down to the sidewalk and opened the carriage door. The President and his wife stepped out, followed by Major Rathbone and Miss Harris. The guard Parker was at hand. The party walked into the theater at about nine o'clock. An usher led them to their box. The audience in their 1,000 seats saw or heard that the President had arrived. They applauded; many rose from their seats; some cheered. The President paused and nodded his acknowledgment of their welcome to him.

On the stage proceeds a play written 14 years before by the English dramatist Tom Taylor; on rehearsal he decided it was not for the British public and later had sent it to the New York producer Lester Wallack, who had told Laura Keene it would fit her. She had put it on, but after a fairly good run it has about reached its limit.

Ford's Theater,
Washington, DC.

Room in the Petersen House where Lincoln lay until his death.

Replica of the bed where Abraham Lincoln died at Petersen House.

The play proceeds, not unpleasant, often stupid, sprinkled with silly puns, forced humor. The story centers around the Yankee lighting his cigar with an old will, burning the document to ashes and thereby throwing a fortune of $400,000 away from himself into the hands of an English cousin. The audience agrees it is not bad. The applause and laughter say the audience is having a good time.

This privacy however is not as complete as it seems. A few feet behind the President is the box door, the only entry to the box unless by a climb from the stage. In this door is a small hole, bored that afternoon to serve as a peephole—from the outside. Through this peephole it is the intention of the Outsider who made it with a gimlet to stand and watch the President, then at a chosen moment to enter the box. Close to the door connecting with the balcony two inches of plaster have been cut from the brick wall of the narrow hallway. The intention of the Outsider is that a bar placed in this cut-away wall niche and then braced against the panel of the door will hold that door against intruders, will serve to stop anyone from interference with the Outsider while making his observations of the President through the gimleted hole in the box door.

At either of these doors, the one to the box or the one from the balcony to the hallway, it is the assigned duty and expected responsibility of John F. Parker to stand or sit constantly, with unfailing vigil. A Ward Lamon or an Eckert on this duty would

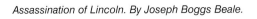

Assassination of Lincoln. By Joseph Boggs Beale.

probably have noticed the gimleted hole, the newly made wall niche, and been doubly watchful.

"The guard . . . acting as my substitute," wrote the faithful Crook later, "took his position at the rear of the box, close to an entrance leading into the box . . . His orders were to stand there, fully armed, and to permit no unauthorized person to pass into the box. His orders were to stand there and protect the President at all hazards. From the spot where he was thus stationed, this guard could not see the stage or the actors; but he could hear the words the actors spoke, and he became so interested in them that, incredible as it may seem, he quietly deserted his post of duty, and walking down the dimly-lighted side aisle, deliberately took a seat."

Either between acts or at some time when the play was not lively enough to suit him or because of an urge for a pony of whisky under his belt, John F. Parker leaves his seat in the balcony and goes down to the street and joins companions in a little whiff of liquor—this on the basis of a statement of the coachman Burns, who declared he stayed outside on the street with his carriage and horses, except for one interlude when "the special police officer [meaning John F. Parker] and the footman of the President [Forbes] came up to him and asked him to take a drink with them; which he did." Thus circumstances favor the lurking and vigilant Outsider.

The moment of high fate is not seen by the theater audience. Only one man sees that moment. He is the Outsider, the one who

FORD'S THEATRE

TENTH STREET, ABOVE E.

SEASON II............WEEK XXXI........NIGHT 191

WHOLE NUMBER OF NIGHTS, 495.

JOHN T. FORD................................PROPRIETOR AND MANAGER
(Also of Holliday St. Theatre, Baltimore, and Academy of Music, Phila.)
Stage Manager................................J. B. WRIGHT
Treasurer................................H. CLAY FORD

Friday Evening, April 14th, 1865

THIS EVENING,

The Performance will be honored by the presence of

PRESIDENT LINCOLN

BENEFIT!

—AND—

LAST NICHT

OF MISS

LAURA KEENE

THE DISTINGUISHED MANAGERESS, AUTHORESS AND ACTRESS,

Supported by

MR. JOHN DYOTT

AND

MR. HARRY HAWK

TOM TAYLOR'S CELEBRATED ECCENTRIC COMEDY

As originally produced in America by Miss Keene, and performed by her upwards of

ONE THOUSAND NIGHTS'

ENTITLED

OUR AMERICAN

COUSIN

FLORENCE TRENCHARD........MISS LAURA KEENE
(Her Original Character.)

Abel Murcott, Clerk to Attorney	John Dyott
Asa Trenchard	Harry Hawk
Sir Edward Trenchard	T. C. GOURLAY
Lord Dundreary	E. A. EMERSON
Mr. Coyle, Attorney	J. MATTHEWS
Lieutenant Vernon, R. N.	W. J. FERGUSON
Captain De Boots	C. BYRNES
Binney	G. G. SPEAR
Buddicomb, a Valet	J. H. EVANS
John Whicker, a gardener	J. L. DeBONAY
Rasper, a groom	
Bailiff	G. A. PARKHURST and L. JOHNSON
Mary Trenchard	Miss J. GOURLAY
Mrs. Mountchessington	Mrs. H. MUZZY
Augusta	Miss H. TRUEMAN
Georgiana	Miss M. HART
Sharpe	Mrs. J. H. EVANS
Skillet	Miss M. GOURLAY

SATURDAY EVENING, APRIL 15,

BENEFIT of Miss JENNIE GOURLAY

When will be presented BOURCICAULT'S Great Sensational Drama,

THE OCTOROON

Easter Monday, April 17, Engagement of the YOUNG AMERICAN TRAGEDIAN,

EDWIN ADAMS

FOR TWELVE NIGHTS ONLY.

Ford's Theatre broadside for Our American Cousin.

John Bright on the Presidency.

John Bright, the "British Reformer," whose efforts in behalf of the United States, in combating the English sentiment in favor of the rebels, have awakened for him love and gratitude on the part of all loyal Americans, has written a letter to Horace Greely, in which, after alluding to the great struggle for liberty, in which we are now engaged, he says:

At this moment, we turn our eyes rather to to the political than to the military struggle; and there is, with us, the same difference of opinion and of sympathy, as regards your coming Presidential election, that has been manifested in connection with your contest in the field.

All those of my countrymen who have wished well to the rebellion, who have hoped for the break-up of your Union, who have preferred to see a Southern Slave Empire rather than a restored and free Republic, so far as I can observe, are now in favor of the election of Gen. McClellan. All those who have deplored the calamities which the leaders of secession have brought upon your country, who believe that Slavery weakens your power and tarnishes your good name throughout the world, and who regard the restoration of your Union as a thing to be desired and prayed for by all good men, so far as I can judge, are heartily longing for the re-election of Mr. Lincoln. Every friend of your Union, probably, in Europe, every speaker and writer who has sought to do justice to your cause since the war began, is now hoping, with an intense anxiety, that Mr. Lincoln may be placed at the head of your Executive for another term.

It is not because they believe Mr. Lincoln to be wiser or better than all other men on your continent, but they think they have observed in his career a grand simplicity of purpose, and a patriotism which knows no change and which does not falter. To some of his countrymen there may appear to have been errors in his course. It would be strange indeed if, in the midst of difficulties so stupendous and so unexpected, any administration or any ruler should wholly avoid mistakes. To us, looking on from this distance, and unmoved by the passions from which many of your people can hardly be expected to be free—regarding his Presidential path with the calm judgment which belongs rather to history than to the present time, as our outside position enables us, in some degree, to regard it—we see in it an honest endeavor faithfully to do the work of his great office, and, in the doing of it, a brightness of personal honor on which no adversary has yet been able to fix a stain.

I believe that the effect of Mr. Lincoln's re-election in England, and in Europe, and indeed throughout the world, will be this: it will convince all men that the integrity of your great country will be preserved, and it will show that Republican institutions, *with an instructed and patriotic people,* can bear a nation safely and steadily through the most desperate perils.

PRESIDENT LINCOLN.

The large audience assembled last evening at the Academy of Music, to hear an address from Rev. Henry Ward Beecher, may be considered as fairly representing the most enlightened and intelligent population of Philadelphia. The welcome to Mr. Beecher was hearty, as it should have been. Every portion of his address was well received; but the loudest applause was given when he spoke in commendation of the course of the National Government in its prosecution of the war against the Southern rebels. An incidental allusion to General Jackson called forth some hearty plaudits. When they ceased Mr. Beecher, in his peculiar quiet way, said "Abraham Lincoln may be a great deal less testy and wilful than Andrew Jackson, but in a long race, I do not know but that he will be equal to him." The storm of applause that followed this seemed as if it never would cease. The turn given to the popular enthusiasm, by the mention of Lincoln's name alongside of Jackson's, was wholly unexpected. But the spontaneous outburst showed how strong a hold the President has upon the popular heart throughout the loyal North. As the time approaches for a new Presidential election, and people cast their eyes about for a candidate, there is no one so generally looked to as Abraham Lincoln. Other men may have the requisite talents and virtues; but none impress the people as being so well entitled to the next term of four years as the man who has so faithfully guided the republic through the terrible storms of civil war. There is a general feeling that after a term of war he is entitled to a term of peace; and that other men, military and civil, must defer their

News clipping found in Lincoln's pocket after his death.

waited and lurked and made his preparations. He comes through the outer door into the little hallway, fastens the strong though slender bar into the two-inch niche in the brick wall, and braces it against the door panel. He moves softly to the box door and through the little hole studies the box occupants and his Human Target seated in an upholstered rocking armchair. Softly he opens the door and steps toward his prey, in his right hand a one-shot brass derringer pistol, a little eight-ounce vest-pocket weapon winged for death, in his left hand a steel dagger. He is cool and precise and times his every move.

The revolver used by John Wilkes Booth to assassinate President Abraham Lincoln.

He raises the derringer, lengthens his right arm, runs his eye along the barrel in a line with the head of his victim less than five feet away—and pulls the trigger.

A lead ball somewhat less than a half-inch in diameter crashes into the left side of the head of the Human Target, into the back of the head, in a line with and three inches from the left ear. "The course of the ball was obliquely forward toward the right eye, crossing the brain in an oblique manner and lodging a few inches behind that eye. In the track of the wound were found fragments of bone, which had been driven forward by the ball, which was embedded in the anterior lobe of the left hemisphere of the brain."

For Abraham Lincoln it is lights out, good night, farewell—and a long farewell to the good earth and its trees, its enjoyable companions, and the Union of States and the world Family of Man he has loved. He is not dead yet. He is to linger in dying. But the living man can never again speak, see, hear or awaken into conscious being.

Near the prompt-desk off stage stands W. J. Ferguson, an actor. He looks in the direction of the shot he hears, and sees "Mr. Lincoln lean back in his rocking chair, his head coming to rest against the wall which stood between him and the audience . . . well inside the curtains"—no struggle or move "save in the slight backward sway." Of this the audience knows nothing.

Major Rathbone leaps from his chair. Rushing at him with a knife is a strange human creature, terribly alive, a lithe wild animal, a tiger for speed, a wildcat of a man bareheaded, raven-haired—a smooth sinister face with glaring eyeballs. He wears a dark sack suit. He stabs straight at the heart of Rathbone, a fast and ugly lunge. Rathbone parries it with his upper right arm, which gets a deep slash of the dagger. Rathbone is staggered, reels back. The tigerish stranger mounts the box railing. Rathbone recovers, leaps again for the stranger, who feels the hand of Rathbone holding him back, slashes again at Rathbone, then leaps for the stage.

This is the moment the audience wonders whether something unusual is happening—or is it part of the play? From the box railing the Strange Man's leap for the stage is slightly interrupted. The draped Union flag of silk reaches out and tangles itself in the spur of one riding boot, throwing him out of control. He falls perhaps ten feet to the stage, landing on his left leg, breaking the shinbone a little above the instep.

Of what he has done the audience as yet knows nothing. They wonder what this swift, raven-haired, wild-eyed Strange

Man portends. They see him rush across the stage, three feet to a stride, and vanish. Some have heard Rathbone's cry "Stop that man!" Many have seen a man leap from a front seat up on the stage and chase after the weird Stranger, crying "Stop that man!" It is less than half a minute since the Strange Man mounted the box railing, made the stage and strode off.

Off stage between Laura Keene and W. J. Ferguson he dashes at breakneck speed, out of an entrance, 40 feet to a little door opening on an alley. There stands a fast bay horse, a slow-witted chore boy nicknamed John Peanuts holding the reins. He kicks the boy, mounts the mare; hoofs on the cobblestones are heard but a few moments. In all it is maybe 60 or 70 seconds since he loosed the one shot of his eight-ounce brass derringer.

Did the Strange Man now riding away on a fast bay horse pause a moment on the stage and shout a dramatic line of speech? Some said he ran off as though every second of time counted and his one purpose was escape. Others said he faced the audience a moment, brandished a dagger still bloody from slashing Rathbone, and shouted the state motto of Virginia, the slogan of Brutus as he drove the assassin's knife into imperial Caesar: "*Sic semper tyrannis*"—"Thus be it ever to tyrants."

A woman's scream pierces the air. Some say afterward it was Mrs. Lincoln. The scream carries a shock and a creeping shiver to many hearing it. "He has shot the President!" Men swarm up to the edge of the stage, over the gas-jet footlights onto the stage. The aisles fill with people not sure where to go.

Some 200 soldiers arrive to clear the theater. The wailing and the crazy chaos let down in the emptying playhouse—and flare up again in the street outside, where some man is accused of saying he is glad it happened, a sudden little mob dragging him to a lamppost with a ready rope to hang him when six policemen with clubs and drawn revolvers manage to get him away and jail him for safekeeping.

Mrs. Lincoln in the box sees her husband seated in the rocking chair, his head slumped forward. With little moaning cries she springs toward him and with her hands keeps him from tumbling to the floor. Major Rathbone has shouted for a surgeon, has run out of the box into the narrow hallway, and with one arm

House where Lincoln died.

bleeding and burning with pain he fumbles to unfasten the bar between wall and door panel. An usher from the outside tries to help him. They get the bar loose. Back of the usher is a jam of people. He holds them back, allowing only one man to enter, a young-looking man with mustache and sideburns, 23-year-old Charles A. Leale, assistant surgeon, U.S. Volunteers.

Dr. Leale holds Mrs. Lincoln's outstretched hand while she cries "Oh, Doctor! Is he dead? Can he recover? Will you take charge of him? Do what you can for him. Oh, my dear husband! my dear husband!" He soothes her a little; he will do all that can possibly be done.

The man in the chair at first scrutiny seems to be dead, eyes closed, no certainty he is breathing. Dr. Leale with help from others lifts the man from the chair and moves him to a lying position on the floor. Dr. Leale lifts the eyelids and sees evidence of a brain injury. He rapidly passes the separated ringers of both hands through the blood-matted hair of the head, finding a wound and removing a clot of blood, which relieves pressure on the brain and brings shallow breathing and a weak pulse.

Dr. Leale bends over, puts a knee at each side of the body, and tries to start the breathing apparatus, attempts to stimulate respiration by putting his two fingers into the throat and pressing down and out on the base of the tongue to free the larynx of secretion. Dr. Charles Sabin Taft, an army surgeon lifted from the stage into the box, now arrives. Another physician, Dr. Albert F. A. King, arrives. Leale asks them each to manipulate an arm while he presses upward on the diaphragm and elsewhere to stimulate heart action. The body responds with an improvement in the pulse and the irregular breathing.

Dr. Leale is sure, however, that with the shock and prostration the body has undergone, more must now be done to keep life going. And as he told it later: "I leaned forcibly forward directly over his body, thorax to thorax, face to face, and several times drew in a long breath, then forcibly breathed directly into his mouth and nostrils, which expanded his lungs and improved his respirations. After waiting a moment I placed my ear over his thorax and found the action of the heart improving. I arose to the erect kneeling posture, then watched for a short time and saw that the President could continue independent breathing and that instant death would not occur. I then pronounced my diagnosis and prognosis: 'His wound is mortal; it is impossible for him to recover.' "

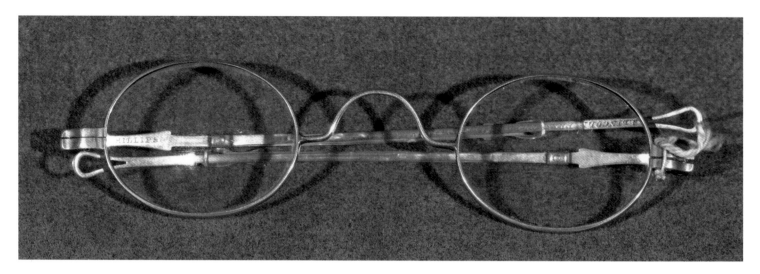

Lincoln's spectacles found in his pocket after death.

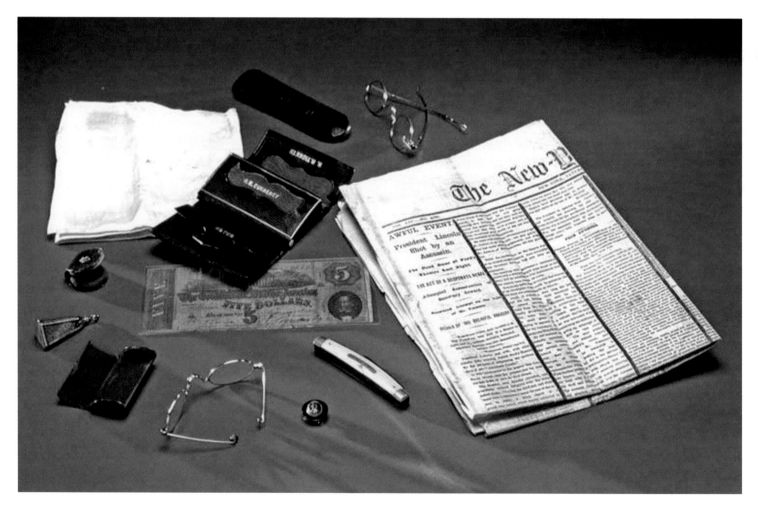

Lincoln realia (contents of Lincoln's pockets) after his death.

Brandy and water arrive. Dr. Leale slowly pours a small quantity into the President's mouth. It is swallowed and retained. While they are waiting for the President to gain strength, wrote Leale later, Laura Keene "appealed to me to allow her to hold the President's head. I granted this request, and she sat on the floor of the box and held his head in her lap. We decided that the President could now be moved to a house where we might place him on a bed in safety."

Four soldiers from Thompson's Independent Battery C, Pennsylvania Light Artillery, lift the President by the trunk and legs, Dr. Taft carrying the right shoulder, Dr. King the left shoulder, Dr. Leale the head. They come to the door of the box. Dr. Leale sees the passageway packed with people. He calls out twice, "Guards, clear the passage!" A captain goes into action with troopers. They show muskets, bayonets, sabers. "Clear out!" rings the repeated order. "Clear out!" they cry to the curiosity seekers, and to some who hesitate and still insist on blocking passage. "Clear out, you sons of bitches!"

Then the solemn little group with their precious freight carried headfirst moves slowly through a space lined by protecting soldiers. At the stair head they shift so the feet are carried first. Two more soldiers join the original four in holding the President and moving him. As they go out of the door of the theater Dr. Leale is again asked if the President can be taken to the White House and answers, "No, the President would die on the way."

Packing Tenth Street straight across from the front door of Ford's Theatre is a crowd so massed that there is no hope of a path for those carrying the President unless something is done. Leale asks the captain to clear a passage to the nearest house opposite. The captain draws a sword, commands the people to make an opening; they move back, and the procession begins its slow crossing. Several times they stop while Dr. Leale removes the newly gathered blood clots on the head wound. A barrier of men forms to keep back the crowds on each side of an open space leading to the house. Now comes the report that this house is closed. At the next house, Mr. Petersen's, No. 453 Tenth Street, Dr. Leale sees a man standing at the door with a lighted candle, beckoning them to come in. "This we did," ran Leale's account, "not having been interrupted in the slightest by the throngs in the street; but a number of the excited populace followed us into the house."

There they lay their stricken Friend of Man in the rented room of William Clark, a boarder in the house of William Petersen—on a plain wooden bed—at about 10:45 o'clock, somewhat less perhaps than a half-hour after the moment the trigger of the little eight-ounce derringer was pulled.

The President lies on his back in the center of the humble walnut bed. Now Dr. Leale holds the face upward to keep the head from rolling to either side. The long knee elevation troubles Leale. He orders the foot of the bed removed. Dr. Taft and Dr. King report it is a fixture. Leale requests it be broken. This it seems cannot be done with any satisfaction. Leale then has Lincoln moved so he lies diagonally across the bed and, propped with extra pillows, is gently slanted with a rest for head and shoulders, finally in a position of repose.

On white sheets lies the unconscious patient still in frock coat and long boots. Under the white sheets is a cornhusk mattress resting on rope lacings. The room fills with anxious people. Leale calls an officer, directs him to open a window, and to order all except the doctors and friends to leave.

After a short rest for the patient Leale decides to make a thorough physical examination to see if there are other wounds. He requests all except surgeons to leave the room. The captain reports all have left but Mrs. Lincoln, with whom he does not feel authorized to speak. Leale makes his wish known to Mrs. Lincoln and she leaves at once. They undress the patient, search the body from head to foot, finding no other wound. The lower extremities are cold; Leale sends a hospital steward for hot water and hot blankets. He sends for a large mustard plaster; this is applied over the solar plexus and to every inch of the entire anterior surface of the body.

The breath comes hard; pulse 44, feeble; the left pupil much contracted, the right widely dilated; both eyes totally insensible to light. The President is completely unconscious, an occasional sigh escaping with the labored breath.

In a nearby room Mrs. Lincoln has the company of Miss Harris, of several women who have arrived, and of the Reverend Dr. Gurley. Major Rathbone has fainted from loss of blood and is taken home.

At intervals Mrs. Lincoln is notified she may visit her husband. Once she cries to him, "Live! you must live!" and again, "Bring Tad—he will speak to Tad—he loves him so."

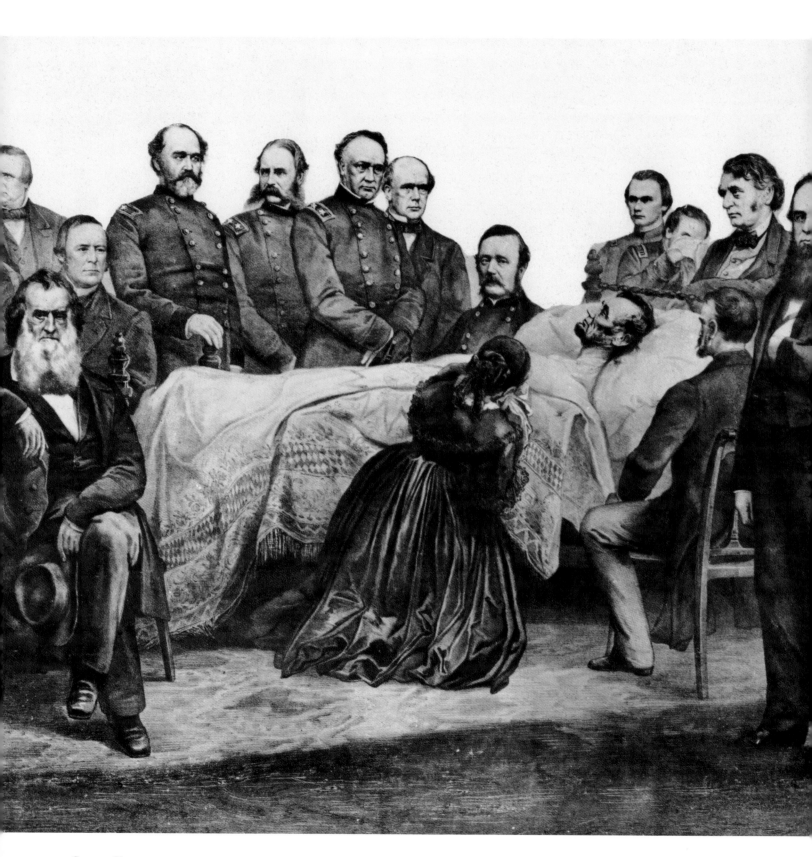

Dr. Robert K. Stone, the Lincoln family physician, arrives, followed soon by Surgeon General Joseph K. Barnes and his assistant Dr. Charles H. Crane, who take charge. Dr. Leale reports to his chief what he has done. At 2 A.M. Dr. Barnes tries to locate the bullet and after a time further exploration for the bullet is considered of no avail.

In the White House Robert Lincoln and John Hay sit gossiping pleasantly, Nicolay away at the Fort Sumter flag-raising. The doors burst open and several voices at once tell them the news. They run downstairs, take a carriage, cannot quite believe what they have heard. Slowly their carriage plows a path through the gathering thousands of people around Tenth Street. Dr. Stone gravely and tenderly tells Robert the worst: there is no hope. He chokes. The tears run down his face. After a time he recovers and does his best during hours of the night at comforting his mother.

At about the same hour and minute of the clock that the President is shot in Ford's Theatre a giant of a young man rides on a big one-eyed bay horse to the door of the Seward house on Lafayette Square, gets off his horse, rings the doorbell, says he is a messenger from the attending physician and has a package of medicine that must be personally delivered to the sickroom of the Secretary of State. The servant at the door tries to stop the young man, who enters and goes up the stairs, suddenly to turn in a furious rush on Fred Seward, beating him on the head with the pistol, tearing the scalp, fracturing the skull and battering the pistol to pieces.

Young Seward grapples with the intruder, and in their scuffling the two of them come to the Secretary's room and fall together through the door. There Fred Seward fades out and for days knows nothing, in a stupor of unconsciousness. The Secretary's daughter and a soldier-nurse, Sergeant George T. Robinson, spring from their chairs. The murder-bent young giant knocks them right and left, gives Robinson a knife thrust, then rushes to the bed where the Secretary of State has lain nearly two weeks with a steel frame about the head and face. He stabs over and again at the throat of the sick man, delivers three ugly gashes in the cheek and neck. The steel frame foils a death

Lincoln's wife at his bedside.

gash. And the quick wit or odd luck of the victim still further foils him; the Secretary of State rolls off between the bed and the wall.

Now the stranger in the house hurls himself down the stairs, slashes an attendant on the way, is out of the front door unhurt, leaps into saddle and rides out Vermont Avenue toward an eastern suburb. Behind him he has left a quiet home transformed into a battlefield hospital, five persons bleeding from ghastly wounds, failing of death for any of them. Behind him too he has left a bloodstained knife, the battered pistol and his slouch felt hat.

Secretary Welles is just falling asleep about 10:30 when his wife calls him. His messenger James Smith has arrived, excited, saying the President has been shot. In the Petersen house at the bedside of "the giant sufferer" Welles' outstanding impressions were: "He had been stripped of his clothes. His large arms, which were occasionally exposed, were of a size which one would scarce have expected from his spare appearance. His slow, full respiration lifted the clothes with each breath that he took. His features were calm and striking. I had never seen them appear to better advantage than for the first hour, perhaps, that I was there. After that, his right eye began to swell and that part of his face became discolored."

One by one the other Cabinet members arrive till all are in the Petersen house except Seward and McCulloch. Vice-President Andrew Johnson comes early for a brief visit.

The one man dominant in the house is Edwin McMasters Stanton. He seems to have lived for this night, for the exercise of the faculties on which he prided himself. Over Washington wild rumors were running that a new uprising of the Confederacy was breaking, a city guerrilla warfare—that secretly armed secessionists were to swarm from their hiding places, take strategic points, and make a last desperate stand for the Confederate cause. "Stanton," wrote one of his friends, "instantly assumed charge of everything near and remote, civil and military." He ordered troops to keep clear the spaces around the house, to let no one enter the house except high Government officers and persons on special business. He sent for the District of Columbia Chief Justice David K. Cartter, who arrived soon and in an adjoining room began taking testimony, with a shorthand reporter present, of persons who might have evidence bearing on the high crime.

To Charles A. Dana, Assistant Secretary of War, who could write shorthand, Stanton dictated telegrams to all parts of the country.

Stanton sent for several army officers to act as aides; directed General Thomas M. Vincent to take charge of affairs in the Petersen house; telegraphed to General Grant at Philadelphia that Lincoln had been shot and to return at once to Washington; telegraphed to Chief Kennedy of New York to send on his best detectives immediately; wrote and dispatched a note to Chief Justice Chase, saying the President could not live and to be ready to administer the oath of office to Vice-President Johnson; notified the Vice-President that the President was dying; and sent to the country and the people bulletin after bulletin concerning the tragedy and the President's condition. Thus, wrote a friend of Stanton, "he continued throughout the night, acting as president, secretary of war, secretary of state, commander-in-chief, comforter, and dictator."

As daylight began to slant through the windows, with its white clarity making the yellow gas jets and lamplights look garish and outdone, it became evident the President was sinking. Surgeon General Barnes, seated near the head of the bed, occasionally held his finger over the carotid artery to note its pulsation. Dr. Stone sat on the edge of the foot of the bed. Dr. Leale held the President's right hand, with an extended forefinger on the pulse.

At 5 A.M. the oozing from the wound ceased entirely and the breathing became stertorous and labored. On the haggard faces of the silent ones circled about, it was written more than once they thought the end had come.

A cold rain began falling. Out of a monotonous sky inexorably gray a cold rain began falling. A little before seven Welles went into the room where a warm Friend of Man was going cold, moving into the final chill that all men at the last must know. "His wife soon after made her last visit to him. The death-struggle had begun. Robert, his son, stood with several others at the head of the bed. He bore himself well, but on two occasions gave way to overpowering grief and sobbed aloud, turning his head and leaning on the shoulder of Senator Sumner."

The last breath was drawn at 21 minutes and 55 seconds past 7 A.M. and the last heart beat flickered at 22 minutes and

10 seconds past the hour on Saturday, April 15, 1865. Dr. Barnes' finger was over the carotid artery, Dr. Leale's finger was on the right wrist pulse, and Dr. Taft's hand was over the cardium when the great heart made its final contraction.

The Pale Horse had come. To a deep river, to a far country, to a by-and-by whence no man returns, had gone the child of Nancy Hanks and Tom Lincoln, the wilderness boy who found far lights and tall rainbows to live by, whose name even before he died had become a legend inwoven with men's struggle for freedom the world over.

The voice of Phineas D. Gurley: "Let us pray." Kneeling at the bedside, his sonorous tones shook with submission to the Everlasting, to the Heavenly Father, with pleading that the dead man's country and family be comforted.

The widow was told. She came in and threw herself with uncontrollable moaning on the body. When later she went away the cry broke from her, "O my God, and I have given my husband to die!"

Over the drawn face muscles Dr. Leale moved a smoothing hand, took two coins from his pocket, placed them over the eyelids, and drew a white sheet over the face. Over the worn features had come, wrote John Hay, "a look of unspeakable peace." Stanton, it was said afterward, pronounced the words: "Now he belongs to the ages." By his wish this became legend.

The Cabinet, with Seward and McCulloch absent, met in the back parlor, arranged to notify the Vice-President and the Chief Justice of the Supreme Court, and to meet again at noon in the room of the Secretary of the Treasury and take action with the newly sworn-in President toward "preserving and promoting the public tranquillity."

Now there was a tincture of deep violet given to the Gettysburg phrases: "We cannot consecrate—we cannot hallow—this ground." Now there was a snow-white fabric crossed with sunset vermilion around the words written to the Boston widow woman: "The solemn pride that must be yours to have laid so costly a sacrifice upon the altar of freedom."

Death-Bed of Lincoln.

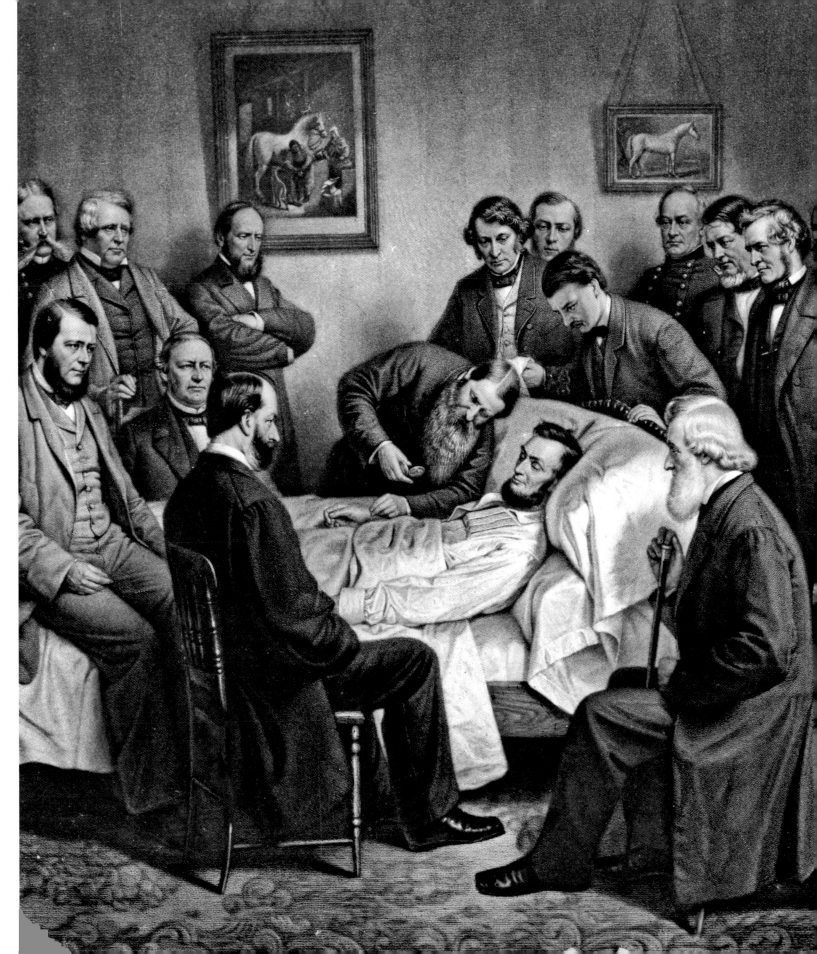

CHAPTER 62

SHOCK—THE ASSASSIN—
A STRICKEN PEOPLE

*Portrait of John Wilkes
Booth, ca. 1862.*

SHOCK—THE ASSASSIN—A STRICKEN PEOPLE

T HE TOLLING of the bells began in Washington. Likewise in New York, Boston, Chicago, Springfield, Peoria, metropolitan centers and crossroads villages, the day had tolling bells hour on hour, flags at half-mast, the gay bunting, red, white and blue festoons brought down and crape or any fold of black put out and hung up for sign of sorrow.

Out on the Illinois prairie of Coles County they went to a farmhouse and told the news to an old woman who answered: "I knowed when he went away he'd never come back alive." This was Sally Bush Lincoln, prepared for her sorrow which came that day.

Edwin Booth, the world's foremost Shakespearian actor, lay abed in Boston the morning of April 15 when a servant came in and told him that his brother, John Wilkes Booth, had shot and killed the President. And as Edwin Booth related it to Joseph Jefferson, his mind "accepted the fact at once," for he thought to himself that his brother "was capable of just such a wild and foolish action." Edwin Booth added: "It was just as if I was struck on the forehead by a hammer." To General Grant's secretary, his old friend Adam Badeau, Edwin Booth on Sunday, April 16, wrote, "Abraham Lincoln was my President for, in pure admiration of his noble career and his Christian principles, I did what I never did before—I *voted* and *for* him!"

The man hunters and the fugitive John Wilkes Booth were second in national interest only to the death of Lincoln. Who was this Booth? Out of a mediocre fame he had now wrapped the letters of his name with a weird infamy. His own Southern heroes almost universally repudiated him as a madman, one who fought foul. And he was that—a lunatic—a diabolically cunning athlete, swordsman, dead shot, horseman, actor. Now his face and name were published with a War Department promise of $50,000 for his capture dead or alive.

John Wilkes Booth was one of ten children born to Mr. and Mrs. Junius Brutus Booth on a big wooded farm 25 miles from Baltimore. Junius Brutus Booth seemed to be a man filled with a compassion that often shook his controls and ran over into the pathetic, the ridiculous, even the comic. When he died in 1852 his feet had wandered before all shrines and altars and paid homage. He was brought up an Episcopalian; he made it a custom to keep some of the sacred days of the Koran; Catholic priests claimed him for one of their own because of his familiarity with their faith; and in synagogues he had been taken for a Jew when he joined fluently in their worship in their own tongue; Masons buried him in a Baptist vault. He was widely accepted as a figure in American cultural life, the supreme Shakespeare player.

The son, John Wilkes Booth, had room to play, a 200-acre wooded farm, an oak-floored bedroom facing the east and the sunrise, on the walls deer antlers, swords, pistols, daggers, a bookcase holding Bulwer, Marryat, Byron, Shakespeare. Over the father's dark spells and grand whims, over Edwin's impenetrable melancholy, over the failings of others of the family, the mother and loyal Asia had no such brooding near to anguish as they gave the boy and youth Wilkes. To the hanging of John Brown went J. Wilkes Booth as a lieutenant in the Richmond Grays. Though he hated John Brown's cause, he was fascinated and spellbound by the dramatic, lone-handed audacity of Old Ossawatomie.

His first stage successes came in Southern cities. As the Southern States moved into secession he moved North as a player. William Winter saw the young star's acting as "raw, crude and much given to boisterous declamation." He delighted in leaps and bounds while acting. The Baltimore *Sun* critic ticketed Wilkes Booth "the Gymnastic actor." Over a piece of scenery more than five feet high, wrote W. J. Ferguson, he saw Wilkes Booth jump "with little effort." These unexpected feats were accepted as part of a "dashing buoyancy" natural to him. He was the idol of women. They would rave of him, his voice, his hair, his eyes.

Portrait of President Andrew Johnson.
Lithographed by Bingham & Dodd, 1866.

From '61 continuously as he traveled the North he spoke as openly as was convenient for the Confederate cause.

In '64 when he was filling fewer engagements because of a failing voice, Booth seemed to have a deepening sense of guilt over keeping himself in safety and comfort while the war raged and the Southern cause sank lower. His broodings took two directions. He would perform a deed saving the Southern cause while at the same time giving the world a breath-taking dramatic performance. In August '64 he won two recruits to "the enterprise," as they termed it.

Samuel Arnold and Michael O'Laughlin, two former schoolmates of Booth at St. Timothy's Hall, after two years in the Confederate Army, considered themselves "engaged" with Booth as leader. The "enterprise," worked out in their talks, designed the "capture" or "abduction" of the President. Having gotten their prisoner out of Washington down to Richmond, they would exchange him for enough Confederate prisoners to win the war.

Most of the time until April 14, 1865, Booth lived in Washington, checking in and out of his National Hotel quarters, taking many trips on errands whose purpose he kept secret. He studied Lincoln's ways and habits, particularly as a theatergoer. At both Grover's Theatre and Ford's, Booth was at home, receiving his mail at Ford's. The entries and exits of these theaters knew him, every door, corner, hall, lobby, passageway, familiar to him. To the stock actors, stagehands, front-office employees, he was a distinguished figure whose nod they valued.

In November he rode a horse over Maryland and Virginia south of Washington, studied the roads, paths and hiding places by day or night. To Asia, in whom he had every trust, he gave an envelope later found to contain some bonds and oil stock certificates—and a letter. This gave the key to his scrambled brain, his vanity and self-importance, his desire to show the South that he was a Confederate hero even though they no longer loved him or cared about him. He referred in passing to his plan for making "a prisoner of this man, to whom she [the South] owes so much of her misery."

Samuel Arnold. Photo by Alexander Gardner, 1865.

Portrait of John Wilkes Booth, ca. 1862.

Michael O'Laughlin. Photo by Alexander Gardner, 1865.

The letter indicated a "master mind," of a sort, holding sway over a little band of schemers and hopers meeting in a boardinghouse on H Street between Sixth and Seventh in Washington. They included a drugstore clerk, 20 years old,

David E. Herold, out of work and seeking a job when Booth found him. Another was a hump-shouldered, scraggly-bearded fellow, dark, sly, fierce of looks though a coward in a pinch; he was of German descent, a carriage-maker at Port Tobacco, Virginia. Booth's promises of gold brought him in.

George A. Atzerodt. Then there was a tall, broad-shouldered 20-year-old athlete joining ox and tiger in his frame, a veteran of Antietam and Chancellorsville, wounded at Gettysburg. In January '65 this youth after nearly four years of hard righting at bloody salients had despaired of the Confederacy and deserted, happening in Baltimore when he was homeless, penniless, in rags, without money to buy food, to meet Booth, finding sympathy, praise, new clothes and money. This was the man known as Lewis Paine (Lewis Thornton Powell), whose entry into the Seward home had resulted in five persons stabbed and the Secretary of State narrowly missing a death wound. The keeper of the boardinghouse where the plotters met was the widow of a Confederate informer and dispatch-carrier, Mary E. Surratt.

Daily Mrs. Surratt saw her boarders acquainting themselves with weapons, holding vague whispered conversations, telling her nothing definite, intimating they would save the sinking Southern cause. The air had a touch of terror. Daily she crossed herself and more often hurried to church to pray.

Mrs. Surratt's son John H., Jr., at first opposed and then gave way to Booth's eloquence. Just old enough to vote, six feet tall, slender but powerful, blond, with eyes sunken under a bulging forehead, he knew his footing more surely than the others. He quit his job as an Adams Express Company clerk to join Booth. With him came one Louis J. Weichmann, a wavering, suspicious

David E. Herold. Photo by Alexander Gardner, 1865.

George A. Atzerodt. Photo by Alexander Gardner, 1865.

Mrs. Surratt (Photographic copy of drawing).

SHOCK—THE ASSASSIN—A STRICKEN PEOPLE

and careful young man who had been Surratt's chum for two years at college when Surratt studied for the priesthood. Weichmann had been a schoolteacher in Washington, later getting a clerkship in the office of the commissary general of prisoners. Of the two former Maryland schoolmates of Booth, Samuel Arnold was a farm hand who hated farm work, rather lazy, a student of books with an unmanageable vocabulary; Michael O'Laughlin was a Baltimore livery-stable worker, fairly good at handling horses and better yet at carrying liquor. The crew filled the seven bedrooms of Mrs. Surratt's boardinghouse. Some of them subsisted on money furnished by Booth, and all except Weichmann were led and lighted by Booth's stratagems and wild-fire eloquence over the glory awaiting them all for their service to the Confederacy.

April 8 Washington is ablaze with flags and the North howling joy over the surrender of Lee's army. Paine, Atzerodt and Herold are left to Booth, awaiting his wish and whim. The evening of April 11 Booth is with Paine on the White House lawn near the window where the President speaks. He is shaken with rage at the President's saying the elective franchise, the ballot, should be given to the colored man, "the very intelligent, and . . . those who serve our cause as soldiers." He urges Paine to shoot the speaker, Paine protesting the risk is too great. The two walk away, Booth muttering, "That is the last speech he will ever make."

On April 14 Booth writes to his mother a letter dated "2 A.M." of that day. "Dearest Mother:" he begins. "I know you hardly expect a letter from me. Excuse brevity; am in haste. With best love to you all I am your affectionate son ever. John." That was all. To his mother, to his brother Edwin, to such friends as John T. Ford and John Deery, no inklings of a deed and a motive for which he is willing to pay with his life. The word "assassin," several commentators were to note, took root from the word "hashish" or "hasheesh," an East Indian drug that inflates the self-importance of the one eating it.

John H. Surratt, son of Mary Surratt.

Between 11 and 12 o'clock of Good Friday morning, April 14, Booth comes to Ford's Theatre for his mail, hears that a messenger from the White House has engaged a box for the President that evening. He goes into action, hires a bay mare for himself to be ready at four o'clock in the afternoon. He calls on Mrs. Surratt just as she with Weichmann is leaving for Surrattsville, handing her a package holding a field glass to be delivered at a tavern there. To the empty Ford's Theatre he goes, seeing the two boxes thrown into one, the rocking chair brought for the President's corner of the box. He inspects locks, bores a hole through the box door, digs a niche in the plastered brick wall.

At seven in the evening Booth leaves his room at the National Hotel. In passing he asks the hotel clerk if he is going to Ford's Theatre this evening. The clerk hadn't thought about it. "There will be some fine acting there tonight," says Booth; he hurries to the Herndon House and sees Paine. They arrange their timing:

George A. Atzerodt. Photo by Alexander Gardner, 1865.

J. Wilkes Booth, ca. 1860.

at the same hour and minute of the clock that night Paine is to kill the Secretary of State and Booth is to kill the President. Atzerodt, run the further plans, is to kill Vice-President Johnson.

Herold is to guide Paine to the Seward home and then hurry to the support of Atzerodt. On the street Booth talks with Atzerodt, who has heard of the righting nerve of Andy Johnson and now tells Booth he enlisted for abduction but not killing. Atzerodt begs and whimpers. Booth storms at him and curses him.

Atzerodt, armed with a revolver he knows he can never use, drifts away, never to see Booth again. Early in the morning on foot headed toward his boyhood home 22 miles west of Washington, in Georgetown pawning his revolver for $10, was a muddled wanderer, one of the only three men in the world who could have told the police beforehand to the hour of Booth's intentions that night.

At a stable near Ford's and close to ten o'clock Booth, Paine and Herold get on their horses and part, Booth to go to Ford's,

David E. Herold. Photo by Alexander Gardner, 1865.

Lewis Payne Powell, alias Lewis Payne, who attacked Hon. W.H. Seward. Photo by Alexander Gardner, 1865.

SHOCK—THE ASSASSIN—A STRICKEN PEOPLE

Herold to guide Paine to the Seward house. At the back door of Ford's Booth calls for the theater carpenter Spangler to hold his horse, enters and goes down under the stage, out of a private door into an alley and therefrom to the street in front of the theater. Spangler meantime calls the door boy John Peanuts to hold Booth's horse. Peanuts says he has to tend his door, Spangler saying if anything goes wrong to lay the blame on him. Out front on the street Booth sees the President's carriage at the curb, a crowd of curiosity seekers on the sidewalk, some of them waiting to have a look at the presidential party when it leaves the theater. The play is more than half over and a stir of voices and laughter drifts out from the windows to the lighted and cheerful street.

Booth walks past the doorkeeper Buckingham and with a pleasant smile and "You'll not want a ticket from *me?*" asks the time, and is pointed to the clock in the lobby. He requests a chew of tobacco from Buckingham, who draws a plug from which Booth takes a bite, as customary a proceeding as gentlemen of a previous generation exchanging snuff. On the street an actor who is to sing a new patriotic song asks the time and the theater costumer steps into the lobby and, looking at a large clock on the wall, calls out, "Ten minutes past ten." Booth opens a door from the lobby into the parquet, takes note of the presidential box, whether there are any visitors. He has seen *Our American Cousin* played and has calculated to fine points the strategic moment for his deed. Soon only one actor will be out front on the stage, only a woman and a boy in the wings. A laugh from the audience usually follows the exit of two ladies, a loud enough laugh perhaps to smother any unusual noises in a box.

Booth goes up the stairs leading to the dress circle, picks his way among chairs behind an outer row of seats, reaches the door of the passageway leading to the presidential box. He leans against the wall, takes a cool survey of the house. Booth opens the door into the narrow hallway leading to the box, steps in, closes the door, fixes the bar in the mortised niche and against the door panel. On soft tiger feet he moves toward the box door, puts an eye to the hole bored through the door, sees his victim is precisely where he wishes and as he had planned. Softly he

Howard's Stable, Washington, DC, where Booth hired the horse on which he escaped.

THE LATE RESIDENCE OF MRS. SURRATT, 541 EIGHTH STREET, WASHINGTON.
[Sketched by E. A. Perkins.]

Robert E. Lee after the war.

swings the door back and with his brass derringer pistol in the right hand and a long dagger in the other, he steps into the box.

Up till that instant any one of a million ordinary conceivable circumstances of fate could have intervened and made the next moment impossible. Yet not one of those potential circumstances arrived. What happened that next moment became world history—not because of him who did what was done, but because of the name, life and works of the victim of the deed.

Residence of the late Mrs. Surratt,
541 Eight St. Washington, DC.

Edward Spangler. Photo by Alexander Gardner, 1865.

Copy of Printed Reward Poster "$100,000 Reward…"

War Department Washington, April 20, 1865,

$100,000 REWARD

THE MURDERER

Of our late beloved President, Abraham Lincoln,

IS STILL AT LARGE.

$50,000 REWARD

Will be paid by this Department for his apprehension, in addition to any reward offered by Municipal Authorities or State Executives.

$25,000 REWARD

Will be paid for the apprehension of G. A. Atzerot, sometimes called "Port Tobacco," one of Booth's Accomplices.

$25,000 REWARD

Will be paid for the apprehension of David C. Harold, another of Booth's accomplices.

LIBERAL REWARDS will be paid for any information that shall conduce to the arrest of either of the above-named criminals, or their accomplices.

All persons harboring or secreting the said persons, or either of them, or aiding or assisting their concealment or escape, will be treated as accomplices in the murder the President and the attempted assassination of the Secretary of State, and shall be subject to trial before a Military Commission and the punishment of DEATH.

Let the stain of innocent blood be removed from the land by the arrest and punishment of the murderers.

All good citizens are exhorted to aid public justice on this occasion. Every man should consider his own conscience charged with this solemn duty, and rest neither night nor day until it be accomplished.

EDWIN M. STANTON, Secretary of War.

DESCRIPTIONS.—BOOTH is Five Feet 7 or 8 inches high, slender build, high forehead, black hair, black eyes, and wears a heavy black moustache.
ATZERODT is Five Feet 6 or 7 inches high, has dark short, curly hair, and a short thick black moustache. He had a light goatee, and his whiskers were much thinner on the side of his face. He has a dark skin, and very dark eyes. He was dressed in a suit of greyish dark color, and wore a gray sack coat and a black kossuth hat. He had common coarse boots, with pants outside of them, and wore spurs.
HAROLD is a little chunky man, quite a youth, and wears a very thin moustache.

Reward poster with portraits of Surrat, Booth and Harold.

SURRAT.   BOOTH.   HAROLD.

War Department, Washington, April 20, 1865,

$100,000 REWARD!

THE MURDERER

Of our late beloved President, Abraham Lincoln,

IS STILL AT LARGE.

$50,000 REWARD

Will be paid by this Department for his apprehension, in addition to any reward offered by Municipal Authorities or State Executives.

$25,000 REWARD

Will be paid for the apprehension of JOHN H. SURRATT, one of Booth's Accomplices.

$25,000 REWARD

Will be paid for the apprehension of David C. Harold, another of Booth's accomplices.

LIBERAL REWARDS will be paid for any information that shall conduce to the arrest of either of the above-named criminals, or their accomplices.

All persons harboring or secreting the said persons, or either of them, or aiding or assisting their concealment or escape, will be treated as accomplices in the murder of the President and the attempted assassination of the Secretary of State, and shall be subject to trial before a Military Commission and the punishment of DEATH.

Let the stain of innocent blood be removed from the land by the arrest and punishment of the murderers.

All good citizens are exhorted to aid public justice on this occasion. Every man should consider his own conscience charged with this solemn duty, and rest neither night nor day until it be accomplished.

EDWIN M. STANTON, Secretary of War.

DESCRIPTIONS.—BOOTH is Five Feet 7 or 8 inches high, slender build, high forehead, black hair, black eyes, and wears a heavy black moustache.

JOHN H. SURRAT is about 5 feet, 9 inches. Hair rather thin and dark; eyes rather light; no beard. Would weigh 145 or 150 pounds. Complexion rather pale and clear, with color in his cheeks. Wore light clothes of fine quality. Shoulders square; cheek bones rather prominent; chin narrow; ears projecting at the top; forehead rather low and square, but broad. Parts his hair on the right side; neck rather long. His lips are firmly set. A slim man.

DAVID C. HAROLD is five feet six inches high, hair dark, eyes dark, eyebrows rather heavy, full face, nose short, hand short and fleshy, feet small, instep high, round bodied, naturally quick and active, slightly closes his eyes when looking at a person.

NOTICE.—In addition to the above, State and other authorities have offered rewards amounting to almost one hundred thousand dollars, making an aggregate of about TWO HUNDRED THOUSAND DOLLARS.

And the one man whose sworn duty it was to have intercepted the assassin—John F. Parker? There were charges brought against him by Superintendent A. C. Richards of the Metropolitan Police Force, "that Said Parker was detailed to attend and protect the President Mr. Lincoln, that while the President was at Ford's Theatre on the night of the 14th of April last, Said Parker allowed a man to enter the President's private Box and Shoot the President." But there was no trial on these charges, and it was not till three years later that Parker was to be dishonorably dismissed from the police force for sleeping on his beat.

In company with Senator Ben Wade went Congressman Henry Laurens Dawes to greet in the Kirkwood House the newly sworn-in President Andrew Johnson. And Wade's greeting, as Congressman Dawes told it to his daughter Anna, ran: "Mr. Johnson, I thank God that you are here. Lincoln had too much of the milk of human kindness to deal with these damned rebels. Now they will be dealt with according to their deserts." This feeling ran through a caucus of the Republican party radicals meeting that day to consider, as Congressman George Julian phrased it, "a line of policy less conciliatory than that of Mr. Lincoln."

Of the new President little was known, and from the Judge Advocate's office, at headquarters of the Department of the South, Hilton Head, South Carolina, John C. Gray, Jr., wrote to John C. Ropes: "He may turn out more of a man than we hope.

The single event of an assassination swept away a thousand foundations carefully laid and protected by the living Lincoln. A long series of delicate roots of human relationships the living Lincoln had nursed and guarded were torn up in a night.

The New York *Herald* on Easter Sunday, April 16, editorialized on the press as no factor of enlightenment, no sobering influence at all. It said directly that newspaper editors shared in the guilt of leading an assassin toward his bloody work. "It is as clear as day that the real origin of this dreadful act is to be found in the fiendish and malignant spirit developed and fostered by the rebel press North and South. That press has, in the most devilish manner, urged men to the commission of this very deed."

Sherman on his way to a conference with the Confederate General Joseph E. Johnston had a decoded telegram handed

Portrait of John Wilkes Booth with devil whispering in his ear.

him from Stanton: "President Lincoln was murdered about 10 o'clock last night." Sherman pledged the operator to say nothing to anyone of the telegram. When Sherman and Johnston sat alone in a small farmhouse, Sherman handed over the telegram. Johnston read. On his forehead slowly came sweat "in large drops," as Sherman watched him, Sherman remembering so clearly and for so long a time afterward how one of the greatest of Confederate captains said that "Mr. Lincoln was the best friend they had" and the assassination was "the greatest possible calamity to the South." In the surrender terms they were to sign, Sherman's motive, according to his keenest interpreter, probably

Apotheosis of Lincoln.
By Joseph Boggs Beale.

SHOCK—THE ASSASSIN—A STRICKEN PEOPLE

ranged around a thought: "Lincoln is dead. I will make his kind of a peace." When later the dread news was given to Sherman's army, many were ready to burn the city of Raleigh to the ground. Logan made speeches against it, other officers intervened, and discipline prevailed.

Now the gentle sister Asia Booth was taken from her Philadelphia home to a Washington prison. Now the brother Edwin announced he would play no more drama for the American public—not for years, if ever again. Now the pursuit of the fugitive Jefferson Davis was urged more furiously by Stanton.

The fugitive Jefferson Davis wrote later of his dominant feeling: "The news [of the assassination] was to me very sad, for I felt that Mr. Johnson was a malignant man, and General Lee at first refused to hear the details of the murder . . . He said that when he dispossessed himself of the command of the rebel forces he kept in mind President Lincoln's benignity, and surrendered as much to the latter's goodness as to Grant's artillery. The General said that he regretted Mr. Lincoln's death as much as any man in the North."

Yet Booth had not entirely miscalculated. A small extremist minority element North and South exulted over his deed. New York, the major draft-riot city, saw more of this tumult than other places. From coast to coast, however, there was a Copperhead minority to whom Booth was a hero. The Lincoln-haters at first had no notion of how crushed with grief, how exquisitely sensitive, were an overwhelming number of Lincoln loyalists.

The North was in grief. Everywhere the eye might turn hung the signs of this grief. The sermons, editorials, talk in streets, houses, saloons, railroad cars and streetcars, the black bunting and the crape—these were attempts to say something that could not be said. Men tried to talk about it and the words failed and they came back to silence. To say nothing was best. Lincoln was dead. Was there anything more to say? A great Friend of Man had suddenly vanished. Nothing could be done about it. Silence, grief and quiet resolves, these only were left for those who admired and loved and felt themselves close to a living presence that was one of them.

Thousands on thousands would remember as long as they lived the exact place where they had been standing or seated or lying down when the news came to them, recalling precisely in details and particulars where they were and what they were doing when the dread news arrived.

Newsboys at their stands cried no headlines, handed the damp sheets from the press to the buyers, one boy noticed as he brushed with his dirty hand the tears from his dirty cheeks. In thousands of stores the merchants told the clerks they would close for the day; in many schools the sobbing teacher could only tell the children, "Go home, there will be no school today." The father, the children, coming home unexpected, the mother asked what was wrong and heard "Mama, they've killed the President" or "Our President is dead." Then the family hunted up crape or black cloth for the front doorway.

Now Father Abraham was gone. Old Abe—there would be no more stories about him, alive there in the White House in Washington. Now there was a memory to keep. That was left—the life he had lived—the meanings and the lights of that life. This could not be taken away.

Like a vast sunset of flame and changing gold ending a day and punctuating a period of time their faraway friend at Washington had vanished into the overhead planets and the same constellations of mist that had taken that long roll call of soldiers no longer answering "Here" to the company sergeant calling the names.

In a million and more American households they sought words that might help and assuage. "The land mourneth, every family apart," ran one Easter Sunday text. Also "The steps of a good man are ordered by the Lord: and He delighteth in his way." Over doorways, in store windows, on arches spanning streets, ran the legend "And the Lord blessed Abraham in all things."

On one arch of crape and white over Broadway in New York ran the sentence "The great person, the great man, is the miracle of history."

CHAPTER 63

A Tree Is Best Measured when It's Down

A Tree Is Best Measured when It's Down

IN GREAT stone cathedrals of the cities, in modest frame churches of small towns, in little cabin churches at country crossroads, in hospital chapels and in at least one state prison, on Navy ships and in outdoor Army camp services, there were Easter Sunday sermons memorializing the dead President.

That Lincoln, without being an affiliated churchman, had by a natural reverence, without affectation, won his way to many hearts of the clergy was evident in pulpit tributes paid him. In Boston the Reverend Samuel K. Lothrop mourned: "Brethren, but one theme can command your attention today . . . I feel almost incompetent to direct your thoughts this morning, as I have scarcely been able for the last twenty-four hours to collect and guide my own. Language is impotent." Over and again were the parallels drawn of Lincoln and Christ in blood of atonement dying for mankind, of Lincoln having his Judas no less than Christ. "The last and costliest offering which God demanded has been taken," said the Reverend C. B. Crane of the South Baptist Church of Hartford, Connecticut. "Jesus Christ died for the world, Abraham Lincoln died for his country."

In scores of sermons before large congregations of the well-to-do and influential, radicals pressed the need for trials and hangings of Southern leaders. In the Protestant churches of Boston such clergymen were in a large majority of the pulpits. In other cities and communities, however, the clergy in the main humbly held themselves to spiritual ministration and kept out of politics. The Reverend Edward Everett Hale in his Unitarian Church in Boston intimated that in the passions of the hour, including his own, it behooved good men to think twice and speak slow: "I dare not trust myself to speak a word regarding this simple, godly, good, great man . . . To speak of him I must seek some other hour."

Henry Ward Beecher threw himself with a flowing vitality into the occasion. Nothing now of that remark of his in Charleston a few days earlier that Johnson's little finger was stronger than

Lincoln's loins. Beecher's Easter Sunday congregation in Plymouth Church, Brooklyn, filled all pews and added chairs in the aisles. Hundreds outside had failed to get in, scores had climbed up on the window sills to stand and listen. Beecher pointed to the murderer as one suckled and nursed in the slave system and its cruel and boisterous passions. Never would men forget that the slavery institution with its "mischiefs and monsters" had martyred one American President. "Never! while time lasts, while heaven lasts, while hell rocks and groans." The most often reprinted passage from sermons of this Easter Sunday was Beecher's closing. He pictured a coffined martyr moving in triumphal march, with cities and states as pallbearers, bells and cannon beating the hours. He intoned a dead march:

"Pass on, thou that has overcome! Your sorrows, oh people, are his peace! Your bells, and bands, and muffled drums, sound triumph in his ear. Wail and weep here; God made it echo joy and triumph there. Pass on!

"Four years ago, oh Illinois, we took from your midst an untried man, and from among the people. We return him to you a mighty conqueror. Not thine anymore, but the nation's; not ours, but the world's.

"Give him place, oh, ye prairies! In the midst of this great continent his dust shall rest, a sacred treasure to myriads who shall pilgrim to that shrine to kindle anew their zeal and patriotism.

"Ye winds that move over the mighty places of the West, chant his requiem! Ye people, behold a martyr whose blood, as so many articulate words, pleads for fidelity, for law, for liberty!"

In black-border crape typography, in editorial comment, letters, poetical effusions, the newspapers went along with the public grief. The weekly periodicals, the monthly magazines, these too wore crape in the national mood. An issue of the New York *Herald* with its remarkable extended biographical sketch and its thorough news coverage in Washington sold out 15 minutes after its arrival. The price for an obtainable copy in Washington next day was $10. Under the heading "The Great Crime—Abraham Lincoln's Place in History" the *Herald* on April 17 published a shrewd and lavish portrayal. He was a *new* figure. All other nations of the human family would study him "as the type man of a new dynasty of nation-rulers," holding that "the best and strongest rule for every intelligent people is a government to be created by the popular will, and choosing for itself the representative instrument who is to carry out its purposes." Gravely the *Herald*, naturally conservative though responsive to both property rights and human movements, noted: "The triumph of the democratic principle over the aristocratic in our recent contest is an assurance that time has revolved this old earth on which we live into a new and perhaps happier—perhaps sadder—era."

An old proverb known to woodsmen was fitting: "A tree is best measured when it's down." Often came the statement that over the world the whole civilized Family of Man shared in regrets or grief for the loss of a hero who belonged to humanity everywhere. The story of the living and actual Lincoln had come to an end. Now began the vast epic tale of the authentic Lincoln tradition mingled with legend, myth, folklore. Believers and atheists, those of fixed doctrine or the freethinkers—both were to argue he was theirs. Letters and pamphlets were to picture him as Freemason or Spiritualist, as Protestant or Catholic or Jew or having Negro blood in his veins. The teetotalers were to claim properly he was theirs because he never drank alcoholic liquors; the saloon crowd amid the sawdust and the spittoons were to say his stories alone put him in their class. Some had one sweeping claim: "He was humanity."

A letter to Mrs. Lincoln signed by Victoria Regina was deeply personal, woman to woman, the Queen saying: "No one can better appreciate than I can, who am myself *utterly broken-hearted* by the loss of my own beloved husband, who was the *light* of my life, my stay—*my all*—what your suffering must be; and I earnestly pray that you may be supported by Him to whom alone the sorely stricken can look for comfort." The House of Lords joined in an official address of sympathy to the American people.

In the French Senate and Chamber of Deputies imperialists and republicans joined in formal expressions of grief. A massive gold medal, bought with two-cent subscriptions from masses of people, was brought to the American Minister by a committee of liberals. It was for Mrs. Lincoln, with their message, "Tell her the heart of France is in that little box." In Germany many *Bunds* and

Walt Whitman, American poet, 1819-1892.

Vereins, workingmen's clubs, co-operative societies, labor journals, spoke their loss. In Austria one parliamentary deputy noted a human memory taking on "supernatural proportions," Lincoln becoming "a myth, a type of the ideal democracy."

In Sweden flags were ordered at half-mast on the ships in harbor at Göteborg and there were expressions as in the *Nya Daglig Allehanda* of Stockholm: "It is a beautiful death, and Lincoln forever will be surrounded by the rays of impeccable glory. The time for impartial judgment will not come for many years." And in the harbor of Stockholm flags hung at half-mast on all ships. Excitement and sorrow rooted partly in Swedish sentiment over the victory of the *Monitor*, designed by John Ericsson and carrying guns invented by Admiral John Adolph Dahlgren.

To the four corners of the earth began the spread of the Lincoln story and legend. What he seemed to mean was reached for, Russia's Leo Tolstoy saying Lincoln had become a world folk legend through "peculiar moral powers and greatness of character . . . He was what Beethoven was in music, Dante in poetry, Raphael in painting and Christ in the philosophy of life. If he had failed to become President, he would be no doubt just as great, but only God could appreciate it." Of all great national heroes and statesmen of history Tolstoy was to say to the journalist James Creelman, "Lincoln is the only real giant." He named heroes but they were lesser than Lincoln "in depth of feeling and in certain moral power." Mystic shadows and a bright aura gathered around Lincoln's memory for the famous Russian. "Lincoln was . . . a Christ in miniature, a saint of humanity whose name will live thousands of years in the legends of future generations. We are still too near his greatness, and so can hardly appreciate his divine power; but after a few centuries more our posterity will find him considerably bigger than we do."

Lincoln, in Emerson's analysis, grew according to need. In the whirlwind of the war he was "He is the true history of the American people in his time. Step by step he walked before them; slow with their slowness, quickening his march by theirs, the true representative of this continent; an entirely public man; father of his country."

Walt Whitman would have blossoms and green branches piled on the coffin—armfuls of roses fresh as the morning—in loaded arms sprigs of lilac just off the bushes—brought and poured on the coffin. He would study sea-blown cities and moving harbor ships, the changing lights of the Ohio River shores and the flashing bosom of the wide Missouri, far-spreading prairies covered with grass and corn—he would in his psalm bring these to the coffin. He would consider the miracle of light so gentle and soft-born from the most excellent sun so calm and haughty—evening and the welcome of night and the stars—these too he would carry along in a threnody of praise to death—lovely and soothing death—the sure-enwinding arms of cool-enfolding death. He had listened to a hermit thrush singing in solemn shadowy cedars and still ghostly pines—under the evening star a carol of death with praise of its serene arrival and its husky whispering to "the huge and thoughtful night." This too he would bring to the coffin as his offertory and benediction, his chant of sane and sacred death. He gave it the title "When Lilacs Last in the Dooryard Bloom'd," in a closing line inscribing it "for the sweetest, wisest soul of all my days and lands—and this for his dear sake."

In thousands of commentaries Lincoln incarnated two results—Emancipation and Union. Two causes directed by Lincoln had won the war. Gone was the property status of the Negro, gone the doctrine of secession and states' rights. Black men could now move from where they were miserable to where they were equally miserable—now it was lawful for them to move. Now too for the Negro no longer was it a crime for him to be found reading a book nor was it any longer a crime to teach a Negro to read.

Out of the smoke and stench, out of the music and violet dreams of the war, Lincoln stood perhaps taller than any other of the many great heroes. This was in the mind of many. None threw a longer shadow than he. And to him the great hero was The People. He could not say too often that he was merely their instrument.

CHAPTER 64

VAST PAGEANT,
THEN GREAT QUIET

Vast Pageant, Then Great Quiet

I N THE East Room of the White House lay the body of a man, embalmed and prepared for a journey. On a platform under a canopy of folds and loops of black silk and crape rested the coffin. Tassels, shamrock leaves, silver stars and silver cords could be seen on facings and edges. A shield with a silver plate had the inscription:

Abraham Lincoln
Sixteenth President of the United States
Born Feb. 12, 1809
Died April 15, 1865

It was Tuesday, April 18, and outside surged the largest mass of people that had ever thronged the White House lawn, the estimate 25,000. In two columns they filed through the East Room, moving along the two sides of the coffin, many pale and limping soldiers out of the convalescent wards of the hospitals, many women and children sobbing and weeping aloud as they passed, pausing only the slightest moment for a look.

On Wednesday, April 19, arrived 60 clergymen, the Cabinet members, the Supreme Court Justices, important officials, foreign Ministers, General Grant with white sash across his breast, the new President Andrew Johnson—600 dignitaries in all. Mrs. Lincoln was still too distracted to be present, but Robert Lincoln came.

Bishop Matthew Simpson of the Methodist Episcopal church offered prayer that smitten hearts might endure, might not be called upon for further sacrifices. A bitter cup from the hand of a chastening Divine Father had been given the mourning nation, said the Reverend Dr. Phineas D. Gurley in the funeral address. "His way is in the sea, and His path in the great waters; and His footsteps are not known . . . We bow, we weep, we worship . . . We will wait for His interpretation . . . He may purify us more in the furnace of trial, but He will not consume us."

The closing invocation was spoken by a Baptist clergyman, chaplain of the U.S. Senate, the Reverend Dr. E. H. Gray. The final ceremonial words spoken in the White House over the mute form of the author of the second inaugural and the Louisiana

Sergent Boston Corbett, 16th N.Y. Cav. who shot John Wilkes Booth. Photo by Mathew Brady.

PRESIDENT LINCOLN'S HEARSE.

Entered according to Act of Congress, in the year 1865, by HENSZEY & CO., PHOTOGRAPHERS, No. 812 Arch St., in the Clerk's Office of the District Court, for the Eastern District of Pennsylvania.

President Lincoln's hearse.

reconstruction speech of April 11 were: "O God, let treason, that has deluged our land with blood, and devastated our country, and bereaved our homes, and filled them with widows and orphans, and has at length culminated in the assassination of the nation's chosen ruler—God of justice, and avenger of the nation's wrong, let the work of treason cease, and let the guilty author of this horrible crime be arrested and brought to justice."

The services were over. The pallbearers took the silver handles. The bong of big bells on cathedrals struck and the little bells of lesser steeples chimed in, as across the spring sunshine came the tolling of all the church bells of Washington and Georgetown, and Alexandria across the river. Counting the minutes with their salutes came the hoarse boom of fort guns encircling the national capital and several batteries sent into the city.

Out of the great front door of the Executive Mansion for the last time went the mortal shape of Abraham Lincoln, 16th President of the United States. On the one-mile route to the Capitol, pavements and curbs were packed with onlookers, who also filled every roof, window, doorway, balcony and stairway. Sixty thousand spectators watched a parade of 40,000 mourners. From his sickbed, sore with his dagger wounds, Secretary Seward gazed from the window with mingled grief and thanks.

In the rotunda of the Capitol, under the great white dome that had come to its finished construction while the war raged, 12 sergeants of the Veteran Reserve Corps carried the coffin to a huge catafalque.

In the morning at ten o'clock the doors opened in special consideration for wounded soldiers from the hospitals, weak and battered men, some with empty sleeves, others on crutches, to file by. Afterward came the public, at times 3,000 to the hour, before midnight 25,000 persons.

AR BUILT FOR PRESIDENT ABRAHAM LINCOLN

Friday morning, April 21, saw the coffin placed aboard a special burial car at the Washington depot. Railroad-yard engine bells tolled and a farstretching crowd stood with uncovered heads as the train of seven cars moved out of Washington for Baltimore.

This was the start of a funeral journey that was to take the lifeless body on a 1,700-mile route which included practically the same points and stops that the living form had made four years and two months before on the way to the first inauguration. Aboard the coaches were five men who had made that earlier journey: Colonel Ward Hill Lamon, Justice David Davis, General David Hunter, John G. Nicolay and John Hay. A committee of Senate and House members included Washburne, Yates and Arnold of Illinois, Harlan of Iowa and Julian of Indiana.

Mrs. Lincoln, Robert and Tad were to undergo an ordeal; with them was their kinsman Ninian W. Edwards. The Illinois delegation aboard included Lincoln's first law partner John T. Stuart and such familiars as Lyman Trumbull, William Bross, Jesse K. Dubois, Shelby M. Cullom and General John A. McClernand. Among state governors aboard were Oglesby of Illinois, Morton of Indiana, Brough of Ohio, Stone of Iowa.

Baltimore wore mourning everywhere and paid reverence; the human outpouring was unmistakable. More than surface changes had come to Maryland in the four furnace years. As the funeral train moved slowly over Pennsylvania soil, at lonely country crossroads were people and faces, horsemen, farmers with their wives and children, standing where they had stood for hours before, waiting, performing the last little possible act of ceremony and attention and love—with solemn faces and uncovered heads standing and gazing as the funeral car passed. In villages and small towns stood waiting crowds, sometimes with a little silver cornet band, often with flowers in hope the train might stop and they could leave camellias, roses, lilies-of-the-valley, wreaths of color and perfume. At York in a short stop six ladies came aboard and laid a three-foot wreath of red and white roses on the coffin.

Through heavy rains at Harrisburg came 30,000 in the night and morning to see the coffin in circles of white flowering almond. At noon on Saturday, April 22, in Philadelphia a half-million people

Railroad car built for
Lincoln with Honor Guard.

Tad Lincoln as a teen, 1869.

Lincoln funeral in front of New York City Hall.

Published by Chr. Kimmel & Forster 254 & 256 Canal St. N.
Shooting of Booth

Shooting of Booth.

were on hand for the funeral train. In Independence Hall stood the coffin. Outside the line of mourners ran three miles.

At Newark, New Jersey, on the morning of April 24 the train moved slowly amid acres of people, a square mile of them. At Jersey City was a like scene. The Empire State formally received the body from Governor Parker of New Jersey. A hearse moved through street crowds. The ferryboat *Jersey City* moved across the Hudson River, neared the wharf at Desbrosses Street. The Seventh Regiment National Guard formed a hollow square into which moved the funeral cortege. The procession marched to the City Hall through streets packed to capacity.

Never before, so everyone agreed, had New York put on such garb and completely changed its look so that it seemed another

Published by Chr.Kimmel &Forster 254 & 256 Canal St.N.Y.

Capture of Harrold and the Shooting of Booth in the Barn of Garaths Farm, by a detachment of the 16th New York Cavalry under the Order of Col Baker.

Capture of Harrold and the shooting of Booth in the barn of Garath's [sic] Farm.

city. On the marble and brownstone fronts, in the ramshackle tenements of "those who live from hand to mouth," came out crape or black folds or drapery or black muslin, rosettes, sable emblems, what the news reporters termed "the habiliments of mourning."

From near noon Monday, April 24, to noon the next day the remains of Abraham Lincoln, horizontal amid white satin, lay in the City Hall. A vast outpouring of people hour by hour passed by to see this effigy and remembrance of his face and form.

At noon on Tuesday, April 25, a procession moved from the City Hall to Ninth Avenue and the Hudson River Railroad depot. Nearly every race, nationality, religion, political faith, was represented among those who marched, near 100,000. The

Funeral of President Lincoln, New York City, 7th Regiment Passing.

Funeral of President Lincoln, New York City, 23rd Regiment Passing.

Funeral of President Lincoln, New York City, April 25, 1865.

troops in Union Army blue alone numbered 20,000. The panoramic show took hours. It was massive, bizarre, spectacular, dazzling—yet somber. A hundred thousand strangers had come to New York to see it. The sidewalk, street, curb and window spectators ran perhaps to a million. At the procession's end came a delegation of 2,000 Negroes, some wearing the Union Army service blue. There had been mutterings from a draft- and race-riot element that they would "never let the damned niggers march." This would have interested the man in the hearse, could he have heard it. It was customary and expected. A telegram to General Dix spoke plain that the Secretary of War desired "no discrimination respecting color." And it was so ordered. At the Union Square exercises following the parade the Roman Catholic Archbishop McCloskey pronounced the benediction, Rabbi Isaacs of the Jewish Synagogue read from their scriptures, the Reverend Stephen H. Tyng of St. George's Church offered a prayer, the Reverend J. P. Thompson intoned Lincoln's second inaugural. Evening had come.

Up the Hudson River east bank the night of April 25 chugged the train of seven cars. On every mile of the route to Albany those on the train could see bonfires and torches, could hear bells and cannon and guns, could see forms of people and white sorry faces. Past midnight of April 25 into the morning hours of April 26 the columns of mourners passed the coffin in Albany.

On this morning of April 26, hunted like a wild beast and cornered like a rat, his broken shinbone betraying him, J. Wilkes Booth met his end. Near Bowling Green, Virginia, in a burning barn set afire from the outside, a bullet drove through his neck bone "perforating both sides of the collar," and he was dragged away from reaching flames and laid under a tree. Water was given him. He revived, to murmur from parched lips, "Tell my mother—I died—for my country."

He was carried to a house veranda, there muttering, "I thought I did for the best." He lingered for a time. A doctor came. Wilkes Booth asked that his hands might be raised so that he could look at them. So it was told. And as he looked on his hands, he mumbled hoarsely, "Useless! useless!" And those were his last words.

Across the Empire State that day and night it was mural

GARRETT'S HOUSE, WHERE BOOTH DIED. — [SKETCHED BY W. N. WALTON.]

Garrett's House, where Booth died.

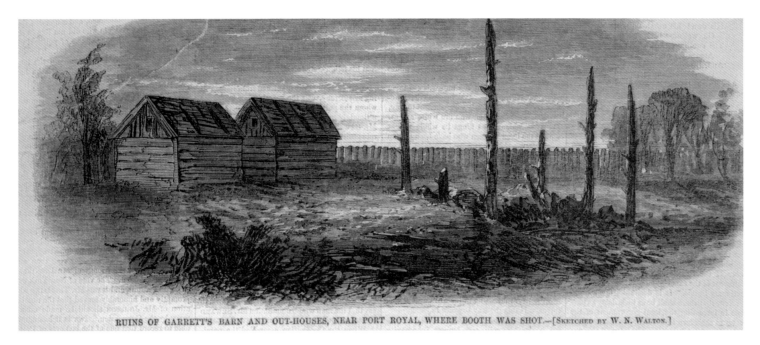

RUINS OF GARRETT'S BARN AND OUT-HOUSES, NEAR PORT ROYAL, WHERE BOOTH WAS SHOT.—[Sketched by W. N. Walton.]

Ruins of Garrett's Barn where Booth was shot.

monotone of mourning, the Erie Canal zone in sober grief with evergreens, flowers, sable emblems. The endless multitudinous effect became colossal. At Buffalo Millard Fillmore, one of the three living ex-Presidents of the United States, attended the funeral, which also was witnessed by the youth Grover Cleveland.

From Cleveland to Crestline the rain kept on in torrents. In the rotunda of Ohio's capitol, on a mound of green moss dotted with white flowers, rested the coffin on April 28, while 8,000 persons passed by each hour from 9:30 in the morning till four in the afternoon. In the changing red-gold of a rolling prairie sunset, to the slow exultation of brasses rendering "Old Hundred" and the muffled booming of minute guns, the coffin was carried out of the rotunda and taken to the funeral train.

The slow night run from Columbus to Indianapolis saw from the car windows a countryside of people thronging to the route of the coffin. At Pleasant Valley were bonfires. Nearly every town had its arch of evergreens, flags and black drapings. At Urbana ten young women strewed roses on the coffin, one of them breaking down in uncontrollable tears. At Piqua were 10,000 at midnight; at Richmond, Indiana, 10,000 again at three o'clock in the morning.

Tolling bells and falling rain at Indianapolis saw the coffin borne into the State House for a Sabbath to be remembered. On the slow night run to Chicago it was as in Ohio, thousands in Lafayette standing mute and daybreak not yet, thousands more at Michigan City. By railway train, by wagon or buggy and on horseback, something like 100,000 people had come into Chicago from all points of the Northwest. The vocal attempts at solemn grief often failed and were overdone. But there was a silent grief—broken only by choked snufflings, by low wailings, by almost inaudible moans—a loss afraid of words. There was a curious dumb sorrow, perhaps deeper than any other.

Slowly at Twelfth Street and Michigan Avenue the funeral train came to a stop. A procession of 50,000 people, witnessed by double as many, escorted the hearse to the courthouse.

All night long Monday, and through the early morning hours and all the day hours of Tuesday, the columns moved in and out

Robert Todd Lincoln.

he had spoken his prophet warnings of the House Divided, stood the casket. Now passed those who had known him long, part of the 75,000 who came. They were awed, subdued, shaken, stony, strange. They came from Salem, Petersburg, Clary's Grove, Alton, Charleston, Mattoon, the old Eighth Circuit towns and villages. There were clients for whom he had won or lost, lawyers who had tried cases with him and against, neighbors who had seen him milk a cow and curry his horse, friends who had heard his stories around a hot stove and listened to his surmises on politics and religion. All day long and through the night the unbroken line moved, the home town having its farewell.

On May 4 of this year 1865 anno Domini a procession moved with its hearse from the state capitol to Oak Ridge Cemetery. There on green banks and hillsides flowing away from a burial vault the crowded thousands of listeners and watchers heard prayers and hymns, heard the second inaugural read aloud. Bishop Matthew Simpson in a moving oration spoke as an interpreter and foreteller: "There are moments which involve in themselves eternities. There are instants which seem to contain germs which shall develop and bloom forever. Such a moment came in the tide of time to our land when a question must be settled, affecting all the powers of the earth. The contest was for human freedom. Not for this republic merely, not for the Union simply, but to decide whether the people, as a people, in their entire majesty, were destined to be the Governments or whether they were to be subject to tyrants or aristocrats, or to class rule of any kind. This is the great question for which we have been righting, and its decision is at hand, and the result of this contest will affect the ages to come. If successful, republics will spread in spite of monarchs all over this earth." Came then from the people, noted the *Illinois State Journal,* exclamations of "Amen! thank God!"

Evergreen carpeted the stone floor of the vault. On the coffin set in a receptacle of black walnut they arranged flowers carefully and precisely, they poured flowers as symbols, they lavished heaps of fresh flowers as though there could never be enough to tell either their hearts or his.

And the night came with great quiet.

And there was rest.

The prairie years, the war years, were over.

of the courthouse. An estimated 125,000 people had taken their last glance at the Man from Illinois. A thousand men with blazing torches escorted the coffin to the funeral car for the slow night run to Springfield on the Alton Railroad.

Then at last home to Springfield. In the state capitol where

Lincoln Monument, Springfield, IL.

LINCOLN CONSPIRATORS' HANGING

by Edward C. Goodman

JOHN WILKES BOOTH originally planned to kidnap Abraham Lincoln and take him to the South to force an exchange of Confederate prisoners. The conspirators recruited to help in the kidnap plan included Samuel Arnold, George Atzerodt, David Herold, Michael O'Laughlin, Lewis Powell a.k.a. "Paine" and John Surratt. They met at the boarding house of Mary Surratt, John's mother. After the war ended, Booth decided to murder the President, Vice-President Johnson and Secretary of State William Seward.

Execution of the Lincoln Conspirators: Bodies Hanging. Photo by Alexander Gardner, 1865.

On July 7, 1865 at approximately 1:15 P.M., the condemned prisoners were walked through the courtyard with their hands manacled and dragging 75-pound balls attached to their leg-irons, past their own graves and up the thirteen steps to the gallows. The gallows was on a ten-foot high platform. The prisoners were seated in chairs while their chains were removed and then white gauze bags were placed over their heads so the audience of 1000 men, women and children would not see their faces turn blue. They were moved to the trap doors or break, and their legs and arms were bound to their bodies with strips of white cloth.

Booth shot Lincoln at Ford's Theatre on Good Friday, 1865. He then leaped to the stage injuring his leg and reportedly shouted "Sic Semper Tyrannis" "Thus Always to Tyrants" and fled on horseback. He met with David Herold and they went to Dr. Samuel A. Mudd who set the leg. They remained on the run until April 26, when Union soldiers tracked them to a barn in Maryland belonging to Richard Garrett. Herold surrendered but Booth refused. Soldiers set fire to the barn and then fatally shot Booth.

Lewis Paine was captured when he appeared at the door of the home of Mrs. Surratt while she was being questioned by police.

Eight of Booth's conspirators were held on board a warship that was being used as a prison. They were kept manacled and had heavily padded bags over their heads to prevent suicides.

The conspirators were tried by a military tribunal which lasted seven weeks with 366 witnesses testifying. The verdicts came on July 5, 1865 with all defendants found guilty. David Herold, George Atzerodt, Lewis Powell "Paine" and Mary Surratt were sentenced to death by hanging while Dr. Mudd, Samuel Arnold and Michael O'Laughlin were given life sentences and Edmund Spangler was sentenced to six years in prison.

General Winfield Scott Hancock read out the sentences and then clapped his hands three times. The supporting post for each break was knocked out and the conspirators dropped about four feet. This proved insufficient to break their necks and they struggled slightly while they suffocated to death. They were finally pronounced dead at 2:15. Mrs. Surratt was the first woman ever executed by the United States government.

The bodies were stripped naked, wrapped in sheets, placed in pine boxes with their names in glass vials in the coffins and buried inside the walls of the fort prison. Their clothes were given to charity. Pieces of the rope were sold as souvenirs along with locks of their hair.

Dr. Mudd, Arnold and Spangler were pardoned by President Andrew Johnson in February 1869. John Surratt escaped to Europe and hid there until his arrest in 1866. His trial ended in a mistrial.

This series of photos taken by Alexander Gardner record the stages of the hanging including the moment the trap was sprung from beneath their feet and the bodies hanging from the ropes of the gallows.

Execution of the Lincoln Conspirators. Photo by Alexander Gardner, 1865.

Execution of the Lincoln Assassination Conspirators. Photo by Alexander Gardner, 1865.

Execution of the Lincoln Conspirators taken from the Roof of the Arsenal. Photo by Alexander Gardner, 1865.

Execution of the Conspirators: Graves, and Coffins Ready for Bodies. Photo by Alexander Gardner, 1865.

Execution of the Lincoln Assassination Conspirators: Adjusting the Ropes for Hanging. Photo by Alexander Gardner, 1865.

Execution of the Lincoln Assassination Conspirators: the Scaffold. Photo by Alexander Gardner, 1865.

EXECUTION OF THE CONSPIRATORS—SPRINGING OF THE TRAP.
[Drawn by A. M℃Callum.]

Execution of the Conspirators: Springing of the Trap. Drawing by A. McCallum.

LINCOLN MEMORIAL
by Edward C. Goodman

THE LINCOLN MEMORIAL is in the form of a Greek Doric temple with 36 columns each 33 feet high that represent the 36 states of the union at the time of Lincoln's death.

The Lincoln Monument Association was formed in 1867 to build a memorial to the assassinated President and a site was finally chosen in 1901. The first stone was laid on Lincoln's birthday, Feb. 12, 1914 and the monument was dedicated on May 30, 1922 by President Warren G. Harding with Lincoln's only surviving son, Robert Todd Lincoln, in attendance.

Lincoln Memorial, Washington, DC.

The monument was designed by American architect Henry Bacon who was awarded the American Institute of Architects Gold Medal for his design in 1923.

The main interior feature is the seated sculpture of a seated Lincoln by Daniel Chester French. It is 19 feet tall and 19 feet wide and was carved in white Georgia marble by the Piccirilli Brothers of New York.

On the south wall is inscribed the Gettysburg Address and on the north wall is inscribed his second inaugural address. On the wall behind the statue is this dedication:

In this temple
As in the hearts of the people
For whom he saved the Union
The memory of Abraham Lincoln
Is enshrined forever.

The Lincoln Memorial is considered to be a Symbol of Freedom.

In 1939, the singer Marian Anderson performed from the steps of the Lincoln Memorial to a live audience of 70,000 and a nationwide radio audience after being denied permission to perform at Constitution Hall because of her skin color.

On August 28, 1965, Martin Luther King delivered his famous "I Have a Dream" speech from the steps of the memorial during the March on Washington.

The Lincoln Memorial is shown on the reverse of the U.S. penny and the $5 bill.

The Lincoln Memorial was listed on the National Register of Historic Places on October 15, 1966 and is administered by the U.S. National Park Service.

Lincoln Statue, Washington, DC.

Aerial view of the Lincoln Memorial, Washington, DC.

Lincoln Memorial, Washington, DC.

Lincoln Memorial, Washington, DC.

Statue to Lincoln at the Lincoln Memorial, Washington, DC. Photo by Charles Zoller, c. 1920.

Statue of Lincoln at the Lincoln Memorial.

U.S. Navy Group for the Lincoln Monument International Exhibition, 1876.

The dedication ceremony of the Lincoln Memorial with Pres. Taft, Pres. Warren G. Harding and Robert Lincoln (l-r). Photo by National Photo Co.

Lincoln Memorial, Washington, DC.

Robert Lincoln, son of Abraham Lincoln snaped while attending the dedication exercises at the Lincoln memorial. //d9/ 5/30/22

Robert Lincoln at the dedication of the Lincoln Memorial, May 30, 1922. Photo by National Photo Co.

IN THIS TEMPLE
AS IN THE HEARTS OF THE PEOPLE
FOR WHOM HE SAVED THE UNION
THE MEMORY OF ABRAHAM LINCOLN
IS ENSHRINED FOREVER

PRESENTATION OF THE GOLD MEDAL
TO HENRY BACON, F.A.I.A.
THE LINCOLN MEMORIAL

AMERICAN INSTITUTE OF ARCHITECTS
FIFTY-SIXTH ANNUAL CONVENTION

WASHINGTON, D. C.
MAY 18, 1923

Henry Bacon's AIA Award for the Lincoln Memorial.

Lincoln Memorial, Washington, DC.

Statue of Lincoln by Daniel Chester French at the Lincoln Memorial.

Sources and Acknowledgments

The chief center of the research on the life of Lincoln before he became President was the Abraham Lincoln Association with its office in Springfield, Illinois, with funds subscribed by a national membership and with outside grants. From 1933 through 1941 the Association published four volumes, each giving "the day-by-day activities of Abraham Lincoln," where he was and what he was doing, so far as known by documents. Harry Pratt's two volumes, *Lincoln Day By Day 1809-1839* and *1840-1846*, are followed by Benjamin P. Thomas' for *1847-1853* and by Paul Angle's for *1854-1861* the four books making a massive, formidable work that will be of use as long as there are sober and anxious students of Lincoln. Approaching the colossal is the nine-volume edition sponsored by the Association, published in 1953, *The Collected Works of Abraham Lincoln*. Heavy, exacting and thorough were the five-year labors of Roy P. Basler, editor, and Marion Dolores Pratt and Lloyd A. Dunlap, assistant editors. Their texts of letters, speeches, documents, are from originals or photostats of originals, except in a few instances which they report and discuss. This carefully documented assemblage of Lincoln utterance is possibly the best historical account by any one man on how and why the titanic war of 1861-1865 arose and was carried through. This utterance record of more than a million words holds the keys or clues to the subtle, wide-ranging personality of Lincoln more than any other work to be read and studied. A large one-volume compilation with an able biographical introduction is *The Life and Writings of Abraham Lincoln* (1940) by Philip Van Doren Stern. The most useful, well-annotated single volume in this field is *Abraham Lincoln His Speeches and Writings* (1946) by Roy P. Basler.

From the Abraham Lincoln Association group and its associates came monographs revealing forgeries of four Lincoln letters printed earlier in books of reputation; they published evidence that the marble-enshrined log cabin at Hodgenville, Kentucky, is not the real and actual birth-cabin of Lincoln but rests on a tissue of traditions; they re-examined the legend of Ann Rutledge and Lincoln, made a strong case that the "romance" rested on conjecture and assumption while the often related grief and borderline insanity of Lincoln at her death were improbable. The Association reproduced in facsimile in 1938 a campaign biography, *Life of Abraham Lincoln* by W. D. Howells, with 14 corrections made by Lincoln's pencil in the summer of 1860; the value of such a book is in the corrections written in it and also in the bulk of statements that Lincoln let stand as fact.

Benjamin P. Thomas' book, *Lincoln's New Salem* (1934), brought to bear his long familiarity with that frontier community; it is the classic on Lincoln's "Alma Mater." Paul M. Angle's *Here I Have Lived: A History of Lincoln's Springfield 1821-1865* (1935) is a master report on Lincoln's home town. William E. Baringer's three volumes, *Lincoln's Vandalia* (1949), *Lincoln's Rise to Power* (1935), *A House Dividing* (1945), represent fresh research, especially on Lincoln in the Illinois Legislature and the intricacies of politics leading to Lincoln's nomination for President in 1860. A research not made thitherto appears in Donald W. Riddle's *Lincoln Runs for Congress* (1948). Harry Pratt's *Concerning Mr. Lincoln: In Which Abraham Lincoln Is Pictured as He Appeared to Letter Writers of His Time* (1944) gives swift and fleeting personal glimpses of Lincoln. Pratt's larger work, *Personal Finances of Abraham Lincoln* (1943), covers more ground than any previous studies of Lincoln's earnings and spendings and his sense about money. From the Abraham Lincoln Association, disbanded in 1953, for nearly 30 years there poured forth bulletins, books, a quarterly magazine, threshing out major and minor phases of the Lincoln story. Logan Hay, who died in 1942, is cherished as the founder and an ever-dynamic force in the Association.

All of the aforementioned books and publications came to print since I was writing *Abraham Lincoln: The Prairie Years*. Also in this period have come the important volumes of James G. Randall, *Lincoln the President: From Springfield to Gettysburg, two volumes* (1945) and *Lincoln the President: Midstream* (1952), this latter one of the most profound and charming studies of Lincoln. *His Lincoln and the South* (1945) and *Lincoln the Liberal Statesman* (1947) hold his keenly searching popular lectures and essays. And it happened that "Jim" Randall, greatly beloved, constantly an inspirational force in the field of Lincoln study, was himself taken away midstream of his great work. His widow, Ruth Painter Randall, published *Mary Lincoln:Biography of a Marriage* (1953), the most elaborately and scrupulously documented narrative of the girl who became wife and widow of Lincoln. There came from David Donald a skilled and brilliant book, *Lincoln's Herndon* (1948), the first book-length biography of Lincoln's law partner for 16 years. *Diplomat in Carpet Slippers* (1945) was Jay Monaghan's floodlight on Lincoln amid foreign affairs. *Lincoln and the Patronage* (1943) by Harry J. Carman and Reinhard H. Luthin has in extensive documented detail, in wide coverage, the

appetites, connivings, whispers, howls of American politics and Lincoln at center. *Lincoln and the Press* (1951) by Robert S. Harper shows the uses of printer's ink in support, praise and defamation of an American President. *Lincoln and the War Governors* (1948) by William B. Hesseltine presents the state executives with whose co-operation or antagonism Lincoln had to deal. Margaret Leech's *Reveille in Washington:1860-1865* (1941) is a pageant of scandal, drama, heroism, vividly written. *Lawyer Lincoln* (1936) by Albert A. Woldman is an advance on former treatments of Lincoln in law practice, his *Lincoln and the Russians* (1952) presenting diplomats, letters, reports. *The First Lincoln Campaign* (1944) by Reinhard H. Luthin is an original and distinctive contribution stressing the economic factors and political personalities that clashed or interwove to make Lincoln the most "available" candidate for President in 1860. Again original and distinctive, probing deep among motives, is David M. Potter's *Lincoln and His Party in the Secession Crisis* (1942). T. Harry Williams is enlightening and worth scrutiny in *Lincoln and the Radicals* (1941) and *Lincoln and His Generals* (1952). The suave, breezy, eloquent, scrupulous Kentuckian, William H. Townsend, has given us *Lincoln and Liquor* (1934) and *Lincoln His Wife's Home Town* (1929), besides monographs of value. The objective viewpoints of a distinguished physician are in Dr. William A. Evans' *Mrs. Abraham Lincoln: Study of Her Personality* (1932). A professor of mathematics, a veteran of two wars, Kenneth P. Williams was fully authorized to write his massive two-volume documented study, *Lincoln Finds a General* (1950). Independent and well written is Bruce Carton's *Mr. Lincoln's Army* (1951). Fletcher Pratt's *Stanton* (1953) is a military history of the war with Stanton as a central figure. John E. Washington in *They Knew Lincoln* (1942) sketches "Billy the Barber" and other Negroes in the personal life of Lincoln. George S. Bryan's *The Great American Myth* (1940) is a re-examination of facts and inventions regarding the murder of Lincoln. *The Mad Booths of Maryland* (1940) by Stanley Kimmel renders in wealth of detail the family and environment from which came Lincoln's assassin. The meditations of an idealist in poetry and philosophy are in T. V. Smith's *Abraham Lincoln and the Spiritual Life* (1951). The new biographies, Francis Brown's *Raymond of the Times* and Helen Nicolay's *Lincoln's Secretary* (1949) have their close-ups of Lincoln, as also does the five-million word *Diary of George Templeton Strong* (1952) edited by Allan Nevins. Basic as document and highly readable is *Lincoln and the Civil War in Diaries* and *Letters of John Hay* (1939) by Tyler Dennett. The controversial Herndon's *Lincoln: the True Story of a Great Life* (1889) in three volumes by William H. Herndon and Jesse W. Weik became available in a one-volume edition in 1930 with an introduction and notes by Paul M. Angle which make it the one Herndon edition most worth reading. Albert J. Beveridge died in 1927 before midstream of his two volumes published in 1928, *Abraham Lincoln: 1809-1858*. Emanuel Hertz died in 1940 shortly after publication of *The Hidden Lincoln and Lincoln Talks*. Oliver R. Barrett died seven months after my book, *Lincoln Collector*, was published in praise of his zeal and intelligence, its pages holding now some of the unity of his notable collection later auctioned. William E. Barton died in 1930, a year after the publication of The *Lineage of Lincoln*, a book two-fifths documents chiefly related to Lincoln kinfolk. The 1860-1861 New York Herald newsletters of Henry Villard, with deletions, are in *Lincoln on the Eve of '61* (1941). In *The American Iliad*, Otto Eisenschiml and Ralph Newman give a narrative of the Civil War by selected eyewitnesses and contemporaries. Eisenschiml's *In the Shadow of Lincoln's Death* (1940) relentlessly asks grim unanswerable questions. In *Legends that Libel Lincoln* (1946), Montgomery S. Lewis throws corrective light on three major libels. *Lincoln's War Cabinet* (1946) is a competent study by Burton J. Hendrick. George Fort Milton's *Abraham Lincoln and the Fifth Column* (1942) covers wide ground as to "Copperheads" and treasonable activities in the North. An elusive sweetheart flits through the pages of *Lincoln's Other Mary* (1946), the facts by R. Gerald McMurtry, the fiction by Olive Carruthers.

Benjamin P. Thomas, a trained historian, a resident of Springfield familiar with all the streets and roads most often traveled by Lincoln, personally acquainted with descendants of characters who figured in Lincoln's life, in 1952 published his one-volume *Abraham Lincoln*. As a narrative and close-up portrait of Lincoln it makes use of all early source materials and also the later accumulations which he often saw in manuscript before their publication; he was one of the most active workers, and at one time secretary, of the Abraham Lincoln Association. Thomas is out of Midwest soil and long broodings over Lincoln. Closing his book, he soberly affirms Lincoln: "Only with the slow march of time would it be given to most of his countrymen to understand the supreme meaning of his life . . . Because to him the American people were the leaders of an awakening of plain people the world over." When he was writing his one-volume Lincoln I told him, "If or when I get written and published a one-volume Lincoln, I hope and believe the two books will stand on the Lincoln shelf as good companions supplementing each other."

None of the foregoing books had been published at the time I was writing *Abraham Lincoln: The Prairie Years*. Most of them have seen publication since I wrote *Abraham Lincoln: The War Years*. All of them, however, have been used in the preparation of this one volume, for corrections or added lights. I have also used the files of *The Journal of the Illinois State Historical Society*, the Lincoln Memorial University's *Lincoln Herald*, the periodicals *Lincoln Lore and The Lincoln Kinsman* written by Louis A. Warren. To the stream of Lincoln source materials was added in 1941 the Herndon-Weik papers made available by Library of Congress purchase, and in 1947 the Robert T. Lincoln collection, a bequest to the Library. From the latter collection in 1948 came from David Mearns two volumes, *The Lincoln Papers*, with selections covering 1809 to July 4, 1861. A reader of these can step back into a generation of vanished Americans and see them in speaking likenesses, a variety of fine persons and odd fools.

In the preface to *The Prairie Years* I mentioned the Daniel Fish bibliography in 1906 listing 1,080 books and pamphlets about Lincoln and that of J. B. Oakleaf in 1925 listing 1,600 items. In 1945, however, came Jay Monaghan's listing of 3,958 items. By now, in 1954, there are more than 4,000 books and pamphlets dealing principally with Abraham Lincoln, his ancestry, wife and kin, even excluding such sources as the indispensable Welles and Browning diaries which deal with Lincoln incidentally. In 13 pages of a foreword to *The War Years* are enumerated and evaluated the array of source materials used in the writing of those four volumes.

The Blue and the Gray: the Story of the Civil War as Told by Participants, two volumes (1950), by Henry Steele Commager is a procession of witnesses and documents, Douglas Southall Freeman joining with others to attest its author as extraordinarily well equipped to present "a history of the Civil War in the words of those who fought it." The background of national events, the storms and the quiet between storms through which the American people moved from the 1847 Congress in which Lincoln had a seat to the 1861 inauguration of Lincoln, are presented as a moving panorama in Allan Nevins' *The Ordeal of the Union*, two volumes (1947), and The *Emergence of Lincoln*, two volumes (1950). These books embody vivid writing and vast research in original sources; they are important if not imperatively requisite for those who seek to know more concretely the wild onrushes of violent events along with quietly inexorable streams of invention, migration, territorial expansion, of those 14 years; they were shaping the national scene where Lincoln was fated to play the somber and leading role.

James O'Donnell Bennett's *Private Joe Fifer* (1936) quotes that Civil War soldier and governor of Illinois as having from Milton Hay the saying of Lincoln, "You can fool some of the people all of the time and all of the people some of the time but you can't fool all of the people all of the time," Fifer adding, "In 1894, after my term as governor, I made a speech in Piatt County, this state, in which I repeated what Milt Hay had told me. The speech was printed in the St. Louis *Globe-Democrat*, the Chicago *Inter-Ocean* and other papers and thus the saying was first given publicity. None of the Lincoln biographers had ever discovered it."

In 1946 came *A Shelf of Lincoln Books* by Paul M. Angle, "a critical, selective bibliography of Lincolniana." He lists and evaluates 81 basic items, reporting their now generally accepted merits and deficiencies. Ralph Newman of the Abraham Lincoln Bookshop in Chicago lists 100 titles of the books he regards as most indispensable to the Lincoln student. In 1947 came Benjamin P. Thomas' *Portrait for Posterity*, a stormy, intensely human story of the procession of Lincoln biographers, their toils, hopes and miseries, their disputes, quarrels and quandaries. Thomas quotes from hundreds of letters they wrote. The book interweaves plots and characters into one of the strangest stories in American literary history. Thomas concludes: "The realist's ruthless searching gives the necessary facts. Yet the realist is ill-advised to scorn the idealist's sensitivity to those soul-qualities of Lincoln which documentary facts alone may not disclose."

PHOTO CREDITS

INDEX

Illustrations are indicated in bold.

A

Abell, Mrs. Bennett, 40, 43
Abolitionists, 104-107
Adams, Charles Francis, 65, 176, 216, 242, 288, 355
Adams, Henry, 144, 224
Adams, John Quincy, 64, 65
African American troops, 206, 236-239, 262, 275, 282, 294, 298, 311-312, 356, 370, 445
Alabama (ship), 312, 313
Alabama, 151
Alaska, 275
Albany *Evening Journal*, 112
Albany, NY, 445
Alton, IL, 44, 88
American Institute of Architects. Gold Medal, 453, **455**
Amnesty Proclamation, 293
Anderson, Marion, 453
Anderson, Robert, 148, 150, 151, 153
Andersonville, GA, prison, 341
Andrew, Governor, 237, 269
Angle, Paul A., iv, v
Annals of Congress, 108
Antietam, Battle of, **196, 200, 201**, 202, 212, 227, 229, 242, 261
Appomattox, VA, 382, **383**, 384
Arkansas, 156, 293-294
Armstrong, Hannah, **32**
Armstrong, Jack, 28, 30
Army and Navy Gazette, 339
Army of Northern Virginia, 260, 297, 383
Army of the Cumberland, 260, 261, 308
Army of the James, 373
Army of the Mississippi, 233
Army of the Ohio, 261, 308
Army of the Potomac, iv, 170, 171, 179, 187, 194, 210, 227, 229, 233, 248, 250-251, 257, 282, 296, 379
Army of the Tennessee, 161, 308
Army of Virginia, 152, 199
Army of Western Virginia, 179
Arnold, Isaac N., 101, 284-285, 366, 439
Arnold, Samuel, 414, **415, 418**, 419, 439, 450
Ashmun, George, 64, 117, 119, 151
Aspinwall, William Henry, 285
Assassination of Lincoln, 390-409, 412-430; conspirators hanging, **450-452**; reward posters, **426-427**
Astor House, NY, 134
Atlanta *Confederacy*, 122
Atlanta, GA, 298, 308, 313, 317-318, 336-337
Atzerodt, George A., **416**, 417, 419, **420**, 450
Austria, 433
Autographed Leaves of Our Country's Authors, 270
Axelrod, Alan, 8-9
Ayres, General, 374

B

Bacon, Henry, 453, 455

Badeau, Adam, 372, 373, 412
Baker, Edward D. "Ned", **58**, 59, 66, 140
Baker, La Fayette C., 244, 325
Ball's Bluff, 182
Baltimore (ship), 184
Baltimore Glee Club, 268
Baltimore *Sun*, 412
Baltimore, MD, 113, 119, 134, 162-163, 290, 294, 300, 302, 305, 313, 439
Bancroft, George, 270
Banks, Nathaniel P., 164, 199, 227, 252, 285, 293, 356
Barnes, Captain, 370, 372, 373
Barnes, Dr. Joseph E., 407, 408
Bartlett, D.W., 119
Bat, The (ship), 370
Bates, Edward, 60, 80, 112, 145, 148, 188, 201, 218, 332
Battery, The, 66
Battle Hymn of the Republic (song), 205
Beale, Joseph Boggs, 18, 26, 28, 133, 139, 223, 377, 399, 428
Beauregard, P.G.T., 150, 165-166, 168, 186
Bedell, Grace, 134
Beecher, Henry Ward, 104, 108, 110, 174, 373, 432
Bell, John, 113
Belmont, August, 123, 152, 285, 316, 318, 332; Mrs., 134
Benet, Stephen Vincent, 8
Benjamin, Judah P., 156
Bennett, James Gordon, 174, 289
Benton, Thomas Hart, 60
Berger, Anthony, 245
Berry, Richard, 13-14
Berry, William F., 31, 32
Bidwell, Daniel D., 308
Bigelow, John, 289
Bingham & Dodd, 412
Bissell, William H., 81
Black Hawk (Chief), 30-31
Black Hawk War, 30-31, 33, 34, 36, 58
Blackwater, MO, 199
Blair, Francis P., 152, 172, 218, 220, 267, 267, 305, 318, 320, 329, 352, 353, 355
Blair, Montgomery, 145, 148
Bleakley & Montgomery, 12, 14
Bledsoe, Albert Taylor, 156
Blyth, David Gilmour, 222
Boell, E., 370
Boone, Daniel, 12
Booth, Asia, 414, 430
Booth, Edwin, 412, 419, 430
Booth, John Wilkes, **398**, 399, 400, 401, 403, **410**, 412, **414**, 417, 419, **420**, 422, **427**, **428**, 430, 436, 450; shooting of, **442-443**, 445; revolver used by, **401**
Booth, Junius Brutus, 412
Boston *Advertiser*, 269
Boston *Journal*, 313
Boston *Transcript*, 144
Botts, John Minor, 64

Boyhood of Lincoln, **16**
Bradford, Gamaliel, v
Brady Studio, 241, 245, 247
Brady, Mathew B., v, 9, 110, 170, 173, 185, 210, 215, 281, 284, 311, 322, 324, 351, 364-365, 436
Bragg, Braxton, 202, 218, 260-261, 274
Brandy Station, 282
Brayman, M., 108
Breckinridge, John C., 119, 120, 133, 162, **164**, 171, 305
Breckinridge, Robert J., 162
Briggs, James A., 110
Bright, John, **217**, 218
Brooks, Noah, 228, 243, 245, 275, 280, 300, 316, 328, 345, 346, 355, 359, 360, 366, 386, 394
Brooks, Preston, 77, 137
Brough, John, 262, 439
Brown, John, 82, **105, 106**, 176, 412
Brown, Joseph, 338
Browning, Orville H., 113, 133, 187, 216, 243
Bryant Cottage, IL, **88**
Bryant, William Cullen, 65, 110, 117, 145, 174, 290
Buchanan, James, 80-82, 113, 125, 140, 148
Buckinham, C.O., 210
Buckner, Simon B., 184
Buell, Don Carlos, 164, 188, 202
Buffalo, NY, 447
Bull Run, Battles of, 168, 171, 174, **175**, 187, 199, 200, 208, 210, 227, 242, 260
Bunn, Jacob, 104
Burnside, Ambrose E., 201, 210, **212**, 227, 227, 237, 242, 261, 267, 274, 282
Bush, Isaac, 15
Butler, Andrew P., 77
Butler, Benjamin F., 163, 164, **165**, 187, 285, 298, 352
Butler, William, 43, 55, 119
Butterfield, General, 228
Butterfield, Justin, 66

C

Cadwalader, George, 163
Calhoun, John C., 33, 65, 68
California, 68, 74, 80; Gold Rush, 74
Cameron, Simon, 123, 124, 145, 148, 152, 165, **180**, 181, 182, 198, 248, 280, 300, 318, 319
Campbell, Frank G., 252
Campbell, John A., 353-354
Camron, John, 27, 28, 34
Canby, E.R.S., 293
Canisius, Theodore, 104
Carpenter, Francis B., 286, 324, 341
Carr, Clark E., 265, 267
Cartes de visite, 324
Cartter, David K., 407
Cartwright, Peter, **56**, 59
Catholics, 75
Central Pacific railroad, 195
Chancellorsville, VA, 228, 236, 242
Chandler, Zach, 251
Chapin, Edwin H., 110

Chapman, A.P., 86
Chapman, Conrad Wise, 147
Charleston *Mercury*, 124, 144, 329
Charleston, SC, 124, 148, 150, 245, 261-262, 373
Chase, Salmon P., 65, 104, 112, 118, 123, 145, 148,
    153, 179, 193, 194, 201, 205, 208, 210, 212,
    216-218, 220, 227, 233, 285, 285, 288-290, 304,
    330, 332, **333**, 348, 362, 408
Chattanooga, TN, 260-261, 274
Cheney, Mary Y., 170
Cherbourg, France, 312
Chicago Daily News, 9
Chicago *Democrat*, 92
Chicago Irish Brigade, 172
Chicago *Press*, 86, 108
Chicago *Times*, 84, 86
Chicago *Tribune*, 86, 120, 174, 270
Chicago, IL, 28, 60, 75, 113, 117, 119, 123, 447
Chickamauga, GA, Battle of, **258**, 260
China, 184
Chittenden, L.E., 133, 325
Chr. Kimmel & Forster, 273
Cincinnati *Commercial*, 233, 268
Cincinnati *Gazette*, 92, 174, 248
Circle of Hosts, 237
City Point, VA, 308, 313, 329, 370, 372-374, 377, 378,
    379
Clary, Bill, 28
Clary's Grove Boys, 28, 30, 31, 32
Clay, Cassius M., 152
Clay, Henry, 27, 37, 59, 61, 65, 66, 68, 70, 71, 162
Clay, James B., 162
Cleveland, Grover, 447
Cleveland, OH, 447
Cobb, Howell, 64
Cochrane, John, 300, **301**
Cold Harbor, VA, 296-298, 300
Columbia, OH, 447
Comager, Henry Steele, 8
Committee on the Conduct of the War, 178, 227
Confederate States of America, 125, 134, 154-159,
    162-166, 253, 262, 341, 344; surrender, 382, 384,
    392
Confiscation Act, 178, 206
Congress (ship), 189
Congressional Globe, 32, 68, 108, 285, 292, 348
Conkling, James C., 257
Conscription Act, 236
Constitutional Union party, 113
Copperheads, 237, 257, 262, 286, 430
Corbett, Boston, **436**
Corinth, 194
Corning, Erastus, 285
Corruption, 177-182
Corwin, Thomas, 60
Couch, General, 228, 248, 267
Crane, Dr. Charles H., 407
Crawford, Andrew, 23
Crook, William H., 324, 362, 370, 372, 377, 378, 394,
    399
Culpepper Court House, VA, 210, 282
Cumberland (ship), 189
Currier & Ives, 114, 123, 186, 192, 301
Curtin, Andrew G., 136, 208, 262, **266**, 267, 286
Curtis, George W., 117, 168, 227, 325

Curtis, S.R., 174
Cushing, Caleb, 176
Cutts, Adéle, 74

D
Dahlgren, John A., 261, 373, 434
Dahms, Virginia, 88
Dana, Charles A., 238, 243, 261, 292, 298, 320, 348,
    390, 408
Dana, Richard Henry, 288
Davis, David, iv, 78, 92, 98, **113**, 117, 119, 133, 172,
    300, 332, 439
Davis, Henry Winter, 305, 345
Davis, Jefferson, 65, 123, 125, 134, 150, 152, **154**, 157,
    188, 198, 208, 232, 233, 243, 252, 262, 274, 275,
    336, 338, **340**, 341, 344, 352, 353, 354, 355, 370,
    372, 373, 377, 378, 392, 430
Davis, Joseph, 233
Davis, Mrs. Jefferson (Varina Howell), **157**, 158
Dawes, Henry Laurens, 428
Dawson, Elodie, 162
Dawson, John, 36, 38
Death totals, 392
Debates on the Federal Constitution, 108
Declaration of Independence (U.S.), 12, 94, 117, 143
Democrats, 36, 38-39, 46-47, 59, 65, 74, 77, 78, 80, 84,
    86, 113, 119, 210, 279, 302, 312, 316-320, 348, 349
Dennis, Elias, 236
Department of the Gulf, 293
Department of the West, 172
Desertions, 237, 262, 338, 368
Detective Bureau, 325
Detroit *Free Press*, 284
District of Columbia. *See* Washington, DC.
Dix, Dorothea, 188
Dix, John A., 164
Dodge, Grenville M., 366
Dorsey, Azel, 23
Douglas, Stephen A., 36, 38, 44, 46, 47, 64, 70-72, **74**,
    75, 80, 82, 84, 86-90, **91**, 92, 107, 108, 110, 113,
    119, 120, 137, 144, 151, 157, 171, 285; death, 162;
    life-mask, **160**
Douglass, Frederick, **234**, 237, 238
Draft riots, 253-254, 257
Draft, 195, 236-237, 262, 311-312, 319, 345
Dred Scott decision, 81, 112
Dresser, Rev. Charles, 50
Dubois, Jesse K., 133
Duncan, Joseph, 27, 36, 39
Dunn, Alfonso, 324
DuPage County Centennial poster, **87**
Eads, James B., 184
Early, Jubal A., 305, 308, 318, 320, 370
Eaton, John, 313
Eckert, Thomas T., 242, 302, 328, **350**, 353, 354, 355,
    399
Edwards, Ninian W., 47, 48, 50, 439
Ehrgott, Forbriger & Co., 222
Eighth Circuit, IL, 55, 68, 78
Elements of Military Art and Science, 194
Elizabethtown, KY, 15
Ellsworth, Elmer Ephraim, 133, 162, 242
Ely, Alfred, 168
Emancipation Proclamation, 205-206, **207**, 208, 220,
    221, **222**, **223**, 224, 236, 275-286, 312, 313, 348

Emerson, Ralph Waldo, 8, 72, 107, 434
English Grammar, 28
Ericsson, John, 192-193, 434
Evarts, William M., 332
Evening Post, 110
Everett, Charlotte Gray Brooks, 265
Everett, Edward, 113, 176, 265, **267**, 268, 270
Execution of Lincoln conspirators, **450-452**

F
Fairfax, D. MacNeill, 174
Farragut, David Glasgow, 187, 312
Fayetteville, NC, 370
Fell, Jesse W., 92, 108, 117, 119
Ferguson, W.J., 401, 403, 412
Fernandina, 134-136
Fessenden, William P., 216, 304, 312, 332
Field, David Dudley, 60, 110
Field, Maunsell, 304
Fifer, Joseph, v, 98
Fillmore, Millard, 70, 71, 80, 81, 447
Five Forks, Battle of, **316**
Florida, 151, 292
Florville, William, 128
Follett, Foster & Company, 108
Foote, Andrew H., 184
Forbes, John Murray, 220
Ford's Theater, Washington, DC, 392, **396**, **397**, **398**,
    399, 400, 401, 403, 405, 414, 419, 420, 422, 428, 450
Forrest, Nathan Bedford, 213, **294**, 340
Fort Donelson, 184, 187, 188
Fort Fisher, 352
Fort Henry, 184
Fort McAllister, GA, 339
Fort McHenry, MD, 163
Fort Morgan, 227
Fort Pickens, FL, 148, 150
Fort Pillow, TN massacre, 294
Fort Stedman, 372
Fort Stevens, 308
Fort Sumter, SC, **146**, 147, 148, 150, 151, 227, 262,
    373
Fort Wagner, 262, 275
Fortress Monroe, VA, 179, 227, 354
Fox, Gustavus V., 245
France, 433
Francis, Mrs. Simeon, 50
Franklin, Abraham, 254
Frederick, MD, 210, 229
Fredericksburg, VA, 212, 227, 236, 242
Freeport, IL, 86
Free-Soil party, 65, 66, 70, 75, 77, 112
Frémont, John C., 80-81, 164, 172, **173**, 174, 179, 181,
    188, 199, 285, 300, **301**, 318
French, Benjamin B., 142, 267, 268
French, Daniel Chester, 453, 455
Fry, James B., 168, 254, 311
Fugitive Slave Law, 68, 70, 104, 165, 176, 179

G
Galena, IL, 80, 88, 184
Galesburg, IL, 8, 88, 90
Gardner, Alexander, 68, 196, 200, 201, 279, 280, 302,
    324, 360, 381, 392, 393, 414, 417, 420, 421, 425,
    450-452

Garrett's house and barn, **442-443**, 445, **446-447**, 450

Garrison, William Lloyd, 373

Gayle, B.B., 202

General War Orders, No. 1, 179; No. 2, 187; No. 3, 187

Generals of the Civil War, **380**

Georgia, 122, 151

Germany, 433

Gettysburg: Address, **268**, **269**, **270**, **271**, 453; Battle of, **248**, **249**, 250, 251, **252**, 253, **254**, **255**; National Cemetery, **250-251**, 265, 267, **268-269**; re-creation of, 252

Giddings, Joshua, 64, 117

Gilbert, C.M., 127

Gillmore, Q.A., 292

Globe Tavern, Springfield, IL, 55

Godbey, Russell, 33

Goldboro, NC, 370

Good Friday schedule, 392

Gordon, John B., 372

Graham, Mentor, 29

Grant, Fred, 279

Grant, Julia Dent, 184, 372, 373, 393

Grant, Ulysses S., iv, 184, **185**, **186**, 187, 194, 227, **230**, 232, 233, 238, 251, 252, 261, 274, 279, 280, **281**, 282, 296-298, 300, 302, 308, 311, 318, 320, 329, 336-338, 340-341, 352-356, 367-368, 370, **371**, 372-374, 378, 379, 382, 283, 384, 390, 392, 393, 394, 430, 436

Great Britain, 433

Great Compromise, 68, 70, 74

Greeley, Horace, 60, 77, 110, 117, 119, 166, 168, **169**, 174, 220, 289, 290, 301, 313

Green, Bowling, 33

Greene, Bill, 40

Greene, S. Dana, 192

Greene, William G., 31, 33

Greensboro, NC, 392

Grigsby, Aaron, 24

Grover's Theatre, 325

Gurley, Phineas D., 405, 408, 436

Gutekunst, Frederick, 378

H

Habeas corpus, 236, 238, 262, 338

Hahn, Michael, 293, 356

Haines Photo Co., 248

Haiti, 178, 206

Hale, Charles, 269

Halleck, Henry W., 164, 194, 201, 212, 229, 233, 245, 252, **256**, 261, 281, 282, 308, 339, 340

Hallowell, E.N., 311

Halstead, Murat, 233

Hamlin, Hannibal, **113**, **114**, 119, 123, 300, 301, 359

Hampton Roads Conference, 354-355

Hancock, Winfield Scott, 450

Hanks, Dennis Friend, 16, 20, 22

Hanks, John, 27, 112, 113

Hanks, Lucy, 12-13, 71

Hanks, Thomas, 112

Hardee, General, 339

Hardie, James A., 229

Hardin, John J., 58-59

Harding, Pres. Warren G., 453, **455**

Harper's Weekly, 117, 270, 290, 301, 318, 324, 325, 345, **349**

Harpers Ferry, VA, 107, 152, 202, 210

Harris, Clara, 396, 405

Harris, Senator, 366

Harrisburg, PA, 136, 439

Harrison, William Henry, 46

Harrison's Landing, VA, 194, 242

Harvard University, 128, 265, 324, 367

Havens, O. Pierre, 200

Hay, John, **126**, 128, 168, 171, 199, 200, 210, 242, 267, 268, 270, 274, 275, 288, 292, 302, 304, 308, 312, 319, 328, 332, 349, 352, 366, 407, 408, 439

Hay, Milton, 94

Hazen, General, 338

Head, Rev. Jesse, 14

Helm, Emilie Todd, 162, 261, 366

Helper, Hinton Rowan, 104

Henning, Fanny, 50

Henry, Dr., 48

Henry, James D., 31, 33

Hermitage, SC, **224**

Herndon, Rowan, 31

Herndon, William, **54**, 55, 65, 71, 78, 82, 98, 104, 108

Herold, David E., **416**, 417, 419, 420, **421**, 422, 427, 450; capture of, **443**

Hesler, Alexander, 86, 118, 122

Hicks, Gov., 163

Hill, Samuel, 28, 34

Hodgenville, KY, 15

Holt, Joseph, 172

Homestead Bill, 195

Hood, John B., 308, 336, 340

Hooker, Joseph, 202, 227, 228, **229**, 242, 261

Howard, General, 339

Howard's Stable, Washington, DC, **422-423**

Howe, Julia Ward, 205

Howells, William Dean, 119

Hugo, Victor, 107

Hunter, David, 164, 205, 439

Hunter, R.M.T., 353-354

I

Illinois Gazette, 92

Illinois Staats-Anzeiger, 104

Illinois State Journal, 448

Illinois State Register, 108

Illinois, 124; Legislation, 36-40

Immigration, 72, 74-78, 104

Impending Crisis of the South, The, 104

Independence Hall, **132**, 136, 442

Indianapolis, IN, 447

Ironclad ships, 184

Irwin, Jared P., 128

J

Jackson, Andrew, 31, 37, 38, 112, 148

Jackson, Calvin, 6, 85

Jackson, Claiborne, 152

Jackson, T.J. "Stonewall," 184, **198**, 199, 201, 202, 228, 294

James River, 298, 372

Jayne, William, 124

Jeffersonian, The, 168

Johnson, Andrew, 64, 301-302, 390, 407, 408, 412, 420, 428, 430, 436, 450

Johnson, Herschel, 119

Johnston, Albert Sydney, 188

Johnston, John D., 23, 27, 70

Johnston, Joseph E., 168, **185**, 186, 187, 194, 199, 282, 308, 352, 356, **358**, 359, 370, 428

Johnston, Matilda, 23

Johnston, Sarah Elizabeth, 23

Jones, J. Russell, 279

Jonesboro, VA, 88

Judd, Norman B., 133, 134, 136

K

Kansas, 72, 75, 77, 80, 82, 107

Kansas-Nebraska Bill, 80

Kearsarge (ship), 312

Keckley, Elizabeth, 188, 189, 243

Keene, Laura, 134, 392, 396, 400, 403, 405

Kellogg, Alexander, 162

Kellogg, David, 162

Kellogg, Margaret, 162

Kellogg, Samuel, 162

Kentucky, 152, 162, 184, 202

Kenyon College, 79, 182

Kerr, Orpheus C., 242

King, Dr. Albert F.A., 403, 405

Kirkham, Samuel, 28

Kirkpatrick, William, 30

Knights of the Golden Circle, 236

Knights Templar, 267

Knob Creek, KY, 20

Know-Nothing party, 75, 77, 80, 112, 316

Knoxville, TN, 261, 274

Koerner, Gustave, 104, 119

Kurz & Allison, 316

L

L. Prang & Co., 317

Lamar, Gazaway B., 156

Lame duck, 325

Lamon, Ward H., 98, 117, 128, **130**, 133, **135**, 136, 148, 265, 267, 268, **388**, 390, 399, 439

Lamson, Mary, 182

Lane, Harriet, 125

Lane, Henry S., 311

Lane, James H., 152

Lane, Joseph, 119

Laury, Mrs., 243

Leale, Dr. Charles A., 403, 405, 407, 408

Leavenworth *Register*, 107

Leaves of Grass, 8, 244

Lee, Custis, 378

Lee, Robert E., 107, 152, 194, 198-202, 210, 212, 228, 229, 233, 242, 248-250, 261, 262, 282, 296-298, 305, 318, 336, 340, 352, 356, 370, 372, 377, 378, **379**, 382, 383, 384, 419, **425**, 430

Leslie's Illustrated newspaper, 94

Leslie's Weekly, 243, 308, 322, 324

Letters of President Lincoln on Questions of National Policy, 257

Lexington, KY, 47-48, 61, 64

Libby Prison, 168, 329, 341, 378

Liberia, 178, 206, 344

Library of Congress, iv, 64, 270

Lincoln & Herndon law offices, **52-53**
Lincoln Birthplace National Historic Site, **14-15, 23**
Lincoln family homestead (Virginia), **13**
Lincoln home, Springfield, IL, 94, **95, 96, 97, 98, 99, 100, 101, 102**
Lincoln Memorial, Washington, DC, **453-455**
Lincoln Monument Association, 453
Lincoln Monument International Exhibition, U.S. Navy Group, **454**
Lincoln speeches: 44, 75, 78, 80, 81; Cooper Union, 108, 110, 112; Election Day 1864, 329; First Inaugural, 130, 140, 143, 144; Gettysburg Address, **268, 269, 270, 271**, 362; House Divided, 84, 107, 108, 120, 362; Lost Speech, 80; Second Inaugural, 360, 362; Springfield Farewell, 130; Victory speech, 386
Lincoln, Abraham (1744-86), 12; homestead, **13**
Lincoln, Abraham, **6**, 8-9, 16-24, 26-34, 36-40, **42**, 43-44, **45**, 46-48, 50-55, 58-61, **62**, 63-66, 68, **69**, 70-72, 74-75, **76**, 77-78, 80-82, 84, **85, 86**, 87-92, 94-102, 104-110, 112, 113, **114**, 115-117, **118**, 119, 120, 122-125, 128-130, **132**-137, **138**-145, 148-153, 158, 159, 162-166, 168-176, 178-182, 184-195, 196-202, 204-208, 210, **211**, 212, 213, 216-218, 220, 221, **221, 222, 223**, 224, 227-229, 233, 236-239, 242, 243, **244, 245**, 248-257, 260-262, **264**, 265, 267, **268, 269**, 270, **271, 272**, 274-276, **278**, 279, **280**, 281, 282, 284-286, 288-290, 292-294, 296-298, 300-302, 304-308, **310**, 311-313, **314**, 316-320, 322, **323**, 324, 325, **326**, 328, 329, 332, 336-341, **342**, 344-346, 348, 349, 352-356, 359, **360**, 362, **363**, 366-368, 370-374, 376-380, **381**, 382, 384, 386, **387**, 390, 392, **393**, 394, 396-409, 412, 414, 428, **429**, 430, 432-434, 436-456; and slaves, **204**, 205, **206**, 207, 208; as postmaster, 31-32, 38, 44; as surveyor, 33, 38; assassination of, **398**, 399-401, 403, 405, 412-430; at Antietam, **196, 200, 201**; autobiography, 108; biographies, 322; books read, 23, 32; boyhood, 14-24; business card, **55**; caricatures of, 315; death of, 399, 405, **406**, 407, 408, **409**; debates with Douglas, 84-92; dreams, 130, 390; early life, 16-24; Easter memorial sermons about, 432; editorials about death of, 432-433; education, 23-23; election campaign (1860), 112-120; election campaign (1864), 300-302, 312-313, 314-320, 328-329; facial hair, 128, 134; first call for troops, 151-152; flat boat trip to New Orleans, **26**-27; funeral, 436, **437, 438-439, 441**, 436-449; funeral train, **438-439**; hearse, **437**; in New Orleans, **29**; Inauguration (1861), 125, 128-137, **138**, 140, **141, 142**, 143, 144, 145; Inauguration (1865), 358-362; journey to Washington (1861), 132-137; last reception, **363**; lawyer in Springfield, 42-48; life masks, **11, 456**; marriage, 50-55; marriage house, **51**; New Salem life, 25-34; reactions to assassination abroad, 433-434; realia found in pocket after death, **400, 404**; religion and, 59-60, 68; Springfield home, 94, **95-102**; State of the Union (1864), 344-345; statues of, **454-455**; studying by firelight, **18**; sum book, **17**; U.S. House of Representatives, 56-61, 62-66; varioloid and, 274; visit to Richmond, **376**, 377, 378; war preparations, 162-166; young legislator, 36-40, 42-48
Lincoln, Bathsheba Herring, 12
Lincoln, Edward Baker "Eddie", 59, 61, 68

Lincoln, John, 12
Lincoln, Josiah, 12
Lincoln, Mary Todd, **46**, 47-48, 50, 55, 61, 70-71, 81, 98-101, 128, 144, 227, 228, 238, **240**, 242, 243, 244, **245**, 261, **276**, 280, 324, 325, 328, 359, **361**, 362, 363, 370, 372-373, 378, 392, 394, 396, **398**, 403, 405, **406**, 408, 433, 436, 439
Lincoln, Mordecai, 12
Lincoln, Nancy Hanks, 12-16, 20, 22, 24, 71, 84, 408
Lincoln, Robert Todd, 55, 61, 110, 128, 243, 253, 324, 366, 367, **368**, 407, 408, 436, 439, 448, 453, **455**
Lincoln, Sarah Bush Johnston, **21**, 23, 24, 34, 70, 86, 128, 412
Lincoln, Sarah, 14, 20, 22, 23; death, 24
Lincoln, Thomas (1812), 20
Lincoln, Thomas "Tad," **69**, 70, 94, 134, 188, **226**, 227, 242, 243, **244, 245**, 267, **298, 324**, 325, 370, 377, 386, 439, **440**
Lincoln, Thomas, 12-16, 20, 24, 70, 94, 408
Lincoln, William Wallace "Willy," 70, 94, 134, 182, 276; burial crypt, **190-191**; death, 188, 189
Lincoln-Douglas debates, 84-88, **89, 90**, 91, 92, 108, 112; Centennial postage stamp, **90**; Centennial poster, **87**
Lincoln-Hamlin campaign, 112-120; button, **117**; banners, **114, 116**
Little Rock, AR, 293-294
Lodge, Nancy, 190, 191
Log Cabin, 168
Logan, Stephen T., 66, 320, 340
London *Dispatch*, 218
London *Morning Chronicle*, 176
London *Spectator*, 245, 329, 345
London *Times*, 224
Longfellow, Henry W., 65, 224
Longstreet, James, **202**, 212, 249, 260, 274
Louisiana, 122, 151, 220, 293, 356
Lovejoy, Elijah P., 44
Lovejoy, Owen, 44, 77, 84, 274, 281, **284**, 285, 286
Lowell, James Russell, 174
Lussier, 74
Lyon, Nathaniel, 171-172

M
Madison, Dolly, 74
Magoffin, Beriah, 152
Mallory, Stephen R., 156
Maltby, Charles, 34
Malvern (ship), 377, 378
Malvern Hill, VA, 194, 199, 212
Manassas, VA, 168, 171, 179, 187
Manifest Destiny, 60
Mansfield, J.K.F., 193, 202
Manual on the Art of War, 171
Marcy, Ellen Mary, 171
Marsh, Matthew, 34, 38
Marshall, Charles, 382
Mary Martin (ship), 372
Maryland, 163
Mason, James M., 174, 176
Masonic Fraternity, 267
Matheny, James, 50, 55
Mather, Thomas, 39, 125
Maxcy, James, 71; Mary, 71

Maximilian, Archduke of Austria, 218
Maynard, Horace, 300
McBride, Robert W., 324
McClellan, George B., **170**, 171, 178, 179, 181, 187, 194, 195, 199, **200**, 201, 202, 210, 212, 227, 229, 242, 243, 260, 262, 285, 315, 317, 318, 320, 328-329
McCormick, Cyrus H., 74, 318
McDowell, Irvin, 168, 187, 194, 199, 201
McLean House, Appomattox, VA, 382, **383**
McLean, John, 80, 112
McNamar, John. *See* McNeil, John.
McNeil, John, 28, 34, 37
McPike, H.G., 285
Meade, George G., 228, 229, 233, **246**, 248-253, 261, 282, 298, 372
Meade, Margaretta Sergeant, 248
Medill, Joseph, 118
Memminger, Christopher G., 156, **159**
Merrimac (ship), 189, **192-193**, 242
Merryman, John, 163
Meserve, Frederick Hill 9
Mexican War, 60, 65
Mexico, 60
Miles, Nelson A., iv
Milledgeville, GA, 338
Milliken's Bend, 236
Mills, Clark, 456
Mills, Henry, 39
Mills, Joseph T., 312
Minnesota (ship), 189, 192
Mississippi, 151, 158
Missouri Compromise, 75
Missouri, 46, 77, 152, 172, 174, 366
Mobile Bay, AL, 312, 313
Molly Maguires, 236
Monitor (ship), **189, 192, 193**, 242, 434
Montana, 75
Montgomery *Advertiser*, 144
Montgomery, AL, 125, 134, 156
Morgan, Senator, 304
Morrison, Mary Anna, 199
Morton, Governor, 319
Mountain Department, WV, 179
Mudd, Dr. Samuel A., 450
Mulligan, James A., 172
Murfreesboro, TN, 218, 260
Murphy, Isaac, 294

N
Nabuco, Joaquin, v
Napoleon III, Emperor of the French, 218
Nasby, Petroleum Vesuvius, 242
Nashville, TN, 340
National Bank Act, 37, 46, 238, 332
National Hotel, Washington, DC, 414, 419
National Intelligencer, 290
National Photo Co., 455
National Register of Historic Places, 453
National Union Club, Philadelphia, 289
National Union party, 290, 300, 302
Nebraska Act, 75, 78
Nebraska, 75
Nevada, 292, 348
New Mexico, 68

New Orleans *Picayune*, 153
New Orleans, La, 27, 29, 187, 356
New Salem, IL, 27-34, 37-38, 40
New York City, 108-110, 128, 134, 153; draft riots, 253-254, 257; Lincoln funeral, **441**, 442-443, **444, 445**
New York *Daily News*, 134, 318
New York *Evening Post*, 117, 145
New York *Herald*, 125, 144, 145, 162, 174, 224, 228, 245, 279, 289, 311, 428, 432, 433
New York *Metropolitan Record*, 318
New York Peace Democrats, 236
New York *Times*, 145, 210, 244, 257, 288, 289, 313
New York *Tribune Almanac*, 275
New York *Tribune*, 60, 77, 81, 108, 117, 118, 119, 120, 134, 144, 145, 166, 168, 269, 289, 301
New York *World*, 238, 285
New Yorker, 168
Nichols, John W., 324
Nicolay, John G., 128, **129**, 148, 168, 181, 227, 242, 267, 274, 275, 280, 281, 288, 302, 308, 312, 319, 332, 348, 349, 354, 366, 373, 407, 439
Norfolk, VA, 120, 152, 192, 193, 220
North Carolina, 156, 370, 373
North Dakota, 73
Nugent, Robert, 254

O
O'Laughlin, Michael, 414, **415**, **418**, 419, 450
Oak Hill Cemetery, IL, **190-191**
Oak Ridge Cemetery, IL, 448
Odd Fellows, 267
Offut, Denton, 27, 28
Oglesby, Richard, 112
Ohio, 133
Oldham, Todd & Company, 61
Olney Times, 92
Olustee River, 292
Opdyke, Mayor, 253, 254
Ord, Edward O., 373, 379
Order of American Knights, 237
Order of the Star Spangled Banner. *See* Know-Nothing party.
Ottawa, IL, 86
Our American Cousin (play), 392, 396, 399, **400**, 401, 422
Owens, Mary, 40, 43
Oxford, MS, 238

P
Pacific Railway Bill, 195
Paine, Lewis (Lewis Thornton Powell), 417, 419, 420, **421**, 422, 450
Palfrey, John G., 64
Palmerston, Lord, 208
Parker, John F., 324, 396, 399, 428
Patterson, Robert, 168
Pea Ridge, AR, 187
Peanuts, John, 403, 422
Pearson, T. Painter, 85
Pemberton, John C., **231**, 232, 233, 251, 252
Pennsylvania, 124, 229, 233
Perry Pictures, 343
Petersburg, VA, 297, 298, 374, 377
Petersen House, Washington, DC, **399**, **402**, 405, **406**, 407, 408, **409**

Philadelphia *North American*, 348
Philadelphia *Press*, 84
Philadelphia, PA, 80, 132, 134, 439, 442
Phillips, Wendell, 107, 119, 174, 352
Pickens, F.W., 150
Pickett, George E., 249-250
Pigeon Creek, IN, 20, 22-23
Pinkerton, Allan, 134-136
Pitcher, John, 23
Pittsburg Landing, TN, Battle of, **186**, 187
Pittsburgh, PA, 133
Pocket veto, 305
Political Text book for 1860, 119
Polk, James K., 59, 60, 64
Pomeroy, Samuel C., 216, 290
Pope, John, 164, 199, 200, 202, 208, 210
Port Hudson, 252
Port Royal, SC, 205
Porter, David D., 187, 201, 202, 232, 251
Porter, Horace, 298, 368, 372, 373, 377, 378, 382
Portrait for Posterity, 9
Pottawatomie Creek massacre, 30, 82
Prisons, 341
Proclamation of Amnesty and Reconstruction, 274-275

Q
Quincy, IL, 88

R
Radford, Reuben, 31
Radical Democracy party, 300
Raleigh, NC, 120
Randall, James G., iv
Rapidan River, 296, 298
Rathbone, Henry Reed, 396, 401, 403, 405
Rawlins, John, 279, 281
Raymond, Henry Jarvis, **288**, 289, 290, 300, 300, 312, 313
Realia from Lincoln's pockets after death, **400, 404**
Reconstruction, 292, 390, 393, 394, 428
Regan, J.H., 156
Regiments, 152
Republican party, 77, 80, 82, 84, 86, 90, 92, 104, 107, 110, 112, 113, 117, 285, 292, 302, 312, 313, 318, 348, 428
Revolver used by John Wilkes Booth, **401**
Reward posters, **426-427**
Reynolds, John, 30
Rhett, Robert Barnwell, II, 65, 124, 125, 156, **158**
Richmond *Inquirer*, 144, 208, 224
Richmond *Whig*, 341
Richmond, Dean, 285, 318
Richmond, VA, 152, 156, 171, 179, 188, 194, 199, 208, 296-297, 300, 352, 374; fall of, 377-378
River Queen (ship), 370, 372, 373, 374
Robinson, George T., 407
Robinson, Jeremiah, 254
Rochester, MA, 238
Rock River, IL, 30
Rock, John S., 355
Rockingham County, VA, 12-13
Rootabaga Stories, 9
Rosecrans, William S., 218, 227, 260, 261
Russell, Andrew J., 307

Russell, Benjamin B., 257
Russia, 275-276, 434
Rutledge, Ann Mayes, 28, 34, 37-38
Rutledge, James, 28, 34
Rutledge, McGrady, 38

S
Sacramento, CA, 74
San Francisco, CA, 74
San Jacinto (ship), 174
Sandburg, Carl, iv-v, 8-9
Sanford, E.S., 194
Sangamo Journal, 30, 36, 37, 38, 43, 44, 50, 77
Sangamon River, 27, 30
Sartain, William, 244
Savannah, GA, 336-337, 339
Sayler's Creek, 379
Schenck, Robert C., 64, 267
Schofield, General, 340
Schwerdt, Christian F., 155
Scott, Dred, 81, 112
Scott, Winfield S., 60, 71, **124**, 125, 130, 137, 140, 148, 164, 168, 171, 172, 198, 324
Scripps, John Locke, 120
Secession, 65, 122-125
Sedgwick, General, 202
Seven Days' battles, 113, 194, 199, 242
Seward, Frederick W., 220, 379, 394, 407
Seward, William H., 66, 70, 71, 75, 92, 107, 112, 117-119, 123, 136, 137, 145, 148, 149, 158, 170, 206, 208, **214**, 216-218, 220, 262, 267, 275, 280, 285, 289, 312, 353, 354, 355, 359, 374, 378-379, 390, 437, 450; assassination attempt, 407, 420, 421, 422
Seymour, Horatio, 210, 236, 254, 257, 267, 318
Seymour, T.H., 317
Seymour, Truman, 292
Shaw, Francis G., 275
Shaw, Robert Gould, 262, 275
Shenandoah Valley, VA, 318, 320, 370
Shepherd, Nicholas H., 63, 77
Sheridan, Philip H., 282, 296, 298, 308, **317**, 318, 320, 329, 370, 372, 374, 378, 379
Sherman, John, 145, 339
Sherman, William Tecumseh, iv, 145, 164, 170, 187, 233, 261, 274, 282, 298, 308, 311, 313, 317-318, 320, 329, **334**, 336-341, 352, 356, 370, 372, 373, 374, 383, 394, 428, 430
Shields, James, 66, 77
Shiloh Church, TN, Battle of, **186**, 187, 194
Simmons, Pollard, 33
Simpson, Matthew, 436, 448
Slave cabins, **224**
Slavery, 39-40, 44, 61, 65-66, 68, 72, 75, 77, 80-82, 104, 107, 110, 178, 204-208, 220-224, 275, 312, 313, 322, 345, 348-349, 354
Slidell, John, 174, 176
Slocum, General, 336
Small, Maynard & Co., 105
Smith, Alexander, 324
Smith, Caleb B., 145, 148, 201
Smith, Kirby, 202
Smith, Rev. James, 68
Soldier vote, 286
Soldiers' Home, Washington, DC, 199, 261, 308, 312

Sons of Liberty, 237
South Carolina, 122, 124, 151
South Dakota, 75
Spangler, Edward, 422, **425**, 450
Sparrow, Elizabeth (Betsy), 12, 16, 20, 22
Sparrow, Nancy. *See* Lincoln, Nancy Hanks.
Sparrow, Thomas, 12, 16, 22
Speed, Joshua Fry, **43**, 48, 50, 58, 60, 123
Spiritualism, 243
Spotsylvania, VA, 296,
Sprigg, Mrs., 64
Springfield *Journal*, 108, 110, 119, 120
Springfield **Republican**, 248
Springfield, IL, 8, 38, 39, 43-45, 66, 68-72, 90;
    Lincoln home, 94-102; Lincoln Monument,
    448
St. Louis, MO, 44, 172
Stanton, Edwin M., 137, **181**, 182, 187, 189, 193, 194,
    201, 210, 212, 216, 218, 236, 244, 267, 280, 282,
    308, 311, 312, 320, 324, 332, 353, 355, 373, 374,
    377, 383, 390, 394, 407, 428
State Bank, Springfield, 43
State Register, 92
Statesmen of the Civil War, 380
Steele, Frederick, 293-294
Stephens, Alexander H., 64, 65, 119, 123, 125, **158**,
    159, 253, 341, **353**, 354, 355
Stevens, Thaddeus, 179, 284, 345, 355
Stewart, A.T., 123, 152
Stockholm *Nya Daglig Allehanda*, 433
Stockton, Thomas H., 267
Stone, Charles P., 182
Stone, Dan, 40
Stone, Dr. Robert K., 407, 408
Stowe, Harriet Beecher, 71, **72**, 239, 368
Stuart & Lincoln law firm, 43
Stuart, J.E.B., 296, **297**
Stuart, John T., 36, 37, 38, 43, 44, 46, 48, 439
Sumner, Charles, 65, 70, 77, **135**, 137, 176, 216, 348,
    355, 356, 366, 378, 408
Sumner, Edwin V., 164
Surratt, John H., Jr., 417, 419, 427, 450
Surratt, Mary E., **417**, 419, 450; house, **424**
Swaney, James, 23
Sweden, 433
Swett, Leonard, 78, 123

T
Taft, Dr. Charles Sabin, 403, 405
Taft, Pres. William, 455
Taney, Roger Brooke, 81, 140, 163, 319
Taylor, Sarah Knox, 157
Taylor, Zachary, 60, 66, 70, 71, 80, 157
Tecumseh, Chief, 46
Tennessee (ship), 312
Tennessee, 156, 184, 220, 339-340
Texas, 68, 151, 156
Thayer, John M., 236
Thirteenth Amendment, 348, **349**, 354
Thomas, Benjamin, 9
Thomas, George H., 260-261, 261, 340
Thomas, Lorenzo, 237
Thomas, Richard S., 58
Thompson, Jacob, 64
Thoreau, Henry David, 107

Thulstrup, Thure de, 186, 317
Todd, Elizabeth, 47
Todd, George, 162
Todd, Levi, 61, 162
Todd, Mrs. Robert S., 261
Todd, Robert Smith, **47**, 61
Tolstoy, Leo, 434
Toombs, Robert, 65, 122, 150, 156, 159
Town, Charles, 107
Transylvania University, 58, 199
Traveler (horse), 383
Tremont House, Chicago, IL, 84, 123
Tremont Temple, Boston, MA, 66, 224
Trent (ship), 174
Trumbull, Julia Jayne, 77
Trumbull, Lyman, 77, 82, 124, 168, 216, 285, 356,
    439
Truth, Sojourner, 237, 322
Turner, Nat, 107

U
U.S. Capitol, 64, 276, 306-307, 359, **360**, 362; Armed
    Freedom statue, 276
U.S. Constitution, 90, 104, 110, 112, 143, 348-349
U.S. House of Representatives, 348, **349**
U.S. National Park Service, 453
U.S. Senate, 112, 348
U.S. Supreme Court, 81, 90, 112; Chief Justice
    vacancy, 319, 332
Uncle Tom's Cabin, 72, 104, 239
Underground Railroad, 39
Union League Club, Philadelphia, 289, 332
Union Lincoln Association, 289
Union Pacific railroad, 195
Union party, 262, 289
Union Progressive Association, 224
Union Relief Society, 237
United States Statutes, 242
Utah, 68

V
Vachon, John, 13
Van Buren, Martin, 38, 46, 65
Vance, John C., 28, 32
Vandalia, IL, 36-37, 38, 44
Vander Weyde, William M., 16
Vicksburg, MS, **231, 232**, 233, 236, 251-252
Victoria, Queen of England, 163, 176, 275,
    433
Virginia, 152, 199, 218, 220
Volk, Leonard Wells, 11, 161

W
Wabash Railroad, 133
Wade, Benjamin F., 168, 178, 305, **428**
Wade-Davis Manifesto, 313
Wakeman, Abram, 253
Walker, Leroy P., 150, 156
Wallace, Lew, 188, 305
War costs, 178-182
Washburne, Elihu B., 279, 355, 439
Washington *Chronicle*, 346
Washington, DC, 8, 64-66, 68, 124-125, 133, 136-137,
    152-153, 168, 187, 200, 206, 242-245, 279-282,
    304-308, 370

Watkins, William, 33
Watson, Henry, 16
Waugh, S.B., 244
Webster, Daniel, 37, 44, 65, 66, 68, 70, 112, 117
Weed, Thurlow, 60, 75, 92, 112, 119, 123, 275, 289,
    300
Weichmann, Louis J., 417, 419
Weitzel, Godfrey, 377, 378
Welles, Gideon, 123, 145, 148, **149**, 150, 189, 193,
    200, 201, 210, 216-218, 228, 251, 261, 304, 312,
    354, 393, 394, 407, 408
Wenworth, John, 92
West Virginia, 171, 218
West, The, 72, 344
Westfield, NY, 133-134
Whig party, 36-40, 44, 46-47, 55, 58-61, 64-66, 71, 75,
    77, 80, 112
White House Landing, VA, 194
White House, 242-245, 362, 366-367, 384,
    386, 436, 437, 439; Lincoln Bedroom,
    367
White, Horace, 302
White, Hugh, 38
White, Martha Todd, 162, 324
Whiteside, General, 30
Whitman, Walt, iv, 8, 244, **433**, 434
Whitney, Henry C., 78, 120
Wide-Awakes political clubs, **115**, 119
Wigwam, Chicago, IL, 117-119, 316
Wilkes, Capt., 176
Willard's Hotel, Washington, DC, 140, 145, 279,
    282
Williams, Archibald,
Williams, Beverly, 265
Williamsburg, VA, 227
Wills, David, 267; house, **265**, 267
Wilmot Proviso, 65, 66
Wilmot, David, 64, 65
Wilson, Mayor, 133
Wilson's Creek, MO, 172
Winchester, VA, 318
Wing, Henry E., 296
Winthrop, Robert C., 318
Winthrop, Robert, 64
Wood, Fernando, 134, 289, 318
Wood, John E., 164
Wool, General, 193
Worden, John, 150, 192, 193
Wordsworth, William, 9
Wright, General, 308
Wyoming, 75

Y
Yancey, William Lowndes, 125, 156,
    159
Yates, Richard, 124, 439
Young Lincoln Studying in the Fields, **19**
Young Men's Lyceum, Springfield, IL, 44
Young Men's Republican Union, NY,
    108
Young, Richard M., 39

Z
Zoller, Charles, 454
Zouaves, 133, 162